"With sympathy for his subject, Griffin details the years of enforced hiding. . . . As he takes Hudson from tongue-tied novice to superstar, Griffin shows that [director Douglas] Sirk wasn't wrong about his star's essential qualities: the ones that colleagues loved, and the ones that neither the camera nor anyone else has ever lied about."
—*Sight and Sound* magazine

"At once the luckiest and unluckiest of men, Rock Hudson finally has the book that his fans have long been waiting for. This richly detailed biography is a revelation. Mark Griffin's thoughtful and compelling *All That Heaven Allows* isn't simply a book about one of the most determined and hard-working movie stars in the history of Hollywood, it also happens to be an insightful look at America in the second half of the twentieth century. Read it and weep."
—Sam Kashner, *New York Times* bestselling coauthor of *The Fabulous Bouvier Sisters* and *Furious Love*

"Rock Hudson's life story mingles the American Dream with nightmarish tragedy. This exhaustively researched book reconstructs the magnificent charade of a screen idol whose double life informed his haunting persona."
—Patrick McGilligan, author of *Young Orson: The Years of Luck and Genius on the Path to* Citizen Kane

"Rock Hudson was the last machine-made movie star, and it couldn't have happened to a nicer guy. Audiences sensed Hudson's basic kindness and responded with a loyalty that never wavered despite his predominantly passive career choices. *All That Heaven Allows* breaks new ground in its revelatory reporting on Hudson's private life and, most important, in empathy for its subject."
—Scott Eyman, author of *John Wayne: The Life and Legend* and *Hank and Jim*

"Mark Griffin paints a vivid portrait of a man who lived a double life in order to maintain his status as a movie star. Griffin's sources are candid but credible, which makes the book a real page-turner. I came away admiring Hudson all the more, and feeling sad for the secret existence that Hollywood demanded of its leading men in the 1950s and '60s."

—Leonard Maltin, author of *Hooked on Hollywood: Discoveries from a Lifetime of Film Fandom*

"A thoughtful exploration of the career and elusive private life of Rock Hudson. . . . An engrossing and carefully documented account of a beloved film icon's life."

—*Kirkus Reviews* (starred review) and a Best Nonfiction Book of 2018

"Griffin provides trenchant cinematic insight and social criticism along with an equally abundant trove of bon mots and anecdotes. Director Douglas Sirk, who worked with Hudson on eight films said, 'The only thing which never let me down in Hollywood was my camera. And it was not wrong about Hudson.' Griffin's lens also puts Hudson in beautifully focused light."

—*Library Journal* (starred review)

"Hudson's rags-to-riches story is revealed by Griffin's comprehensive overview of Hudson's filmography as well as his frank but objective discussion of Hudson's complicated personal life."

—*Booklist*

ALL THAT HEAVEN ALLOWS

ALSO BY MARK GRIFFIN

A Hundred or More Hidden Things:
The Life and Films of Vincente Minnelli

MARK GRIFFIN

ALL THAT HEAVEN ALLOWS

A BIOGRAPHY OF

ROCK
HUDSON

HARPER

NEW YORK • LONDON • TORONTO • SYDNEY

HARPER

In Memory of
Charles Silver
and
Rolande Griffin

CONTENTS

AUTHOR'S NOTE

t was just the way things were," an eighty-nine-year-old actress told me. "In Hollywood—back in Rock Hudson's day—you were expected to keep secrets, just as you were expected to learn your lines. Nobody said anything to you but it was all understood . . . this is how the game is played."

During our interview, Hudson's former costar expressed all of this rather matter-of-factly and even punctuated her remarks with a shrug. The detached tone was unsettling, given the fact that we had been discussing the code of silence that existed in Hollywood during that period of American cinema now longingly referred to as the "Golden Age."

It's true that era was responsible for some of the finest films ever made, but it was also a time when gays were forced to play straight, studio executives passed starlets around like hors d'oeuvres, and casting couches of every persuasion were constantly occupied.

In those days, a major studio might take a chance on an aspiring actor with no experience if he came equipped with the kind of chiseled features the camera loved. The new recruit would be placed under contract and rigorously groomed for stardom. Eventually, this would pay off in the form of fan adulation and magazine covers—the silver-lining side of the deal, in other words. But all too often, there were strings attached. Sadly, studio moguls and other powerbrokers often made demands on young hopefuls that went far beyond having their teeth capped or noses fixed.

It was understood that if a freshman contract player succumbed to the sexual advances of an agent, producer, or head of production (or in some cases all three), their star would rise more rapidly and shine more brightly than if they resisted. Typically, an actor who was uncooperative or outspoken would eventually see their screen career relegated to the B-movie junk heap before sliding headlong into oblivion.

From our politically correct perspective, this scenario is so off-the-charts egregious that it's hard to reconcile the fact that such behavior was once considered "business as usual" in Hollywood. In these more enlightened times, most people readily assumed that such sexually exploitative business practices had long ago gone the way of silent movies.

That is until the day in 2017 when Oscar-winning producer Harvey Weinstein was fired from his own multimedia company. More than eighty women, including several well-known actresses, accused Weinstein of rape and sexual assault. Immediately following these allegations, scores of other high-profile actors, directors, and media professionals faced accusations of sexual misconduct.

While tallying up the alleged abuses, many journalists took the opportunity to remind the public that although these revelations were genuinely disturbing, this type of exploitation had always existed in Hollywood. One of the names invoked as an example of a serial predator was that of the agent Henry Willson, who represented a stable of all-American heartthrobs that included his most successful client—Rock Hudson.

"If you want to get into films, I can help you," Willson told countless young men eager to establish themselves in the industry. Once Willson's latest discovery had been signed, the agent would do everything possible to help launch his career—though the support came at an especially high price. "Everybody who went with him had to sexually express himself to Henry," Tony Curtis told Willson's biographer.

In light of the Weinstein scandal and the many firings and resignations that followed, Henry Willson's notorious brand of star-making seems deserving of its own hashtag. Even so, it's important to remember that Willson was commodifying his clients in an age before social media movements and in a place where open secrets seemed to flourish.

This is the way things were in Rock Hudson's day, and perhaps better than anyone, he understood how the game was played.

INTRODUCTION

On the second day of October in 1985, there was no shortage of newsworthy events happening around the globe. Soviet leader Mikhail Gorbachev had made his first trip abroad. An Israeli air raid on PLO headquarters had killed sixty-eight people. In southwest Sudan, a train carrying famine relief supplies had derailed. While all of these stories warranted international coverage, they would be bumped off the front pages by another headline—the death of a movie star. Rock Hudson, who had appeared in over sixty feature films and defined all-American manhood for an entire generation, had died of AIDS-related causes at the age of fifty-nine.

On television, images of Hudson saturated not only the likes of *Good Morning America* and *Entertainment Tonight* but all of the network news broadcasts. The tributes included glimpses of Rock in his matinee idol prime—punching out James Dean in *Giant*; making out with Doris Day in *Pillow Talk*. These classic clips were intercut with footage of Hudson at a press conference just three months earlier when he reunited with Day to publicize her new cable series, where Rock was almost unrecognizable—gaunt, glassy-eyed, and disheveled. Although Hudson had been the most photographed actor of his generation, it would be these heartbreaking final images of him, looking ravaged and cadaverous, that would remain lodged in the collective consciousness.

Following his appearance with Day, Hudson would not be seen again publicly, although his "mystery illness" would continue to be a major story worldwide. After Rock was admitted to a Paris hospital, the official word was that he was being treated for "fatigue and general malaise," though gossip columns and "insider exclusives" said otherwise. Finally, after weeks of unconfirmed rumors and tabloid innuendo, Rock's French publicist, Yanou Collart, would tell reporters gathered in front of the American Hospital of Paris, "Mr. Rock Hudson has Acquired Immune Deficiency Syndrome."

The announcement that Rock Hudson had AIDS and the presumptive gay outing that accompanied it were so shocking—if not to his show business colleagues then at least to unsuspecting housewives in Peoria—that coverage of his last days seemed to obliterate everything that had come before. When a gravely ill Hudson flew back to America in a chartered 747, this was anything but a happy homecoming. It was clear that Rock had come home to die. In just a matter of weeks, a tragic and untimely death would overtake a rare and extraordinary life.

Symbolic of this was the sight of dozens of photographers—first encircling, then engulfing the unmarked van carrying Hudson's lifeless body away from his Coldwater Canyon home. Rumor had it that an American tabloid was offering six figures to anyone who could produce a close-up photo of Rock Hudson's corpse. Such was the fate of an individual who had valued his privacy above all else. In 1972, Rock had been appalled by the media barrage that had accompanied the funeral of his close friend, the actress Marilyn Maxwell. After that experience, Hudson told his then companion, Tom Clark, that when his own time arrived, the send-off should be quiet and dignified. No three-ring circuses allowed. In the end, he almost got his wish.

Although Rock's memorial service would be attended by such celebrity friends as Elizabeth Taylor, Carol Burnett, and Angie Dickinson, every attempt was made to keep the event low-key and respectful. Despite the good intentions, Myra Hall, a neighbor of Hudson's, charged members of the press $300 each to temporarily take up residence on her lawn. Throughout the proceedings, a helicopter hovered over Hudson's yard as a videographer did his best to capture footage of the memorial. As publicist Roger Jones once said of his most famous client, "He is the center of the storm—dead or alive." Though given the incredible circumstances, how could the death of Rock Hudson be anything less than a high-profile global event? It represented so much.

First, there was the passing of a beloved movie icon—one who had appeared in his first film when he was twenty-three, his last as he was nearing sixty. Millions of people had watched Hudson grow up before their eyes and moviegoers came to feel that Rock belonged to them. From the beginning, they had responded to what director Douglas Sirk had described as Hudson's "straight goodness of heart and uncomplicated directness." The actor's death signaled another important passing—the metaphoric demise of the Hollywood studio system, which in its heyday had brilliantly manufactured and marketed "Rock Hudson." By 1985, it was painfully clear that the kind of stardust and glitter that had enveloped the careers of Hudson and his contemporaries had gone the way of the neighborhood Bijou. Universal, the studio that had produced some of Rock's finest melodramas, like *Written on the Wind* and *The Tarnished Angels*, had now segued to *Halloween III: Season of the Witch*.

For most screen stars, achieving pop culture immortality and closing the book on Hollywood's Golden Age would be enough of a legacy, but Rock Hudson would transcend mere celebrity by becoming the poster boy for a global pandemic. With the disclosure that Hudson had AIDS and not anorexia nervosa (as had been rumored), his own physician, Dr. Michael Gottlieb, would describe Rock as "the single most influential AIDS patient ever."

Although AIDS had been identified several years earlier, President Ronald Reagan seemed not to grasp how significant the epidemic was. "He accepted it like it was measles and it would go away," said Brigadier General John Hutton, a White House physician. This kind of head-in-the-sand indifference would result in the Reagan Administration being widely criticized for its nonresponsiveness to the crisis. That is until Rock Hudson—a friend of both Ronald and Nancy Reagan—told the world that he was battling the disease. Suddenly, from the White House to Frank's Diner in Kenosha, everyone knew someone who had AIDS.

"If Rock Hudson can have it, nice people can have it. It's just a disease, not a moral affliction," said William F. Hoffman, who wrote *As Is*, one of the first plays to focus on the epidemic. Ironically, having the disease would turn Rock Hudson, silver-screen hero, into a real-life hero. And although it had been implied rather than stated, Hudson's "coming out"—such as it was—had made him the most recognizable gay person on the planet (or bisexual, depending on who you talked to). Even if Hudson's gay admission had been an involuntary one, the *New York Times* noted that the actor had now been recast "in his most paradoxical role—that of a model for other gay men." The fact that rugged, red-blooded Rock Hudson—who had been butch enough to share the screen with John Wayne in *The Undefeated*—also happened to be homosexual instantly shattered stereotypes and challenged people's perceptions of what "gay" meant.

In a few short months, the public had been jolted by one Rock Hudson bombshell after another. If all of the shocking revelations, conflicting accounts, and attempts at concealing the truth were unsettling to even die-hard members of his fan base, this was Rock's reality. In a sense, the dramatic events playing out on the world stage were a magnification of daily life at "The Castle," as Hudson's sprawling Beverly Hills home was known. While it had provided the backdrop for many A-list Hollywood parties, The Castle was also the setting for some especially contentious court intrigue.

As Hudson's health began to fail, there would be an intense power struggle among the members of his inner circle. At times, the plots and counterplots that unfolded were so intricate and intertwining that one former staffer would describe the atmosphere as "Shakespeare for queens." None of Hudson's trusted advisors seemed to trust one another. Old flames found themselves cohabitating with new loves. Close friends became bitter enemies as some damning accusations were made.

Ross Hunter, who had produced several Rock Hudson blockbusters, including *Pillow Talk*, had remained close to the star he had helped create. When Hudson began declining rapidly—both physically and mentally—a concerned Hunter phoned actor George Nader and his partner, Mark Miller. As Hudson's closest friends and caretakers, didn't they know that the whole town was talking? If not, the producer would oblige them by repeating one of the more incendiary rumors circulating throughout the Hollywood community.

"I hear Rock's being drugged by staff," Hunter told Nader.

After recovering from the shock, Nader and Miller, who had befriended Hudson more than thirty years earlier, were outraged. "Queens will make anything up," Nader wrote in his journal. "Regarding Rock being drugged by staff at The Castle, it was so ridiculous that it was funny. Their little lie is ludicrous and libelous at the same time."

Since Rock had returned home, there was no denying that life behind the walls of The Castle had become increasingly surreal. Tom Clark, a Hollywood press agent and Rock's former companion, had been summoned back to The Castle after having been banished a few years earlier. Clark would now be living under the same roof with Marc Christian, another of Rock's former boyfriends. Although Christian had been asked to leave the house, he chose to remain. An already tense household became even more strained.

As Tom Clark had once been a stabilizing and supportive presence in Hudson's life, many friends readily welcomed his return, feeling that if anyone could bring Rock some comfort at the end of his life it would be Clark. But by the mid-80s, Clark's alcoholism had progressed to such a degree that his once clear-eyed judgment had been significantly impaired. "Tom Clark has turned Rock's last days into an obscene circus of a publicist's wet dream," George Nader bitterly noted.

If celebrity well-wishers like Elizabeth Taylor and Roddy Mc-Dowall were welcomed in, some family members claimed that they were shut out. "I was kept out of the loop because the entourage took over my brother's life," says Hudson's adoptive sister, Alice Scherer Waier, who believes that Miller and Nader hindered her attempts to communicate with Rock. "They didn't want me to be acknowledged as any living relative . . . I was used, lied to, threatened and abused by them, to the point that I backed away."

Though the intimidation tactics that Waier described didn't stop her from suing her brother's estate. The suit filed by Waier a year after Rock's death alleged that he had been "unduly influenced" by associates when he excluded her from his will. Waier also claimed that some of Hudson's intimates had impeded her efforts to write or telephone her brother and "forced him into a lifestyle contrary to his traditional upbringing."

Waier's lawsuit had been preceded by another, which was explosive, endlessly debated, and groundbreaking. Only a month after Hudson's death, Marc Christian, who claimed that he had been intimately involved with Rock for three years, filed a $10 million lawsuit against Hudson's estate. The thirty-two-year-old Christian maintained that although Hudson had been diagnosed with AIDS in June of 1984, the actor withheld this information from him and they continued having unprotected sex for a period of eight months.

Hudson's AIDS admission had, for the most part, garnered Rock much heartfelt public sympathy. The 45,000 letters of support he had received in the last months of his life were a testament to this. However, Christian's lawsuit made no bones about it—if anybody was entitled to sympathy, it was the wronged lover and not the morally bankrupt movie star.

"If you have AIDS and continue to have sex with someone as if nothing is wrong, I see it as like . . . attempted murder," Christian told an interviewer.

Was it possible that the same Rock Hudson who was held in the highest possible esteem by his coworkers, friends, and relatives had been capable of exposing a partner to a potentially deadly disease in exchange for sexual gratification? If Christian's allegations were true, Hudson's betrayal was unconscionable.

Four years would pass before a jury would reach a decision in the Marc Christian case. In the meantime, even more controversy erupted with the publication of a memoir entitled, *My Husband, Rock Hudson*. Phyllis Gates, who had been married to Hudson from 1955 to 1958, claimed that Rock and his omnipresent agent, Henry Willson, had ruthlessly manipulated her into participating in a sham marriage.

Gates, who had been Willson's secretary, would contend that she had been unwittingly used as a pawn to silence the rumors about Hudson's homosexual proclivities while keeping scandal sheets like *Confidential* at bay. In her book, Gates laid all of the blame for the disintegration of her marriage on Hudson. If Rock's gay predilections were common knowledge even among Hollywood's extras and bit players, Gates had somehow missed this. In a not-so-surprising revelation, she described Hudson's lovemaking as "routine and perfunctory." Gates then proceeded to take her deceased ex-husband to task for his "dark moods," "uncontrollable temper," "male chauvinist" tendencies, and "a strain of jealousy" in his nature. What's more, she recalled that Hudson didn't like to brush his teeth because he found the routine "boring."

In two years, Rock Hudson had morphed from movie icon to gay icon to The Face of AIDS. Somehow, even after his death, the reinvention continued. Only now—if Marc Christian were to be believed—Hudson was no longer a victim but an attempted murderer. And if Phyllis Gates had been completely forthcoming in her tell-all, it would appear that a widely respected and well-loved star had actually been a shamelessly manipulative con artist. Were these disparaging portrayals the unvarnished truth or the vilest form of character assassination?

For those who thought the real Rock Hudson had finally been unmasked at the end of his life, guess again. "Remember that movie, *The Three Faces of Eve*? That was my brother. This man led so many different lives, and kept them all separate from one another," says Rock's sister, Alice Waier. "Think about it—he had his family, he had his professional life, and he had his private life, and he had to portray a different person in each of those realms. Trying to please everyone but himself. I mean, he was a great performer—not only in acting but throughout his entire life."

All of the conflicts, betrayals, and deception that had been so much a part of Rock Hudson's life did not end with his death. For an individual who wanted to be an actor more than anything, there had been drama every step of the way. And it had started from the very beginning.

CHAPTER 1

WINNETKA

Young Roy Scherer, Jr.,
during his toddler years in Winnetka.
(*Photo courtesy of Diane Markert*)

Appropriately enough for one who embodied the American dream, Rock Hudson's story began in an idyllic small town in the Midwest.

"If one must live in Chicago, then one should eat, sleep, love and pray in Winnetka," said A. W. Stevens. Around the turn of the century, the writer had visited the picturesque village in northeast Illinois, located along the shores of Lake Michigan—only twenty miles away from "The Windy City."

Many of the German immigrants who had landed in the area in

the 1830s were from Trier—in the western part of Germany—so they referred to their adopted land as "New Trier." In 1869, the city was officially named Winnetka, after a Native American phrase supposedly meaning "Beautiful Land."

Much of Winnetka's natural beauty was attributable to its trees. Several streets were virtually canopied by American elms. The tall, stately oaks and flowering dogwoods shading the main part of town turned it into what has been described as "a living arboretum." As Judge Joseph Burke once remarked, "In order to have a street named after you in Winnetka, you must be from a very old family, or else be a tree."

In 1925—the same year that ground was broken on Winnetka's New Village Hall—Roy Harold Scherer, Jr., was born.[*] The delivery took place on November 17 at 2:15 a.m. in a rented room at 794 Elm Street, where his parents lived. Junior's father, Roy Scherer, was a twenty-six-year-old mechanic employed at the nearby Elm Street Garage. His mother, Katherine Marie Wood, was a twenty-five-year-old housewife.

By all accounts, it had been a very difficult birth, with Kay's on-again, off-again labor stretched out over five agonizing days. Roy Senior's older sister, Pearl, was a registered nurse. She assisted Dr. Gilbert Lowe—whose office was directly across the street from the Scherers' apartment—with the delivery. "I was right there when Dr. Lowe spanked the breath of life into him," Pearl Scherer recalled years later. "The first night I heard him squall, after his birth, I knew that he'd always be heard the rest of his life."

Although Roy Junior was born healthy—weighing *five* and a half pounds and not nine or thirteen as he would later tell unsuspecting colleagues—there would be an unusually long recovery

[*]Some references list 1924 as the year of Rock Hudson's birth, while others suggest that his given name was "*Leroy* Harold Scherer." Retrieved from the Cook County (Illinois) Bureau of Vital Records, the official birth certificate reveals that 1925 is the correct year and that Roy Harold Scherer, Jr., is how his name was recorded by the attending physician.

period for Kay after her exhausting ordeal. The agony Kay endured giving birth to Roy would haunt him for the rest of his life. "He told me that he had difficulties because he felt that he had ruined his mother's body," recalls actress Diane Ladd, who portrayed Kay in a 1990 television movie. "I said, 'What are you talking about, Rock?' He said, 'I was too big a baby . . . nine pounds. I ruined my mother's body trying to get born . . . I have horrible guilt.' I said, 'Who told you that?' He said, 'My mother.'"

Some recently unearthed evidence suggests that even before he was born, Roy Junior had caused some significant problems for his parents; though once he became a Hollywood star, all of the details would be carefully concealed. In an authorized 1956 fanzine entitled *Star Stories*, writer Jane Ardmore promised her readers Rock Hudson's "true life told in exciting story form." Ardmore described the Scherers' Elm Street residence as their "honeymoon apartment," one that Roy and Kay had moved into "a year and a half after their wedding." While this may constitute exciting story form, it bears only a passing resemblance to true life.

Roy and Kay's long buried marriage certificate is dated March 17, 1925, only eight months prior to Roy Junior's birth in November. This would suggest that the young couple had to get married— shotgun style—in order to save face. In many ways, Winnetka was a small town and news—especially any containing the slightest hint of scandal—traveled fast. Several years later, Kay's family would find this out the hard way.

When first married, it seemed as though Roy and Kay were well matched. Not only did they make a handsome couple, but both husband and wife would be remembered as "friendly and fun loving." Born in 1899, Roy was of average height and pleasant looking, the second eldest in a family of seven. Kay, who was born in 1900, would be described in *Photoplay* terms as, "a handsome, dark-haired woman with the fun-loving temperament and good humor of the Irish as well as an English reverence for thrift and industry." Others remembered both Kay and Roy as impulsive risk-takers.

"Your father loved the gaming tables and your mother loved the ponies," publicist Roger Jones once observed in a letter to their famous son.

Both the Scherers and the Woods were working-class families of modest means. Roy Senior's parents, Theodore and Lena Scherer,* owned a 160-acre farm in the township of Preston, roughly five miles north of downtown Olney. As he grew up, Roy Junior would spend many summers visiting Grandpa Scherer's farm.

"Rock's grandfather, Theodore, was a farmer all his life," says Jerry Scherer, another grandson. "He was the hardest worker you've ever seen. He had 152 acres that he made a living on and the other eight acres of his land went to the railroad that went by on the east side. Granddad always used a team of horses to plow. He didn't have a tractor. He was out there doing everything by himself . . . When people say, 'How could Rock have worked as hard as he did and make all these movies out in Hollywood?' That's because he grew up seeing his grandparents work their own farm. From an early age, he learned what it took to survive."

Relatives remember that Roy Junior would spend his summers riding the plough horse, chasing after his dog Crystal and attempting to assist with some of the daily chores. "One day, my grandmother asked him to feed the chickens," says sister Alice Waier. "I don't know how many chickens they had but I'm sure it was many. So, he went out to the coops and threw down their feed. Much to everyone's surprise, they all died. Instead of chicken feed, he had thrown down lye. Well, my dad was furious. Not Grandma Scherer. She told everyone not to lay a hand on Junior. It was all a mistake. To say the least, my brother was horrified. But Grandma just took

*Rock Hudson's paternal great-grandfather, Adam Scherer, was born in Bavaria, Germany, and arrived in America in 1836 at the age of two. Rock's paternal grandfather, Theodore Scherer, was born in Richland County, Illinois, in 1870. Rock's paternal grandmother, Lena Blatter, was born in Richland County in 1874; her father was Swiss born while her mother was from Illinois.

him under her wing. They got more chickens and she showed him how to feed them. She was always looking out for Junior."

In the latter half of the 1920s, Roy and Kay had managed to scrape by on what Roy took home from the Elm Street garage as well as the occasional handout from Kay's family, but all of that changed in the fall of 1929. Even an affluent community like Winnetka wasn't immune to the Depression. Some indication of the family's precarious financial situation can be found in a census report from 1930. By that time, the Scherers had moved to more affordable lodging at 1027 Elm Street, where they rented rooms for $50 a month. Roy Senior's twenty-three-year-old brother, Lloyd, "a gas station helper," was now residing with them.

After Roy lost his job, he, Kay, and five-year-old Roy Junior suddenly found themselves moving out of their Elm Street apartment and in with Kay's parents. The Woods lived in a modest gray stucco bungalow on Center Street in Winnetka. In addition to the three Scherers, Grandpa and Grandma Wood were already housing their youngest son, John, his wife and their four children. *Eleven* people, all tightly packed under one roof. There was one bedroom, one bathroom, and no privacy. Although conditions at the Wood home were cramped and often chaotic, these circumstances were hardly unique at a time when eight million Americans were out of work.

Kay's father, James Wood, had managed to hold on to his job at Winnetka Coal & Lumber. Born in Armitage, England, Grandpa Wood was over six feet tall and powerfully built, though he never played the commanding patriarch. Instead, he let his charismatic wife take control of their overpopulated household. Kay's mother, Mary Ellen Enright, had been born in Shermerville, Illinois, though her parents were from "the old country"—Ireland.

If the adults in the house were preoccupied with money woes and the unrelentingly grim headlines, young Roy was having the time of his life. The boy with the Buster Brown bob and mischievous smile was clearly Grandma Wood's favorite. "He got away with murder," remembered one cousin. This included taking a single bite out of every apple in the ice box and consuming a pound of uncooked bacon. Although it was obvious who was the culprit, Roy allowed his cousins to take the fall for his antics. Whenever another of Roy's misdeeds was reported to her, Grandma Wood simply looked the other way. Clearly, the woman who enjoyed her dessert before dinner sensed that her disobedient grandson was very much a kindred spirit.

As family lore had it, Kay's doctor had played phonograph records to soothe her during her torturous delivery, which resulted in Roy Junior's early and lifelong love of music. When visiting the Scherer farm, he loved to pump the player piano. At Grandma Wood's, he'd crank up the gramophone and listen to Al Jolson's recording of "There's a Rainbow 'Round My Shoulder" over and over again. And even when he wasn't listening to music, young Roy would still monopolize Grandpa Wood's radio. Every week, he faithfully tuned in to *The Witch's Tale*, listening intently as "Old Nancy, the Witch of Salem," introduced yet another terrifying episode.

If his son was totally oblivious to the troubled times they were living in, Roy Scherer was all too aware of them. Ever since the Elm Street garage had closed, Roy shuffled through his days, feeling useless. Attempts to find work led straight to nowhere. Moving in with Kay's parents had been even more humiliating. He felt like a charity case. With each passing day, Roy grew less hopeful. After mulling it over for weeks, he finally decided it was time to leave. He'd go off and make a fresh start somewhere. It was no good talking it over with Kay. This was something he had to do by himself.

As it happened, Roy Junior was away at Grandpa Scherer's farm in Olney on the afternoon in 1931 that his father walked out. Nearly seventy years after the fact, his cousin Dorothy Kimble remembered Scherer's departure vividly: "I was home from school sick at the time . . . Uncle Roy came out of their bedroom carrying a suit-case, and gave me a nickel not to tell anyone he was going. I cher-ished that nickel. I didn't say a thing. I watched him walk down the street and that's the last I saw of him."*

Scherer walked out on everything that day—his wife, his young son, his extended family, and virtually everything he knew. Though he apparently didn't have any connections on the West Coast, he decided that moving there was his best hope for starting over. But were hard times the real reason Scherer decided to take a walk? Sev-eral family members have suggested that something else may have prompted his departure. It was said that it was Roy Junior who was the real cause of his father's abrupt exit. "There was family gossip that [Kay] was so devoted to Roy [Junior] that she ignored her hus-band, and that's why Scherer left," said Kay's nephew, Edwin Wood.

While his father's abandonment was a subject that Rock Hud-son never discussed publicly, the editors of a 1950s fan magazine concocted their own version of Roy Senior's departure. As a result, one of the most painful episodes in the star's life was reenacted as a sudsy Ross Hunter–produced melodrama. The kind that usually starred Rock Hudson . . .

"You don't understand, Kay, I can't face it, I'm going away to make a new start."

"Oh, but Roy, take me with you. I want to go, too."

"Kay, you don't understand, I'm bankrupt. I spent my last nickel on a railroad ticket . . ."

"All aboard. All a . . ."

"Kay, I've got to catch the train. I'll write you. Goodbye, say goodbye to Sonny . . ."

---

*Kay's mother remembered September 2, 1931, a bit differently. In March of 1933, Mary Ellen Wood testified as a witness in Kay's divorce hearing and told the court that on the day Scherer walked out "he packed his things and left, never said a word to anybody . . . [He went] across the street and got into a car that he had stationed there."

Fanzine writers outdid themselves attempting to turn this desperate act into something glossily cinematic. Though in reality, Scherer's desertion was anything but a tender love scene. He just left and never came back. In official retellings, The Great Depression would always be blamed for Scherer's walkout. Though Mark Miller, one of Rock's closest friends, claimed that Kay told him the real reason for her husband's abrupt departure.

"I was on an airplane with Rock's mother, Katherine. After she had a couple of martinis, she said, 'Mark, there is something I want to tell you . . .' After another sip, she continued, 'Roy Scherer was *not* Roy Junior's real father. I was having an affair with a very tall boy who pumped gas down on the corner.' After another sip, she said, 'I never learned of his name. Then I married Roy not knowing I was pregnant. Roy Junior was actually born seven months after I married Roy. When Roy found out five years later, he deserted us.'"

Truth or martini-fueled fantasy? Roy Junior's birth certificate lists Scherer as his biological father. In some photographs, there's an undeniable family resemblance, despite the fact that Mark Miller's stunned response to Kay's confession was, "I've always wondered why Rock looked nothing like Roy Scherer." The date of Kay's marriage certificate corroborates the fact that she was already pregnant when she married Scherer, which lends some credence to her story. As for "the very tall boy who pumped gas down on the corner," is it credible that in 1920s Winnetka Kay would have had a dalliance with an anonymous lover? And what—if anything—should be made of the fact that Scherer's younger brother, Lloyd (who lived with Roy Senior and Kay at one point), and Roy Junior's future stepfather, Wallace Fitzgerald, both worked as gas station attendants?

Regardless of why Scherer left, what must it have been like for a sensitive six-year-old boy to attempt to process the sudden and inexplicable disappearance of his father? Not only had he left without saying goodbye, but nobody seemed to know exactly where he had gone. Although everyone kept telling Roy Junior that his father would be back—in a few months, when business picked up, by next Christmas—he eventually figured it out. His father was gone for good. And no matter what Roy Junior did, or how many questions he asked, or how well behaved he was, his father had not only moved on without him but, if some of the whispers were to be believed, *because* of him.

Around this time, young Roy entered the first grade at the Horace Mann School. A faded photograph snapped in the schoolroom shows a forlorn, pouty-faced Roy. His expression seems to suggest that he'd rather be back on the Scherer farm in Olney. In later years, Rock Hudson would look back on the days he spent there as some of the happiest of his life. One memory in particular would always stay with him. He came in from playing one afternoon to find Grandpa and Grandma Scherer—who were not usually demonstrative in front of others—sitting on the couch, holding hands, and talking to each other in German.* Even at a young age, he found this touching. Though he also wondered why he'd never seen his own parents behaving so tenderly with each other.

While she was still legally married, Kay was now essentially a single woman with a young son to support. At a time when jobs were scarce, she took work wherever she could find it. At one time or another, she was employed as a waitress, a babysitter, a live-in domestic, a telephone operator, and an organist—providing the musical accompaniment for silent movies. Even on those rare days when she wasn't working, Kay would return to the theatre as a patron. And Roy Junior was always by her side. "Whatever my mother wanted to see was what I saw, every Saturday," Rock Hudson would later recall. "The only trouble was, my mother was hopelessly in

---

*"My father said that when he and his siblings were youngsters, they spoke mostly German in the home," says Rock's cousin Gaylord Scherer. "However, after they reached a certain age, my grandmother Lena said they were no longer going to speak German. They were American citizens and, therefore, they were going to start speaking English at home and on their farm."

love with John Boles. I was dragged off to sit through every movie John Boles ever made, when I was dying to see Robin Hood or Fu Manchu or Buck Jones."

It was most likely that at one of these Saturday matinees Roy had his first notion that he wanted to do what those people up on the screen were doing. Though he kept this a secret. As he explained to an interviewer toward the end of his life: "Back in a small town, I could never freely say, 'I'm going to be an actor when I grow up,' because that's just sissy stuff. You know, 'Don't bother with that. You ought to be a policeman or a fireman.' So, I never said anything. I just kept my mouth shut."

This was the beginning of Rock Hudson's life as a covert operation. And it was this phrase—*I just kept my mouth shut*—that he would repeat over and over again in interviews spanning decades. From an early age, he learned that you could talk about pretty much anything—except what you truly felt and what you really wanted. Like a father. Weeks and then months had passed without any word from Roy Senior. Still, Kay held out hope that he would eventually come back. Convinced that his return was only a matter of the right kind of coaxing, she began setting some money aside. In August of 1932, Kay sent her absentee husband a one-way bus ticket, which Scherer promptly returned, indicating that he had no intention of coming back.

Undaunted, Kay decided that if Scherer wouldn't come to her, then she and young Roy would go to him. Surely the sight of his own child would snap him out of this—whatever *this* was. Mother and son boarded a Greyhound bus for California. Kay managed to track Scherer down through the Priscilla Tea Room, a little restaurant in downtown Los Angeles, where he had been receiving his mail. However, when they reached the boarding house in Pasadena where Scherer was last known to be living, they were surprised to discover that he had suddenly vacated his room. When Kay finally caught up with her husband, she asked him to return home with her and Roy. He refused.

Kay and young Roy returned to Winnetka completely defeated. It was time to face facts. The marriage was over. In December, Kay's attorneys issued a bill of complaint against Scherer. Though he was summoned to appear at the Cook County Courthouse, he was a no-show. The divorce decree that followed spelled everything out:

"The defendant, Roy H. Scherer, wholly and utterly disregarding his marriage vows and obligations . . . willfully deserted and absented himself from the complainant without any reasonable cause . . . It is therefore ordered, that the bonds of matrimony existing between the complainant, Katherine Scherer, and the defendant, Roy H. Scherer, be dissolved . . . It is further decreed that the complainant shall continue to have the sole care, custody and education of the said child, Roy H. Scherer, Jr."

On March 18, 1933, Roy Junior's parents were officially divorced. Although Roy was reassured by relatives on both sides that his parents' divorce had nothing to do with him, he was convinced that he was responsible for the breakup. As the first in a series of lifelong betrayals, his father's desertion would leave him with a gnawing feeling of incompletion. Kay did her best to compensate. "She was mother, father, and big sister to me," Rock Hudson would later say. "And I was son and brother to her, regardless of who she was married to."

WHILE STILL RECOVERING from the collapse of her marriage and struggling to stay afloat, Kay met a handsome, tough-as-nails marine named Wallace Fitzgerald. Originally from Greenland, New Hampshire, Fitzgerald had first enlisted in 1930 when he turned twenty-one. When he and Kay began dating, Fitzgerald was serving as a private at the US Naval Training Station in Great Lakes, Illinois. Friends of the couple recalled that Fitzgerald cut an impressive figure in his military uniform and that Kay was quickly swept off her feet.

Fitzgerald was a powerful presence—the kind of commanding, take-charge type that Kay may have felt she needed to fill the void left by Scherer. What's more, Kay thought that Roy Junior should have a strong authority figure to stand in for his absentee father. Kay's new beau seemed like the perfect candidate. But Wallace Fitzgerald was hardly the clean-cut, all-American hero that he appeared to be. Far from it, in fact.

When Fitzgerald was eighteen, a New Hampshire grand jury charged him with larceny after he was accused of stealing a ring from the home of a Greenland neighbor. He pled not guilty and was released on bail. Three years later, *The Portsmouth Herald* reported that Fitzgerald and a female companion, Mrs. Myra Cameron, were involved in an alleged assault against another Greenland resident. In October of 1931, Fitzgerald's commanding officer charged him with desertion after he went missing for twelve days. While on leave, Fitzgerald had gone on an epic bender, winding up behind bars in Yuma, Arizona.

Kay was apparently unaware of Fitzgerald's criminal history, but all too soon she became aware of his drinking binges. Early in their relationship Kay may have written this off as the curse of an enlisted man, but giving Fitzgerald a pass where his chronic drunkenness was concerned would prove to have dire consequences. Despite the warning signs, Kay decided to take the plunge and on March 17, 1934, she married Wallace Fitzgerald in Waukegan. A year later, the hot-tempered marine adopted nine-year-old Roy.

Almost immediately, Roy's stepfather exhibited an open hostility toward him. Fitzgerald seemed irrationally jealous of the amount of attention Kay lavished on her only child. Determined to make a man out of him, Fitzgerald cracked the whip. He enrolled Roy in a local Boy Scout troop, confiscated any toys that he considered too childish, and smacked away any behavior that he perceived to be effeminate.

The heterosexualizing of Rock Hudson started long before he landed in Hollywood and met Henry Willson, the agent who reconditioned him into a presumably straight leading man. Even as a pre-adolescent, Roy was forced to conform or there would be hell to pay.

"I once asked my stepfather if I could have drama lessons," the adult Rock Hudson recalled. "The old man said, 'Why?' When I said I wanted to be an actor . . . *Crack!* And that was that."

The more Fitzgerald drank, the more violent he became—lashing out at both Kay and Roy. Rock's cousin Edwin Wood didn't mince words: "He was a drunk . . . He used to beat Roy and Katherine." Another cousin, Helen Wood Folkers, claimed to have seen evidence of this. "We used to see Roy covered with bruises . . . One day, Auntie Kay showed up with two black eyes." A once cheerful, free-spirited Roy suddenly became sullen and withdrawn. First nail-biting became a problem, then bed-wetting. Ultimately, Roy began staying away from home as much as possible.

Just as the local movie theatre had been a refuge for Kay after Scherer walked out, it now provided the same kind of sanctuary for her son. One picture that completely captivated Roy was *The Hurricane.* Directed by John Ford, this South Seas melodrama was pure escapist fantasy, intended to give Depression-era audiences a much-needed lift. In the case of one wide-eyed audience member, it more than achieved its purpose. For a couple of hours, Roy was free to roam around the island of Manukura, his own tropical paradise.

The eye candy wasn't only confined to the breathtaking location photography. Bare-chested and outfitted only in an abbreviated sarong for most of the movie, leading man Jon Hall would become young Roy's first man crush. Watching Hall execute a masterful swan dive from a crow's nest into a shimmering lagoon, Roy was transfixed.* Sitting in the dark and hypnotized by the flickering

*After Roy Fitzgerald became Rock Hudson, he told several interviewers that Jon Hall's spectacular diving had inspired him to become an actor. Then he made an important discovery. As he told Kevin Thomas of the *Los Angeles Times*: "Years later, I was skin diving with Paul Stader, the stuntman, and I told him this story. He said, 'Why, that was me, not Hall.' I said, 'So you're the one responsible for getting me into this whole crazy thing.'"

images, he thought to himself . . . *Well, that cinches it, doesn't it? I've got to go to Tahiti. The only way to do that is to become an actor.*

Beyond any homoerotic longings that Hall's Polynesian sailor inspired, *The Hurricane* also touched upon another area of Roy's life that he couldn't share with anyone. It's not too much of a stretch to imagine an abused twelve-year-old closely identifying with Hall's unjustly imprisoned native, who is whipped and beaten after being sentenced to hard labor by a sadistic governor. Abandoned by one father and abused by another, Roy felt betrayed by virtually everyone in his immediate family—even Kay. How could she have subjected him to a monster like his stepfather? If most of the time she was an over-controlling, even manipulative force in Roy's life, at other times was he basically left to fend for himself?

In a surprisingly candid interview with *Modern Screen* in 1955, Kay described her first two marriages as "horrible nightmares." When asked about her second husband, Kay claimed that she was unaware that Fitzgerald was regularly pummeling her son while she was away at work: "He used to beat Roy savagely and the boy never told me about it until after I was divorced. Then he told me everything. I feel very sorry for that man if he ever crosses Roy's path."

During this bleak period of his life, Roy had few trusted friends. "Skokie Junior High. That is where we met," remembered Suzanne Guyot. "I think he worked hard to be happy and always, there was this shadow and he was so shy. He was really a loner. I was his best friend and he was mine. For a while, I was his best girl and that was nice until I threw him over for someone else." Guyot remembered hearing "horror stories" concerning Fitzgerald's extreme cruelty to Roy: "It wasn't a happy childhood, that's for sure."

Instead of hardening Roy, his stepfather's abuse seemed to make him even more compassionate when he encountered others being bullied. "We were in the same class," Edward Jenner recalled. "I was the poor little rich kid, driven to public school by the chauffeur each morning. There were a bunch of hoodlum types going to the school, and they would tease and bully me. But Roy stuck up for me and told them to lay off. After Roy intervened, the others accepted me. When things were tough, he was the only friend I had."

As a reward for Roy's gallantry, Jenner's mother paid to have him enrolled in Alicia Pratt's dance classes at the Winnetka Women's Club, where Ed was already a student. Wallace Fitzgerald was outraged that his stepson was now waltzing away his afternoons, though Kay was thrilled that Roy was associating with one of Winnetka's wealthiest families.

"We used to sleep over at each other's houses," Jenner said. "When he came to my house, he was overwhelmed—we had a swimming pool, and our house was like a country club without the dues." For several reasons, Jenner remembered that staying over at Roy's house wasn't nearly as agreeable: "His house had just two little bedrooms, and was tiny." By this time, Roy had also become a chronic bed-wetter. One evening, when Roy and Ed were preparing to bunk together, Kay instructed Jenner to wrap a towel around himself so that he wouldn't get soaked in the middle of the night. Roy was understandably humiliated.

Jenner also remembered being aware of some of the simmering tensions at his friend's house. "At that time, the stepfather was quite a drinker, and when he went on his little toots, he'd beat up Roy and his mother. That tore Roy apart." Neighbors of the Fitzgeralds became accustomed to calling the police to intervene in what were politely described as "family quarrels." During her seven years of marriage to Fitzgerald, a terrified Kay would frequently turn up at her mother's house, where she would display her latest bruises and scratches. Sometimes she would be alone, but very often Roy was with her.

"I remember when Roy was having some terrible problems with his stepfather, he'd spend quite a bit of time at our house," remembers Robert Willett, whose sister, Louise, became one of Roy's trusted confidantes. "He was looking for some help and support during a difficult period and my sister was a very compassionate and understanding girl. Another reason they were compatible is height. That may sound strange, but Roy had been this very scrawny kid. Suddenly, he had a growth spurt and just grew like crazy. Louise was the tallest girl in her class. Height is very important to kids, so that connected them. But the real reason is he needed someone to talk to when his parents were having all of these difficulties."

As Fitzgerald's drunken tirades became worse, Kay's friends began asking her the obvious question—why stay? In the Midwest in the early 1940s, being a single mother with a pair of divorces was practically unheard of. In fact, an especially devout sister-in-law already refused to associate with Kay because she was a divorcee. And back in 1937, a messy divorce had figured in a very public scandal involving Kay's younger brother.[*] In a small town like Winnetka, this was shocking stuff and a great embarrassment to the family. All of this may have factored into Kay's decision to stick it out with Fitzgerald as long as she could. Though, finally, in the spring of 1941, two particularly disturbing episodes prompted Kay to head back to the Cook County Superior Court.

In her divorce complaint, Kay charged Fitzgerald with "extreme and repeated cruelty." She described the first incident as "a severe beating . . . He came home from work intoxicated and he struck me very severely . . . He choked me, which resulted in calling a doctor." Two months later, there was a second assault that again involved choking and that also required medical attention. Kay's neighbor Catherine M. Dahl testified that throughout his marriage to Kay, Fitzgerald had been "cruel" and "generally abusive."

On July 22, 1941, Judge Charles A. Williams ruled in Kay's favor and granted her a divorce. "It is further ordered that the plain-

---

[*]"Burning Love of Carol G. for Fireman Told" is how an exposé in the *Chicago Daily Tribune* was headlined: "The epic of the Woods of Winnetka and the mysterious Carol G. who entered their lives eighteen months ago went unrolling itself in court. Captain David J. Wood of the Winnetka fire department is suing his wife, Gertrude, for divorce, and she is seeking separate maintenance on a cross-complaint charging adultery with Carol G."

tiff, Katherine Fitzgerald, have the care and custody of the minor child, Roy Scherer Fitzgerald, now aged fifteen years. It is further ordered that the defendant, Wallace Fitzgerald, pay to the plaintiff the sum of $2,000 in semi-monthly installments of $32.50 in full settlement of plaintiff's claim for alimony and support money."[*] Fitzgerald was also ordered to surrender his 1937 Dodge sedan to his wife.

[*]A year after Kay's divorce hearing, the Superior Court of Cook County filed the following addendum on September 24, 1942: "Upon the court being advised that the defendant desires to offer his services to the United States Marine Corps, and the plaintiff having demonstrated to the court that she desires to release said defendant into the service of her country, it is ordered that all provisions requiring payments of alimony be suspended for the duration of the war."

CHAPTER 2

GREEN GIN

Roy Fitzgerald's Navy induction photo, 1944.

n June of 1939, Roy had enrolled in a summer school program at New Trier High School, one of the finest high schools in the country in terms of scholastic achievement. Though Roy Fitzgerald would ultimately emerge as one of New Trier's most famous graduates—alongside Charlton Heston and Ann-Margret—he was never one of the school's most distinguished scholars.

"At New Trier, Roy sat behind me in Latin class," recalls classmate Bill Markus. "He really struggled with the subject. He asked me for help once in a while, which I was able to give him. I remember him as a very shy, soft spoken person. He was still growing and filling out in those days and he may have felt awkward about that.

I remember that he kept to himself and he didn't participate much in school activities."

Although New Trier's varsity track team, The Triermen, regularly won suburban league meets and the dramatics department staged ambitious productions like *The Yeomen of the Guard*, Roy Fitzgerald was far too busy to participate. "Why was he not in activities at school? You have to remember that Roy worked," says classmate Philip "Bud" Davis. "When I knew him, he had a job at White's Drug Store, just a couple of blocks west of New Trier. So, when classes were over, he didn't have time to fool around. The guy had work to do. Though I don't think it was generally known that he did work. All of a sudden, Roy would just disappear after school."

Unlike the majority of his classmates, who were from some of Winnetka's wealthiest families, teenage Roy was already in a position of having to support himself. In addition to managing a full course load, Roy held down a number of part-time jobs. If he wasn't stocking groceries at the Jewel Tea Store or serving up Green Rivers as a soda jerk at Hammond's Ice Cream Parlor, he was caddying at Skokie Playfield. Roy was also an usher at the Teatro del Lago movie theatre, where he had an opportunity to see his heroes, Spencer Tracy and Tyrone Power, for free. "There were very few movie stars I didn't like," he'd later say. "One was Errol Flynn. It was a silly thing. He reminded me of my stepfather, whom I didn't like at all." Little did Roy know that one day, after becoming Hollywood's new romantic idol, his portrait would grace the theatre's lobby.

While most of Roy's surviving classmates remember him as a loner, he did have two close friends in high school: Jim Matteoni and Pat McGuire. In 1952, after Roy Fitzgerald had morphed into Rock Hudson and he was being honored on *This Is Your Life*, the one guest he was clearly most excited to see was Matteoni. And why did they hit it off so well? "We laughed all the time," Matteoni said. "We had some great times together back in high school. You know, most people take one lunch period. Well, that wasn't enough for us. We took three."

Occasionally, all three boys—Roy, Jim, and Pat—would venture to the south side of Chicago. Matteoni remembered that they scoured secondhand shops looking for blues records. One jazz disc in particular—the haunting "Green Gin" by Ernie Andrews—would elude Roy for years. In fact, he couldn't afford to obtain a copy until after he became famous. According to Pat McGuire, there was an ulterior motive connected to some of their musical pursuits: "If we could get near a dance floor someplace, we'd go looking for dancing girls. And just generally look for women. All three of us were single, so that was our main occupation."

According to his best friends, in those days Roy seemed as interested in female companionship as they were. "He chased girls with great care and perseverance," Matteoni recalled. And Pat McGuire remembered that there were "no overtures or insinuations" during sleepovers at Roy's house: "If we had been out late, I would flop at his house. We had no kind of sexual relationship. I'm not gay and I was shocked to find out later that he was."

"When I knew him and he was in high school, he never exhibited to anyone in any way that he was gay," says Bud Davis. "I guess the only way you could say he did is the fact that he did not date very much. Perhaps he was aware of his sexuality then and who knows, maybe confused by it." And, as Roy himself pointed out so often, even if he was starting to feel attracted to other men, he knew enough to keep his mouth shut. Long before he landed in Hollywood, he understood that if he wanted to be accepted, the very essence of who he was would have to be edited out of the frame.

For a small-town boy to admit that he had theatrical ambitions was equivalent to announcing that he wanted to be a prima ballerina. The closest Roy came to revealing his secret longing was when he talked Matteoni and McGuire into joining him in assisting the Threshold Players, Winnetka's community theatre group. They would serve the troupe as prop boys and scene changers. In this way, Roy would get as close as possible to acting without actually going all the way. "Roy was more taken by the whole thing than either me or Pat," Jim Matteoni admitted. "The glamour lasted in him longer than it lasted in us . . . I think one of the reasons Roy became so enamored of the movies and the stage was as a way to escape the pressures and hardships at home."

Even with his stepfather out of his life, Roy still had to contend with an overprotective and domineering mother. Pat McGuire recalls that Kay didn't think that her son should be spending so much time with him. "She and I were enemies," McGuire says. "She didn't like me and I didn't like her. Kay was bound and determined that Roy should associate with wealthy people. My family was not wealthy. Far from it. So, I was considered a waste of time for Roy. I remember that Kay had a rather sharp mouth on her. Sometimes that would cause a few little arguments. Although I have to say that Roy always defended her if there were any battles going on. They had been through so much together and Roy was protective of her. I mean, a better guy you couldn't find."

In both the 1943 and 1944 New Trier yearbooks, Roy Fitzgerald is listed as a senior.[*] Pat McGuire remembers that he and Roy were forced to repeat a semester. "We both had a little problem with absence from school and bad grades. So we didn't have the necessary credits to graduate on time," McGuire says. "I mean, what the hell did we know in those days? We were just a couple of dumb kids."

On January 29, 1944, Roy Fitzgerald voluntarily enlisted in the U.S. Navy as an Apprentice Seaman. His induction photo says it all: *Somebody please help me.* Though he would later pose for thousands of pictures as one of the most photographed actors of his

---

[*]According to New Trier records, Roy was expected to graduate in June 1943. However, he voluntarily withdrew in June 1942 (after his junior year). The official reason for withdrawal is listed only as "Los Angeles, California." At one point, Roy intended to move in with his father and complete high school on the West Coast, though he later changed his mind. There is no reenrollment date listed but there are grades on file for the 1942–43 school year and the first semester of 1943–44. Roy finally graduated from New Trier on February 4, 1944.

generation, this has to be the saddest image ever captured of him. The expression is both deeply wounded and grimly determined. Active duty was yet another ordeal he had to overcome. And it was one more thing standing in the way of his dreams. His boot camp training took place at the Great Lakes Naval Base in Lake County, about thirteen miles from Winnetka. The same location where his stepfather had once been stationed.

In October of 1945, Roy was transferred to the U.S. Naval Air Base in Samar, a mountainous island in the Philippines. According to legend, as Roy shipped out, the new Doris Day hit "Sentimental Journey" came pouring over the loudspeakers, leaving all of the young servicemen, including Day's future Hollywood costar, in tears. Once on base in Samar, Roy was assigned to an aviation repair and overhaul unit, his chief duty as a technician being the unloading of naval planes from carriers.

Roy's service in the Philippines was undistinguished, but in later years he found a way to make it sound noteworthy. For years, he told people that while checking the multiengine bombers on a B-26 Marauder, he made the mistake of revving up two motors on the same side first. Before he could apply the brakes, the plane "sliced a Piper Cub into kindling wood." In 1952, when Roy was spotlighted on *This Is Your Life*, he recounted this embarrassing episode, delighting a captive audience. Host Ralph Edwards inquired, "For this exploit, you were rewarded in what way, sir?" "I was transferred to the laundry," Roy replied. Great story. Even if it wasn't true. "People wanted exciting anecdotes and I didn't have any," he later admitted.

According to Roy's military file, he was involved in two different disciplinary matters during his term of service. In April of 1944, he was declared a straggler when he failed to return to base in a timely manner. While on leave, he had contracted pleurisy and Kay brought him to the military hospital at Great Lakes. Due to a clerical oversight, Roy was tagged AWOL and the Shore Patrol was dispatched. When they finally discovered Roy recovering in a hospital bed, the case against Seaman Fitzgerald was officially closed.

Then, on July 8, 1944, Roy attended a department party with other enlisted men in the Norwood Park neighborhood of Chicago. A few weeks later, he was interviewed concerning his social interactions at the party and the loss of his liberty identification card, which was never recovered. It's unclear why this episode warranted such scrutiny, though it's been suggested that while he was in the service, Roy started having sex with other men. "He told me that he'd had a couple of experiences in the Navy, since he couldn't get to a female anywhere," said Bob Preble, Roy's roommate in the early 1950s. "And he didn't find the experiences he had with males in the Navy all that unenjoyable. So, it was probably something that he had an underlying need for anyway."

On May 14, 1946, Roy was honorably discharged at Camp Shoemaker in Pleasanton, California. Once home in Winnetka, he completed a "Questionnaire Covering Individual War Service." Line 19 of the form inquired about "Number of children, if any, as of this date," to which Roy responded, "None." To this day, many people question whether this was the correct answer.

After his death, articles with sensationalistic titles like "The Search for Rock Hudson's Secret Son" began turning up in tabloids such as the *National Enquirer* and *Star* magazine. The scandal sheets launched investigations into what they termed "a baffling mystery." While rumors had circulated for years that Rock Hudson's "love child" was roaming the streets of Winnetka, the story didn't become tabloid fodder until two of the people closest to Rock started talking. Allegedly, Kay told Hudson's longtime companion, Tom Clark, that while Rock was in the Navy, he had come home on leave and had a weekend fling ("a quickie," in *Star* parlance) with the mother of a New Trier classmate.

According to Clark, Kay recalled receiving a letter at one point from a woman in Winnetka claiming to be the mother of Rock's child. Kay acknowledged that it was within the realm of possibility that the lady was telling the truth. Though some of those closest to Hudson, including his high school buddy, Jim Matteoni, weren't buying it. "If Roy had a son, I would have been the first to know," Matteoni said. "He confided in me about everything. I was his best friend. We were inseparable. Roy didn't have a steady girlfriend in all the time I knew him. We just had platonic friendships with the girls in our bunch."

Even so, the tabloid stories kept on coming. Each "shocking exclusive" claimed to offer new details, insisting that when Rock was still Roy and all of nineteen, he had "sired a secret son while he was in the Navy in 1944." In Clark's memoir, he wrote that Hudson was aware of the rumors that he may have fathered a child. For a time, he even considered returning to his hometown with a meeting in mind. But the mother was married now. What if this stirred things up for all concerned? Or what if the basis for these stories was only some lonely Rock Hudson fan's delusional fantasy?

More than thirty years after his death, the debate over Rock Hudson's paternity continues. In 2014, a sixty-nine-year-old woman named Susan Dent[*] filed a lawsuit against Hudson's estate. Dent sought no financial remuneration but only an order establishing paternity. At one point, DNA testing was conducted and it reportedly revealed a match between Dent and some of Rock's relatives on both sides of the family. Dent's suit was initially dismissed, but in 2017 the dismissal was reversed by the California Court of Appeal. Although Dent's attorneys didn't submit any DNA results with their initial filing, they planned to include this evidence in a new trial.

According to Alice Waier, other evidence exists which confirms that young Roy Fitzgerald had fathered a child: "I have a letter that

[*]In recent years, Susan Dent has met with Hudson's relatives, friends, and estate manager and virtually all of them find her story credible. More than one individual interviewed for this book insisted that while Hudson was in the Navy, he actually fathered *two* daughters—by different mothers—though no evidence has been produced to support these claims.

my brother wrote to a friend in November of 1945. He was still in the service at that point but he'd just heard from this girl that he'd gone to school with. It sounds like they had a one time fling. Now he finds out the girl is pregnant and that she plans to give the child up for adoption. In this letter, he tells his friend everything. When I read it, I thought 'this couldn't be my brother,' because it was somewhat cold. But then I have to go back to his age. There was a war going on. He has no way to support this child. He's got a domineering mother. I can see his predicament . . . and I'm sure Kay handled the whole damn thing because he wasn't even at home."

Once Roy was stateside again, it's unclear if he made any attempts to contact the young woman who may have given birth to his child. Assuming any responsibility—parental or otherwise—seemed to be the furthest thing from his mind. "After my discharge, I returned to Winnetka. I wanted a vacation," he would later tell a reporter. "For nearly a year, I just drifted around, drawing down my $20 a week from the government." At Kay's urging, he completed a Civil Service examination and accepted a position as a substitute mail carrier. "When Rock worked for me, he was always on the job," said Winnetka's postmaster Arthur Kloepfer. "He was a very determined fellow." Roy's determination only lasted so long, however. "Delivering the mail was not for me," he later admitted. "I stood about three months of it and then my feet and back started begging for mercy."

During the Christmas season, he landed a temporary position in the gift-wrapping department at Marshall Field's, Chicago's biggest department store. While working there, Roy attracted lots of attention—though it wasn't for his gift-wrapping expertise. Since returning home, his once willowy frame had filled out nicely. Now his striking looks, towering height, and muscular physique started turning heads. And according to one satisfied customer, it was Roy's abilities off the sales floor that truly impressed.

Samuel Steward—novelist, DePaul University professor, pulp pornographer—included twenty-one-year-old Roy Fitzgerald in his now notorious "Stud File." This was Steward's meticulously detailed cataloging of his homoerotic exploits, from the Turkish baths to Room 111 in the Hotel Medford in Milwaukee. After every tryst, Steward would document the specifics of the encounter as well as his impressions of his sex partners. The entries are unabashedly explicit and often hilarious:

"Davey, John—1952, Paris . . . Stupid NBC announcer. 'Imagine—all those letters just because I said 'Back' instead of 'Bach'!"

"Lt. Wm. Leland Harden—Chicago, 1943—8x Whoosh! Whatta Bitch!"

By comparison, a future Hollywood legend was let off rather easily after an alleged assignation in a Marshall Field's freight elevator which Steward had stopped between floors:

"Fitzgerald, Roy—Chicago, XII-46, 1X . . . Tall ex-sailor. Ami de John Scheele.* Worked in gift wrap dept. Black curly hair. V. gd.-lking."

Despite his popularity at Marshall Field's, Roy found himself idle again after the holidays. Having spent time in exotic locations overseas, Winnetka now seemed rather ordinary. "After I got out of the Navy . . . I thought, 'This place is not for me. Now is the time to do what I want to do.' Mind you, I never told anybody."

Even if Roy had never revealed to Kay his plan for pursuing an acting career, she must have recognized that her son had reached a crossroads in his life and needed a push. Characteristic of both, Roy dreamed big while Kay did something about it. She decided it was time for them to move. She had attempted to put this in motion a year earlier, but Roy had talked her out of it. Employed as a telephone operator at the Glenview Naval Air Station, Kay had requested a transfer to San Francisco in the hopes that she could persuade Roy to relocate there with her once he was discharged. At the time, Roy preferred to return to Winnetka so that he could regroup and catch up with his buddies.

---

*Scheele managed the bookstore at Marshall Field's, where Samuel Steward was also temporarily employed.

Though after a year of drifting, Roy was getting angsty. San Francisco was out of the question in terms of launching an acting career. So it was either Broadway or Hollywood. "I didn't quite flip a coin," he remembered. "I did know one person in Los Angeles and I knew nobody in New York." California eventually won out. For there, not one but two unspoken goals could finally be realized: becoming a screen actor and reuniting with his father. Fifteen years had passed since Roy Scherer had walked out of his son's life. During that time, they had occasionally corresponded, though there had been relatively few visits. In 1945, while on leave, Roy had spent the holidays with his father, who by that time had relocated to Long Beach and remarried.

If Roy had been hoping to forge a more meaningful relationship with Scherer, it didn't happen then. Though maybe, if they were living together, his father might come around. With this in mind, Kay arranged for a job transfer to Pasadena, where she would eventually settle with her third husband, a retired Winnetka civil servant named Joseph Olsen. Roy would temporarily move in with his father while deciding what his next move should be. As Roy quickly discovered, even though they were, at last, under the same roof, the distance between them remained.

CHAPTER 3

A UNIQUE APPEAL

Roy Fitzgerald in the late 1940s.

hey weren't exactly the closest father and son," says Rock's cousin Jerry Scherer. "Rock wanted to be closer to my Uncle Roy, in the same way that he was close to my own dad ... The reason Rock liked my dad so well is because he was always nice to him, he'd listen to him, he'd go and do things with him. This was the sort of thing he may have been looking for with his own father but it just wasn't there."

Also, Roy would now have to compete for his father's attention. In 1933, Scherer had married his second wife, Florence Palmer, and they had recently adopted a little girl named Alice, who was not yet a year old. Initially, Roy had intended to enroll at the University of Southern California under the G.I. Bill of Rights. The campus was only a couple of blocks from his father's house. He would major in dramatics. Already his father wasn't the least bit impressed. "Not very stable stuff" was Scherer's blunt assessment. Having finally worked up the courage to tell his father what he really wanted to do with his life, Roy's entire future had been shot down with a few words.

"First of all, my father was not at all happy with my brother's career decision and never wanted him to go into show business," says Rock's sister, Alice Waier. "My father was totally against it. He wanted my brother to work with him in his business and help him grow it. The acting stuff was not something that my father encouraged. No, none of that went over very well at all."

Despite his father's disapproval, Roy forged ahead. USC proved to be too expensive, so Roy shifted his attention to UCLA. "With the G.I. Bill, everybody was trying to enroll in college," he remembered. "They couldn't handle everybody and they had to raise the entrance requirements to a B plus. And, of course, I was a C minus or a D plus, so forget it!"

Postwar business was steady at Scherer's electrical-appliance store. Why didn't Roy give him a hand by selling tank-type vacuums door to door? All too soon, it became clear that this was yet another dead end. "Rock vacuumed for six months and never sold a single vacuum cleaner," recalled Hudson's friend, Mark Miller. "He was always talking the customer out of a purchase because he knew the vacuum cleaners were junk. His last line to the lady would be, 'You don't want to buy this . . .' His father fired him and kicked him out of his home."

Keeping a close eye on his finances, Roy moved into the "sack suite" of a rooming house. "I had a room but I had to share it with three other guys. You had to hide your valuables, you know—your brass cuff links—or they'd steal them." Within a few weeks, a friend of Scherer's helped Roy land a job as a truck driver for Budget Pack. He'd now be earning sixty a week and overtime for hauling packaged macaroni and dried fruit all over East Los Angeles.

Roy was accustomed to making the best of bad circumstances, but as he made his daily rounds, he wondered if he'd be forever outside looking in. Sure, he was in Hollywood. But what was he doing? Breezing by the major studios in his Budget Pack truck, wasting time delivering shriveled apricots when he should have been signed up and in front of the cameras, winning acclaim as Winnetka's answer to Cary Grant.

In Tinseltown terms, he was a complete unknown but that didn't mean he wasn't getting noticed. People seemed to constantly comment on how handsome he was. Sometimes it was just like they had read his mind and come to the same conclusion that he had. Roy Fitzgerald belonged on a movie screen. Finally, he found the courage to actually state his ambition out loud: "I thought, 'I'll never get anywhere unless I speak my piece. So I said, 'I want to be an actor' and nobody laughed at me, which was encouraging. They said, 'Oh, really? That's wonderful!'"

Though, of course, all of this was easier said than done. Where were all of those talent scouts he had heard so much about? Whatever happened to the guy who had discovered Lana Turner while she was downing that milkshake at Schwab's? Roy decided that it was time that Hollywood took a good, long look. Between deliveries, he would park his truck at the back gates of one of the majors—Columbia or Paramount—and try to look like the working man's Robert Taylor.

"In my mind, this has to be one of the most erotic images of Rock that I can imagine," says Hudson's friend Ken Maley. "Just think about the young Rock Hudson—this big stud standing up against his truck outside the studio gates. He'd roll up his sleeves and just stand there, like some giant ad for sex, waiting to be noticed day after day."

Maybe it was the Budget Pack uniform that was throwing

everybody off. How could he ever be taken seriously in that? He bought a tan gabardine suit—though only $55, it still ate up almost an entire week's wages. Once he was suited up, he stepped up his plan of action. Now he'd park his truck and promenade in front of MGM's main gates in Culver City. Surely, at some point, Louis B. Mayer would get up from his desk, as gleaming and polished as one of Fred Astaire's dance floors and go over to the window to survey the entire magic factory over which he reigned supreme. While taking it all in, he would spot Roy Fitzgerald in his new suit.

The mogul, who knew true star potential when he saw it, would immediately recognize that Roy was a diamond in the rough. He'd then pick up his executive phone and say, "Sign up the kid from Winnetka." Only it would never happen that way. Nobody noticed.

———————

Toward the end of his life, Rock Hudson would tell an interviewer that his early years in Hollywood were marked by frustrated ambition and loneliness: "It was very difficult for me to make friends out here . . . Then I got to know a guy who was an older brother of a guy that I was overseas with. It was one of those things, 'If you're ever in Los Angeles, look me up.' So I called him."

Handsome, viciously witty, and snappily attired, Kenneth Hodge was in his prime when he met the young Roy Fitzgerald in the summer of 1947. At the time their paths crossed, Hodge had already made his mark in broadcasting. Several years earlier, he had served as an assistant producer for two of CBS's most popular radio programs, *Amos 'n' Andy* and *Lux Radio Theatre*. Though when he was introduced to Roy, Ken was taking a break from radio and managing several Long Beach rental properties for his Aunt Bernadette. Nevertheless, with his industry connections and celebrity contacts, Hodge seemed perfectly positioned to help an aspiring actor get a foothold in the business. And Roy Fitzgerald was keenly aware of this: "I kind of talked to him a little bit, kind of edged in sneakily, that I would like to become an actor and he began inviting me down to his place at Long Beach and we became best friends." Not to mention lovers. Though this was something of an open secret even among the members of Hodge's close-knit family. "When I was young, it was not only a big deal that Rock Hudson was gay but that he had been involved with my Uncle Kenneth, who started his whole career," says Hodge's niece, Kare Grams. "It was only later that I found out about the romance because none of that was ever discussed in our family. Nothing gay ever was. As far as the family was concerned, that just didn't exist."

Like virtually all of the Rock Hudson partners to follow, Ken Hodge didn't conform to any gay stereotypes. "You would never guess with Uncle Kenneth, just as you wouldn't with Roy," says Grams. "Uncle Kenneth had hemophilia and that was always cited as the reason he never got married."

Given the trauma he had endured with both of his fathers—real and adoptive—it's not surprising that young Roy Fitzgerald would gravitate toward an older man, though over the years, various sources have exaggerated the disparity in their ages in either direction. "He was, I guess, about four or five years older than I, at the most," Rock Hudson would incorrectly surmise during an interview in 1983. In reality, Hodge was thirty-three years old when he first met Fitzgerald, who was still several months shy of his twenty-second birthday.

Even though he was only eleven years older than his protégé, Hodge seemed far more sophisticated and worldly. He was also something of a one-man finishing school. "I could definitely see that Uncle Ken would be very influential for Rock in a constructive, positive way," says Richard Hodge, Ken's nephew. "He was that way with me. I had this typical 1950s dad. Republican. Baseball. All that kind of stuff. But then I had this amazing Uncle Ken that lived up in Hollywood. He took me to musicals and Buddhist temples. He gave me books to read. He really opened up a big chunk of the world to me and I'm sure he did the same thing for Rock."

It was Ken who began smoothing away some of Roy's rougher

edges and smartening up his appearance. Though like Henry Willson after him, Hodge was careful not to ritz up Roy so much that his Midwestern charm and boy-next-door approachability would be sacrificed.

Shortly after meeting, Ken and Roy began living together at the Chateau Marmont—not the legendary Los Angeles hotel but an apartment building in downtown Long Beach that Hodge managed. They would occupy the penthouse apartment, which Ken had tastefully furnished with many valuable antiques. The Chateau Marmont was in walking distance from the Villa Riviera, a far more luxurious apartment building. Only minutes from the beach, the Villa Riviera attracted many young gay men and not only for its proximity to the ocean. Even postwar, the Villa Riviera was referred to as the "Home of the Admirals," as there were so many naval officers in residence, a fact not lost on either Roy Fitzgerald or his benefactor.

"Kenny liked sailors, and often had them lined up in his living room," remembered Rock's friend Mark Miller. "But Rock was the one guy that he really fell for. I'm sure that Kenny did all that he could for Rock. He had some gay connections in Hollywood and he really tried to help him but I think there was only so much that he could do at that time."

Herbert Millspaugh befriended both Hodge and Fitzgerald during their Long Beach days. "They were a good team but so different from one another," Millspaugh remembers. "Ken was very cultured, very polished. Roy was this great, big, gorgeous farm boy. Smart in his own way but not at all sophisticated. Ken was looking for a way to get back into the business in Hollywood and when he met Roy Fitzgerald, he decided that he would be Roy's agent and they would go back to Hollywood, which they eventually did."

In what may have been a concerted effort to get Roy closer to the studios and casting directors, Hodge and Fitzgerald moved into a bungalow in the Hollywood Hills. This was a second residence for Hodge, who referred to the hillside property as his "shack." According to Hodge's niece, this time they had company. "At some point, Uncle Kenneth and Roy were living with another friend named Leon Hall, who worked for Technicolor," says Kare Grams. "He wasn't really an uncle but we all called him 'Uncle Leon.' He was an orphan and he was always in my Uncle Ken's life. They had been together forever."

Friends remember that at one point, Hodge dipped into his savings to host an especially extravagant bash, the sole purpose of which seemed to be the public "unveiling" of his beloved protégé. *You Oughta Be in Pictures* being the underlying theme of the party. Roy Fitzgerald was introduced to anyone with even the remotest connections to show business that Hodge had managed to corral. Almost certainly, it was at one of Hodge's soirees that Roy Fitzgerald first encountered his future agent, the infamous Henry Willson. From the moment they met, each saw something they could use in the other.

"The story that I always heard is that when things started moving with Rock and a big deal agent took him under his wing, Rock left Ken, both professionally and personally," says Richard Hodge. "I think Rock was very ambitious and motivated and when he saw bigger fish in another pond, he knew it was time to move on."

According to Herbert Millspaugh, Roy Fitzgerald moved on without so much as a backward glance, ripping the rug out from under his first mentor: "Ken was pretty devastated. He moved back to Long Beach and sold most of his furniture and antiques. Then he signed on with Armed Forces Radio." Roy's abrupt departure was not unlike the one that occurred years earlier when Roy's own father had walked out. In either case, the loss was deeply felt by the one left behind. Friends remembered that after Roy left, Hodge began drinking heavily.

"Part of the heartbreak was that it was very unexpected," says Kare Grams. "After Roy left, Uncle Kenneth went to Europe for at least a year and tried to leave it all behind. I think that he was really broken hearted. He never had another important relationship that anybody knew about. Or other close friends, other than Leon. I think maybe he didn't trust people after Roy said goodbye."

"DISGUSTING," "DIABOLICAL," AND "Predatory" were among the terms of endearment that Hollywood insiders used to describe Henry Willson. If those descriptions were a bit too subtle, others took it a step further. "He was like the slime that oozed out from under a rock you did not want to turn over," said actor Roddy McDowall, counting himself lucky that he had decided not to sign with Willson early in his career.

Though even those who found Henry Willson completely repugnant as a person would readily admit that as an agent, he was first rate. "I'd say that Henry Willson was one of the top three agents in Hollywood for an actor," said television star Jack Larson. Veteran publicist Dale Olson, who would handle P.R. for Rock Hudson later in his career, felt that Willson's contribution to the film industry went far beyond peddling a fresh face and collecting his 10 percent: "Henry Willson was much more than an agent. He was Hollywood's first manager." And it seemed that virtually every aspect of Willson's life experience had thoroughly prepared him for that role.

Born in 1911 in Lansdowne, Pennsylvania, Willson was raised in New York and surrounded by stars from an early age. As his father was vice president of the Columbia Phonograph Company, Willson got to rub elbows with the likes of Will Rogers and Fanny Brice. As star-struck as young Henry Willson was, his unappealing looks immediately ruled out an acting career. Thick, overgrown eyebrows arched over heavy-lidded eyes. Then there was an aggressive nose, a protruding lower lip, and a receding chin.

The fact that he was no threat to Clark Gable wasn't about to stop Henry Willson. After all, there was more than one way to break into show business. The ever-resourceful Henry discovered that there was a market for all of the juicy celebrity gossip that he and his family members were privy to. While still in high school,

Willson began writing backstage tidbits for *Variety*. Henry may have been thrilled to be writing for the "showbiz Bible," but Horace Willson was concerned that his son's all-consuming interest in theatrical lore didn't seem very manly.

In an effort to butch him up, Willson's father shipped him off to an all-male boarding school in North Carolina. "One way or another, my dad got it into his head that the company of all those other boys would turn me into a real man." As miserable as Henry may have been backpacking through the Blue Ridge Mountains, even this misguided attempt at heterosexual conversion would prove useful later on. *"He won't be gay when I get through with him!"* Willson was frequently heard exclaiming whenever he was confronted with a client who seemed a bit light in the loafers.

Once he returned from his "vacation in purgatory"—as he would later refer to his exile to the hinterlands—it was right back to star-gazing. In the early 1930s, Willson relocated to Hollywood, where he began profiling actors for fan magazines like *Photoplay* and the *New Movie Magazine*. Henry churned out one adoring puff piece after another, increasingly aware of the fact that a movie star's "real life" was usually an elaborate fiction, as carefully scripted as any role that actor played on screen.

Willson couldn't help but notice that once his interview with a star was over, the matinee idol's fixed smile quickly faded. And what if the public knew—as Henry did—that a demure ingénue was really a hell-raising dope fiend? Or that leading men like Ramon Novarro, William Haines, and Cesar Romero—all of whom romanced women on the screen—were frequently out cruising for male lovers? Willson learned firsthand that even after the cameras stopped rolling, Hollywood was fueled on illusion.

In 1943, Willson would become the head of talent for David O. Selznick's production company, Vanguard Films. Having scored back-to-back triumphs with *Gone With the Wind* and *Rebecca*, Selznick was not only the most acclaimed producer in Hollywood but one of the most powerful individuals in the business. Working with

Selznick would not only offer Willson an invaluable education in film production but a master class in unrestrained self-indulgence.

"Henry learned a lot about the business from Selznick but he also picked up some bad habits during his apprenticeship," says Willson biographer Robert Hofler. "The whole thing about drug-taking, that's something that Henry picked up from Selznick, who was severely addicted to Benzedrine. Henry needed to keep up with Selznick, so he starts taking amphetamines . . . Then there was a whole pimping thing that Henry learned from him. Selznick would send Henry a memo and it would say, 'There's a girl posed by a surf board on page twelve of the *Los Angeles Times*. Get her in here. I think she's a good bet.' It was Selznick who started this whole thing with Henry picking up people, whether it was on the beach or in a nightclub. All of that sexual stuff started with Selznick, who was the ultimate womanizer and eventually Henry became the ultimate 'manizer,' if there is such a word. And in his case, there should be."

The two men shared many of the same personality traits. Both were fiercely driven, exceedingly generous and nurturing (if one was in favor), and determined to control virtually everything and everyone in their orbit. Despite being married to Irene Mayer, who was the daughter of MGM mogul Louis B. Mayer, Selznick was an incorrigible skirt-chaser, one with an impressive list of conquests.

In the name of equal opportunity lechery, Willson began pursuing any attractive young man he considered to be "a good bet." Whether it was on the dance floor at the Trocadero or in the midst of a bustling studio commissary, he could always spot them. A terrific-looking guy with untapped potential; a diamond in the rough in need of the Willson polish. "I can always tell within ten minutes if the person has it or not," Willson told a reporter. "With this inner sense of mine, I know if he has picture potential." If Henry had any lingering doubts regarding a prospective client's future, he would invite the young man over to his house in Beverly Hills. They would have drinks. And if the new discovery played his cards right, he would depart the next morning, confident that he had not only found an agent but a surrogate father and supportive friend.

As preproduction work began on the World War II tearjerker *Since You Went Away*, David O. Selznick and Henry Willson would each find an obsession. Selznick began to exert a Svengali-like control over star Jennifer Jones, while Willson would become fixated on his own object of desire. It was at a *Lux Radio Theatre* broadcast that Henry spotted a "demigod" seated in the audience. A vision in his navy whites, the young sailor was so extraordinary that Henry had to force himself to occasionally avert his gaze. The fresh-faced twenty-one-year-old with the splendid physique was just on "the right side of rugged" and his name was Robert Moseley.

The rigorous grooming process that other Willson clients—Tab Hunter, Troy Donahue, Rory Calhoun—would be subjected to was launched with Moseley, the hunk for whom the term "beefcake" would be coined. Although he would appear on screen for only a matter of minutes in *Since You Went Away*, Willson worked Moseley over as though he'd be carrying the entire picture. The first thing that needed fixing was his name.

Henry decided that the former telephone lineman would be introduced to moviegoers as "Guy Madison." "I always give a green actor the gimmick of a trick name to help him get known while he's learning his trade," Willson explained. "I named Guy Madison for a signboard advertising Dolly Madison cakes—all that boy thinks about is food." Although Henry never tired of seeing Guy in uniform, he knew it was time to introduce his protégé to a pair of cuff links. Willson took his favorite client shopping. Guy tried on dress shirts and dinner jackets while Henry selected an inoffensive cologne for him. The sailor's sun-bleached locks were carefully cut and colored at Comb 'n' Shears. They needed to be ready when *Photoplay* beckoned.

"Some of Henry's boys really had nothing going for them outside of their good looks," says Robert Hofler. "You take someone like Guy Madison, who was a sailor or Rory Calhoun, who was an ex-con—Henry would tutor these guys, groom them and give them manners. He would always take them out to restaurants and show them what fork to use or how to behave in public. Henry Willson was like Henry Higgins but it's a better story than *My Fair Lady* because he didn't have one Eliza Doolittle. He had a few hundred." And out of the hundreds of hopefuls that Willson mentored over the years, one would stand out above all the rest. It was in the summer of 1947 that Willson met the young man who would become his most celebrated invention.

Roy Fitzgerald was the perfect specimen and everything that Willson could have hoped for in a client—devastatingly handsome, extremely ambitious, and almost effortlessly manipulated. Henry quickly cued into the fact that at six foot four, Fitzgerald may have been physically imposing but his clumsiness combined with a boyish sweetness and vulnerability made him completely nonthreatening. Then, too, Willson simply recognized the obvious: "I also saw a face that had the possibility of flipping a lot of women."

It took Henry all of ten minutes to figure out how to sell the slouchy hunk in front of him. A decade later, *Look* would sum up Willson's approach with an insightful analysis of the gentle giant's movie star aura: "He's wholesome. He doesn't perspire. He has no pimples. He smells of milk. His whole appeal is cleanliness and respectability—this boy is pure." What's more, there was something for everyone—men would like him because of his easygoing masculinity, while women and nancy boys would fantasize about him as a romantic idol. It was more than just the twinkle in his eye. Willson sensed that beneath the placid surface, there were plenty of unexpressed feelings churning around. That kind of stuff was great for actors. But, hold on a second, could this kid even act?

As the story goes, during their first meeting, Henry asked Roy if he had any acting experience. Before he could stop himself, Fitzgerald had blurted out, "No." After listening to one newcomer after another babble endlessly about their summer stock experience,

Willson found the unguarded response refreshing. "He liked my honesty when I said, 'I have no training . . .'" Roy remembered. "He said, 'You're the only one who's ever told me that.' So, points for me, right?"

It's uncertain how quickly the relationship between mentor and protégé segued from professional to personal, but considering Henry's track record and Roy's extraordinary ambition, *immediately* is a safe bet. Fitzgerald now had a powerful player in his corner, an influential insider who would take a very personal interest in the progress of his career. Just as David O. Selznick transformed Phylis Lee Isley of Tulsa into Jennifer Jones of Hollywood, Willson went to work on Roy Fitzgerald. As with Guy Madison before him, the first thing to go was the name. Thinking big, Willson combined the Rock of Gibraltar with the Hudson River (or was it the economy-sized Hudson convertible?) and *Rock Hudson* was born.

Once the name was in place, actor Robert Stack said Willson then proceeded "to develop a character that fit the name." But Roy Fitzgerald, being all too human, occasionally slipped and displayed one of the effeminate traits that his stepfather hadn't managed to obliterate. There was a girlish curl to his upper lip whenever he smiled. Instead of a manly guffaw, there was that fluttery giggle. And at times, there was an uncomfortably high pitch to his voice. None of this said "Rock Hudson." In addition to stomping out any vestiges of Roy's inner sissy, Willson tried to get his client to stop plucking at his fingernails. "Rock Hudson" should be stoic and uncomplicated. Never neurotic or insecure.

The overhauling of Roy Fitzgerald had only just begun. Next there would be drama lessons with Florence Cunningham, who subdued his Midwestern drawl, straightened his stooping posture, and taught him how to relax—or at least give the impression that he was relaxed. There were voice lessons with Lester Luther, a rotund former opera singer. Hudson always said that he owed his seductive baritone to Luther, who advised him to wait until he had a cold and then head into the mountains and holler like a banshee.

This would "break" the vocal cords, and when they healed he'd sound like Franchot Tone on his best day. While Rock would retell this story in dozens of interviews, it's been rumored that early in his career he had surgery on his vocal cords, which eradicated the high pitch and left him with a more sensual sounding low tone.

With his new name, deeper voice, and more confident posture, Henry's client seemed ready for the marketplace. But as they made the rounds in the late 1940s, they were met with one disappointment after another. Selznick said no, as did independent producer Walter Wanger. The common refrain: "He's too green, Henry. Bring him back when he's gained more experience." At MGM, Lucille Ryman Carroll, the studio's head of talent, rejected the fledgling actor for reasons other than his inexperience. "He stumbled and giggled, and I can't tell you what made me know that he was gay, but it was there," Carroll recalled. "I suspected that Henry and Rock were lovers, from the way he held Rock's hand when he stumbled. I just felt it . . . The studio was very anti-gay when it came to hiring stars . . . There was no way I could have taken on someone like Rock with even the possibility of his being gay."

Rock was greatly discouraged, but not Henry Willson. He knew that if he could get his client in front of the right individual, one who could see beyond the awkwardness and inexperience, they would be going places. All it would take is someone who could look into the future.

BY THE TIME Rock Hudson met Raoul Walsh, the "one-eyed bandit" was more than halfway through his fifty-year career in Hollywood. As an actor, Walsh had played John Wilkes Booth in *The Birth of a Nation*. As a director, Walsh's films—*The Roaring Twenties, High Sierra, White Heat*—were virile, unpretentious, hard as nails. Not unlike Walsh himself. "Raoul was tough as a fucking boot," says actor L. Q. Jones. The black pirate patch the director wore over his right eye (jackrabbit through the windshield) only enhanced his reputation as a "colorful roughneck," as Gregory Peck put it.

Accounts differ regarding how Walsh first met Hudson. In the most plausible version, Henry Willson arranged for Hudson to visit the director at his office on the Warner Brothers lot. "I tend to believe the story that Rock turned up in Walsh's office," says Marilyn Ann Moss, the director's biographer. "It just sounds like the way Walsh would have dealt with a newcomer hungry for work."

Willson was well aware that Walsh had not only made some of Hollywood's finest Westerns, but the director had once been a cattle herder himself. By the time Henry was through, Hudson looked as though he had detoured to the interview on his way to a gunfight at the O.K. Corral. Rock's chinos were replaced with a pair of weathered blue jeans; his customary loafers swapped out for a pair of leather boots. Willson stopped short of borrowing a buckskin jacket from Western Costume, but even without it Hudson filled the eye.

"Walsh just saw this towering figure before him and said, '*Wow!* . . . who is this guy?'" says Moss. "With that perfectly symmetrical face and his strong jawline, it was the equivalent of what we'd now call eye candy."

After giving Hudson the once over, Walsh knew that the young man would mesmerize the camera, in much the same way the director's earliest and most important discovery had. "It must have been like seeing the young John Wayne all over again," Moss says. "Walsh always said that Wayne was one of the most beautiful creatures he'd ever seen. And then Rock walks in. Walsh is introduced to this big, beautiful man and he's thinking maybe he'll be the next John Wayne." Or, "At the very least, he'll be good scenery," Walsh muttered.

Eighteen years earlier, the director had pulled Marion Morrison, a former USC football player, out of the Fox property department, renamed him John Wayne, and put him in *The Big Trail*. Eventually, Wayne would become one of the best-known and most successful stars in Hollywood history. Could lightning strike twice? Walsh had a good feeling about Rock Hudson, green as he was. Despite the director's reservations about Rock's lack of experience, Walsh put him under personal contract. He'd give Hudson a bit part in his next picture. Basically, Rock would be set dressing, but Walsh would see to it that he was given a few lines. Maybe even an entire scene.

For Walsh, this first assignment would serve as an elaborate screen test for his new protégé. For Hudson, it was the fulfillment of his unspoken dreams. At last, he was going to make his debut as an actor. The movie was called *Fighter Squadron* and it was the kind of hard-boiled, two-fisted action picture that Warner Brothers specialized in. Robert Stack, Edmond O'Brien, and John Rodney were cast as the "gallant warbirds" whose personal lives become entangled as D-Day approaches. Whereas Stack would collect $1,750 per week for starring in the film, Rock would earn a comparatively modest $175 a week. But at least it was a start.

Like Hudson, actor Jack Larson (best remembered as Jimmy Olsen in *The Adventures of Superman* series) would also make his movie debut in *Fighter Squadron*. As Larson recalls: "It was considered a big film at that time. The reason everyone was carrying on so much about it is because [studio chief] Jack Warner, who had been this sort of bogus colonel in the air force, had managed to get all of the Technicolor footage of D-Day, which was quite rare. Warner turned to two of his top people, [producer] Seton Miller and [writer] Marty Rackin and assigned them to concoct a film around this D-Day footage."

The authentic combat footage was not so seamlessly blended with the saga of U.S. airman Ed Hardin (Edmond O'Brien). Stationed at an American air base in England in 1943, the headstrong Hardin is nearly court-martialed after disobeying orders during a bombing raid over Germany. Although Hardin downs more enemy planes than any of his fellow officers, his recklessness continually puts the entire unit at risk.

Rock makes his inauspicious debut about thirty minutes into *Fighter Squadron*. He's one of a group of flyboys listening to a captain bragging about his sexual exploits: "Did you ever have a lovely, tall blonde covered with perfume from heaven entice you into a $14,000 limousine?" In an uncredited role that is the very definition of a bit part, Rock is fleetingly glimpsed in a few scenes in which members of Hardin's squadron gather in the base canteen. "Get out the good dice, I have $400 burning a hole in my pocket . . ." is his only substantial line,* though every time the boyishly handsome Hudson appears, he manages to catch the eye. Jack Larson remembers that Rock was originally supposed to have made even more of an impression in the picture.

"Rock had one very good scene that was cut from the film," Larson remembers. "That scene was with my character, Lieutenant 'Shorty' Kirk. We shot it over and over for a day and a half. He just couldn't do it. In this scene, my character is in his private air corps cubicle and he's shaving. Rock's character pays me a visit and says, 'You're too young to shave . . .' I tell him that I'm shaving because it's my birthday and I'm now old enough to do so. The camera zooms in on a calendar. It's not only my birthday but it's also D-Day. The music swells."

The scene didn't present Rock with much of an acting challenge, but as Walsh and his crew prepared to shoot what should have been a routine sequence, Hudson worked himself up into a state of complete panic. He agonized over his minimal dialogue, fretted about hitting his marks, and obsessed over completing basic bits of stage business. The simple act of knocking on a door was enough to completely immobilize him.

"I could tell he was sweating. The poor guy was just terrified,"

---

*Over the years, Hudson would tell a number of interviewers that he had repeatedly flubbed one of his few lines in *Fighter Squadron*. For a sequence in a recreation room, Rock was supposed to say, "Pretty soon you're going to have to get a bigger blackboard," only he kept saying "bligger backboard." When Hudson first told the story, it was twenty takes that were ruined, later it was *thirty-eight*. However, in the Warner Brothers Archives, there doesn't appear to be any evidence supporting this. Neither the *Fighter Squadron* production files nor the assistant director's daily reports mention Hudson blowing his lines. However, in his 2005 memoir, actor Tab Hunter recalls visiting the set and that an "incredibly nervous" Rock "blew many takes, *dozens*."

Larson says. "He had never really been in front of the camera and here was this great director determined to make a star out of him." Larson remembered that Walsh went to great lengths to help Hudson, instructing the actor to silently count to ten before knocking. When this didn't work, the director even installed a light beside the door to cue him. "When the light comes on, you knock," Walsh told Hudson. Places were called. Cameras rolled. The cue light came on. And as before, Rock froze.

As Larson remembers: "Finally, after many takes and Rock still not doing anything, Walsh yelled at him, 'Damn it, you big lug. Don't just stand there like a tree! Get out of the middle of the shot, for Christ's sake.'" For the record, leading man Robert Stack remembered it as "a *goddamned Christmas* tree."

"It was very sad and I felt awful for him," says Larson. Though not quite as awful as Hudson himself. Decades later, he was still embarrassed. "I remember when I first saw myself on screen, in the dailies. My God! What a clumsy, tongue-tied galoot I was!" Hudson told journalist Rowland Barber. "After that, every extra cent I made, I started putting into acting lessons and voice lessons and body-movement lessons."

When *Fighter Squadron* was released in November of 1948, it received mixed reviews. Given his practically nonexistent screen time, the critics took no notice of newcomer Rock Hudson, who wasn't even listed in the credits.* Back in Winnetka, however, Roy Fitzgerald's screen debut had not gone unnoticed. The fact that the shy, soft-spoken New Trier graduate had been cast in a major Hollywood movie was nothing short of astounding. Old friends Jim Matteoni and Pat McGuire were dumbfounded. "I just couldn't believe it," says McGuire. "Jim and I used to mumble about Roy and his sudden success. That was all we could do because he was on a completely different planet from us now."

---

*In the official cast list, Hudson is billed generically as "Lieutenant," while Rock's studio contract refers to his character only as "Second Pilot."

Not nearly as impressed with Rock's screen debut was his mother. "When I took her to that movie, she had no idea," Hudson recalled. "She thought I was still driving a truck. None of her business. I was over twenty-one. I'll do what I damn well please." As she would always be her son's staunchest supporter and severest critic, Kay Olsen's reaction when the lights came up was unusually candid: "Save your money."

While Rock hadn't exactly burned up the screen in *Fighter Squadron*, at least now he had a picture under his belt. Based on his looks alone, Warner Brothers was prepared to offer Hudson both a studio contract and a starring role in Raoul Walsh's next production, a Western redux of one of the director's biggest hits: "I remade *High Sierra* as *Colorado Territory* because Warners was stuck for a release," Walsh remembered.

High Sierra had supplied Humphrey Bogart with one of his best roles as the renegade prison parolee "Mad Dog" Earle. For an inexperienced newcomer like Rock Hudson, this would be a tough act to follow. Even so, Warner Brothers was willing to roll the dice as long as Walsh would be calling the shots. Rock could hardly believe his ears. A big studio contract? Playing the lead in only his second film? Although he hadn't been out of Winnetka all that long, Hudson knew there had to be a catch—and, of course, there was.

If Warners was graciously offering Hudson the chance to follow in Bogie's footsteps, he'd have to sign a seven-year studio contract to demonstrate his gratitude. Suddenly, the offer didn't sound so appealing. Besides, Rock already had a contract—with Walsh. Hudson felt a loyalty to the man who had given him his first big break in the business. Though he was hardly in a position to turn anyone down, Rock found himself telling Warners "No thank you . . . ," and the doomed hero in *Colorado Territory* went to Joel McCrea.

Even though Hudson wouldn't appear in the film, Walsh insisted that he tag along when the company started shooting in a small town appropriately named Gallup: "I took him on location to New Mexico . . . I put a couple of cowboys with him. I said, 'Show this bum how to get on a horse and how to get off and how to ride. And rough him up.' I asked, 'Fellas, what time do you get up in the morning?' They said, 'We get up at five.' I said, 'Get him up at five.'"

But according to the film's leading lady, Virginia Mayo, Rock did not get up at five. Or anything close to it. "He would wander onto the set around noon, after the rest of us had been working since 6 a.m., and Raoul would say, 'Rock, you have to get on the set and work with the cowboys at dawn. You do not just decide to show up at noon or one o'clock.' He would show up finally and then just goof around. He liked to play! He was just a huge kid. Raoul would scold him, but Rock would just pour on that gigantic, charming grin routine and all would be forgiven—until the next time."

Considering the *Fighter Squadron* debacle and Hudson's unprofessional antics during the making of *Colorado Territory*, it's not surprising that Raoul Walsh began to wonder if his protégé had any kind of future in Hollywood. With considerable time left on Rock's contract, the director decided that Hudson should continue to assume a variety of roles—although none of them would wind up on a movie screen.

At one point, columnist James Bacon remembered seeing Rock chauffeuring Walsh around town. When he wasn't occupying the driver's seat, Hudson could be found painting the director's house or watering his lawn. Despite the fact that things didn't look promising, Henry Willson was undeterred. In July of 1949, the agent arranged for Rock to screen test at 20th Century-Fox. The test would be directed by writer-producer Richard Sale (*Father Was a Fullback*) and would also feature actress Kathleen Hughes.

"He was certainly very handsome, no question about that and he was also very pleasant but there was just no spark there," Hughes says of Hudson. "I mean, there was really no chemistry with us. He did not appeal to me as a man or as someone that I would want to date. I didn't get much of an impression of him at all, except that he was just another good-looking actor. I was much more interested in the director of the screen test. In fact, I had a huge crush on him. But Rock Hudson, no."

In the test, Rock plays an ex-soldier named "Vic," who compares his entire platoon being wiped out to a month-long estrangement from his fiancée: "The last winter of the war, over in Germany, for thirty days and nights, we took a steady beating . . . but that was nothing compared to the beating I've taken these last thirty days and nights. The score adds up to this—you're all there is for me."

Contrary to later reports that Rock's test was so bad that Fox regularly screened it for freshman contract players as an example of what *not* to do when appearing before the cameras, he is as believable as anyone could be, given the material.

Upon reviewing the test, an unnamed executive jotted down his thoughts on Hudson: "Very photogenic. Likeable. Voice—Good. Needs training—he might have a unique appeal." In a sense, the test offered a preview of the distinctive movie star aura that audiences would eventually respond to so strongly. Here was a tall, dark, handsome heartthrob who managed to be vulnerable and tender without forfeiting an ounce of his masculinity. "Unique appeal" indeed. Moviegoers would be drawn to a certain duality in Hudson without realizing how deep the divide really went.

Despite Fox's favorable assessment, the studio did not put Rock under contract. But even if Darryl Zanuck didn't bite, Warner Brothers and Universal did. Both studios offered to buy Hudson's contract from Raoul Walsh, with the latter emerging as the high bidder. In August of 1949 and only a year after personally signing him, Walsh would sell Hudson's contract to Universal-International for $9,700. The newcomer would be earning $125 a week.* At the time, it seemed like a real bargain as Hudson hardly seemed poised to give Spencer Tracy or Clark Gable a run for their money.

---

*This is more than likely the correct amount, though some sources state that Hudson was earning $75 a week when he was initially put under contract to Universal.

None of those involved in negotiating the deal with Universal—not Henry Willson, not Raoul Walsh and certainly not Rock himself, could have ever imagined that in a few short years, he would not only be Universal's top star but the number one box office attraction in the world. Rock Hudson . . . *king of the movie stars?* The same guy who had inordinate difficulty opening a door on cue? Go on.

CHAPTER 4

UNIVERSAL

Winnetka's own as an Arab in *The Desert Hawk* (1950)
(Courtesy Everett Collection)

W hen Rock Hudson first arrived at Universal in 1949, the studio was in the throes of its latest identity crisis. Cash-strapped and operating under a deficit of $4.3 million, Universal's once promising postwar future suddenly seemed very uncertain.

In recent years, the studio had transitioned from producing folksy, unpretentious crowd-pleasers (*Pardon My Sarong, The Egg and I*) to distributing loftier prestige pictures (*Great Expectations, Hamlet*). This sudden change had earned Universal critical acclaim and Oscar attention but not desperately needed profits. Though this was hardly anything new. Over the years, Universal's fortunes seemed to ebb and flow in accordance with the unpredictability of popular taste as well as the studio's own internal upheavals. And it had been that way since the very beginning.

Founded in 1912 by exhibitor turned producer Carl Laemmle, Universal had been operating under the same business model since its earliest days, when one-reelers were cranked out on the 230 acres of farmland north of the Hollywood Hills that Laemmle had purchased for $165,000. In 1915, Laemmle welcomed exhibitors to what he described as "the biggest moving picture plant in the wide, wide world." And this was no empty boast. From day one, Universal City Studios was a fully integrated organization. Production, distribution, and publicity were all managed in-house. The joke around town was that Carl Laemmle did everything but sell you the popcorn.

If competitors MGM and Paramount catered to the metropolitan moviegoer with sumptuous musicals and sophisticated comedies featuring A-list stars, Universal couldn't be bothered with anything quite so high-minded. Laemmle promised his audiences pictures in which "we blow up bridges, burn down houses, wreck automobiles and smash up things in general." As film historian Ethan Mordden has noted, Universal could lay claim to "the least ambitious aesthetic of all the major studios."

It was Universal's innocuous escapist fare that kept audiences coming back for more. Teenage soprano Deanna Durbin's pictures saved the studio from bankruptcy during the Depression. And Universal's series of horror movies—*Frankenstein*, *Dracula*, and *The Mummy*—not only kept the ledgers in the black but became the one genre where the studio excelled.

In 1946, Universal merged with the independently operated International Pictures. Once the reorganization was complete, the studio had a new head of production, William Goetz, who was not only International's founder but also the son-in-law of Metro's all-powerful Louis B. Mayer. When Goetz took control, the studio was awkwardly rechristened Universal-International. Goetz intended that the name change would be a signal to both the industry and the ticket-buying public that a new day had dawned at the studio.

A Universal-International production would now outclass the competition with adaptations of acclaimed Broadway dramas. The radical shift resulted in more urbane fare being doled out to audiences in Podunk who had grown accustomed to seeing *La Conga Nights* or *Bride of Frankenstein*. Not sure quite what to make of the latest "highbrow" pictures screening at the neighborhood Bijou, audiences stayed away.

By the end of the 1940s, everything possible was being done to return Universal-International to a state of fiscal stability. Lowbrow series featuring the likes of Francis the Talking Mule, Abbott and Costello, and Ma and Pa Kettle once again dominated the production schedule. If Universal-International found itself in a precarious position at the end of the decade, the situation wasn't much better for twenty-four-year-old Rock Hudson, whose own future was unsettled. What if he blew it at Universal just as he had at Warners? After much wrangling, Henry Willson had negotiated Hudson's $125-a-week contract with Universal. The pressure was on.

Nervous executives were taking a close look at any contract players who didn't seem to be doing their bit to improve the bottom line. While at the same time, studio manager Edward Muhl (who had joined Universal back in the silent era as a $50-a-week accountant) was keeping a close eye on any newcomers who seemed to exhibit genuine star potential. In time, Muhl would not only become head of production at Universal but also one of Rock's most powerful allies. But all of that was still in the future.

In the summer of 1949, Hudson was all too aware of how expendable he was. There were constant reminders from Henry Willson, who advised his favorite client to play ball with the studio, no matter how outrageous the demands might be. If Universal wanted him to drop the "k" from his first name and become "Roc" (just like the mythological bird of prey), he should do it. If the publicity department asked him to pose shirtless while washing his car, grilling steaks, or playing solitaire, he should suck his stomach in and gladly oblige photographers. In the event that producers made friendly advances, it was understood that he should willingly submit. In every way possible, Rock—or "Roc" if they insisted—simply had to become the model contract player.

Ken Hodge, Henry Willson, and Raoul Walsh may have all played an important role in molding an ex-truck driver into an employable actor. But the most miraculous part of the transformation would be completed in Universal's stock-player training program. "Universal in those days was almost 'collegiate,'" says actress Julie Adams. "Especially for the younger people who were under contract. They had programs so that you could come to the studio and take dancing lessons, you could take singing lessons, and they had horseback riding on the back lot . . . In those days, the studio offered a young actor every opportunity to learn something new."

One of the key people helping new contract players find their way was Sophie Rosenstein. The author of *Modern Acting: A Manual*, Rosenstein was Universal's head of talent and the studio's chief acting coach. She was unwavering in her belief that good acting was based on two cardinal principles: "Absolute sincerity and absolute simplicity. There is no substitute for genuine emotion." When she wasn't guiding performances in her classes, the diminutive Rosenstein also played den mother to her new recruits.

Rock would attend Rosenstein's diction and drama workshops alongside such rising stars as Tony Curtis, Piper Laurie, Hugh O'Brian, and Mamie Van Doren. While other performers were more polished or self-assured, Rosenstein zeroed in on the bashful young man who always seemed to be gnawing at his fingernails. Clearly there was much work to be done, but Rosenstein sensed that there was something there. While watching Hudson play a few scenes, she took inventory: "His biggest asset is stamina," Rosenstein declared. "His biggest failing, shyness. It's torture for him to get up and act before an audience, even this audience of other young players in the workshop, but he keeps doing it. He talks too fast and he doesn't stand straight but he's learning and he's willing. He'll make it."

Another staunch supporter during his early days at the studio was actress Piper Laurie. "I first met Rock before either of us was under contract," Laurie recalls. "They decided to screen test both of us and see if they wanted us under contract. So they put us together in this very dramatic, romantic scene. I was seventeen but I looked fourteen, with experience that matched. With a straight face, I had to look up at him and say, '*I love you like this, all stirred up with fire in your eyes.*' Well, we could barely get through it. We couldn't stop laughing. But they signed both of us anyway and we became very good friends during that period."

After their unintentionally hilarious love scene, Laurie later observed Rock playing another with very different results: "One of the few times I got to sit in on the acting workshops, I watched Rock do a love scene with an actress. And I often thought back to this years later. In the physical moment, with the kissing and the touching and all that, there was a quality about it that sort of stunned me. It was a little violent. It was physically energized beyond any love scenes that I'd seen between a man and a woman and I'd seen a lot of movies. Looking back, I wonder if that came out of his real sexuality. I think guys are probably different when they're with other guys. I don't want to be a smartass here, but I was aware that there was something special about the way he touched the woman. I'd never seen anything quite like it."

DOING EVERYTHING HE could to jump-start Hudson's career at Universal, Henry Willson began feeding the press one publicity item after another. In October of 1949, the *Chicago Daily Tribune* dutifully announced: "Newest Chicagoland contribution to Hollywood is 24 year old Roc Hudson, New Trier High school and navy graduate who, after a bit part in *Fighter Squadron*, has been placed under personal contract to Raoul Walsh. He'll make his starring debut in Universal's *The Big Frame*."* While Walsh and Hudson had already parted company—at least contractually—Willson knew that it didn't hurt to keep Hudson's name linked with the director's in the columns.

For his first U-I assignment, William Castle's noirish *Undertow*, Hudson was billed in ninth place and generically credited as "detective." The real star of the film is Scott Brady, who plays an ex-convict framed for the murder of a mob boss. Enlisting the aid of school teacher Peggy Dow, he rummages through some of Chicago's shadiest corners in pursuit of the real killer.

Undertow is populated by Castle's trademark assortment of oddballs—a hulking garage attendant with a hair-trigger temper, an overly inquisitive landlady, a tow-headed simpleton who goes berserk upon spotting Brady's Nambu. Appearing only once, "Roc" plays a colleague of seasoned detective Bruce Bennett and his dialogue includes such banalities as "No prints on the bullets?" It wasn't much of a step up from *Fighter Squadron,* but after a year he was back on the big screen and at least it was a foot in the door at Universal.

The title *I Was a Shoplifter* proved to be the best thing about Rock's next film. Mona Freeman stars as a kleptomaniac librarian who is released after her first offense but is forced to sign a confession, which is later used to blackmail her. Hudson appears briefly, at the beginning and end of the picture as a store detective. If Rock barely registers on-screen, Tony Curtis, playing a dim-witted thug, makes a much greater impression, especially when uttering the film's only memorable line: "Women, horses and steel companies ain't to be trusted."

Finally, Rock was assigned to a picture that proved to be a cut above. *Winchester '73* was the first of eight films teaming star James

---

*The Big Frame was the working title of Rock Hudson's first film for Universal-International. Midway through production it was retitled *Undertow.*

Stewart and director Anthony Mann. Some of Stewart's postwar pictures (*On Our Merry Way, You Gotta Stay Happy*) were uninspired, lightweight trifles and the Oscar-winning leading man knew it was time to steer a completely new career course. Stewart started looking around for dramatically compelling projects with an edge.

At first glance, *Winchester '73*—which traced the journey of a prized precision firearm as it passes from one owner to another—may have looked like any of the sagebrush sagas that Universal was churning out in the early 1950s. But *Winchester '73* would prove to be anything but typical. Alongside *High Noon* and Mann's *The Furies, Winchester* would usher in an era of "psychological westerns." This new breed of introspective cowboy movie would elevate the genre by peering into the darkened corners of the American psyche.

In this case, a riveting variation on the Cain and Abel story unfolds as frontiersman Lin McAdam (Stewart) pursues the notorious outlaw Dutch Henry Brown (Stephen McNally) from Kansas to Texas. Dutch is not only the murderous gunslinger who stole the coveted Winchester rifle from McAdam, he also happens to be Lin's estranged brother. A sibling rivalry in spurs.

Into this fraternal showdown, Universal inserted several of its promising contract players, including Rock Hudson, who would play for the first—though not the last—time in his career an Indian chief. One named Young Bull. Although he was wearing an uncomfortable wig, a prosthetic nose, and Bud Westmore's best approximation of war paint, Hudson never complained, even though he felt badly betrayed by his director.

"Anthony Mann was a fair action director," Rock would recall some thirty years later. "He wasn't a good director as far as acting is concerned. Nor was he a good human being. He took advantage of my stupidity. And he had me doing, in that movie, my own stunts. I was doing these horse falls, full gallop, with a loincloth. I didn't know that there were stunt men—A; and B, that they wore padding. And this is gravel and rocks. Yuck! And I did it twice, like an ass. I should have just said, 'No' looking back on it. But I was eager and he took advantage of that. That's not a nice man. That's a prick."

The sly dialogue exchanges that Borden Chase wrote for Jimmy Stewart and Shelley Winters ("*I know how to use it . . .*" Winters says with a knowing look when Stewart hands her a really big gun) were more inspired than what Hudson was given to work with. "*This is gun I want . . .*" is Rock's most memorable line, delivered in pure Hollywood Comanche.

But was anyone actually paying attention to what Rock Hudson was saying? Outfitted only in an abbreviated loincloth, Hudson's rangy, muscular physique is on ample display. While his role is almost as brief as his costume, Rock is spotlighted in a couple of scenes that were masterfully composed by Greta Garbo's cinematographer of choice, William Daniels. In a climactic sequence, Hudson's Young Bull has fallen from his horse after being killed in battle. As chaos and brutality rage all around the fallen chief, Daniels zeroes in on Young Bull—now obliviously at peace.

"He did a very good job as the Indian chief," star Jimmy Stewart would say of Hudson some four decades after they both appeared in *Winchester '73*. "I didn't get to talk to him very much but I think everybody realized that he not only knew his job but as it turns out, he knew how to do it very well." Made for $918,000, *Winchester '73* would ultimately return more than $2 million to Universal. For the first time since *Fighter Squadron*, Rock Hudson had appeared in a certified hit.

————

"The best thing about Rock was that his mother was a wonderful cook," Vera-Ellen once confided to a friend. If his mother's culinary skills were all Rock had going for him, what does this say about his supposedly torrid love affair with Vera-Ellen? The one that the fanzines exhaustively explored beneath headlines like "Will Vera and Rock Find Happiness?" or "A Wedding Within the Year."

Columnists had managed to make one of their first encounters at the Mocambo sound like something out of a fairy tale—this despite the fact that "pert, pixyish" Vera-Ellen had been escorted by another man and Rock, "the gentle giant," was, as usual, in the company of Henry Willson: "Six feet four inches of manhood went slightly pink under the tan. He strode across the dance floor, tapped Vera's escort on the shoulder and said, 'Pardon me . . . may I?' No one was more surprised than Rock when he found himself holding Vera's little figure close and light against him . . . they fell in love. Hollywood began to talk."

Yet most of the industry chatter focused on how shrewd Henry Willson was to pair his relatively unknown client with an established star who was starting to be billed alongside the biggest names in the business. A former Rockette, Vera-Ellen had made her movie debut in *Wonder Man* opposite Danny Kaye, though it was her magnificent dancing in MGM musicals—teamed with Gene Kelly and Fred Astaire—that would win Vera her greatest acclaim.

"Cuteness incarnate" is how one critic had described Vera-Ellen; her lithe figure and elfin features played well against Rock's towering height and strapping physique. Henry Willson made sure that they were photographed together at every opportunity—whether they were dancing at Ciro's or attending the opening of a show at El Capitan. But Willson would score his greatest triumph in October of 1949 at the Flashbulbers Ball, a star-studded benefit for the Hollywood Press Photographers Association.

Enlisting the aid of MGM's makeup department, Rock and Vera would attend as "Mr. and Mrs. Oscar." A couple of walking, talking Academy Awards. He would be outfitted in skin-tight latex swim trunks and a skullcap; she would be clad in a simple satin bathing suit. Each would be armed with a gilded broadsword. To complete the effect, both would be slathered in pore-clogging gold paint from head to toe. As Vera recalled, "We went into a paint store for the gold paint and when the salesman wanted to know *what* we were going to paint, Rock said 'ourselves.' I'll never forget the expression on the man's face."

The salesman's dazed expression was nothing compared to the stunned reaction caused by Rock's and Vera-Ellen's grand entrance at the ball. Members of the press corps, who had seen everything in their day, were speechless. Flashbulbs popped. Columnist Louella Parsons summoned the ravishing statuettes over to her microphone for an exclusive interview.

The images of Rock and Vera-Ellen as "Mr. and Mrs. Oscar" would turn up in newspapers all over the country, sparking further interest in them as a couple. Readers of *Modern Screen* knew that Vera was divorced from fellow dancer Robert Hightower. They also knew that while Rock adored Vera, he was already blissfully wed to his career. Though as any subscriber to *Photoplay* could tell you, once Hudson had made some legitimate headway in the industry, he and Vera planned to elope. "The minute I get that first big part," Rock assured his fans.

Some sources say that the stars were involved in a real love affair, while others insist their dates were primarily for show. The mystery surrounding their relationship was compounded by Vera-Ellen herself. She told one choreographer that she planned to marry Hudson. To another friend, she confessed that all was purely platonic; even before their initial meeting, she knew that Rock "didn't prefer women."

Vera-Ellen's biographer, David Soren, believes the connection was a close friendship. "Vera's family always told me that they were just very good friends," says Soren. "He was always a gentleman on a date and she liked that about him. Also, he was very sweet and kind and funny. These dates were initially arranged by agents or by the studios and one shouldn't read too much into them. But clearly, they had a genuine liking for one another."

Actress Peggy Dow believes that the romance wasn't only trumped up for the fan magazines. "Rock was absolutely stricken and madly in love with Vera-Ellen," Dow says. "We double dated and they were just precious together. Then, all of a sudden she became involved with this young guy who just spirited her away from Rock and encouraged her to leave MGM, which was the biggest mistake of her life. I think if this other young man hadn't come between Rock and Vera-Ellen, they probably would have gotten married. They were just that mad for each other. She married this other young man and Rock, all of a sudden, just went in a different direction, God love him."

Within a couple of years of their meeting, Rock and Vera-Ellen's paths would diverge. After she married her second husband, millionaire Victor Rothschild, in 1954, Vera-Ellen would be portrayed as "the girl who got away" in virtually any story printed about Hudson's ill-fated love life.

———

In a Technicolor trifle entitled *Peggy*, Rock would make his romantic debut as an Ohio State fullback wooing Diana Lynn on his way to the Rose Bowl. Critics dismissed the practically non-existent plot as "nutty as fruitcake," but Universal took notice of the fact that Hudson's first screen kiss resulted in his first batch of fan mail. "It was right then that we started to get requests about Rock," recalled Universal publicist Betty Mitchell. *The Desert Hawk* was next. This was a quickie remake of Universal's Persian epic *Arabian Nights*, which had starred Rock's boyhood crush, Jon Hall. Outfitted in a stylish keffiyeh and sporting a goatee, Rock is nearly unrecognizable when he briefly appears as Captain Ras. The only thing giving him away is his twangy Midwestern drawl.

And so it went. A line here. A line there. After trooping and trucking his way through one Universal programmer after another, Rock had made no real progress. Any good-looking Moe could hold the door open for the real star or raise a tomahawk and say he made movies. But this wasn't acting. How would he ever make the transition to more substantial parts? The dramatic coaches at Universal weren't miracle workers. And yet the drive to succeed was there, always gnawing away at him. If only somebody saw things his way.

In between his undistinguished assignments, Hudson continued to sit in on Sophie Rosenstein's acting workshops. Periodically, the contract players would put together a production consisting of scenes they had been working on in class. Universal would invite casting directors and producers from all of the major studios to see if any of the young actors piqued their interest. If so, Universal would essentially rent them out for a picture or two.

During one of these productions, *"Evening of '52,"* Rock appeared opposite his fellow Winnetkan, Hugh O'Brian, in *A Sound of Hunting*. While O'Brian may have been the more assured performer, the audience couldn't take their eyes off Hudson, who managed to capture attention by virtue of his quiet presence and what one reviewer described as his "almost startling masculine beauty."

Rock would also pair off with a young starlet named Susan Cabot for a scene from *The Four Poster*. "She was madly in love with him," recalls actress Kathleen Hughes. "Susan was my best friend at the time and she was always telling me that she wanted to marry him and that Rock even took her home to meet his mother once. Susan was really hoping to end up with him but I had already heard that he was gay, so as gently as possible, I told her, 'I don't think it's going to happen, honey.'"

Apart from the obvious reason that Cabot's love would remain unrequited, Hudson was too busy bouncing from one picture to the next to even notice that anyone was pining for him. Universal continued to test him out in various small roles, allowing him to gain experience while racking up screen credits. The minuscule parts seemed to be in direct proportion with how Universal's front office felt about their handsome but seemingly unexceptional contract player.

"In those early years before he got any decent parts to play, he was still playing Indians and overgrown teenagers," Piper Laurie remembers. "There was a period of time when they were very rough on him. He did like to eat and he would plump up and it wasn't becoming to him. As he was standing in the commissary, waiting to get a table, I overheard the studio heads evaluating him, as they did all of us . . . they'd talk about you almost like you weren't human. In his case, they were hard on him about his weight and I know he was very sensitive about it. He really did not have an easy time of it when he was getting started."

IN 1951, ROCK was introduced to a young actor named Bob Preble. A twenty-three-year-old native of Newton, Massachusetts, and a fellow client of Henry Willson's, Preble arrived in Hollywood hoping that the stage success he had enjoyed back east would translate to an important film career. While studying drama at the University of Maine, Preble had appeared regularly at the Camden Hills Theatre and won acclaim for his performances in *Hamlet* and *Macbeth*.

But after moving to the West Coast and signing with Willson, Preble discovered that innate talent and single-minded determination weren't quite enough. If Rock Hudson was willing to do whatever it took to ensure his footing in the business, Bob Preble was not. As countless boys fresh off the farm had discovered, the obligatory fling with Henry Willson was almost an industry initiation rite. Preble said that he found the idea of "being nice" to Mr. Willson totally abhorrent: "Henry was a guy that you always wanted to look right in the eye. I don't think I would have trusted him for a minute behind my back. His behavior was offensive to me."

If Preble wasn't willing to give Willson considerably more than his 10 percent, the actor's uncooperative attitude would result in an unusually short list of screen credits. Though he was a contract player at 20th Century-Fox, Preble managed only bit parts in the Bette Davis drama *The Star* and John Ford's *What Price Glory*; he was loaned out to Columbia for the sci-fi thriller *It Came from Beneath the Sea.*

With his film career at a standstill, Preble found himself working odd jobs and sharing a house in Malibu with four other guys. At the time, Rock was scraping by as the sole occupant of a small apartment on Woodrow Wilson Drive. After all of the hubbub at the studio, Hudson found coming home to an empty nest unnerving. It was Henry Willson who suggested that Hudson and Preble move in together. This arrangement would give Bob some breathing room and Rock some after-hours companionship.

Willson made a point of telling Bob that Rock was gay. According to Preble, "He just tossed that in as part of the conversation. It didn't surprise me. As it turned out, Rock never bothered me and I never got in his way." Hudson and Preble moved into a one-bedroom house off Mulholland Drive, the first of four residences they would share. The official reason given for their extended period of cohabitation was economy.

In a 1952 *Photoplay* layout entitled "Bachelor's Bedlam," the magazine ran photos of a shirtless "Rip Van Hudson" lounging in bed as Preble stands over him, attempting to rouse his sleepy housemate after the alarm clock has failed to do so. Although the accompanying article is attributed to Preble, it was almost certainly the work of a Universal publicist, who was careful to note that Bob's own room was "down the hall" from Rock's. In fact, the resourceful bachelors had pushed two single beds together to create one large bed spacious enough to accommodate both of them.

Photoplay wanted to know if Rock and Bob ever competed for the same girl. Presumably with tongue in cheek, Preble responded, "We're never attracted to the same types." According to several friends, Rock was most attracted to extremely masculine men, preferably those who self-identified as straight or were at least known to go "both ways." As actress Mamie Van Doren put it, "I think it was a challenge to get a straight guy and see if he could swing him. And I'm sure he did. If anybody could swing a straight guy, Rock could do it." This was certainly the case with Preble, who admitted to "a little experimenting, on a couple of occasions after we'd had a few drinks . . . I guess he hoped the barriers would come down. The situation did come close to spilling over to something that would have been foreign to my whole being, my whole behavior."

Even so, Preble would remember his rooming with Hudson as "a blast—one great glorious good time." He would also describe his best friend as "moody at times, usually when he's depressed about his work. And he has a temper that simmers for weeks, then comes to a boil and finally explodes. But it's over in a hurry. He picks up something—anything—and throws it, and a minute later, he's putting a record on the phonograph."

As close as Hudson and Preble were, Rock wanted a friend with whom he could freely be himself. Instead he found two. In January of 1951, Hudson was introduced to actor George Nader and his partner, Mark Miller. For the next thirty-four years, the three would be virtually inseparable. A seemingly endless parade of lovers, short-term boyfriends, and one-nighters would pass through Rock's life, but Nader and Miller managed to provide him with something more enduring—a sense of continuity and a kind of surrogate family.

"We were called 'The Trio,'" says Mark Miller. "We were together from the beginning to the end but never sexually . . . Regardless of how hard people tried, no one ever succeeded in destroying our friendship." The threesome harkened back to the days when Roy Fitzgerald, Jim Matteoni, and Pat McGuire were haunting the halls at New Trier High School. The Hudson-Nader-Miller bond was forged through a similar sense of humor, a love of music (Rock's favorite song was the Patti Page hit "Mockin' Bird Hill," which he played at every opportunity), and several epic miniature golf competitions.

An important part of The Trio's camaraderie involved regaling one another with tales of their frequent sexual conquests—from airline pilots to studio executives. "When sex was involved, Rock loved all the stories and that theme lasted throughout the entire thirty-four years of our friendship," Miller said. "He was always amused with sexual tales and wanted to know all the details . . . He also told me all of the details of his encounters, which, of course, were fun."

On the flip side, there was also the shared misery of the closet. Like Hudson, George Nader didn't conform to any limp-wristed stereotypes and often found himself in the company of unsuspecting producers or studio executives who regularly cracked fag jokes or openly ridiculed the effeminate hairdressers and choreographers on the lot.

According to Miller, The Trio instinctively knew when they could cut loose and freely be themselves or when the mask of heterosexuality had to be firmly in place. Rock and his boyfriend of the moment couldn't ever accompany Nader and Miller to a restaurant. "Because instantly, it's two couples," said Miller. "So, we went three—not a problem. Nobody said anything." But just in case, they all carried briefcases, so that everyone understood their get-together was strictly business.

Unlike Roy Fitzgerald's humble beginnings, George Nader had been born into a life of wealth and privilege in Pasadena in 1921. Though very much like Rock, George's relationship with his father—who was a broker for Signal Oil—tended to the theoretical. A mistress in Santa Barbara occupied most of Nader, Sr.'s leisure time. And as for George's overly attentive mother, the elder Nader once told his son: "Ignore her . . . I do."

Just like the young Roy Fitzgerald, Nader had served in the Navy during World War II. Upon being discharged, George graduated from Occidental College with a Bachelor of Arts degree in theatre. Even out of his uniform and back in civilian clothes, Nader was movie star material. Strikingly handsome and in peak physical condition, he tended to draw attention wherever he went. Reserved and somewhat shy, Nader was often oblivious to the effect he created simply by walking down the street.

The third member of The Trio—Mark Lincoln Miller—was born in Macedonia, Iowa, in 1926. In sharp contrast to Nader's posh upbringing, Miller grew up in an abandoned house, built in the

1870s, that offered neither an indoor bathroom nor electricity. Miller's father, Claude, was a bus driver who worked nine months out of the year.

Despite the grim circumstances, Miller says that his father never lost his sense of humor and managed to impart to his son an off-the-wall camp sensibility. As they were growing up, Claude would refer to Mark and his younger brother, Philip, as "Phyllis and Nadine." Amused rather than insulted, Claude's sons simply returned the favor. "We called him 'Claudia,' which always made him laugh," Miller recalled. "There didn't seem anything unusual about this at the time, but then again, I have been homosexual ever since I could remember."

Whenever the rest of the family was away on shopping expeditions, "Phyllis and Nadine" would turn the living room into a low-rent version of the Cotton Club. "We would get in drag," Miller recalls. "By using black shoe polish on our faces, we'd imitate the great black singers, Lena Horne and Ethel Waters . . . since the family was gone about two hours and it took an hour to get the shoe polish and our sister's Tangee lipstick off, it was a fairly short concert. During one songfest, I said to Philip, 'We've got to get out of Iowa and off this farm and get to New York or Hollywood, I don't care which!'"

After relocating to California, Miller met George Nader in 1947 while both were performing in a production of *Oh, Susannah!* at the Pasadena Playhouse. "There he was, my Prince Charming! I said to myself, 'I don't care if he's straight,' I'll make him 'one of the boys,'" Miller recalled. After introducing himself, Miller asked Nader, "'Did you see my picture on the front page of the *Times Mirror* today? I'm Miss World Trade Queen. I was crowned in Long Beach two days ago.' [He] shrugged and turned away. We didn't speak again that evening but I knew he was mine . . . A week later, I got him in the back seat of his father's 1937 Buick sedan . . . I did him in the parking lot of Biggars Furniture Store and we were together from that moment on, only to separate for work."

At the time that Nader befriended Hudson, neither had made much progress in terms of their respective film careers. Though at least Rock was under contract to one of the majors, whereas George found himself bouncing from one studio to another as a freelancer. Later, when George was cast in lead roles, they tended to be in Poverty Row productions like *Robot Monster* or the so-bad-it's-brilliant *Sins of Jezebel*, which had been shot in only three days.* In his best films, Nader turns in perfectly respectable performances but he is devoid of the one quality that Rock Hudson had in spades . . . star charisma. According to Mark Miller, even after Nader signed with Universal, there were reasons why his screen career never flourished in the same way that Hudson's did.

"Rock went much further at Universal Studios than George because George refused to play the sexual game. Rock played it to the hilt. Therefore, Rock got all the good parts, the best costars, and the best directors. George got just the opposite—mediocre scripts, and not a single top director. None of the directors gave any direction to him at all. He was known as the one-take actor. Rock, on the other hand, was given every chance to improve a scene. Of course, George had a master's degree in theatre arts and had done twenty-five stage plays before he arrived at Universal. Rock had a master's degree in truck driving."

If Rock was single-mindedly determined to become a major film star and was willing to do whatever it took to achieve the dream, Nader had a loathing of publicity and tended to keep a low profile. He was willing to work hard but not *that* hard. And no matter how many hours Hudson put in at the studio, his paycheck always seemed to be coming up short. "Rock was under contract to Universal for $75 a week, but only for forty weeks a year," Mark Miller says. "He was always strapped for money because he

---

Sins of Jezebel was a camp favorite of Rock's friend, the actor Roddy McDowall, who could recite some of the more outlandish dialogue from memory. The film's low-budget look inspired a memorable review from the *Toledo Blade*: "The desire was strong but the cash was weak."

couldn't make enough to cover the three months he had off in a year."

In the early 1950s, Hudson was renting a house in Sherman Oaks owned by Nader's Aunt Marilyn. The $150 a month was often hard to come by. "He couldn't always pay the rent," says Miller, who claimed, "In those days, I had to pay the rent for both Rock and George." Miller's generosity to Hudson at the beginning of his career further cemented their friendship, though it may have also created a feeling of eternal indebtedness. Years later, when their circumstances were reversed, Rock would pay Mark back— and then some.

Looking the way he did, Hudson found plenty of quick sex available but not the kind of emotionally fulfilling partnership that Nader and Miller shared. In so many ways, Hudson's friendship with the couple helped fill the void.

ROCK'S NEXT ASSIGNMENT for Universal was *The Fat Man*, adapted from a popular radio drama of the same name starring J. Scott Smart. The title refers to Brad Runyan, rotund gourmet-detective, who solves capers between generous forkfuls. In a storyline best described as highly original, Runyan investigates the murder of an eminent dentist and the subsequent disappearance of an incriminating X-ray plate.

Making his way through a shadowy underworld populated by "two-timers," "two-bit phonies," and thugs named Shifty, The Fat Man's deductive reasoning takes him all the way to the circus, where he meets a clown played by Emmett Kelly and things get even weirder.

In one of his most assured early performances, Hudson played Roy Clark, a petty criminal whose molars and incisors seem to hold the key to the entire mystery. "Is the doc around?" Hudson asks no-nonsense nurse Jayne Meadows. "This toothache's killing me." *Killing* being the operative word. Many years after *The Fat Man*'s release, Rock screened the film at his home for some friends. An unintentionally hilarious scene inspired a major Hudson laughing jag. In a sequence in which his ex-con character meets up with his girlfriend, played by Julie London, he admits to a laundry list of misdemeanors, capping the confession with, "I did time in the state prison for six years." Without missing a beat and apparently unfazed by her boyfriend's extensive criminal history, London's character dreamily responds, "I love you, Roy. I want to cook for you."

Under the direction of William Castle, *The Fat Man* started production in August of 1950, with a breakneck eighteen-day shooting schedule and a proposed budget of $354,600 that seemed modest even by Universal standards. When it opened, the *New York Times* gave *The Fat Man* a surprisingly positive review, deciding that "its heavyweight hero is a man who should be seen as well as heard." *The Hollywood Reporter* wasn't impressed with the film in general ("It has all the elements of a top murder mystery except an exciting story"), but one of the supporting players was singled out for praise: "Rock Hudson . . . in his most important role to date, shows exceptional talent."

Just as Rock was beginning to make some headway—slight though it may have been—there was suddenly a crisis to contend with. Publicist Roger Jones would never forget the day when Sam Israel, Universal's publicity director, called Jones into his office and delivered some unwelcome news: "Stop whatever you have working for your boy, Rock—we're letting him go!"

Although Hudson's contract option still had three months to go, Universal executives decided that they had given the actor more than enough time to prove himself. Tony Curtis, who had received the same training and publicity buildup as Rock, had recently scored a hit with *The Prince Who Was a Thief.* Despite some encouraging reviews, Hudson didn't seem to be taking off in the same way.

"I remember Rock saying, 'I'll never be a star at Universal. They're doing everything they can for Tony Curtis,'" remembers actress Joyce Holden. "I used to say, 'Aw, come on, Rock, you've got more going for you than Tony. Don't be down-hearted.' I tried my best to build his confidence but he was starting to wonder if his career was ever going to happen the way he wanted."

Roger Jones remembered that he was "totally devastated" when he found out that the studio was cutting Hudson loose. Jones thought of himself as a surrogate father, a trusted advisor. "Sam, you can't do this!" Jones pleaded with his boss. "This studio has never had its own male star. We always borrow them. The only female star we ever made was Deanna Durbin and she brought this studio out of the red and into the black. Rock Hudson can do the same!"

Sam Israel waved Jones away. He returned to his office. Maybe it was time to resign. After all, MGM had recently made him an offer to handle publicity for two of its most important stars, Gable and Garland. As he was weighing his options, there was a soft tap on the door. It was a totally despondent Rock, needing to talk. After a few minutes of exchanging hopeless glances, Jones suddenly blurted out, "Do you want to be a star?" Without a moment's hesitation, Rock responded, "Yes!"

Decades after their conversation took place, Jones could still vividly recall Rock's "goddamned soulful eyes" welling up with tears, moved that Jones was willing to make a last-ditch effort to resurrect his career at Universal. "I felt so sorry for him," Jones recalled. Right then and there, I made my decision to stay with Universal and fight for him. I said, 'O.K., *we go!*' I had three months to make Rock Hudson a star."

Over the course of several months, Hudson's face would grace the pages of countless national magazines. There was a *Saturday Evening Post* profile entitled "How to Create a Movie Star." This was followed by a feature in *Cosmopolitan*. An interview with *Redbook*. None of this was lost on Universal's front office, which started to reconsider its decision to drop Rock from their roster of contract players.

Unbeknownst to Hudson, there had also been some divine intervention from someone else at the studio. When Rock had received word that Universal was through with him, he shared his miseries with fellow contract player Piper Laurie, who by then had graduated to some starring roles. "He was very unhappy, really very depressed," Laurie recalled. "He expressed it to me and I had the ear of an important producer there."

Whomever Laurie met with—and all signs point to Ross Hunter—he obviously agreed that Rock was being wasted in throwaway roles. What he needed was a substantial part in a thoughtfully planned production that would really showcase his abilities. Between Piper Laurie pulling strings behind the scenes and Roger Jones's publicity barrage, Universal renegotiated Rock's contract.

———

"I've found making lots of friends here not easy," Hudson revealed to columnist Hedda Hopper in the early 1950s. Although the fan magazines had him out on the town virtually every night of the week and in the company of Hollywood's beautiful people, Rock's grueling schedule—up at four, home by nine—left next to no time to cultivate meaningful friendships. Superficial, agent-arranged, good-for-your-career friendships, yes. Genuine, emotionally fulfilling, mutually supportive friendships, not so much. George Nader and Mark Miller being the exceptions, of course.

So, when Rock's teenage cousin, Jerry Scherer, needed a change from the day-to-day back in Illinois, Hudson didn't hesitate to extend an invitation. During their time together, Rock introduced Jerry to his fellow Universal contract player, James Best. They chatted up Piper Laurie and visited with Raoul Walsh and his wife. Though the one celebrity who made the most lasting impression on Scherer was Vera-Ellen. "Rock was dating her at that time and it seemed like a real romance but I can't say for sure," Scherer says. "But she was such a gentle, sweet lady. I had my eighteenth birthday out there and Rock and Vera-Ellen took me to the Tail o' The Cock to celebrate. The night we were there, who's sitting at the bar but John Wayne. He didn't know who I was or even who

Rock was in those days but he sang 'Happy Birthday' to me, which is not the kind of thing you ever forget." Scherer also remembers that that evening Rock and Vera told him that they intended to get married but they had not yet set a date.

Scherer also recalled visiting the set of Rock's latest effort, a boxing picture entitled *Iron Man*. "I remember the guard at the studio gate questioned Rock as we drove in, *'What are you here for? What set are you working on?'* and so forth. After we did get in, Rock said, 'I'll bet you one of these days, he won't be stopping me and asking me who I'm bringing in here. He'll just wave me through.' And, of course, that came to pass, just like he said."

"A FIGHT STORY . . . all that slugging and grunting business" is how star Evelyn Keyes remembered *Iron Man*. The *New York Times* also found the film shrug-worthy, finding it only "standard for the course." Yet *Iron Man* was the movie that would finally gain Rock Hudson both widespread attention and lifelong fans. Among the new converts was a nineteen-year-old movie buff from Colfax, Washington, named Robert Osborne. "I'd say the first time that I really noticed Rock on screen was in the movie *Iron Man*," Osborne remembers. "He had a secondary role in it, but he was very impressive as the young prizefighter. Terribly handsome, of course, and he really stood out. The other thing that I liked about him—and at this point, I wasn't aware of whether he was a good actor or not—is that he didn't seem to push the performance further than his talents allowed him to. So, he never came off as dishonest in what he did. There was always a sincerity there."

Iron Man was Universal's remake of its own ringside melodrama. The original, which had starred Lew Ayres and Jean Harlow, had turned a tidy profit for the studio in 1931. In director Joseph Pevney's updating of the story, Jeff Chandler is Coke Mason, a poor Pennsylvania coal miner who is persuaded to earn some quick cash prizefighting. The ordinarily docile Mason becomes a ferocious fighting machine once he steps inside the ring ("I'm like an animal . . . I want to kill"). Having at last graduated to fourth billing, Rock was granted a decent amount of screen time.

As Tommy "Speed" O'Keefe, a friend of Mason's who ends up pitted against him in a bout for the heavyweight title, Hudson finally made a genuine impression on-screen. Clearly, some of the attention was attributable to the fact that in *Iron Man*, Rock's sex appeal was on full display. Shirtless and outfitted in form-fitting boxing shorts, "The Beefcake Baron" was unleashed.

While Rock would maintain an athletic physique throughout most of his career, trainer Frankie Van had gotten him into peak condition. "The studio executives were taking a big chance because he didn't know how to box," Van remembered. "But I had faith in him. I put him in training and you never saw a boy work any harder." In six weeks, Hudson had shed ten pounds as a result of his intense workouts and daily sparring sessions with costar Jeff Chandler. Van also had to teach a left-handed Rock how to throw punches with his right hand. As a result of Rock's tenacity, Van recalled that Hudson was "suddenly more like Gene than Gene Tunney."

SHE REFERRED TO him as either "Igor" or "Dear Old Dad." He called her "Fortuna Divine" or "Magda Upswitch." After they worked together on a number of films in the early 1950s, Rock and script supervisor Betty Abbott Griffin became close friends. Griffin's own tenure at Universal predated Hudson's and she thought of Rock and her other colleagues as extended family. "I was a messenger girl before I became a script girl," says Griffin. "In those days, the studio had a very family feeling to it. When I was delivering the mail, I got to know everybody. They were like your uncle or your brother and it was wonderful." Actually, Betty really did have an uncle gainfully employed at Universal—Bud Abbott, the "straight man" half of the cross-talking comedy team Abbott and Costello.

"Rock fit right into this family atmosphere," says Griffin. "He was great fun, with this wonderful, wild sense of humor. Between takes, he was a real devil, always playing tricks on people. But with me, he became like a big brother. Very protective." Rock was drawn to Betty's unaffected, down-to-earth personality. Not only did they share an absurdist sense of humor but they both worshipped the same screen siren.

"He had a tremendous crush on Lana Turner and I thought Lana was the greatest thing since you-know-what," Griffin says. "I remember once, he and I didn't have much money but we went to the market and bought anchovy paste and Saltine crackers. We went down to Los Angeles to see a Lana Turner picture and we sat there, eating our anchovy paste and crackers for dinner because we had spent all of our money just so that we could see her. In those days, we had no money but it didn't matter because he made everything we did such fun."

It wasn't long before *Photoplay* took note of "a camaraderie seldom seen in Hollywood" and magazines were devoting lengthy articles to "Rock's Mystery Girl," who was described as "a lovely, vivid blonde . . . with warmth and understanding and a rare gift for gayety." Suddenly, the fanzines had turned a devoted friendship into a full-blown romance. *Modern Screen* didn't mince words: "Despite the diplomacy, the hedging, the shying away from any talk about marriage, Betty Abbott is the number one girl in Rock Hudson's life." Rock's mother was even called upon to give her carefully worded blessing in print: "I surely hope that Rock marries Betty, if he marries anyone. I would love to have that girl as my daughter-in-law."

Countless teenage girls may have been heartbroken when a magazine ran a photo of their idol captioned: "Heading for a Wedding?" But Betty Abbott Griffin says that she and her "intended" had a very different reaction whenever they read that wedding bells were about to chime: "We would laugh our heads off," Griffin says. "It was publicity. Nothing more, nothing less than that."

CHAPTER 5

"WE WANT HUDSON!"

Rock and director Raoul Walsh during the making
of *The Lawless Breed* (1952)
Courtesy of Universal Studios Licensing LLC

Along a thousand miles of majestic river roars this epic of the opening of our last untamed frontier!" blared the trailer for *Bend of the River.* Two years after *Winchester '73*, star James Stewart, director Anthony Mann, and producer Aaron Rosenberg would all reunite—this time in glorious Technicolor—for a widescreen adaptation of Bill Gulick's bestselling novel, *Bend of the Snake.*

In 1840s Oregon, Glyn McLyntock (Stewart), a former Missouri border raider, is guiding a wagon train of peaceful settlers intent on becoming ranchers and establishing their own community. Along the way McLyntock reunites with Emerson Cole (Arthur Kennedy), his former partner, who has a nasty habit of stealing provisions intended for impoverished settlers and selling them for profit.

Many familiar faces from Universal's roster of contract players, including Julie Adams and Lori Nelson, would appear in Mann's sweeping production. Fourth-billed Rock Hudson, having graduated from Young Bull, was now playing professional gambler Trey Wilson of San Francisco, whom McLyntock describes as "a right handsome fella."

While on location in Oregon, Hudson had an opportunity to observe Stewart at work. Rock was impressed with how much time and effort the actor invested in his portrayal of a man attempting to redeem himself while struggling with the dual sides of his nature. Although Stewart worked diligently in terms of building a character, he typically gave a performance that seemed effortless and unaffected. There were no false gestures, no self-consciousness.

Early in his film career, Stewart had discovered the secret of using his own inner life to make his characters—no matter how thinly drawn or poorly conceived—seem fully human and totally believable. Even while cranking out four pictures a year at MGM, Stewart had managed to combine his stage training with his own idiosyncratic brand of Method acting, without a single Strasberg in sight.

Hudson marveled at Stewart's ability to somehow make audiences share his feelings and have even the tritest dialogue sound as though it had just tripped off his tongue. How much of Stewart's technique was absorbed and later appropriated by the twenty-seven-year-old Rock Hudson? His costars remember Rock watching Stewart very intently, especially when he was preparing for a particularly dramatic scene.

"I remember watching Jim and thinking, he's not really 'doing' anything," recalls leading lady Julie Adams. "Yet when we looked at the rushes later, *everything* was there . . . I have no doubt that

Rock was paying very close attention to all of this and filing everything away for later. He was just like a sponge that way."

If *Bend of the River* would prove to be another hit for the unbeatable team of Stewart and Mann, this tale of redemption can also be credited with giving the career of Rock Hudson an important boost at a crucial moment. Not only was this the first time that Hudson's name appeared above the picture's title, but it was his first opportunity to share scenes with an established star. *Iron Man* may have succeeded in exploiting Rock's sex appeal, but *Bend of the River* would legitimize him. *Hey, there's that good-looking kid from Universal holding his own with Jimmy Stewart. How about that?* And thanks to the efforts of Universal's publicity team, "Rock Hudson" was quickly turning into a salable commodity with a steadily growing fan base.

Rock would always remember the reception he received when he attended the world premiere of *Bend of the River* in Portland, Oregon. Along with James Stewart and Julie Adams, Hudson rode in a procession of convertibles as they made their way to J. J. Parker's Broadway Theater, where the film was screened. *The Oregonian*'s Phyllis Lauritz reported that an estimated 10,000 movie fans "pushed, pulled, clutched and clawed" cast members and there was one star in particular that everybody wanted to see. "Handsome Rock Hudson's arrival sent the bobbysoxers into a chant of '*We want Hudson!*' that not even the subsequent presentation of other feature players and studio dignitaries could subdue."

Later, at a podium outside of the theatre, each star was asked to say a few words before entering. As Rock remembered it, the crowd applauded and cheered him more enthusiastically than the film's top-billed star. "It went to my head," Hudson recounted in his memoir. "I was floating! *Me over Jimmy Stewart?*"

While it wasn't surprising that the young Rock Hudson would inspire some appreciative squealing, it is unusual that a supporting player would receive this kind of rousing welcome. It's been suggested that Universal publicists may have planted a few in-house "fans" (studio employees) among the real ones. As for Jimmy Stewart, the local press did report that he was "mobbed" by autograph seekers and nearly pulled off the platform by his more ardent admirers.

Bill Gulick, author of the novel on which the film was based, liked Rock's performance but he wasn't pleased with the rest of the picture. He told *The Oregonian* that the screen version substituted Hollywood spectacle for historical accuracy: "The movie makers threw my book away and retained only three words of my title. If someone mislaid his steamboats and Shoshones, it wasn't I."

WHEN U-I EXECUTIVES viewed the rushes from the otherwise unimpressive *Tomahawk*, it occurred to them that Yvonne De Carlo and Rock Hudson—two of the screen's great beauties—might make for a perfect couple in a modestly budgeted drama. The picture the studio assigned them to, *Scarlet Angel*, would mark Hudson's first film as a romantic lead. Rock's latest vehicle would be camouflaged just enough so that it wasn't instantly recognizable as a quasi-remake of Rene Clair's *The Flame of New Orleans*, in which an impoverished Marlene Dietrich masquerades as a countess.

For *Scarlet Angel*, screenwriter Oscar Brodney retained the New Orleans setting but shifted the action from the eighteenth century to just after the Civil War. Taking over from Dietrich, De Carlo is scrappy dance-hall hostess Roxy McClanahan, who is "about as subtle as a tropical cyclone." Shortly after meeting rugged, barbrawling sea captain Frank Truscott (Hudson), Roxy makes off with his bankroll as well as the baby of a deceased war widow, whose identity she assumes.

During the making of *Scarlet Angel*, Hudson completely charmed costar Bodil Miller, who played the doomed widow. "I first met Rock when we were both enrolled in Sophie Rosenstein's drama classes," says Miller. "We studied together. He was a great friend and a wonderful person . . . I really liked Yvonne De Carlo, too. She had a tremendous charm about her. Actually, I think she had a bit of a crush on Rock but he seemed to be too busy in those days to respond."

This was the third film in which De Carlo and Hudson had worked together and the leading lady had noticed a change for the better in her costar. "He was doing leads now and had come a long way since *Tomahawk*," De Carlo said. "He was no longer awkward before the camera, and I was sure now—a bit late—that Rock was on his way to movie stardom."

In complete agreement was budding film historian Robert Osborne, who now made a point of seeing each new Rock Hudson movie as soon as it was released. "After he gained some attention in the early films, like *Iron Man* and *Scarlet Angel*, it was wonderful to watch him grow as an actor," Osborne said. "So often there were people starring in films simply because of the way they looked. They would be given wonderful opportunities but their talent didn't really grow. Over time, Rock was one who really did grow as an actor, as did Tony Curtis. They became wonderful actors, and that was really an exciting thing to see."

Although the pictures were now coming one right after another, Rock always seemed to be scraping by financially. So, he could only laugh when informed that his next film would be entitled *Oh Money, Money*. Joseph Hoffman's screenplay fondly recalled "the happy days and the mad fads" of the Roaring Twenties. In this era of bobbed hair, raccoon coats, and speakeasies, good times flowed as freely as bathtub gin. At least until everything came crashing down on Black Tuesday. As it was essentially a lighthearted comedy with musical interludes, the movie was eventually retitled *Has Anybody Seen My Gal* after one of the popular tunes of the day. Despite the title change, the film's focus is obvious from the very beginning. A silent movie–style title card flashes on-screen and it doesn't mince words: "This is a story about Money . . . *Remember It?*"

In Rock's latest vehicle, an eccentric millionaire named Samuel Fulton (Charles Coburn) intends to leave his vast fortune to the family of a deceased paramour named Millicent, who spurned his marriage proposal some forty years earlier. Fulton tracks down Millicent's daughter, Harriet Blaisdell (Lynn Bari), who is not so blissfully wed to small-town druggist Charles (Larry Gates).

Posing as a painter named "Mr. Smith," Fulton rents a room from the Blaisdells so that he can closely observe the effects his anonymous gift of $100,000 will have on this "typical" middle-class family. The results are hardly what Fulton had hoped for. Once she's well-off, Harriet wastes no time mutating into a snobby social climber. She evicts Mr. Smith and decides that poor soda jerk, Dan Stebbins (Hudson), isn't good enough to marry daughter Millie (Piper Laurie). Meanwhile, Charles sells the drugstore and begins playing the stock market while son Howard (William Reynolds) takes up gambling. What should be the family's darkest moment proves to be their salvation. When Charles loses everything in the '29 crash, the Blaisdells end up flat broke but everyone is genuinely happy once more.

"It was a charming movie," says Piper Laurie, "but I personally felt that soda jerk part was beneath Rock . . . Here's this six-foot-four hunk and they had him saying lines that sounded like they belonged in a teenager's mouth." Even so, Hudson is as ingratiating as the movie itself. Whether teaching old-timer Charles Coburn how to serve up a strawberry surprise or doing the Charleston with Piper Laurie, Rock makes the most of a role that would have been instantly forgettable in other hands. *Has Anybody Seen My Gal* would be the first of two successful screen teamings for Rock and Piper. Even more significantly, the picture would bring Hudson together with Douglas Sirk, the director who would prove to be more influential than any other in terms of molding Rock's screen persona.

Born Hans Detlef Sierck in Hamburg in 1897, Sirk was "lost to the theatre," as he put it, after the first play he directed became a surprise success in 1922. Many of the signature touches that would later distinguish his Hollywood films were first introduced in his stage work. Whatever the medium, Sirk would excel at presenting what he called "dramas of swollen emotions"; his visually arresting production design provided ironic commentary on the plight of his characters and their often conflicted states of mind.

"Mr. Sirk was an absolutely fascinating person, and in time he became very much like a surrogate father to Rock," says Betty Abbott Griffin, who worked as a script supervisor on several of the director's films. "He and his [second] wife, Hilde, had a fantastic background. He was the great director and she was an actress— sort of like the Shirley Temple of Germany. Hilde was of Jewish descent, so during the war they had to make arrangements to leave Europe." Once in Hollywood, Hans Sierck became Douglas Sirk, and by 1950 he was under contract to Universal. Almost immediately, the director found his muse.

"I saw a picture Rock was playing in, with Jeff Chandler in the lead [*Iron Man*]. He had a small part, and he was far inferior to Chandler, but I thought I saw something. So, I arranged to meet him, and he seemed to be not too much to the eye, except very handsome. But the camera sees with its own eye. It sees things that the human eye does not detect . . . I gave him an extensive test, and then put him into *Has Anybody Seen My Gal*. The only thing which never let me down in Hollywood was my camera. And it was not wrong about Hudson."

"I think that Mr. Sirk found something that other people didn't find in Rock, which was the intensity to not only become an actor but a fine actor," says Griffin. "The patience that Mr. Sirk had was just incredible. I think that had a lot to do with it. He was impressed by the fact that Rock was really trying very hard and that he wanted to succeed."

With *Has Anybody Seen My Gal*, Sirk's camera was trained on not one future superstar but two. Twenty-one-year-old James Dean briefly appears as one of Rock's customers. Dean delivers his one line ("A choc malt, heavy on the choc, plenty of milk . . .") in his trademark sulky style.

"Nobody knew Jimmy then," says Piper Laurie. "He was just

sitting at the counter and nobody paid any attention to him. Extras were just extras. I was very into my own work and I didn't socialize a lot on the set. Years later, my Uncle Maury called me from New York, said he was watching the movie on television and asked me, 'Do you know who that was sitting in the drugstore?'"

Only three years later, Hudson and Dean would work together again, though each would be a major player in Hollywood by that time, appearing in one of the most important films of each of their careers. But Rock's participation in a prestige project would have to wait. For now, it was on to a pair of B-Westerns. Although director Budd Boetticher would eventually be acclaimed as a master of the genre and some of his stark, pictorially striking Westerns of the 1950s are considered classics, *Horizons West* isn't one of them.

Neal Hammond (Hudson) and his older brother, Dan (Robert Ryan), survive the Civil War, but once they return to Texas they lead very different postwar lives. Neal settles down on his father's ranch while power-hungry Dan turns to rustling, ruthlessly seizing control of the territory. Every bit of character development is not only telegraphed but followed by an exclamation point: "I'm going to have land and the land will be covered with cattle and cotton! I'm building an empire!" the corrupt Hammond proclaims. "When I'm on the top, people will swear that I've done nothing wrong!" To which one of his lackeys responds, "This reconstruction period is made to order for you! No Texas rangers. Very little law!"

"*Horizons West* bites the dust before anybody in it," the *New York Times* said in its thumbs-down review. However, *The Lawless Breed*, which came next, would prove to be an important vehicle for its star. For once, Rock's character offered him a legitimate acting challenge. And for the first time, he'd be portraying a real person on screen—namely the notorious gunslinger John Wesley Hardin, a ruthless desperado "so mean, he once shot a man for snoring."

Born in Texas in 1853, Hardin boasted in his autobiography that he had killed forty-two men (thirty-four more than Billy the Kid, for those keeping score). Apart from Hardin's quite obvious character flaws, there were some unusual dualities in the outlaw's life that Hudson could use in terms of building a compelling characterization. Ironically, one of the most infamous criminals of the Old West was the son of an especially devout Methodist preacher. At least according to Bernard Gordon's screenplay, Hardin's father "carried his Bible like a six gun" and attempted to bullwhip the fear of god into his rebellious son—shades of Wallace Fitzgerald here.[*]

The scenes of Hardin gunning down sheriff's deputies and Texas rangers were contrasted with sequences in which he was presented as a loving husband and responsible father. At one point, Hardin becomes so incensed by the sight of his sixteen-year-old son handling a gun that he backhands the boy. If the complexities of Hardin's personality didn't already present enough of an acting challenge, the gunfighter would age from eighteen to forty-two over the course of the story. Considering all of this, could Rock Hudson—who had never carried an entire picture before—deliver the goods? Raoul Walsh, who agreed to direct, thought so.

Just because the director had faith, didn't mean that he had patience, too. At one point, Hudson turned to Walsh for guidance regarding how to play the scene in which Hardin reunites with his wife, Rosie, after he's been imprisoned for sixteen years in the Texas State Penitentiary. By way of response, the famously brusque director told Rock to stop holding up the entire company and to get on with it.

"He had a wonderful way of directing me," Hudson later said. "Because I was so busy with acting class and learning the technique and all this junk that you really should just throw out, his

[*]In May of 1952, Universal's publicity department issued a bizarre press release concerning *The Lawless Breed*: "Rock Hudson is one of those young actors who will go all out for his art . . . The script requires John McIntire, in the role of Hudson's stern father, to whip Rock with a leather strap. McIntire tried some experimental blows. 'Harder,' said Rock, and McIntire laid on with more vigor. After the realistic scene was filmed, McIntire, curious, asked Rock to remove his shirt. Hudson did, and his torso and arms were a mass of welts."

attitude was, 'Don't bother with that. Just do it.' That was Raoul Walsh's attitude. When he said that, he just made it this surmountable problem. Instead of climbing this hurdle, it was like a step down to do. It made it so simple in my head. Great acting lesson, I thought."

The Lawless Breed was one of six films that Rock would appear in with fellow contract player Julia Adams, who would soon change her first name to "Julie" and achieve pop culture immortality courtesy of *Creature from the Black Lagoon.* In the years that they worked together, Adams noticed that the higher the bar was set for Rock, the better the end results would be.

"You had to give him something meaningful to play," Adams says. "*The Lawless Breed* gave Rock a real opportunity to show that he was more than just this handsome hunk . . . I think his great strength as an actor was that he always brought a sense of reality to whatever he was doing. He seemed completely real and many times, you work with actors who are very obviously 'acting.' Not Rock. You always had a feeling that the person he was portraying was a real human being, and that was impressive to me . . . I really believe that he was a better actor than he was given credit for."

The reviewer for *The Hollywood Reporter* paid tribute to Hudson's "absorbing sincerity and conviction" and felt that *The Lawless Breed* presented Rock with his "best role to date." Other critics weren't quite as sold. In his *Los Angeles Times* review, Phillip K. Scheuer found Hudson's characterization only "fairly acceptable . . . He's a likeable-appearing fellow, except that his face isn't exactly the kind that registers indelibly. I was never quite sure he was he, especially after he sprouted a mustache, till I had looked twice."

Even if some of the critics were on the fence about his first legitimate star turn, *The Lawless Breed* was the picture that would eventually lead to his being cast in the most celebrated role of his career. Still, Hudson didn't seem to retain any special fondness for *The Lawless Breed.* Decades after the picture's initial release, film historian Eric Spilker told Hudson that he was planning to screen the movie for a group of students who had never seen it. Rock's reply was unsparing: "The best thing you could do with that picture is to burn it."

———————

"It was a tumultuous affair, which didn't turn out well," Mark Miller would say of Rock's next relationship. "The guy was funny, wonderful to be around . . . His name was Jack Navaar." The new man in Hudson's life was a friend of Nader's and Miller's. Unlike the quick fling he had with a carhop named Jimmy Dixon, Rock's affair with Navaar would prove to be of greater consequence.

Navaar was a twenty-two-year-old Korean War veteran. A willowy, blue-eyed blond, Navaar was bisexual and despite his tender age, well-versed in fielding passes from both men and women. Not surprisingly, Henry Willson was among those who pounced. He eagerly signed Navaar to his agency, bestowing upon the young man one of his favorite uber-macho screen names: Rand Saxon. While remarkably handsome, Jack was sorely lacking in two areas that were essential for Hollywood stardom—ambition and vanity. Nevertheless, Henry enrolled Jack in acting classes; interviews were arranged with casting directors. But before Willson had Navaar playing bellboys and traffic cops in a succession of Universal comedies, Rock claimed the young man for himself.

Hudson's long-term roommate, Bob Preble, moved out of their Avenida del Sol house in May of 1953 when he married actress Yvonne Rivero. Almost immediately, Jack Navaar moved in, though at Navaar's urging, he and Rock would soon relocate to a more spacious home on Grand View Drive in Studio City. Though Jack had a job at Hughes Aircraft, Rock managed to persuade him to give it up, preferring to have his partner all to himself when he was between pictures.

Apart from dinners with Nader and Miller, Hudson and Navaar kept their socializing to a minimum. And this may have been a self-protective measure on Rock's part. As he closed in on thirty, what would the press make of the fact that he had recently swapped one male roommate for another? If Bob Preble had been introduced to Hudson's fans in the pages of *Photoplay*, Jack Navaar would deliberately be kept out of sight. "We lived a very reclusive life and we were very involved with each other," Navaar would later say. "Rock made me feel secure and loved."

Despite this, friends remember that the relationship was extremely volatile. It seemed that no matter what Hudson did, it set Navaar off. "If he did nice things for me, I was angry, and if he didn't do nice things and ignored me, I would be angrier. I was an angry young guy," Navaar admitted. When a totally plastered Rock came home from a party at three in the morning, Jack first kicked him out of bed and then, out of the house. If partying with Joan Crawford until all hours wasn't bad enough, Hudson then had the audacity to come home and start snoring the moment he hit the sheets.

As time went by, the shouting got louder and the arguments intensified. One evening, Rock phoned Jack to say that he would be late coming home from the studio. They needed to reshoot a scene. Navaar wasn't buying it. Surely some good-looking extra or stuntman had caught Hudson's eye. Starting at annoyed, Navaar quickly moved on to enraged. As it got later, he worked himself into a state of nearly operatic hysteria. When Hudson finally made it home—several hours after he was expected—he could only look on in horror as Navaar tossed his priceless collection of 78 records off the back deck and down the hill.

———

In June of 1952, Universal announced that it was signing Rock Hudson to a new term contract of one year with a forty-week guarantee. The new deal, which had been negotiated by Henry Willson, included options for six additional years with salary increases. While this was encouraging, Rock was surprised to learn that for the first time since he had joined Universal, he was being loaned out to another studio, in this case RKO. Also, for the first time, he would be shooting a picture in a foreign location, in this case the Channel Islands of Guernsey and Jersey, off the coast of Normandy.

Hudson's leading lady would once again be Yvonne De Carlo and his director would once again be Raoul Walsh. Adding to the feeling of déjà vu, *Sea Devils* had already served as the title of a flag-waving action yarn which had been released sixteen years earlier, albeit with an entirely different plot.

This version of *Sea Devils* was set during the Napoleonic era. Rock played Gilliatt, a rugged young Channel Island fisherman-turned-smuggler who meets an alluring but mysterious woman named Drouchette. The seaman agrees to transport Drouchette to the French coast after she reveals that she's on a mission to rescue her imprisoned brother. As Gilliatt later discovers, Drouchette is actually a British agent, intent on thwarting Napoleon's threatened invasion of England. Or, put in the very succinct lingo of Universal's advertising department: *"A Man Built for Action! A Woman Born to Kiss! Gripped tight in the dangers of desperate intrigue!"*

Far from Hollywood and the prying eyes of gossip mavens Hedda Hopper and Louella Parsons, Rock was not nearly as circumspect as he was back home. When some of his more flamboyant gay friends paid a visit to the location, director Raoul Walsh griped to Yvonne De Carlo: "I don't like the birds he's traveling with. You know— birds of a feather?" To her credit, De Carlo didn't play along. "I had nothing to contribute to Raoul's comments. I only knew that Rock was Rock . . . and he was a very, very nice guy. Anything beyond that would be conjectural."

Another of Rock's costars, Bryan Forbes, didn't have to do much speculating. Forbes, who would later transition from actor to director, said that he and Rock became inseparable during the making of *Sea Devils*. In fact, two years after the film was released, Forbes wrote an article for *Picturegoer* magazine in which he detailed the intimacies of their friendship.

In a piece entitled "Rock's All Right," Forbes said that after being inundated with Hudson's early "Beefcake King" publicity, he had expected to be introduced to "six feet four inches of nothing but corn-fed conceit." Instead, Forbes found that Hudson had "a fine sense of self-deprecation and can take, as well as give, a joke on the set."

Forbes recounted how he and his girlfriend "double-dated" with Rock and Sharman Douglas, daughter of the United States Ambassador to Great Britain. After that, Forbes took Hudson to dinner in Soho, to his parents' home in Essex (where Rock "quickly established a lasting friendship with Grandmother, who insisted on a signed photograph") and to a tailor, where they ordered Hudson his first Savile Row suit. Conspicuously absent from these reminiscences, though, was the fact that Rock had attempted to take the friendship with Forbes a step further: "I shared rooms with Rock and was somewhat amazed one night when over dinner he confessed he was in love with me. I told him it was very flattering but I did not swing that way, so I suppose I was one of the first to know of his homosexuality."

De Carlo remembered that both on the set and off, Rock was in need of guidance—the kind of fatherly support that Raoul Walsh had once provided freely but now seemed to withhold. "I didn't feel hurt when Walsh would end a take with a grunt rather than an accolade," De Carlo said. "With Rock, it was more difficult. He was doing well by that stage of his career but he still wasn't the most secure actor in Hollywood, and he needed direction and personal nudges at times." Some of the nudges being quite literal. After *Sea Devils* wrapped, Hudson and De Carlo were sent to Belgium to promote the film. Having made *Hotel Sahara* in England and *Sombrero* in Mexico, De Carlo knew all too well how merciless the foreign press could be with American movie stars.

In an effort to protect Rock from a hardline interrogation, De Carlo devised a plan that she would give him a light kick in the shins if she felt the line of questioning was venturing into dangerous territory. This led to one unusually abrupt interview, as the actress recalled in her autobiography: "As they started to close in on questions about his love life, I let him have it, kicking him so hard he doubled over and said something like, 'Ooof!' It may not have been the answer the reporter wanted, but at least it wasn't something they could quote out of context."

In his *New York Times* review of *Sea Devils*, Bosley Crowther dismissed the movie as "completely undistinguished" and "a flat and pedestrian walk-through of a lot of adventure-film clichés . . . in which the square-jawed, bare-chested Mr. Hudson and the low-bodiced Miss De Carlo get into and out of scrapes . . . Actually filmed on the coast of France, it could as well have been filmed in a studio tank."

After romping around in the open air, it was right back into the studio tank for Hudson. His next picture, *The Golden Blade*, almost seemed to revel in its own artificiality. Cartoonish and vibrantly Technicolored, this light-hearted Arabian Nights yarn is Ali Baba courtesy of Roy Lichtenstein. The pop art elements of the movie aren't surprising given that it was directed by Nathan Juran, who was later responsible for the infamous *Attack of the 50 Ft. Woman*.

Outfitted like Universal's best approximation of Rudolph Valentino in *The Sheik*, Rock is a brave youth from Basra named Harun, who travels to Baghdad to avenge his father's death. Once there, he meets the ravishing but mischievous Princess Khairuzan (Piper Laurie), "whom trouble follows like a faithful dog." Harun also discovers the mythical "Sword of Damascus,"* an enchanted weapon that renders its owner invincible. The blade is coveted by the evil vizier Jafar (George Macready, as splendidly villainous here as he was in *Gilda*).

---

*The film was originally titled *The Sword of Damascus* and both Farley Granger and Tony Curtis passed on the role ultimately played by Hudson. Several years before she made a splash in Fellini's *La Dolce Vita*, Anita Ekberg appeared as one of Piper Laurie's handmaidens. Future *McCloud* star Dennis Weaver can be briefly spotted as the "Rabble Rouser."

There are jousts, scantily clad harem girls, and kooky comic book dialogue like, "By Zeus! I knew I was right . . ." or "Ten thousand devils, no!" More than sixty years after she costarred with Rock in *The Golden Blade*, Piper Laurie says that her initial impressions of the picture have evolved over time.

"When we were shooting it, I thought it was really stupid. And initially, when I saw it years ago, I hated it. But I happened to see it recently and I thought it was very funny and spirited. I actually laughed out loud. It was very much a silly fairy tale and they used all the clichés that existed, like pulling the sword out of the column . . . But I thought Rock was really terrific in that movie. He managed to bring some reality to a fairy tale, as he did it with such conviction. And the exteriors on the back lot were so good that years later, when I got married and I went to Morocco on my honeymoon, it was like being right back at Universal again."

Rock would eventually classify *The Golden Blade* and *The Desert Hawk* as "movies to die by," films that he'd made early in his career that he'd just as soon forget. "They serve a purpose, though," Hudson told the *New York Daily News*. "I can invite friends in, get good and smashed and giggle over them."

Another loan-out, this time to Columbia, offered Rock a temporary change of scenery but not much else. *Gun Fury*, Hudson's fourth film for director Raoul Walsh, was another routine Western, though it would be shot in picturesque Sedona, Arizona, and in the gimmicky new 3-D process (the illusion of depth not being an effect especially well-suited to a one-eyed director).

The cinematic equivalent of a dime novel, *Gun Fury* features Hudson as a heroic Civil War veteran pursuing a gang of notorious desperadoes who have kidnapped his beautiful bride-to-be. Donna Reed was cast as Hudson's fiancée, future star Lee Marvin would play one of the heavies, and twenty-four-year-old newcomer Roberta Haynes would portray fiery cantina owner Estella Morales.

"I really didn't want to make that movie," says Haynes. "When

I went to Columbia, I had been promised the part of the prosti-tute in *From Here to Eternity* but they gave that to Donna Reed instead . . . then they put us both in *Gun Fury*. I thought it was a horrible movie and not only was it a complete waste of time but it was even in 3-D, if you can believe it."

Between takes, Haynes befriended some—but not all—of her costars. "Lee Marvin was very protective of me," says Haynes. "I think he was already an alcoholic but a really nice guy. As for Rock Hudson, I never heard anyone say a bad word about him . . . Sure, people in Hollywood knew that he was gay but the rest of the world didn't. There were so many people in that sort of predicament in those days. And it wasn't just actors. There were writers, producers, directors. They were all married. All in the closet. And nobody really cared. It was just the way things were."

On the last day of shooting, while riding at full gallop, Hudson suffered an appendicitis attack. Upon returning to Los Angeles, Hudson checked into St. John's Hospital. The doctor was insistent that an appendectomy be performed immediately. Rock waved him away. The studio was deep into preparations for what was being touted as his breakthrough film—one in which he'd be playing, ironically enough, a physician. Hudson feared that if he were ab-sent from the studio for even a week, Tony Curtis and Jeff Chandler would start to look better and better to the powers that be. It was only after his doctor insisted, that Rock underwent surgery.

While recovering, Hudson made good use of his time in the hos-pital. With his upcoming role in mind, he studied how the doctors interacted with patients and staff and he badgered his attending physician with questions concerning surgical procedures. If he was going to be stuck in the hospital, he may as well get some work done.

Before Rock could be entrusted with that long promised "A" pic-ture, there were a few more routine vehicles to slog through, includ-ing Douglas Sirk's only Western, which was being produced by Ross

Hunter. The reteaming of Hudson and Sirk was all part of Hunter's long-range plan. Before they all moved on to a more ambitious endeavor, he wanted star and director to join forces on a B-picture. "So that they can get to know each other," Hunter explained. "They can live together. They can feel each other's thoughts. They can know whether their chemistry is right."

CHAPTER 6

DOUBLE TECHNICOLOR

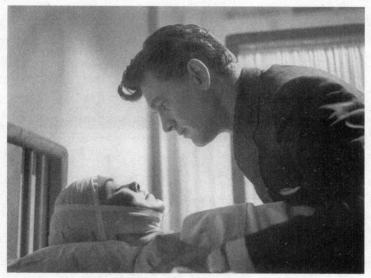

"A damned crazy story, if ever there was one," is how director
Douglas Sirk described *Magnificent Obsession*. Part Sunday school
lesson, part Harlequin romance, all perfectly insane.
(Photo courtesy of Photofest*)*

t was 118 degrees. War paint was running down his neck. Every
time he jumped on a horse, his wig fell off. Each time he flubbed
a line, the crew glared at him. After *Winchester '73*, he thought
he'd never play another Indian and yet, here he was . . . a six-foot-
four Apache from Winnetka, Illinois, complete with a Midwestern drawl.

Although Hudson could scarcely believe it, he was *Taza, Son
of Cochise*. "I looked like Joe College with a long wig and dark
make-up. It was ridiculous," Hudson would later say. As he sweated

it out on location in Utah's Moab Desert, all he could think of was that his friends, Jim Matteoni and Pat McGuire, would have a good laugh at his expense when his latest epic finally turned up at the local movie house back home.

Even so, Rock was willing to endure all of the snickering if playing Taza meant that he was that much closer to becoming a leading man. In a sense, *Taza* was a feature-length screen test. If he worked well with Douglas Sirk, he'd be reteamed with the director for *Magnificent Obsession*, the vehicle that had been painstakingly planned as his breakthrough.

Despite the great talent involved, Hudson knew that *Taza* was only a notch above average. The picture would be redeemed by Sirk's psychological layering and a pro-Indian stance, which was unusual for Hollywood in the early 1950s. Set in the Arizona Territory in 1874, the story begins with the death of Cochise,* an old Apache warrior. Before taking the "Big Sleep," Cochise appoints his elder son, Taza, as the new tribal leader. Peace-loving Taza vows to live in harmony with the "White Eyes," though his younger brother, Naiche, believes the tribe should join forces with Geronimo and resist any attempts at containment by the United States Cavalry.

Sirk worked closely with screenwriter George Zuckerman on developing the script. Throughout the narrative, Taza struggles with his divided allegiance—he's torn between protecting the members of his tribe and obeying the commands of the cavalry leaders he has promised to assist. This is neatly summarized in a sequence in which Taza heads off to battle, wearing half Indian garb and half of an officer's uniform. This was the kind of "split" character that Sirk was intrigued by and one that the director knew that Rock

*Jeff Chandler had played the Indian chief in both *Broken Arrow* (1950) and *The Battle at Apache Pass* (1952). When Douglas Sirk invited Chandler to reprise the role in *Taza*'s opening sequence, the actor balked: "My God, I'm a star! Just to do five minutes and then die!" Chandler eventually gave in, though as Douglas Sirk remembered, this involved "a large sum of money" as well as a reference to Chandler's character in the title.

would immediately identify with. In fact, who better than Hudson to play a protagonist torn between his natural instincts and a more conformist existence?

If the sweltering conditions—shooting outside in the desert, in the dead of summer, under the blazing sun—weren't bad enough, the entire company had to endure lengthy setups and camera tests, necessitated by the use of 3-D equipment, which Sirk considered a nuisance. For a climactic battle sequence, which took Sirk and cinematographer Russell Metty a week to shoot, real Native Americans were employed as extras. To the director's delight, they "hadn't been spoiled by [John] Ford." The fact that the Indians weren't of the Hollywood variety caused Hudson even greater embarrassment. "I felt like such a fool and a complete imposter," Hudson would later tell George Nader.

When *Taza* was released in February of 1954, *Variety* commended Sirk for his "forceful" direction and ability to make "every scene an eye-filling experience." The leading man, however, was only faintly praised: "Rock Hudson suffices in action demands of his role as Taza, but character is none too believable."

"It's double-Technicolor," is how Rock would describe *Magnificent Obsession* nearly twenty years after he had appeared in the film. While full of praise for costar Jane Wyman and director Douglas Sirk, Hudson felt that the movie was too saccharine (even for an old-fashioned weepie) and that it didn't completely hold up. "It comes off as trite—each line is just dripping with love," was Rock's surprisingly candid assessment.

And yet, he knew that *Magnificent Obsession* was one of those films that fans wholeheartedly embraced—whether they took it at face value or appreciated it for its countless camp delights. Whatever the case, when all was said and done, it was the movie that made Rock Hudson a star. Though he nearly blew his big break.

Only two weeks before production launched, Hudson, Jack

Navaar, George Nader, and Mark Miller piled into Rock's car and headed off to Laguna Beach. While riding the waves in an oversized black inner tube ("like an ass"), Hudson was picked up by a giant swell, which dropped him ("like a match") headlong onto the beach. His collarbone was broken. As he waited for the ambulance, Rock started sobbing—less because of the physical pain and more because he was terrified that the studio would recast his part.

"How long before it's healed, doc?" Hudson asked the grave-faced bone specialist, who was hovering over him, looking unusually concerned.

"Hard to say, Rock. We'll have to wait for X-rays. But I'm thinking eight to twelve weeks at the outside. You really ought to be in traction, son."

Out of commission for nearly three months? Impossible. Universal would never delay the start of shooting for that long. Rock suddenly had nightmare visions of Tony Curtis taking possession of *his* role. Now, all of the time, effort, and energy he had spent working up to this moment may have been wiped out in a single afternoon.

"I called the studio in a panic. It was a plum role and a good chance for advancement for me," Hudson recalled. "So many people at the studio went to bat for me when one of the executives wanted me replaced. The head of the studio, Bill Goetz said, 'No, that part's for him and he's going to do it. Nobody else.'—which I loved."

If the rumor mill is to be believed, there may have been some divine intervention from another corner of Universal's administration building. Edward Muhl, who had just been promoted to vice president in charge of production, made an executive decision that single-handedly saved Rock Hudson's career. "Without Muhl, Rock would have been dropped from *Magnificent Obsession*," Mark Miller says. According to Miller, Muhl had fallen hard for Hudson and would occasionally meet with Rock behind closed doors for afternoon assignations. "Not true," says Alexandra Muhl, Edward Muhl's eldest daughter. "They never even socialized."

Regardless of what went on (or didn't) behind the scenes, Rock remained in the movie. "I did it with a broken shoulder," Hudson told an interviewer. "I had a figure eight bandage on and it criss-crossed around behind my back . . . Poor Jane Wyman, we'd do these love scenes and the broken bone would creak and make her sick. But she kept right on as we were doing this love scene, you know. She gets a chevron for that."

Even in 1953, when Rock's remake went into production, *Magnificent Obsession* was already considered something of a warhorse. Back in 1929, Lloyd C. Douglas, a Congregational clergyman, had published a bestselling novel by the same name about redemption and the transformative power of anonymous philanthropy. The themes Douglas explored had originated with one of his own essays, the clinically titled "Personality Expansion through Self-Investment in the Philanthropic Rehabilitation of Others." In other words, paying it forward. In adapting *Magnificent Obsession*, screenwriter Robert Blees wisely jettisoned several subplots, though he retained the essence of Douglas's novel. However, even a streamlined version of the story read like an especially sudsy episode of *The Guiding Light*.

Spoiled, good-for-nothing playboy Bob Merrick is seriously injured when he crashes his speedboat. A resuscitator is used to save Merrick, which means it isn't available to help another desperately in need of it. That would be Brightwood Hospital's overworked chief, Dr. Wayne Phillips,* renowned as "the most important figure in the field of brain surgery on the continent." A pillar of the community, Dr. Phillips has performed countless good deeds for those in need—though always anonymously.

After the saintly Dr. Phillips succumbs to a heart attack, Merrick attempts to absolve his guilt by paying off Phillips's widow, Helen, with a sizable check. She rejects the offer and later, while

---

*In the 1954 version of *Magnificent Obsession*, the surname of Helen's unseen late husband was changed from "Hudson" to "Phillips" as Universal didn't want to create any confusion between the dead character and a leading man the studio frequently touted as the picture of robust vitality.

fleeing from Merrick, she's hit by a car and blinded. Merrick then meets spiritually attuned painter Edward Randolph (Otto Kruger), who teaches the young carouser how to establish contact with "the source of infinite power," the same spiritual wellspring that had inspired the late Dr. Phillips to give to others so unselfishly. Soon after, Merrick introduces himself to an unsuspecting Helen as "Robbie Robinson," and she immediately falls for the unusually attentive stranger.

Attempting to atone for his past transgressions, Merrick dedicates himself to becoming Helen's "eyes," by secretly financing several of her operations. In another act of redemption, he saves the cash-strapped Brightwood Hospital from bankruptcy. After completing medical school, Merrick becomes one of the world's foremost neurosurgeons. Although he's certified just in time to save a gravely ill Helen, Merrick is apprehensive. What if the surgery fails? Helen could die. After some encouraging words from Randolph, Merrick saves Helen's life, restores her sight, and vows that they will courageously face the future together.

It may have been totally improbable schmaltz, not to mention the saltiest of tearjerkers, but *Magnificent Obsession* was a blockbuster in whatever form it appeared. The first successful screen adaptation of the bestseller had been released by Universal in 1935. Robert Taylor, on loan-out from MGM, became a star by playing Bob Merrick. Could lightning strike twice? Universal was banking on it. Decades after it was produced, there would be a lingering debate about who first came up with the idea for a Rock remake of *Magnificent Obsession*. Several insiders were quick to claim credit.

Joseph Pevney, who had directed Rock in *Iron Man*, said that Universal's chief, William Goetz, asked him to dust off the property. Douglas Sirk insisted that it was Jane Wyman who had first suggested a remake; the actress shrewdly recognized that playing a blind widow virtually guaranteed her a second Oscar. "Everybody has taken credit for *Magnificent Obsession* and I am here to say that

I brought that idea to everybody at the studio and they all turned it down except William Goetz," recalled producer Ross Hunter. "I said . . . 'I believe this picture could make a star out of Rock Hudson. All you're doing is putting him into action pictures and he's not that type of boy. He's a good-looking, clean cut man that young people all over the world will fantasize about.'"

Douglas Sirk wasn't nearly as enthusiastic. "My immediate reaction to *Magnificent Obsession* was bewilderment and discouragement," Sirk recalled. "But still, I was attracted by something irrational in it . . . because this is a damned crazy story, if ever there was one."

In what was an unusual move for the studio, Universal executives granted Sirk six weeks of rehearsal. Most of this time would be devoted to carefully molding Hudson's performance. "Rock Hudson was not an educated man but that very beautiful body of his was putty in my hands," Sirk would later comment. Although he had found a director he trusted, Hudson would also turn to his leading lady for guidance and support.

"Rock was new in the business and he was scared, of course, because we were in a big 'A' production now," remembered Jane Wyman. "He wanted so much to learn. Rock was a sponge. He just sopped up everything and pigeonholed it and used it when he could. And by the end of the picture, he was a pro."

Universal contract players Barbara Rush and Gregg Palmer were cast as Helen's stepdaughter and beau. Like Hudson, Palmer was grateful that he had found his way into one of Universal's rare prestige productions: "Rock and I were both scared as hell. We knew that we had to be on our game in *Magnificent Obsession* because there were some real heavyweights in that cast with Jane Wyman, Agnes Moorehead, and Otto Kruger. I was just starting out in the business and I was very taken with all of these people and their professional abilities. I know that some of my contemporaries had a very different experience with Sirk but I liked him and found it easy to work with him . . . I could see that he was very supportive of Rock and why shouldn't he be? We all knew this was Hudson's big chance . . . I mean, for him, this was sink or swim."

Hudson was feeling the pressure so intensely that he came close to dropping out of the production. While on location at Lake Arrowhead, publicist Roger Jones was awakened with a distress call at one o'clock in the morning. It was a terrified Rock, who had talked himself into a full-blown panic attack. When Jones arrived at Hudson's bungalow, he found the actor packing and ready to bolt. *"I'm no actor . . ."* Hudson muttered to himself, furiously digging at his fingernails. *"I can't do anything . . . I'm going to quit now . . . I'm going home . . . I'm going to get out of this business!"* As he had done so many times before, Roger managed to calm Rock down, this time by launching into a discussion about the character Hudson would be playing.

As Jones recalled, "[Rock] began to relax a little, and laid down on the bed. I got the book out, sat down and started reading to him, so he could get the feel of this character. Finally, I realized he was asleep, so I unpacked his suitcases and hung everything back up. I picked up my shoes and went back to my own bungalow. It was three a.m. Somebody from the crew had seen me tiptoeing, as it were, out of Rock's bungalow. The next morning, the propaganda had already started. I was supposed to be having an affair with Rock." As the rumor mill had it, Hudson had seduced his married publicist in an effort to ensure that his star-making performance would get the extra attention it deserved. "It was all quite strained on the set," Jones remembered. "Little did they know that *Magnificent Obsession* had lost its leading man for a while!"

From the first strains of the angelic chorus heard over the main titles to the final fade-out in a private sanitarium (one named Shadow Mountain, no less) *Magnificent Obsession* is part Sunday school lesson, part Harlequin romance. All perfectly insane. Wisely, Sirk doesn't try to legitimize the story or attempt to make the plot seem more credible. Instead, he fully embraces the melodramatic lunacy, even as the story leaps from one completely implausible plot development to the next.

In *Obsession*, Ross Hunter finally presented Rock Hudson as the romantic idol that so many of his fans had fantasized about. "Women wanted to go to bed with him, to put it very crudely," says film historian David Thomson. "I do not think that virtually any of them read or saw or felt the real Hudson that we now know existed off camera. To me, it's the most interesting thing about him. Despite the fact that he's this big, strong, awe-inspiring guy, there's a gentleness and a tenderness about him. He has a very special relationship with the women in his movies and I think female audiences loved it."

On the evening of May 11, 1954, *Magnificent Obsession* premiered at the Westwood Theater in downtown Los Angeles. Rock escorted Betty Abbott Griffin, while Jack Navaar was paired off with starlet Claudia Boyer. As the lights came up after the screening, there was no question that both the movie and its leading man had scored a triumph. "There was this great burst of applause, number one, but also this feeling of genuine excitement," recalls Betty Abbott Griffin. "Everybody was pulling for him." Except maybe Jack Navaar.

Instead of being allowed to sit alongside his own boyfriend, he was seated next to Ross Hunter's boyfriend, designer Jacque Mapes. As Rock basked in the glory, everything felt stage-managed to Navaar. His "date" had been supplied by the studio. Even the tuxedo he was wearing had been borrowed from George Nader. At the post-premiere party at La Rue restaurant, Navaar made no secret of the fact that he was unhappy. When he and Rock finally met up at home later that evening, he laid into Mr. Hollywood: "You said we'd be sitting together. I felt like a fool. Like you're the star and I'm the jerk!" Rock attempted to explain that Ross Hunter had rearranged the seating at the last minute, but Jack wasn't buying it.

Once *Obsession* went into wide release, Hudson continued to receive widespread acclaim. The reviewer for the *Los Angeles Examiner* hailed Rock's performance: "Released for the first time from formula two-fisted adventure and derring-do, Hudson proves himself an actor of unsuspected sensitivity and emotional maturity." In the *New York Journal-American*, Jim O'Connor was equally enthusiastic: "At last, Rock Hudson has a part which permits him to do some acting. His is a fresh and not-too-maudlin approach . . . He plays Bob Merrick with conviction."

The critical accolades offset the fallout from the scene Jack Navaar had made the night of the premiere. Up till then, Rock's industry colleagues had done their best to look the other way where his private life was concerned. But now, to a certain degree, it had been dragged into the open and, suddenly, the knives were out.

One day, publicist Roger Jones overheard a director regaling his associates with tales of Rock and his "fairy friends" camping it up at a restaurant. "The director was saying Rock and a 'couple of the boys' were sitting in the booth next to him, raising all sorts of faggot hell. With that, I jumped into the group and said, 'That's a goddamned lie! He spent the evening with my wife and I at our apartment, playing the piano until two a.m., and if you don't cut out this crap, I'll spread some phony stories about you, so knock it off.'"

But now the floodgates were open. One morning, Jones was pulled aside by Universal's makeup supervisor Bud Westmore. "Bud was very anxious to talk to me," Jones recalled. "He told me that a policeman friend of his in downtown Los Angeles had called to say that the studio had better do something about Rock Hudson, who was in jail at that moment on a homo charge. I told Bud that was impossible. [Rock] was home in bed." When Jones reached Hudson by phone and relayed the news, the actor immediately knew what had happened: "'That goddamned Henry—he's in the cooler again on a homo charge, and he puts his name on the police blotter and then in large letters, "Rock Hudson's Agent" and all they see is Rock Hudson.' So I handed the phone to Bud . . . he apologized."

IF *MAGNIFICENT OBSESSION* had been thoughtfully and meticulously designed as Rock Hudson's breakthrough picture, his next film was nothing more than a formulaic adventure, a bit of period nonsense that Hudson was assigned to only after another actor had bowed out—and not just any actor, but a leading man that Rock stood in awe of and would consciously pattern his own career after.

Tyrone Power was set to star in *Bengal Brigade*, in which he was to have played a dashing British army officer attempting to prevent a Sepoy rebellion in nineteenth-century India. In July of 1953, *Variety* reported that Power was dropping out of the picture, citing too many professional commitments. Power's full plate included the stage production *John Brown's Body*, which two decades later would be revived for Rock Hudson, earning him some of the best reviews of his career. *Bengal Brigade* was another story. If the project had been tailor-made for Power, it was in some ways an ill-fitting hand-me-down for Hudson. While he could certainly handle the matinee idol heroics, Hudson had not yet cultivated Power's grace or suavity.

Dialogue that may have tripped off the tongue of Tyrone Power sounded stilted and unnatural when spoken by Rock Hudson. What's more, Rock's Midwestern twang would simply not give way to an English accent. As a result, Hudson's character, the very British Captain Jeffrey Claybourne, sounds as though he received his military training in Great Lakes, Illinois. As far as Rock was concerned, the only good thing that emerged from *Bengal Brigade* was his lifelong friendship with costar Arlene Dahl.

"When we were on the set, we got along like sister and brother," Dahl says. "He had a great sense of humor and I like to think I do, too. We just had a great time, although Laslo Benedek, our director, was Hungarian and very 'Achtung!' about everything. You know . . . *Do this. Do that.* Like a drill instructor . . . I remember Rock and I had a long talk about where he came from and where he wanted to go and I said, 'If you want to be a big star, and you can, Rock, you've got to take the acting seriously and study with somebody.' I had a wonderful coach and I told him about her. I don't know if he went to see her or not, but he really started taking his career seriously after we made *Bengal Brigade.*"

As Rock continued working on his latest picture, Universal's publicity department was flooded with requests for interviews. After the release of *Magnificent Obsession*, the public suddenly had an insatiable interest in all things Rock Hudson. Even respected news outlets succumbed to what had been termed "Rock Fever." Feature-length articles were devoted to scrutinizing Hudson's dietary habits ("Hollywood's most eligible bachelor is a good cook, broils a spectacular steak") and wardrobe preferences ("He likes single-breasted suits, wears wool socks the year round"). The fan magazines also made an issue of his bachelorhood. *Modern Screen* ran a photo of Hudson, which suggested that the unattached actor was being hunted down as though he were an escaped convict: "Wanted! Evading Wedlock: Rock Hudson. Description: 6'3 [sic], 197 lbs., brown hair, brown eyes . . . has always made clean get-a-way before being taken to the altar."

In just a few short years, he had gone from being a barely visible bit player to an instantly recognizable movie star. Now that he was in the spotlight, Rock realized that he had to be extremely careful. If he said something, it would be quoted. If he did something, it might wind up in a column. If he was having a fling with a male costar—as he reportedly was during the making of *Bengal Brigade*—he had to continually watch his back. All of the unrelenting pressures that came with Hudson's newfound stardom, coupled with the stress of having to conceal any gay liaisons, made for one incredibly anxious leading man.

"I noticed that he was biting his nails all the time," says Arlene Dahl. "So, I thought, 'Well, we can't have this.' I said, 'You can't

TOP: Rock's mother, Katherine Wood.

ABOVE: Rock's biological father, Roy Scherer.

LEFT: Eight-year-old Roy Scherer, Jr. *(Photo courtesy of Diane Markert)*

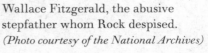

Wallace Fitzgerald, the abusive stepfather whom Rock despised. *(Photo courtesy of the National Archives)*

Fourteen-year-old Roy Fitzgerald in Glenview, Illinois, July 1939. *(Photo courtesy of Robert L. Willett)*

Seaman Roy Fitzgerald stationed in Samar (in the Philippines) during World War II. *(Photo courtesy of the Winnetka Historical Society)*

Rock (far right) and his Navy buddies in the Philippines. "He didn't find the experiences he had with males in the Navy all that unenjoyable," said Hudson's roommate, Bob Preble.

Father and son: Roy Scherer poses with a teenage Roy Fitzgerald. *(Photo courtesy of Diane Markert)*

Ken Hodge, Rock's companion and mentor in the late 1940s. *(Photo courtesy of Kare Grams)*

Rock's controversial agent, Henry Willson.

Rock and Vera-Ellen were a sensation outfitted as "Mr. and Mrs. Oscar" at the Flashbulbers Ball in 1949. *(Photo from the Lou Valentino Collection)*

Rock and longtime roommate Bob Preble in the early 1950s. *(Photo from the Lou Valentino Collection)*

Rock with close friend George Nader, whom Hudson first met in 1951. *(Photo from the Lou Valentino Collection)*

Mark Miller, George Nader's partner, and one of Rock's closest friends.

Rock camping it up in the early '50s. *(Photo courtesy of Jerome Scherer)*

Rock and his "Mystery Girl," Universal script supervisor Betty Abbott. *(Photo from the Lou Valentino Collection)*

Rock caught between Amanda Blake and Yvonne De Carlo in *Scarlet Angel* (1952). The *Hollywood Reporter* described Hudson as "a big, good-looking chap with definite leading man possibilities." *(Photo courtesy of* Photofest*)*

In *Has Anybody Seen My Gal* (1952), Rock was teamed with close friend Piper Laurie. The film also marked the first of eight collaborations between Hudson and director Douglas Sirk.

(Photo courtesy of Photofest*)*

"A strange romance" is how *Photoplay* described Rock's close relationship with actress Marilyn Maxwell. *(Photo from the Lou Valentino Collection)*

Rock and Arlene Dahl in a scene from *Bengal Brigade* (1954). "If you want to be a big star, you've got to take the acting seriously," Dahl told Hudson. *(Photo courtesy of* Photofest*)*

"It's a little bit naughty," Rock would say of the May-December romance in *All That Heaven Allows* (1955). Here, Hudson, Jane Wyman, and Agnes Moorehead gather around director Douglas Sirk. *(Photo courtesy of* Photofest*)*

Hudson and Julie Adams in a scene from *One Desire* (1955). *(Photo courtesy of* Photofest*)*

bite your nails, Rock. They're down to the nub. You're a star now. People are going to notice.' He said, 'Oh, I want to stop.' I said, 'I'll tell you what I'm going to do. Every day on the set, you'll present your nails to me and I'll give you a star if you haven't bitten them overnight.' So, every day, Rock presented his nails to me and he absolutely stopped biting them. He really earned the sterling silver mug that I gave him."

If only the critics had been as kind. Reviewing *Bengal Brigade* in the *New York Times*, Bosley Crowther found it no better than run-of-the-mill: "There is nothing remotely original in this straight assembly-line color film—which is probably as intended, since it appears to be aimed at the double-bill trade . . . Rock Hudson performs the injured captain in a handsome, emotionless way."

IN THE SUMMER of 1954, Rock found himself with two weeks free before shooting began on his next film, *Captain Lightfoot*. As the movie would be the first ever shot entirely on location in Ireland,[*] Hudson knew that the European setting would provide him with an opportunity to do something he had always wanted to do—tour the continent.

Even though Rock was ostensibly on vacation, Universal kept close tabs on him and the studio issued a flurry of press releases documenting his every move. Once Hudson reached Italy, there were almost daily dispatches issued, alerting Hudson's fans that he was gorging on Neapolitan pizza whenever he wasn't making the rounds of the Florentine museums. One columnist noted— presumably with a knowing wink—that Hudson had been completely "mesmerized" by Michelangelo's *David*.

In fact, all of Rome made such a favorable impression that the thought of eventually having to return to Universal's backlot

---

[*]Both Frank Launder's *Captain Boycott* (1947) and John Ford's *The Quiet Man* (1952) featured some exterior sequences that were shot in Ireland, while other scenes were completed on studio soundstages.

seemed wholly uninviting. By late June, yet another update was announced: "Rock Hudson was so captivated by Italy in a pre-shooting trip there, that he asked Universal-International for a year's leave so he can take up residence in Rome." Rock's plan was that upon completion of *Captain Lightfoot* in August, he would return to Italy.

The official reasons cited were that Hudson wanted to attend the Venice Film Festival as well as resume his sightseeing. Of course, the real reason Rock wanted to spend more time in Italy was never going to find its way into one of U-I's press releases.

At some point during his grand tour, Hudson had been introduced to a strikingly handsome Italian actor. By some accounts, Rock's affair with the young man would endure, on and off, for a number of years, overlapping with some of Hudson's other relationships. For years, the actor's identity has been the source of much speculation. In various memoirs, a number of clues have been dropped. The actor in question was described as having "a deeply tanned face and bleached hair." He typically wore a silk suit and was said to be a close friend of the actress Anna Magnani. When presented with these leads, one of Rock's other boyfriends cracked, "Jesus, that describes just about every actor in Rome."

In recent years, one writer claimed that he had actually interviewed the mystery man and that his name was "Massimo." As a result, unsubstantiated rumors circulated that it was the late Massimo Girotti, who starred in *Ossessione*, an unauthorized Italian version of *The Postman Always Rings Twice*. Others have suggested that "Massimo" was actually the late Massimo Serato, who appeared in *The Naked Maja* and fathered a child with Magnani. Yet, the author who interviewed "Massimo" said that the actor died in Paris at the age of sixty-nine in 2002. This seemed to leave both Girotti (who died in 2003) and Serato (who passed away in 1989) out of the running.

In 2017, the same author who claimed to have interviewed "Massimo" announced that he was finally terminating the suspense by publishing a rare photo of Rock Hudson's Italian paramour. A revelation it wasn't. In the published image, the figure identified as "Massimo" is actually the non-Italian leader of the Limerick Pipe Band, who loaned his busby to Hudson as they posed for photographers in June of 1954. Rock was in Limerick to promote *Captain Lightfoot*. The author not only disappointed with this bizarre "exclusive," but in the photo caption, he even managed to misidentify Hudson's costar, Barbara Rush, as "Barbara Hale."

Whoever Rock's Italian boyfriend really was, he made Universal's publicity team extremely nervous. When Hudson and his lover were spotted out in public on several occasions, Rock's studio figured that it wasn't a bad time to dash off another press release, reminding everyone that their resident heartthrob had a real eye for the ladies: "Rock Hudson has resumed a romance, which began two years ago in England with Jill Clifford, London heiress . . . During time off from *Captain Lightfoot*, he flies to London every possible occasion to be with her. One of England's prettiest girls, Jill has brown hair and blue eyes."

The studio breathed a sigh of relief when Rock met up with his *Lightfoot* colleagues Barbara Rush and Betty Abbott in Paris. These were "safe" traveling companions and Hudson's publicists could fully exploit his outings with two beautiful young women. The trio didn't seem to care that every leg of their journey became fodder for the fan magazines. "Oh, we had great fun on that adventure," says Betty Abbott Griffin. "We got caught in this bicycle race in the southern part of France. Then we went on a tour of Ireland, the three of us. We kissed the Blarney Stone and Barbara and I fell into the [stinging] nettle, which amused him no end. I just remember a lot of laughter."

After two weeks of seeing the sights, it was time for Hudson to report back to work on his latest production. Set during the Irish Rebellion of 1815, *Captain Lightfoot* chronicles the exploits of Michael Martin, a Robin Hood-ish revolutionary who robs from rich Englishmen and gives everything to poor Irish peasants. The charismatic rebel leader John Doherty, better known as Captain Thunderbolt, makes Martin his second-in-command. Thunderbolt tutors his young protégé in the fine arts: wall-scaling, bar brawling, and how to convincingly masquerade as an aristocrat.

Martin is not only blind with love for his country but also smitten with the beautiful but headstrong Aga Doherty, Thunderbolt's daughter. Their newfound love is tested when Martin is arrested by the British and extradited back to his hometown of Ballymore, where he is ordered to stand trial. Assisted by his fellow patriots, Martin escapes from prison and resumes command of the rebel forces.

All of the elements were in place to ensure that *Captain Lightfoot* would triumph at the box office. Ross Hunter to produce. Douglas Sirk to direct. Technicolor. Cinemascope. Add to this the fact that budget-conscious Universal had taken the unusual step of greenlighting a production shot entirely on location.

Although Ross Hunter had gone to great lengths in terms of scrupulously preparing his latest production, one important detail had somehow been overlooked—the weather. "Most of it was shot in the rain," recalled Douglas Sirk. "It came out handsomely, even though it was practically all shot in the drizzle." Ireland's unpredictable climate ultimately worked to the film's benefit. "In Hollywood, you have a light which is really too strong, too splendid" said Sirk. "The constant change of light in Ireland in a way, matched the course of the story. The good are the bad and the bad are the good."

As with many of Hudson's later films, *Captain Lightfoot* features role-playing or impersonation as an important plot point. After Thunderbolt takes Michael Martin under his wing, he spruces him up, outfits him in the most elegant finery, and passes the once disheveled highwayman off as a purebred aristocrat.

More than likely, Rock didn't play the title role with any degree of self-reflexive awareness, but it's very likely that Douglas Sirk, who certainly knew the score about Hudson, nudged his leading man toward characters who are in the throes of an identity crisis. Whether it was Rock's portrayals of sinner turned saint in *Magnificent Obsession* and *Battle Hymn* or the alcoholic newspaperman who yearns to be one of the aerialists he's covering in *The Tarnished Angels*, Sirk understood that a character at odds with himself was one that Rock would connect with emotionally.

Sirk was also one of the first to recognize that there was a largely untapped side to Hudson's talent. After watching the rushes of the pistol duel in which Captain Lightfoot demonstrates his lackadaisical attitude toward the proceedings by lighting up a cigar and shooting a scarecrow, the director realized that the sequence hinted at what was to come: "Hudson was playing comedy and I realized that his talents might lie there."

Although the producer, director, and stars of *Magnificent Obsession* had all been reunited for *Captain Lightfoot*, the picture did not duplicate the blockbuster success of the earlier film. Still, the critics couldn't help but notice that Rock seemed more natural on-screen than ever before. As the *Los Angeles Times* noted, "Hudson is developing some ability as an actor, except when his face falls into repose. Fortunately for him, there's small time for that. [*Captain Lightfoot*] seethes with action—*so much* indeed, that after a while one begins to yearn for a little peace and quiet. One doesn't get it."

After the failure of *Bengal Brigade*, Universal's advertising team did its best to sell *Captain Lightfoot* as a tender romance instead of a rollicking adventure. Posters for the film depicted Hudson embracing Barbara Rush against the wind-lashed moors. With both stars looking very contemporary, there was no indication that this was Rock's second costume drama in a row. When *Captain Lightfoot* performed respectably but not sensationally at the box office, Hudson would find himself locked into a succession of romantic melodramas—not all of which were confined to the screen.

CHAPTER 7

IS ROCK HUDSON
AFRAID OF MARRIAGE?

If Rock Hudson was the boy next door, his future bride had to be a
fresh-faced, all-American girl like Phyllis Gates. Some friends were
convinced that the relationship was legitimate, while others insist that
it was a carefully arranged corporate merger.
(Photo courtesy of Photofest*)*

ife proclaimed Rock "Hollywood's Most Handsome Bachelor"
when he became the magazine's cover story on October 3, 1955.
After informing readers that "Rock Hudson Gets Rich Alone,"
it became obvious that promoting Hudson's latest picture was
not *Life's* top priority. The editors immediately got down to

business, laying it on the line in the first paragraph of their accompanying profile: "Fans are urging 29-year-old Hudson to get married—or explain why not."

For years, columnists and fan club members had been asking themselves the same question: If "The Beefcake Baron" was such a terrific catch, how come he had never even been engaged? After all, Hudson was regularly photographed with some of the most beautiful ingénues in Hollywood on his arm. Surely one of these glamour girls was a suitable candidate for marriage? Well, maybe for some other lucky guy. As Rock gallantly pointed out, it wasn't the ladies who were lacking in any way. It was him. Hudson's demanding work schedule and his "traumatic breakup" with Vera-Ellen were typically cited as the reasons why the matinee idol remained "marriage shy."

Even so, Henry Willson knew that the public and the press could be stalled for only so long. The drumbeat was getting louder and the pressure was on. Rock's aversion to matrimony being examined in a mainstream magazine like *Life* was one thing, but a threatened *Confidential* exposé was another matter entirely. Fifty years before the advent of *Access Hollywood* and TMZ, *Confidential* magazine—which boasted a monthly readership of more than four million—dared to go where no other publication would. "Tells The Facts and Names the Names" read the catch phrase on the front cover.

Through the thinnest of veils, *Confidential* plied its readers with stories about Judy Garland's drug dependency, Desi Arnaz's extramarital affairs, and Robert Mitchum's naked pool party shenanigans. More often than not, a *Confidential* exposé had some basis in reality. However, when the magazine's informants weren't able to come through with any juicy exclusives, the editors had no qualms about stretching the truth or fashioning one of their "uncensored and off-the-record" reports out of whole cloth.

"It Was The Hottest Show in Town When Maureen O'Hara Cuddled in Row 35 . . ." read one headline from March of 1957.

According to *Confidential*, the actress engaged in a steamy interlude with a "south-of-the-border sweetie" during a screening at Grauman's Chinese Theatre. In the purplest of prose, the article described how O'Hara and her Latin lover were thrown out of the theatre after an usher "got the shock of his life." The star of *How Green Was My Valley* was found "spread across three seats—with the happy Latin American in the middle seat."

Up until this time, the press-shy O'Hara had steered clear of any scandal, but when the issue of *Confidential* detailing her alleged indiscretions hit newsstands, the story was even picked up by nationally syndicated columnists. "The descriptions of our alleged behavior were so lewd and obscene that they were talked about all over Hollywood," O'Hara said. The widespread reaction to the story clearly demonstrated how destructive *Confidential* could be. With one salacious headline, an entire career could be wiped out. Thanks to the magazine and its latest "scoop," Maureen O'Hara's wholesome image was suddenly shattered.

As it turned out, "the facts" that *Confidential* regularly promised readers just didn't add up in O'Hara's case. Not only were the eyewitness accounts vague and contradictory, but O'Hara's passport proved that she wasn't even in the United States when the alleged incident supposedly occurred. The outraged actress sued *Confidential* for libel. Although O'Hara would ultimately be vindicated, the vicious gossip and lurid headlines the story generated were not the kind of publicity that any star wanted. Rock Hudson especially.

By the mid-1950s, Rock was finally where he wanted to be. After a long and grueling climb, all of his hard work and countless sacrifices were beginning to pay off. The previous year, *Modern Screen* had named him "The Most Popular Star." And it wasn't only magazine publishers and theatre exhibitors who were taking notice of his enormous popularity. The editors of *Confidential* had been waiting for the perfect moment to pounce on Hollywood's white knight.

Confidential founder Robert Harrison decided it was time to expose Rock Hudson as a "Lavender Lad," just as he had done a year earlier with Van Johnson ("The virile hero of the big muscle and the fierce embrace was a scared, lonesome boy locked in his secret"). The European tour that Rock had embarked on in 1954 had stirred Harrison's interest. The publisher of *Confidential* knew that Hudson and Henry Willson had not only stayed in the same hotel, but that the two men had even shared a suite.

One of Harrison's Hollywood tipsters kept him well informed regarding Henry's antics, especially any escapades involving Willson's platoon of B-list hunks. A fact not lost on the publisher of *Confidential* was that even with this eye-filling assortment at his disposal, Willson seemed to prefer the company of his star client. And now, the most popular scandal sheet in America would be sharing Rock and Henry's carefully guarded secrets with the ticket-buying public.

Robert Harrison, whom Humphrey Bogart dubbed "The King of Leer," freely admitted that his stock in trade was "sin, shame and suicides." *Confidential*'s owner could always smell a good story and, in early 1955, he gave one of his top writers a plum assignment: Expose Rock Hudson. At first, the usual tricks were employed. Extras, bit players, and assistants were paid for whatever privileged information they might have. Hudson's former roommate, Bob Preble, was offered $10,000 to talk. "*Confidential* approached me and wanted to do an exposure article on him," Preble said. "'We know this man is gay, Mr. Preble, and we'll help fatten your wallet a little bit if you'll tell us everything you know about this gay bird.' But I turned them down. I said no." As did Jack Navaar, who could have really used the money.

Undeterred, Harrison assigned photographers to surreptitiously trail Hudson wherever he went. *Confidential* spies phoned in if Rock seemed to linger at Montgomery Clift's table at the Mocambo or if he seemed a bit too familiar with Victor Mature at a premiere. The information *Confidential* collected through its regular channels was more than enough to expose Hudson, but Harrison had heard rumors that some truly damning evidence existed. A gold mine, in fact. A former boyfriend claimed that he was in possession of an incriminating photo of Rock. The image may have been grainy and blurred but it was unmistakably the star. In a compromising position. This was exactly the kind of irrefutable proof that *Confidential* would need to legitimize their story on "Rock Hudson's *Magnificent Obsession* . . . After Hours." Harrison hadn't seen the photo, but if it actually existed, he was willing to pay a small fortune to obtain it.

"It was really terrifying living in Hollywood before Stonewall and the advent of gay liberation," says photographer Michael Childers, the longtime partner of director John Schlesinger. "When I met John in 1968, it still wasn't accepted for two men to go to a premiere or an industry party together without a woman along as a beard. The expected thing would be for him to take a friend, like Natalie Wood, as a cover. There was this curtain up in terms of what was considered acceptable behavior. I can see why the cover-ups and the hiding happened with people like Rock and Tab Hunter. It was just a mean, scary time to be gay. Magazines like *Confidential* and even certain gossip columns would pay huge money to get all the smut on stars that they could. They'd do everything possible to destroy you."

When Henry Willson was tipped off that *Confidential* was planning a cover story on Rock, panic set in. Hudson was a leading contender for an epic that Warner Brothers was preparing. And there were already back-to-back projects lined up for Hudson at Universal, MGM, and 20th Century-Fox. If Willson was going to kill the *Confidential* story on Rock, he knew that he had to move swiftly and with great precision.

So is the legend true? Did Henry Willson sacrifice a couple of former clients to *Confidential* to preserve Rock Hudson's reputation? Some insiders swear that this is exactly what happened, while others wonder whether *Confidential* was open to that kind of boardroom-style "negotiation." Mark Miller insisted that it was

Universal's head of publicity, Jack Diamond, who intervened. Others have said that the type of bartering involved was quintessential Willson. Some accounts claim that the mob was called in. Another rendition says that hush money was exchanged. Whatever the case, instead of the planned front-page exposé of Rock Hudson, *Confidential* blew the whistle on two other popular heartthrobs.

In May of 1955, the magazine's cover story featured the headline, "Rory Calhoun, But For The Grace of God, Still a Convict!" The exposé dished the dirt regarding Calhoun's armed robbery conviction, which dated back to 1940. Then it was Tab Hunter's turn: "It is the racy story of a night in October, 1950 when the husky Hunter kid landed in jail, along with 26 other good-looking young men, after the cops broke up a pajama party they staged—strictly for boys." As Hunter had fired Henry Willson only a few months prior to the pajama party story hitting newsstands, many feel this implicated the agent as a stool pigeon.

Despite all evidence to the contrary, rumors persist to this day that it was George Nader who was the sacrificial lamb. As Hudson made Nader the primary beneficiary in his will, some observers have suggested that this was payback—on a grand scale. But not only was George Nader never a client of Henry Willson's, *Confidential* magazine never outed the actor in its pages. Something which also proved to be true for Hudson. "Every month, when *Confidential* came out, our stomachs began to turn," Nader recalled. "The amazing thing is that Rock, as big as he became, was never nailed. It made me speculate that Rock had an angel on his shoulder, or that he'd made a pact with the devil because he seemed under supernatural protection."

Although *Confidential* had been pacified—at least for the moment—Henry Willson knew that there was only one way to silence all of the rumors about Hudson's homosexuality. It was time for Rock to get married. And fast. Though who was truly worthy of being the king's consort? Surely, there had to be a card-carrying member of the Screen Actors Guild who would be ideal casting as

Mrs. Rock Hudson. And if the young lady didn't happen to exist in precisely the same way the public may have envisioned, Willson could always redesign her to his own specifications. To hear Henry tell it, the task of finding a wife for Rock had been comparable to the exhaustive search that Willson's former employer David O. Selznick had undertaken to find the perfect Scarlett O'Hara.

Several candidates could be instantly eliminated as they were either too old or too bobby-soxer. If a contender had even one divorce on her resumé, Willson ruled her out. Same for party girls, peroxide blondes, and gum-snappers. If Rock Hudson was the boy next door, his wife should be the sort of all-American girl who reminded one of church socials and county fairs. Someone sweet, unspoiled, and down-to-earth. Ordinarily, Vera-Ellen or Betty Abbott Griffin would have been ideal, but the fan magazines had already exhausted their supply of stories in which Rock had wined and dined them. All of that seemed like old news. And when Hollywood's most eligible bachelor finally tied the knot, it had to be *front-page* news.

It was clear to Willson that a fresh face was needed; a dewy ingénue that the public wasn't too familiar with and yet felt like family. As it turned out, the best candidate wasn't smiling back at Henry from the cover of *Modern Screen* but sitting right under his nose. Willson's secretary, Phyllis Gates, was a thirty-year-old native of Dawson, Minnesota, whose background was so quintessentially Middle American it almost seemed scripted. The youngest of five children, Gates grew up in a farmhouse equipped with only one oil-fed heater.

By the time she was a teenager, Phyllis was handling most of the chores on the family farm, including driving the tractor. As she recalled in her memoir, "I spent my entire summer bouncing and jiggling over those dusty fields." When she wasn't milking cows or baling hay, Gates taught Sunday school classes at Our Savior's Lutheran Church. So far, so good.

If Rock Hudson's dream girl should read as down-home as possible, this did not mean that she should be dull. A natural beauty was required and once again, Gates didn't disappoint. Phyllis had placed second in the Dayton Company's annual beauty contest and, during her years as a secretary in New York, she had caught the eye of the young Marlon Brando.

The first time Henry Willson met her, he told Gates, "I shouldn't hire you as a secretary. I should get you a studio contract." And Willson wasn't the only one who thought that Phyllis exhibited genuine star quality. When Gates accompanied one of Henry's clients to an audition at 20th Century-Fox, the casting director took one look at her and decided that it was Phyllis, and not the young hopeful by her side, who should be screen-tested. Gates declined the offer, explaining that she had no interest in becoming an actress.

Despite this, Henry Willson had big plans for her, which did not include opening his mail. From the moment Phyllis joined the agency, Henry seemed extremely eager to introduce her to Rock, though that would have to wait. Gates had never met Willson's most important client as Hudson was halfway around the world shooting *Captain Lightfoot*. Even so, that wasn't going to stop Willson from playing matchmaker. Demonstrating why he was considered one of the craftiest agents in the business, Henry decided it was time to get the show on the road. Literally.

"Why don't you and Phyllis take a trip? Rock's away. And you're just sitting there," Willson said to Jack Navaar. He convinced Jack that escorting Phyllis back to Minnesota so that she could visit her family made perfect sense. Why worry about what Rock might think? He was away on location doing god only knows what. It was no secret that the bisexual Navaar had a crush on Gates, so spending several days alone with her sounded pretty terrific. And as Henry was quick to point out, Rock's yellow Lincoln Convertible, which had been loaned to the actor by the Ford Motor Company for publicity purposes, was just sitting idle while its owner was away. Why not put it to the test by driving it cross-country?

As Navaar had already palled around with Gates and considered her a friend, heading out on the road with her seemed like a great idea. As they drove along, Navaar found himself strongly attracted to the woman who was, in a sense, his rival. "I enjoyed her company," said Navaar. "And I felt secure doing this because Henry had proposed it. Later, I realized Henry had instigated the trip to alienate me from Rock." It seemed that whenever Henry Willson was handling the negotiations, there was always some sort of catch.

Before reaching Phyllis's very conservative hometown, she suggested to Jack that they shout out every four-letter word they knew. Better to get the cussing out of the way before they had to play it straight in front of the folks for a few days.

Navaar recalled that on the way back to L.A., Gates requested a detour to Kansas City. Phyllis wanted to catch up with some old friends she had met during her days as a stewardess for Mid-Continent Airlines. Gates took Navaar to a party where women danced with one another and there were very public displays of affection. To Navaar, this was hardly surprising. Months earlier, Phyllis, Jack, and Mark Miller had spent a weekend in Laguna Beach. At a bar called Camille's, which catered to gays of both genders, Gates met a woman at the bar and promptly disappeared for the rest of the weekend. "I'll catch up with you . . ." was Phyllis's reply whenever Jack and Mark invited her to hit the beach or join them for dinner. Despite her repeated promises, Phyllis never did seem to catch up.

Upon returning to the West Coast, Navaar and Gates discovered that news of their cross-country trip had somehow traveled overseas. A furious Hudson phoned long distance to chew out his young lover. Rock had discovered that after Jack had hosted some wild parties at the Grand View house, it had been ransacked. And not only had Jack taken the yellow convertible without Hudson's permission, but there had been disturbing transatlantic reports that Navaar had been seen cruising around in it, yelling out obscenities with a female companion. Was this any way for Rock Hudson's "roommate" to behave?

"I wasn't even in town!" Jack bellowed. "You son of a bitch, how dare you ask me those questions." But it was too late. Coming so soon after Navaar's post-premiere tantrum, these latest offenses sealed his fate. Suddenly, Jack's monthly allowance disappeared. As did Phyllis. Rock wouldn't return any of his phone calls. Henry Willson washed his hands of the once promising "Rand Saxon," informing him: "The studio is capable of taking extreme measures to protect a property." Jack's mind was reeling. Had this whole trip been set up by Henry Willson in an effort to get him out of the picture so that Rock could hurry up and marry Phyllis Gates? Was Hudson complicit in all of this? Had that whole angry tirade over the phone been . . . *rehearsed*? Understandably confused, yet all too aware that he had fallen out of favor, Navaar moved out of the Grand View house while Hudson was still away.

If Jack Navaar was out, Phyllis Gates was in. Once *Captain Lightfoot* wrapped and Rock had returned home, Henry Willson saw to it that Hudson became much better acquainted with his secretary. "I gave Rock a nice background on Phyllis Gates," Henry recalled, making it sound as though he had handed his client an especially favorable investment portfolio.

Prior to meeting Hudson, Gates claimed that she had seen only one of his films—*Magnificent Obsession*—though it made an indelible impression. It was, she said, "a movie that made me weep like a school girl." Phyllis's first evening out with Hudson was just as memorable. Cocktails at the Cock 'n Bull included a meet-cute sequence straight out of a Frank Capra comedy. As Rock made his way through the dimly lit barroom to the table that Gates was occupying, he tripped over a chair, nearly landing on the floor. Later at dinner, Henry Willson held court while Hudson made some fumbling attempts at small talk.

"I discovered that Rock Hudson in person was nothing like Rock Hudson, the self-assured hero of the movie screen; he was terribly shy," said Gates, making the same surprise discovery that scores of Hudson's male partners would over the years. This sheepish, submissive guy was . . . *Rock Hudson*, the idol of millions of moviegoers? Whatever happened to Taza, Son of Cochise?

An innate shyness, which masked a driving determination, was a trait that Hudson and Gates shared. And like Rock, Phyllis could be irresistibly charming and seductive, especially if it might help to open some doors. "I could understand why Rock thought he could fall in love with her because I could have," said Jack Navaar. "She knew how to make a guy feel fabulous. She had a marvelous laugh and an incredible personality. You'd meet her and in ten minutes, you'd feel you were the most important person in her life."

In the early days of their relationship, Gates would see Hudson at the office, on his way in to a meeting with Henry. Along with contract negotiations and P.R. strategies, was Phyllis part of what they discussed behind closed doors? Had it already been decided that Gates answered the question *Is Rock Hudson Afraid of Marriage?*

Years later, Phyllis would claim that she had no idea that she was being "manipulated" into a relationship with Rock. Others insist that Gates not only knew the whole score but that she compliantly moved as directed by her employer. Whether she was aware of it or not, Phyllis's first dates with Rock, which the press would later describe as "impromptu, spur-of-the-moment" get-togethers, were all carefully engineered by Henry Willson. And Willson's involvement didn't end there. To observers who found the Hudson–Gates pairing dubious, the fact that Henry usually tagged along on their dates only confirmed their suspicions. And if being a constant presence in his client's life wasn't already enough, Willson was now insisting that Hudson had to get married.

After Rock made and canceled several dates with Gates, she wasn't feeling quite as starstruck. Hudson had cited professional commitments, though it's possible that Rock may have been having second thoughts about becoming involved with his agent's secretary. True, he always did as Henry instructed, but the thought of *marrying* Gates—as opposed to just being photographed with her—qualified as above and beyond, even if his career was at stake.

Couldn't he just "date" Phyllis? Did he actually have to marry her? It seemed like an awful lot to go through in the name of keeping his fans happy.

On the other hand, Rock was used to being handed a script he didn't particularly like and asked to make it work. In some ways, wasn't getting married an acting job like any other? Perhaps, Rock reasoned, he would get into character, kiss his leading lady as directed, and publicize his latest effort the same way he would any other Hollywood production. Besides, getting married would please everyone. The studio. The ticket-buying public. Henry. Hedda and Louella. His mother. The happily married man was the one role that everyone wanted him to play. As for real happiness—the kind not usually found within the pages of *Photoplay*—well, there didn't seem to be a clause for that in his contract.

Which was too bad as, according to Mark Miller, Hudson had recently found a more agreeable playmate than Phyllis. While Rock was supposed to be courting Gates, he was "dallying" with another Henry Willson client. Blond, blue-eyed, and boyishly handsome, Cragill Fowler had been working as a lifeguard in La Jolla when one of Henry's assistants snapped his photo. Within a matter of weeks, Fowler had been rechristened Craig Hill and he was under contract to 20th Century-Fox. Hill was not only being groomed for stardom by Willson, but he seemed very much Rock Hudson's preferred dish.

Gates recalled an awkward scene when she happened to bump into Hudson and Hill while they were doing some Christmas shopping. Rock was so flustered by Phyllis discovering them together it was almost as though she had caught them in bed. Not long after this incident and seemingly to make amends, Hudson finally followed through on a long-promised dinner with Gates. However, this proved to be anything but a romantic rendezvous. Not only did Henry Willson join them, but he even brought a prospective client along. Phyllis said she felt slighted and shut out. "I finally gave up trying to join in," Gates said. "I could hardly wait to leave the dinner and return to my apartment."

Whether to make it up to Phyllis or please Henry—or both—Hudson began spending more time with Gates. And Henry made sure that whenever they stepped out, columnists would chronicle their every move. "Rock Hudson has been enjoying hideaway dinners with Henry Willson's purty secy. Phyllis Gates," read an item in Mike Connolly's column in *The Hollywood Reporter*, which almost certainly had been dictated by Willson himself.

Even if they had been Willson-orchestrated, Gates would recall her outings with Hudson as though they were clips in a romantic movie montage: Dancing at L'Escoffier . . . candlelight dinners at a quaint French bistro . . . listening to their favorite pianist at the 881 Club in Beverly Hills . . . attending the premiere of *Captain Lightfoot.*

In recalling these episodes, Phyllis would present herself as the ultimate wide-eyed innocent. The self-portrait is so determinedly *Alice in Wonderland* that it's easy to forget that Gates was a Hollywood insider, working for one of the most notorious power brokers in the industry. Surely she couldn't have been that naïve, despite this passage from her memoir: "He brought me home at midnight and gave me a warm kiss on the doorstep. I lay in bed sleepless for an hour, savoring the pleasures of the evening. Still, my Midwestern conservatism interrupted with the caution: 'Now, Phyllis, don't overdo. Just because you had one lovely date with a movie star doesn't mean anything more serious is going to follow. Go to sleep now.'"

Of course, something more serious did follow. One morning, Rock walked Phyllis through a two-bedroom Pennsylvania Dutch–style cottage, which he called "the house of my dreams." It was located in an exclusive neighborhood in the Hollywood Hills, nestled between Beverly Hills and Sunset Plaza. The area was known for its "Bird Streets"—Blue Jay Way and Skylark and Oriole Lane; the house Hudson had fallen for was on Warbler Place. Surrounded by pine trees and Scotch broom, the barn-red house seemed like a cabin tucked away in the mountains, even though it was only a fifteen-minute drive to Universal. Hudson surprised Gates by asking her to move in with him, an invitation she initially rejected. "I was thunderstruck," Phyllis recalled. "Nothing Rock had said or done had prepared me for this. He had never said he loved me."

Hudson still hadn't uttered those all-important words when he showed up at Henry Willson's office one afternoon and handed Gates a diamond ring. He was up-front about the fact that he had received the ring as compensation for appearing on a television show. But was it actually intended to be an engagement ring? Gates wasn't sure. Rock muttered what seemed to Phyllis to be only an indifferent "You can have it . . ." as he offered it to her. Phyllis felt that Rock remained coolly detached throughout the proposal—if that's, in fact, what it actually was.

To some, it seemed totally appropriate that Rock Hudson and Phyllis Gates got engaged—or something like it—in the office of the agent who had brought them together. To those in Rock's inner circle who believed that his romantic interest in Phyllis Gates was his best acting job to date, the dispassionate betrothal seemed to prove them right. According to the future Mrs. Hudson, it exhibited all of the warmth and tenderness of a corporate merger. And more than a few people believed that's exactly what it was.

––––––––

If *Captain Lightfoot* had afforded Hudson an opportunity to play a different kind of character and temporarily stray beyond the Universal backlot, his next assignment represented a return to form as well as the confines of the studio.

As produced by Ross Hunter, *One Desire** seems like a calculated

---

*When production launched in November of 1954, the movie was entitled *Tacey*, which was closer to the title of the bestseller it was adapted from, Conrad Richter's 1942 novel, *Tacey Cromwell*. By late December of 1954, the title had been changed to *One Desire*, which Universal's publicity department felt "would provide more potent romantic appeal, especially since we have Rock Hudson in the lead."

blending of Rock's two most successful genres, the Western and the romantic melodrama. Key elements of the story seemed reminiscent of previous films. The character of Clint Saunders, described as "an empty pockets, unrespectable lug," was sort of a variation on the cardsharp that Hudson had played in *Bend of the River.* Restless and independent, Saunders is determined to find a better way of life beyond his existence as a dealer at the White Palace, a bustling dance hall that's equal parts casino and bordello.

The same day Clint loses his job at the betting table, his runaway kid brother Nugget (Barry Curtis) turns up in dire need of some surrogate parenting and a safe place to call home. Lucky for Clint, the White Palace comes complete with a whore with a heart of gold who happens to be crazy about him and likes kids. When Oscar-winner Anne Baxter makes her first appearance as Tacey Cromwell, she's wearing a dress so brazenly red that she's practically a walking scarlet letter ("*Men gave her everything . . . but a good name!*" is how the film's tag line put it.). But beneath Tacey's feathers and tough talk, there's a loving woman longing for some respectability. "I got a yen to wear clothes that don't scream at you for a change and go to ladies' tea parties," she confesses to her infatuated pimp.

Tacey's prayers are answered when Clint suggests that they pack up and, with Nugget in tow, move to a booming Colorado mining town and start over. Once they land in Randsberg, Tacey becomes a model housewife and a citizen so upstanding that she takes in orphaned ragamuffin Seely Dowden (seventeen-year-old Natalie Wood) and raises her as her own.

Clint, on the other hand, sets new standards for bold-faced ambition. Within minutes of hitting town, he charms a senator and his daughter, Judith (the inevitable Julie Adams). Unlike Tacey, the ruthless and possessive Judith doesn't believe in sharing any of her holdings. "When I was a young girl, I would never share my pony with my cousins," Judith tells Clint. "If I can't have something that's all my own, I just don't want it." This includes Clint, who fast-talks his way into a job at the bank Judith's family owns.

Determined that Clint will remain hers exclusively, Judith hires a private investigator and learns all about Tacey's tawdry past. In the film's most dramatically satisfying scene, Tacey tearfully pleads with a stone-faced judge to allow her to keep Nugget and Seely after the court threatens to take them away. Unmoved, the judge not only brands Tacey morally unfit, he turns the kids over to Judith for safe-keeping.

Although Rock received second billing for *One Desire*, he has relatively little to do in the picture besides periodically scan the horizon in search of a brighter future. Baxter and Adams have the showier roles, and they managed to upstage Hudson—not only on-screen but off.

"I take full credit for almost burning down one of Universal's biggest sound stages," Julie Adams says. For a climactic sequence—in which a drunken Judith sets her bedroom ablaze—things didn't go exactly as planned. As Adams recalls, "I remember I threw this candlestick just as we had rehearsed it but this time the flames shot up to the top of this long curtain and kept right on going into the rafters . . . I started to move away but the assistant director began yelling, 'Julie, get back in there! What are you doing? We have to get this shot in the can today . . .' The fire then set off all of the sprinklers and we were drenched."[*]

Anne Baxter had caused her own costly production delays because of "meticulous attention to her hairdressing and makeup." After a meeting was called with Baxter's agent, Russell Birdwell, Baxter picked up the pace considerably. If director Joseph L. Mankiewicz had cast Baxter in *All About Eve* because of her "bitch virtuosity," Jerry Hopper makes the most of her warmhearted vulnerability in

[*]Universal production reports from December 27, 1954, back up Adams's account: "While photographing the fire scene on Stage 18, the fire got out of control at approximately 6 p.m., [special effects advisor] Nick Carmona received back burns from hot water, but otherwise there were no injuries . . . Grips, propmen, electricians, laborers all pitched in to minimize the danger and damage."

One Desire, a fact not lost on the critics. It's too bad the rest of the movie wasn't as well reviewed as Baxter. "*One Desire* is nothing more than a plodding, old-fashioned soap opera," said the critic for the *New York Times*. "Some spectators may find themselves tuning in, eyes closed, to the familiar train of events, dialogue and musical effects."

In the midst of bouncing from one production to the next, Rock did something he would almost never do during his long tenure as a Universal contract player—he made a request. According to a studio memo from November of 1954: "Rock Hudson had requested that sleeping accommodations be placed in his dressing room so that he could remain at the studio overnight during this period when he is under pressure of two pictures." Universal's executive committee turned him down.

READERS IN UNIVERSAL'S story department had been scouring the shelves in search of a suitable property that would readily lend itself to a reteaming of Rock Hudson and Jane Wyman. After the tremendous success of *Magnificent Obsession*, the studio had received hundreds of letters—not only from members of Rock's poodle-skirted fan base but from theatre exhibitors across the country. Everyone, it seemed, was demanding an immediate follow-up.

As it focused on a May-December romance uncannily reminiscent of *Magnificent Obsession*, Edna and Harry Lee's 1952 novel, *All That Heaven Allows*, seemed to provide the best excuse for Hudson and Wyman to be "rapturously reunited" (as the ads put it) in another Ross Hunter–produced tearjerker.

"In spite of a poor story—a nothing of a story, really, I got interested in that film," director Douglas Sirk would say some two decades after being assigned to *All That Heaven Allows*. "Beyond what I had been doing in *Magnificent Obsession*, I put a lot of my own handwriting into that film. For the first time, I put in my mirrors, my symbols, my statues, my literary knowledge . . . I was trying to give that cheap stuff a meaning, you know."

While reviewers at the time tended to dismiss Sirk's movies as nothing more than Technicolored histrionics, by the 1970s his work would undergo a thorough reevaluation. The same Douglas Sirk who had once been written off as a studio hack would find long-delayed acclaim for turning that "cheap stuff" into his own unique brand of high art. And *All That Heaven Allows* would eventually be considered a prime example of Sirk at his subversive best.

On the surface, the story was the quintessential "women's picture." Cary Scott has recently been widowed after twenty years of marriage. Tucked away in the family homestead in an idyllic New England suburb, Cary is well-off, yet cast adrift. With her two adult children, Ned (William Reynolds) and Kay (Gloria Talbott) away at college, fortyish Cary suddenly finds herself alone with "nothing but time."

In terms of regular companionship, Cary is constantly reminded that her only viable options appear to be submitting to a sexless union with a "remarkably civilized" graying hypochondriac (Conrad Nagel) or getting herself a new television set—which a well-meaning friend describes as "the last refuge for lonely women." Both alternatives seem designed to lull the widow Scott into a state of stupefied semiconsciousness until death can officially take over. Which doesn't sound all that different from daughter Kay's studies of ancient Egypt, where in the days of the pharaohs, there was a time-honored tradition of "walling up the widow alive in the funeral chamber of her dead husband along with all of his possessions."

Salvation arrives in the form of Cary's ruggedly handsome tree surgeon, Ron Kirby, who is fifteen years her junior. The picture of robust, red-blooded health and clean living, Ron seems to have emerged directly from the pages of a vintage L.L.Bean catalog. A self-reliant disciple of Thoreau, Ron is so attuned to nature that wild deer obediently eat out of his hands, and he gets misty-eyed while extolling the virtues of a silver-tipped spruce. After Cary tours a rickety old mill that Ron dreams of refurbishing, love blooms.

While the happy couple couldn't be more content spending time together, their *Lady Chatterley*–style romance sparks outrage and fierce opposition from everyone in Cary's world. Ron is . . . too young, too working class, too earthy. And unlike Cary's geriatric suitor, he practically oozes testosterone. "That tan . . . I suppose that's from working outdoors. Of course, I'm sure he's handy indoors, too," snarls the town gossip.

More than anything else, the fact that their widowed mother still maintains a healthy sexual appetite seems to rankle her children ("How long must she be a widow . . . Before she can be a Woman again?" was the all-important question posed in the film's ads.). "I think all you see is a good-looking set of muscles," an indignant Ned tells Cary. An Oedipus complex in argyles, her only son then threatens to stop visiting her if she follows through on her plans to marry Ron.

The emotional blackmailing doesn't end there. Daughter Kay discourages Cary's interest in Ron after she's harassed at school about her mother's new companion. The gang at the country club turns smug and spiteful. Before a lynch mob appears, Cary calls off her engagement to Ron. Not long after, a television set is wheeled into the widow's living room.

As *Magnificent Obsession* had been so popular with audiences, Universal executives wondered if their follow-up would be as warmly received. Rock Hudson, for one, seemed to prefer *All That Heaven Allows* to his previous pairing with Wyman. "I found it a rich experience because it was, I felt, a much more playable story," Hudson reflected decades later. "*All That Heaven Allows* was very playable, and a hell of a good role and rather daring. There was a woman with a young gardener and she's not well-to-do but comfortable. In those days, it simply wasn't done. So, it's a little bit naughty."

Geoffrey Shurlock, chief executive censor at the Motion Picture Association of America, found *All That Heaven Allows* more than a little bit naughty. In a letter to Universal's William Gordon, Shurlock voiced his concerns that even after reading a revised version of the screenplay, "We still feel the relationship between Cary and Ron includes an unacceptable treatment of illicit sex . . . We are particularly concerned with the dawn scene in which the couple is shown lying down . . . with the scene concluding on a very intimate embrace."

Five films into their eight-picture collaboration, Hudson had become extremely comfortable working with Sirk (something that other actors on the Universal lot considered an impressive achievement in its own right). Their working relationship was so simpatico that Sirk's direction of Hudson had become almost telegraphic.

"*Scared puppy* . . ." were the only words Sirk said to Rock before they shot a scene in which, after a period of estrangement, Ron encounters Cary as she's shopping for a Christmas tree. When he saw the rushes, Sirk called Hudson to express his approval. It was a gesture that Rock would never forget, telling an interviewer years later: "You know, when you're scared and new and you're trying to figure out this picture business and suddenly, an older man reaches out to you and says, 'There, there, it's okay . . .' That makes all the difference. That was Douglas Sirk."

Cast as Wyman's son, William Reynolds had last appeared with Rock in *Has Anybody Seen My Gal*. In the interim, Hudson had changed says Reynolds: "Rock had matured as an actor . . . I also attribute the change to the fact that he was now a star. When you're a star, people pay attention to you. You say something and it has meaning. All of a sudden, his own values became ascendant by virtue of his stardom. Thankfully, he had not changed as a person. He was quite a guy and I liked him a lot."

With two of his favorite actors assuming the lead roles and his signature very much evident throughout, Sirk turns the film into a tour de force and, by far, his most personal statement. As a result, *All That Heaven Allows* emerges as the director's masterpiece—an intriguing mix of German expressionism, high Hollywood gloss, and Freudian angst. Beneath the Ross Hunter syrup and Day-Glo colors, there lurks a sharp-eyed indictment of 1950s conformism. Wyman's widow is practically burned at the stake for stepping outside of societal bounds and associating with a green-thumbed iconoclast.

In 1954, the year that *All That Heaven Allows* was in preproduction, Red-baiting and government-sanctioned efforts to winnow out any behavior that smacked of radicalism were still front-page news. Nicholas Ray's bizarro Western *Johnny Guitar*, released the same year, is often cited for its veiled references to the McCarthy witch hunts. Nevertheless, Sirk's melodrama has an even sharper edge, as its witch-hunting isn't removed to some windswept no-man's-land but centered right in the heart of small-town America.

Within the framework of a "women's picture," Sirk also explores gender roles and finds that if postwar society isn't insisting that a woman's place is in the kitchen, it might be in the living room. In a sequence that's pure and quintessentially Sirkian, Cary breaks down on Christmas Eve and admits to a newly engaged Kay that she's given up Ron for all the wrong reasons. As she's pouring her heart out, Ned wheels in a Christmas gift for his mother . . . a television set. As her own forlorn expression is reflected back in the screen, the TV salesman tells Cary that with this easy-to-operate model, "You have all the company you want . . . life's parade at your fingertips."

And who better to star in a movie about the consequences of partnering with a socially unacceptable lover than Rock Hudson? Just as Sirk's movie appears to be one thing on the surface (a routine weepie) and something quite different underneath (a damning social critique) so, too, is Hudson a walking anomaly. At first glance, he's a generous slice of all-American virility, but behind the flannel-shirted exterior lies the only thing more threatening to postwar conformism than a card-carrying pinko or a racially integrated school system: a deceptively macho homosexual who could easily pass for straight.

"In *All That Heaven Allows*, Sirk is quite brilliant in terms of how he uses Rock Hudson," says actress and film historian Illeana Douglas. "The character Rock is playing is a kind of deviant. He represents the outsider point of view in this upper middle-class environment, not only because he's the gardener but because he represents something that is dangerous—this kind of unleashed sexuality. It could be said that there's this undercurrent of homosexuality in the artistic nature of Hudson's character, who is living this bohemian life that is unencumbered by capitalistic values. Not only is Jane Wyman punished for enjoying a relationship which is outside the norm but the gardener is punished for introducing sexuality to this world that is very cloistered. Add to the equation that Rock Hudson was asked to portray the ultimate heterosexual throughout the 1950s and, underneath that, he's infusing it with the emotions of a gay man and all those layers become very interesting."

While *All That Heaven Allows* wasn't quite the blockbuster that *Magnificent Obsession* had been, it was still one of the highest-grossing films of 1955 (earning over $3 million in its initial release). As with the first Hudson-Wyman teaming, the reviews were mixed. "As laboriously predictable as it is fatuously unreal," declared the *Monthly Film Bulletin*. Though in *The Hollywood Reporter*, Jack Moffitt wrote that the rematch had been "produced with smartness and good taste . . . Hudson is excellent in a well-written part that could have easily gone sour in the hands of the wrong actor. With no obvious actors' tricks, he completely sells the idea that this man is a free spirit . . . It's the most exacting role he's played in some months and he demonstrates his increasing maturity as an actor in his handling of it."

In the *Saturday Review of Literature*, Hollis Alpert delivered the most entertaining review, which took the form of an open letter to Rock's alma mater: "Dear Universal Pictures Corporation: I am writing this letter on behalf of my Aunt Henrietta, who went with me to see your new picture, *All That Heaven Allows*. She wishes me to thank you for giving her the kind of heartfelt emotional experience she so rarely gets from movies these days . . . The end of the picture was real dramatic, with Rock falling off the snow embankment and getting himself a brain concussion. And then, when he opened his eyes and Jane said, 'I've come home, darling,' the lump in my throat was as big as a goose egg. I don't mind telling you, I *cried*."

NEVER A STUDIO to tamper with a winning formula, Universal immediately cast Hudson in yet another turgid melodrama. *Never Say Goodbye* looks and sometimes feels like a Douglas Sirk movie, which is understandable given that he made uncredited contributions to it.* However, as the bulk of the film was directed by Jerry Hopper, it is missing the subversiveness and ironic commentary of Sirk's best work. What's left is pure potboiler.

Never Say Goodbye is a remake of the 1945 Merle Oberon vehicle *This Love of Ours*, which in turn was inspired by a play by Luigi Pirandello. With each incarnation, the story seemed to become more grossly sentimental. Brimming over with tragic accidents, chance encounters, and tearful reconciliations, *Never Say Goodbye* seems intent on achieving maximum bathos. Taking the tearjerker to an entirely new level, every frame of the film seems to ooze with a kind of treacly goo.

Hudson is Dr. Michael Parker, a widowed surgeon so dedicated to furthering orthopedic research that he maintains a state of the art diagnostic laboratory in the basement of his own home—complete with a young Clint Eastwood as his attentive lab assistant.

Parker's young daughter, Suzy (Shelley Fabares), is so single-mindedly devoted to her father, she's diagnosed as having "an advanced Electra complex." Although her heart belongs to daddy, Suzy

---

*Sirk was responsible for bringing the film's female star, Cornell Borchers, over from Germany. After completing some preliminary work on *Never Say Goodbye*, Sirk turned his attention to *Written on the Wind* and only returned to *Never Say Goodbye* during the final stages of production. This included reshooting several scenes featuring George Sanders.

also finds time to create a needlepoint shrine to her long-departed mother. Dr. Parker's chauffeur and housekeeper talk about his German-born wife—who went missing in the Russian zone just after the war—in only the most hushed, reverent tones. While attending a medical conference in Chicago, Parker joins some colleagues at Timmy's Tavern, where Lisa (Cornell Borchers), the wife he long assumed was dead, is not only very much alive but providing piano accompaniment for the house caricaturist, Victor (George Sanders, at his most languid).

Within moments of this unexpected reunion of husband and wife, an overwhelmed Lisa dashes into the street and is struck by a car. She may have survived years of deprivation behind the Iron Curtain, but with a punctured lung the chances of her pulling through surgery are slim to none. Paging Doctor Parker. With weepy violins underscoring every lachrymose flashback, it's all Hudson can do to keep a straight face while delivering lines like, "You could have at least closed one door when you married me . . . the door to your lover!" or "I like to dream my dreams when I'm wide awake."

With Rock's popularity surging, *Never Say Goodbye* became one of the top-grossers of 1956. The film proved to be critic-proof, which is a good thing as the reviews were hardly raves. *Variety* noted that the picture was overloaded with "the ingredients of misunderstanding and mother love which appeal to those gals who go for soap opera and magazine romance."

CHAPTER 8

GIANT

Rock and his bride-to-be, Phyllis Gates, on the set of *Giant*
in the summer of 1955.
(Courtesy of Wally Cech)

think Rock Hudson worked best with a big background," says film historian Steve Hayes. "A big melodrama against a big landscape. He was such a big presence and the camera caught how strapping and stalwart and dependable he was. You don't lose him in the Pacific Ocean when he's on a schooner. You don't lose him in the vineyards when they're on fire. He's the ultimate hero and you feel like he's big enough to take all of that on."

Hudson's next production would be big in every way. It took more than three years to make. And even then, it ran forty-four days overschedule. It cost far more than its initial budget of $3 million and at 210 minutes, it was longer than its projected running time of two and a half hours. As Hollywood epics go, *Giant* was a film of mammoth proportions—as grandiose and immense as the Texas it depicted. It would even be advertised as "a story of big things and big feelings."

After director George Stevens read Edna Ferber's novel, which spanned almost thirty years in the life of a wealthy ranching family, he knew that the Pulitzer Prize–winning saga would form the basis for his next film.

In 1955, Stevens was a fifty-year-old army veteran and his career in motion pictures had been going strong for over thirty years. As one of the most prolific and dependable craftsmen in the business, Stevens had directed classics in virtually every genre, including *A Place in The Sun, Gunga Din, Alice Adams, Swing Time*, and *Shane*. While the projects he was attracted to were typically panoramic in scope, Stevens was also intent on making movies that explored the human condition in intimate detail.

During World War II, Stevens was recruited by the U.S. Army Signal Corps. The director supervised a film unit which documented D-Day as well as Nazi atrocities at the Dachau concentration camp. Upon his return to Hollywood, the kind of riotous battle of the sexes comedies Stevens had made before the war (*The More the Merrier, Woman of the Year*) suddenly didn't seem as appealing to him. "I guess I wasn't in a very hilarious mood," the director told his colleagues. Recognizing that the cultural climate in postwar America had shifted, Stevens wanted to make more serious-minded, socially conscious pictures.

With its sweeping scale and themes of racial intolerance, capitalistic excess, and feminism, *Giant* seemed tailor-made for George Stevens and the perfect property with which to launch his own independent production company. The sensitive social issues that Ferber had focused on in her novel may have scared off some of his contemporaries, but not Stevens. The director seemed to like the fact that Ferber's searing indictment of Texas's arrogance and racism had generated plenty of controversy when *Giant* was published by Doubleday in 1952.

Many irate citizens from the Lone Star State felt that "a little old lady from Kalamazoo" had humiliated and betrayed them. One El Paso newspaper went so far as to suggest that Ferber be hung in effigy in bookstore windows. "The reaction was quite violent in some quarters," Ferber recalled at a press conference a year after *Giant* was published. "They called me names that were unprintable—but they printed them."

When a syndicated columnist asked readers if they'd like to see Ferber's much discussed novel turned into a movie, a Dallas newspaper responded that if Hollywood filmed the book, bullet holes would fill the screen wherever *Giant* was shown in Texas; and given the intense reaction to Ferber's latest effort throughout the state, this was no idle threat.

None of this ruffled Stevens, who understood that all of the outrage was good for business: "To my mind, all of this bombast meant controversy, a healthy and provocative thing. And as such, it seemed to add to my enthusiasm for putting the subject on to the screen in the best and most forceful possible form."

In November of 1953, Stevens's appropriately named Giant Productions acquired the screen rights to Ferber's novel, which thanks to all of the ballyhoo, had become a runaway bestseller. A month later, Stevens signed a contract with Warner Brothers for the financing and distribution of what the trades were already touting as "the biggest and most important picture since *Gone With the Wind*."

When Stevens announced that he was about to begin casting *Giant*, his office was deluged with letters and telegrams from readers all over the country who had very definite ideas about which actors should fill *Giant*'s leading roles: headstrong cattleman Jordan "Bick" Benedict, his socially conscious wife, Leslie, and their surly ranch hand, Jett Rink, who becomes a well-to-do oil baron in the latter half of the film. In Ferber's novel, Bick Benedict is described as a mass of contradictions: "There was nothing regal, certainly, in the outer aspect of this broad-shouldered figure in the everyday clothes of a Texas cowman. Yet here was the ruler of an empire . . . His was a deceptive gentleness; soft spoken, almost mild. The eyes were completely baffling; guileless, visionary; calculating, shrewd."

The actor playing Bick would have to portray him at three different stages of his life—as an ambitious young rancher, then as a middle-aged husband and father, and, finally, as a graying grandfather in the film's final hour. Bick undergoes a transformation from entitled bigot—who treats the minorities working for him disdainfully—to proud defender of his half-Mexican grandson.

Ferber saw Burt Lancaster, the robust veteran of dozens of Westerns, as Bick. Others felt that Alan Ladd's career-defining performance in Stevens's *Shane*, made him the most logical choice. Meanwhile, Clark Gable let Stevens know that he was interested in the role—provided that he would get a percentage of the grosses. Gable would have come with the kind of "marquee insurance" that movie studios prize, but at fifty-four he was a bit long in the tooth to play Bick as a younger man.

The fact that most of Hollywood's established stars were over forty prompted Stevens to move in a different direction. Instead of resorting to gauzy lenses and strategic lighting to make over-the-hill actors appear thirty years younger in the opening scenes, Stevens decided to cast actors in their twenties and age them for the second half. With this new approach in mind, Stevens continued to search for his leads.

"We thought about Bill Holden very seriously, at one time," Stevens recalled. Warner Brothers liked the idea of reteaming Holden and Audrey Hepburn in *Giant*, as they had been paired very successfully in *Sabrina* a few years earlier. This dream casting quickly fell apart, however. After Hepburn met with Stevens in July of 1954, it was decided that the star of *Roman Holiday* was "too sophisticated" for Leslie. As for Holden, he was intent on starring in the forthcoming United Artists production of *Elmer Gantry*. In the kind of ironic twist that Hollywood seems to specialize in, Burt Lancaster ended up playing Elmer Gantry, making Holden once again available for *Giant*; only now Stevens had moved on.

One morning, the director got a call from Joan McTavish, a casting agent at Universal and the woman who would later become Stevens's second wife. "Have you thought about Rock Hudson?" McTavish asked him. She had recently seen Hudson in *The Lawless Breed* and remembered being pleasantly surprised by his performance. At McTavish's urging, Stevens screened the biopic, in which Rock portrayed John Wesley Hardin from youth to old age. When the picture ended and the lights went up in his screening room, Stevens knew that he had found his Bick Benedict.

"He's the best young star in pictures," Stevens would say of Hudson. "He's big and strong and fits the physical qualifications 100 percent." The only problem was, Rock Hudson was not at liberty to star in a George Stevens production. Universal-International essentially owned Hudson under the terms of an ironclad seven-year contract. The studio wasn't about to let their most important asset walk out the door.

"When I first went to the [Universal] front office with the idea of *Giant*," Hudson recalled in an interview in 1981, "they said, 'Well, we can't have you go to Warner Brothers, Rock. That'll be six months and we can make two pictures with you here in that time. It's out of the question.'" Hudson rarely used his star power to get his own way, but he wanted to appear in *Giant* so badly that he insisted on another meeting with top brass.

Rock was granted an audience, but once inside Universal's executive board room he found himself being subjected to the ultimate game of Hollywood hardball. The studio would release Hudson to appear in *Giant*, but they would demand a then-impressive $100,000 for his services. What's more, Rock had to agree to renew his contract with Universal for four more years. "They were really bastards!" Hudson recalled years later. "But it was worth it . . . If it wasn't me, it was going to be Holden. And every actor in town wanted the role."

Stevens announced Hudson's casting in November of 1954. "Wonderful, wonderful news. Am walking in clouds," Hudson cabled Stevens. Long before the cameras rolled, director and star got down to work. "I was very grateful because he did all of the directing with me before the picture began," Hudson said. "First of all, he got me thinking I was the richest son of a bitch in the world. And he got me all puffed up and full of myself by making me believe my opinion was important to every aspect of the picture. And he got me so bigoted, talking about the squalor and filth of the Mexicans . . . that I hated them. From then on, he hardly said a word."

Stevens also took Rock on an educational field trip—to, of all places, the Wiltern Theatre in downtown Los Angeles. Perched in the balcony, Stevens and Hudson watched movies starring Spencer Tracy and Gary Cooper. Hudson remembered that Stevens offered minimal commentary. Once, while an early Cooper feature was being shown, the director remarked, "Look at the way Cooper reacts—he doesn't move a muscle but you can see what he feels."

Through a kind of cinematic osmosis, Rock Hudson would achieve an unaffected naturalness, quiet authority, and newfound subtleness in *Giant* that had only been hinted at in some of his previous performances. All of those qualities had been lying dormant from the beginning of his career, but, with the exception of Douglas Sirk, few of Hudson's directors had encouraged the actor to tap into them.

With his Bick Benedict finally in place, Stevens turned his attention to finding a bankable and popular—though not too sophisticated—actress to play Leslie Lynnton Benedict. Moviegoers had lined up for Rock Hudson and Jane Wyman. Why not reunite them for *Giant*? Stevens kept the Oscar-winning Wyman in mind while pursuing an even bigger star. "Frankly, I would rather have had Grace Kelly for the part at that time," the director recalled years later. "She sort of suited it better and she was the most important female star at that time." But when Stevens approached MGM about borrowing the future "Serene Highness of Monaco" for his latest production, the answer from studio chief Dore Schary was swift and emphatic: "We are not going to loan Miss Kelly for *Giant* or any other picture. End of discussion."

Then, as Stevens would later diplomatically phrase it, "Liz Taylor cast herself in *Giant.*" Rock Hudson, for one, was delighted. Although they had never had an opportunity to work together, Hudson and Taylor had socialized a bit and found that they enjoyed each other's company.

May 19, 1955, marked the first day of principal photography and the pivotal third role of Jett Rink had been cast only a few days earlier. For months, Stevens was bombarded with casting suggestions for Jett Rink. They ran the gamut from the inspired (Robert Mitchum) to the absurd (Frank Sinatra). As it turned out, the ideal actor had been visiting Stevens's office on the Warner Brothers lot on a regular basis. He was a displaced New Yorker. A bongo-playing, motorcycle-riding disciple of Marlon Brando. In his cruddy blue jeans and scuffed cowboy boots, he already seemed dressed for the part of Bick Benedict's adversary. The uniquely talented oddball with the slouching stance was named James Dean.

Although he had already starred in Elia Kazan's production of *East of Eden* for Warners, the film had not yet been released. Word around the studio was that Dean had delivered—and then some—with a riveting, star-making performance. Stevens told screenwriter Fred Guiol, "We should think about this boy for Jett. He's very different from anybody that we have thought about."

Very different was right. If eager-to-please Rock Hudson had been buffed and polished into a kind of gleaming but impenetrable form of matinee idol perfection, Jimmy Dean was the anti-star—an ill-mannered, mercurial, intensely neurotic loner who almost single-handedly personified the edgy intensity of the Actors Studio.

Alongside Marlon Brando and Montgomery Clift, Dean was a

poster boy for the Method, a supposedly more "authentic" approach to acting, in which the performer accessed their own emotional memory to bring a character to life. Director Lee Strasberg and other practitioners of the Method believed this technique resulted in a more realistic, multilayered portrayal. In other words, it was as far from Hollywood's cardboard theatrics and glycerin tears as one could get. And the same could be said for Marfa, Texas, where cast and crew of *Giant* converged in early June.

Vast and remote, this West Texas town of 3,500 had been founded as a railroad water stop in 1883. As one scenic designer put it, "Marfa was 3,856 square miles of blank page." Desolate and drought-stricken as it may have been, Marfa and its people would supply *Giant* with its atmospheric heart and soul. Although some exteriors had already been shot in Keswick, Virginia, it was in Marfa where virtually the entire company and all of George Stevens's meticulous preplanning finally came together. Along with reporters from *Look, Life*, and Marfa's own *Big Bend Sentinel*, as many as 700 curious onlookers would observe shooting on any given day.

In Stevens, Hudson found a supportive and inspired director. In Elizabeth Taylor, he found a soul mate. Almost immediately, the two stars became inseparable. So much so that rumors started flying. "At the time it was suspected there was a romance between Elizabeth Taylor and Rock Hudson," says Joe Duncan, owner of the El Paisano Hotel, where the stars were temporarily housed. "Taylor's husband, actor Michael Wilding, showed up from Hollywood with their two dogs to investigate the rumor. He and Elizabeth had a blow-out fight in the main room that could be heard for miles."

Although Elizabeth confided in Rock about some of the problems in her marriage, the legendary Hudson-Taylor camaraderie seems to have been more about cutting loose than getting reflective. "Rock made me laugh," Taylor would say after his death. "We spent most of the time chatting and laughing and being silly. Just before he died . . . I remember making him laugh by recalling a night in Marfa, Texas, when it was hailing. The hail was like golf balls. We were running out, getting conked on the head . . . making chocolate martinis. So you can imagine the state we were in."

In addition to bonding with Taylor, Rock went out of his way to ingratiate himself with the rest of the cast, which included Carroll Baker (debuting as Bick's daughter), Dennis Hopper (playing son Jordan), Earl Holliman (as son-in-law Bob Dace), and Sal Mineo (as fallen war hero Angel Obregon). The same kind of sociability didn't seem at all possible with James Dean. Even though Rock, Jimmy, and character actor Chill Wills were sharing a house on location, Dean couldn't have been more remote. "I don't mean to speak ill of the dead, but he was a prick. Pardon my French," Hudson would tell an interviewer in 1974. "He was selfish and petulant, and believed his own press releases. On the set, he'd upstage an actor and step on his lines. Arrogant. But let him alone and he was brilliant."

"It was like night and day with those two," says Jane Withers, who played Bick's neighbor Vashti Snythe. "But that shows you how conscientious George Stevens was as a director. The characters Rock and Jimmy played were enemies . . . he knew exactly who to cast."

Dialogue coach Bob Hinkle, who would spend several months on the picture helping Hudson and others perfect their Texas twang, remembers that the animosity between Hudson and Dean was obvious. "Jimmy was jealous of Rock because Rock had all of the good dialogue," says Hinkle. "And Rock was jealous of Jimmy because *East of Eden* had just been released and Jimmy was getting all of the media attention. They never had words, but you could feel the jealousy."

Dean was annoyed that Hudson—who was not a member of the Actors Studio—had achieved such stature in films. Rock worried that Jimmy was stealing focus—with the press, squealing fans, and their director. "Stevens is throwing the picture to Dean, I know he is," Rock complained to Phyllis Gates, who paid a visit to Marfa and witnessed the rivalry up close. "Stevens is giving Dean all the close-ups. I'm left out in the cold."

It's also been suggested that there was some unresolved business between the two stars. Hudson knew that like himself, Dean had once been kept by an older gay man. Jimmy's benefactor, Rogers Brackett, was an advertising executive who happened to be friends with Henry Willson. Rock may have had this association in mind when Jimmy turned up on the set of *Has Anybody Seen My Gal*. Dean's friend, William Bast, remembered, "It was after his first day of shooting on that picture that Jimmy confided in me his contempt for Mr. Hudson, based on nothing more than Hudson's hypocritical pose as straight on the set while privately trying to hit on him."

Carroll Baker, who knew Dean from their days at the Actors Studio, says that there was yet another source of friction between the men: Elizabeth Taylor. A still photographer visiting the set captured a revealing image of *Giant*'s trio of stars: Taylor, who is in the midst of a conversation with Hudson, is being "lassoed" by Dean—his lariat encircling her neck and hands.

"We were all having a wonderful time and then Jimmy arrived and he stole Elizabeth away from us," Baker says. "She went off mysteriously each evening with Jimmy and none of us could figure out where they went." Shrewdly recognizing that Taylor, for all her glamour and movie star trappings, was instinctively drawn to outcasts and misfits, Dean instantly won her over with his lost-boy vulnerability. "I don't think there was a romance of any kind there. I really don't," says Baker. "But I think it was his way of saying, 'Hey, Rock, I can take Elizabeth away from you. I'm the third character in this film and just like in the film, she's yours. Well, off screen, she's not yours. She has my attention.'"

September 30, 1955, marked the 110th day of shooting. The company, now back on the Warners lot in Burbank, had wrapped for the day. George Stevens was screening rushes with some of the cast when he received an urgent call in the projection room. "The lights came up in the theater and George was on the phone and he was absolutely pale," Carroll Baker remembers. "You just saw all the blood drain out of him and he turned to us and said, 'Jimmy's dead.' I remember we just sat there with the lights up for the longest time. There wasn't crying. There wasn't talking. There wasn't anything, there was just dead silence."

Dean and his mechanic, Rolf Wütherich, had been traveling to a sports car competition in Salinas when his Porsche collided with a vehicle driven by Donald Turnupseed, a twenty-three-year-old college student. Wütherich and Turnupseed both survived the crash, but Dean sustained massive internal injuries and was pronounced dead on arrival by the time the ambulance reached Paso Robles War Memorial Hospital.

While their relationship had been adversarial and fiercely competitive, Rock reacted to the death of James Dean in a completely unexpected way. "I had never seen him so sorrowful before, and it frightened me," Phyllis Gates recalled. "His big frame was convulsing in sobs . . . I asked him why the news had shattered him." Gates said that Hudson responded, "Because I wanted him to die . . . Because I hated him. I was jealous of him because I was afraid he was stealing the picture from me. I've been wishing him dead ever since we were in Texas. And now he's gone." According to Gates, "It was days before Rock overcame his black depression . . . Rock couldn't be reached. He was overcome by guilt and shame, almost as though he himself had killed James Dean."

Although Hudson and Taylor were in no condition to work after learning of the tragic death of their costar, the order came down from Jack Warner himself: The show must go on. Stevens was painfully aware that the picture was thirty-four days overschedule and that shutting down an already over budget production to allow for a grieving period simply wasn't practical. On October 1, Hudson, Taylor, and Chill Wills began shooting the final scene of the film in which Bick reveals to Leslie that he believes that his entire life has been a failure. It was one of the most demanding, emotionally wrenching scenes in the film, and the fact that it was being shot only a day after Dean's death made for a very somber atmosphere on the set.

"Elizabeth, the Earth Mother, took Jimmy's death very hard," Hudson remembered. "She was grief-stricken and crying and sobbing and George made her work . . . Now, I'm trying to play a scene with a woman who is sobbing. He said, 'Action. Cut. Print.' It was merciless . . . He was being—I thought at the time—cruel. He wasn't. He was trying to get her to stop thinking about it . . . but it didn't work, not with Elizabeth."*

Stevens would end up reshooting this entire sequence days later, and once this was completed, principal photography on *Giant* finally wrapped, nearly four months after it began. On May 22, 1956, the first preview screening of the film was held at the California Theatre in San Diego. *Giant* ran three hours and thirty-five minutes without an intermission, making it the longest picture ever to be released by Warner Brothers up to that time. Despite the extended running time, 307 of the 383 preview cards rated the film "excellent" and the performances of the three leads were universally praised.

After the first preview and between five others (in San Francisco, Riverside, Bakersfield, Long Beach, and Encino), a steady stream of detailed memos poured forth from Jack Warner's office . . . Could Stevens possibly excise fifteen minutes of footage without damaging the narrative? (He could.) Could Stevens please remove the scene where Taylor's character criticized the 27½ percent tax depletion on oil revenue? (He couldn't.) Could Stevens clarify Dean's

---

*In addition to mourning Dean, Taylor was plagued with ailments throughout production, including a throat infection, acute bladder pain, laryngitis, sciatica, and what was either a bout of appendicitis or complications from her recent caesarean section. In a Warner Brothers memo dated August 31, 1955, production manager Tom Andre reported that Taylor complained that she had "a very bad headache." In response, an exasperated Warners executive scrawled "Hangover!" in the margins.

unintelligible dialogue during a climactic drunk scene? (He could and did, by bringing in Dean's *Rebel Without a Cause* costar Nick Adams to rerecord thirty lines of Dean's dialogue for $300).

Then Ben Kalmenson, Warners' chief distribution executive, got into the act, publicly blasting Stevens for making what he described as "a communist picture" and demanding that the director remove the last scene of the film in which a white baby and a Mexican baby are shown together in the same crib. Stevens shrugged off Kalmenson's objections and the scene remained.

When *Giant* opened in theatres in Texas on October 18, the screens were not filled with buckshot and George Stevens was not hung in effigy in the lobby. Instead, the film actually went on to break box office attendance records in the Lone Star State. When the movie went into wide release across the country on November 24, the reviews were, for the most part, outstanding.

"*Giant* . . . is a strong contender for this year's top-film award," Bosley Crowther proclaimed in the *New York Times*. "Every scene and every moment is a pleasure . . . Such things as the great ranch house standing in the midst of an empty plain . . . or the funeral of a Mexican boy killed in the war are visioned with superlative artistry." *The Hollywood Reporter* hailed *Giant* as "an epic film in a class with the all-time greats" and its leading man was singled out for praise: "Hudson is powerful in perhaps the best portrayal of his career, a real acting job that goes under the skin of the character and gives substance to the most important single role in the picture."

As critics had grown accustomed to seeing Hudson in Universal quickies such as *One Desire* and *Never Say Goodbye*, it's no wonder that a fully realized performance in a first-class production like *Giant* seemed like a revelation. During a tender moment of reconciliation between Bick and Leslie, Hudson is genuinely moving as a man who must swallow his pride and admit his failings. "Are you ready to come back to your old, beat up cowhand?" Bick asks his long-suffering wife. It was moments like these that inspired the critic for *Variety* to write, "With *Giant*, Hudson enters real star status."

In the early morning hours of February 19, 1957, the Oscar nominations were announced and *Giant* received ten nominations, including a nod for Best Picture. As expected, there was a posthumous nomination for James Dean, which the film community roundly applauded. Rock was also in the running for Best Actor, putting him in direct competition with his deceased costar as well as Yul Brynner for *The King and I*, Laurence Olivier for *Richard III*, and Kirk Douglas's acclaimed portrayal of Van Gogh in *Lust for Life*. While the trades predicted Douglas would go home victorious, a *Photoplay* magazine poll revealed that fan support was clearly in Hudson's corner.

As it turned out, both Hudson and Dean lost to Yul Brynner's bravura turn as the King of Siam. "I think Rock Hudson was robbed that year," says film critic Kevin Thomas. "He really is the lynchpin of that entire movie. Elizabeth Taylor and James Dean are superb but they are supporting Rock. He is the key to the whole film and if anybody deserved that award, it was him." George Stevens was named Best Director and his win softened the blow that came after. In a decision that still has Oscar historians scratching their heads, the Academy inexplicably chose style over substance, naming the all-star travelogue *Around the World in 80 Days* the Best Picture winner over *Giant*.

The acclaim and attention that Rock Hudson received for his performance in *Giant* ensured that he would remain one of the most sought-after screen actors of the era. Even as he was preparing to appear in a new picture several years later, *Giant* was still very much on his mind. In May of 1962, Hudson wrote to Stevens:

> *Dear George:*
> *I thought you might be interested to know that the old house set in "Giant" has not become something of the past but is very much something of the present. I was in a B-52*

bomber in a refueling operation and took off from the SAC base in Roswell, New Mexico. The crew asked me if I would like to experience [an] assimilated bombing attack. I said yes, naturally, and guess what the target was! The bombardier asked me if I would like to make a bomb run and I said yes again ... scored a bull's eye on the first try.

Just as the exterior façade of Bick Benedict's ranch house, Reata, would be left behind after the *Giant* company headed back to Hollywood, the summer of 1955 seemed to linger in Marfa, Texas. Although Liz, Rock, and Jimmy were only in town for a little over a month, they left an indelible impression. And the movie they made together has not only aged gracefully but continues to cast a very long shadow.*

*The long shadow cast by *Giant* has been explored in a number of works, most notably Ed Graczyk's play, *Come Back to the Five & Dime, Jimmy Dean, Jimmy Dean.* Robert Altman directed a 1982 film version in which Sandy Dennis, Cher, and Karen Black play members of a James Dean fan club who reunite in 1975, twenty years after the actor's death. In 1961, Billy Lee Brammer published an acclaimed novel, *The Gay Place,* in which a wily governor visits the set of a movie being made in the desert. Brammer covered *Giant*'s Marfa shoot for the *Texas Observer.*

CHAPTER 9

WRITTEN ON THE WIND

Mr. and Mrs. Rock Hudson pose with a pair of Korean orphans
on the set of *Battle Hymn* (1957).
(Bettmann/Getty Images)

O n November 9, 1955, Rock Hudson and Phyllis Gates were
married in a bungalow in the Biltmore Hotel in Santa Barbara. In several ways, the ceremony had a rushed, last-minute
feeling about it. For years, Hudson had told persistent interviewers that he would get around to marrying when he was
thirty. Now his nuptials seemed to be occurring in the nick of time;
only eight days before his thirtieth birthday, in fact.

Notifying the best man that his services were required was left
until the eleventh hour. In the middle of the night, Rock phoned

Jim Matteoni, his best pal from Winnetka. Could Jim and his wife, Gloria, pack up and get on a plane to California in a matter of hours? Then, on the day of the wedding, Rock was ticketed $27 for speeding on his way to the license bureau in Ventura. The frantic pace had less to do with the fact that the couple were anxious to be wed and more to do with the fact that Hudson's next picture, *Written on the Wind*, was scheduled to start production at the end of November. As always, career came first.

At Phyllis's insistence, a Lutheran minister officiated. Besides Jim and Gloria Matteoni, the only others in attendance were Gates's friend Pat Devlin and of course, Henry Willson, who was credited with arranging every detail of the wedding, from blood tests to bridal bouquets. He had even remembered to have a three-pound bag of rice at the ready. Although Willson had also meticulously planned the couple's Jamaican honeymoon, he stopped short of joining the newlyweds in the Caribbean.

After the wedding ceremony, the first calls made were not to relatives of either the bride or the groom but to Hollywood's high priestesses of dish, Hedda Hopper and Louella Parsons. Willson knew that if they phoned in the news early enough, both columnists would have time to make the afternoon editions of their respective papers. Once the news broke, everyone everywhere would be talking about Rock Hudson finally tying the knot. What even Henry Willson could not foresee was that people would still be talking about the marriage decades after the couple exchanged vows.

"The question of whether the marriage was real or phony is the central conundrum of Rock Hudson's life," writes Sara Davidson in the memoir she authored for Hudson.

"Phyllis Gates and Rock Hudson began to be companionable, and not, so help me, solely for the sake of appearances," said Hudson's friend, actor John Carlyle. "Their laughter and giggles . . . in the bedroom, in restaurants, and everywhere else, became constant and nonstop enough to make their friends feel excluded." The observations of another close friend, director Stockton Briggle, are no less emphatic: "That was an arranged marriage from the get go. It was obviously never going to work. One of the few things he ever said to me about that was that he always resented being manipulated like that and it was a very dark period in his life." So which interpretation of the Hudson-Gates marriage comes closest to the truth?

Phyllis presents "The Sham" version of events in *My Husband, Rock Hudson*, published two years after Hudson's death. After 200 pages of missed signals and red flags, she finally pieces everything together in a chapter entitled "Revelation": "The whole thing was too nightmarish to comprehend. Was Rock a homosexual? I couldn't believe that. He had always been the manliest of men . . . Had our marriage been a cover-up for Rock's true nature? Impossible. I *knew* that Rock had loved me, during the courtship and in the early stages of our marriage."

Most people who knew either Rock or Phyllis or both aren't sold on Gates's "I was duped" defense. MGM's head of talent Lucille Ryman Carroll says, "I don't know how that's possible. I knew people who knew Rock very well during the time he was married to Phyllis, and he was in and out of every gay singles bar in town. He was notorious."

Many of Rock's friends tend to ascribe to "The Arrangement" theory. In this version of the coupling, Henry Willson shrewdly paired off an essentially gay man and an essentially lesbian woman in an arranged marriage where both participants agreed to play house in the name of job security. "What I heard from Rock is that when they were married, they both knew of each other's sexual proclivities," says Martin Flaherty, Hudson's estate manager. "In their relationship, it was agreed that they could both pursue their other interests as long as it wasn't talked about or brought into the home. Sort of like, 'don't ask, don't tell.' The problems started when Phyllis wouldn't give up her harem but she wanted Rock to give up all of his guys. Of course, this was unfair but he went along with it for a while because in his own way, he really did love her."

Others agree that Gates reneged on her end of the deal. "Phyllis behaved, I think, very badly," says actor Christopher Riordan. "When I first came to Hollywood, I was very good friends with a couple of ladies who knew her. They told me Henry Willson came to Phyllis and said, 'We need to do this for Rock and this is what's going to happen if you'll agree to go along with it.' So, Phyllis knew everything but she didn't live up to her end of the bargain. Then she wrote a book about their marriage, which annoys me. She could have been more honest about the whole thing and just said, 'Well, it was a different time and it was something that had to be done . . .' Everybody knew that Rock was gay and that was fine, but nobody ever discussed things like that in those days. 'Being gay' was something that you did after the party was over."

If Douglas Sirk had found the relatively tame *Magnificent Obsession* "a combination of kitsch, and craziness and trashiness," what must he have thought when he was handed an outline for *Written on the Wind*? Albert Zugsmith, who would go on to produce everything from *Touch of Evil* to *Sex Kittens Go to College*, owned the rights to the novel *Written on the Wind*, and he believed that the material was ideal for Sirk. And, as improbable as it seems, "this drama of psychic violence" (as Sirk would eventually come to refer to it) had been inspired by actual events.

In 1932, Zachary Smith Reynolds, the twenty-one-year-old heir to the R.J. Reynolds Tobacco Company, and husband of troubled torch singer Libby Holman, died under mysterious circumstances after a party at his North Carolina estate. The ensuing scandal inspired novelist Robert Wilder to write *Written on the Wind*, which was praised for its "you-can't-put-it-down readability" when it was published in 1945. In Wilder's thinly disguised version of the Reynolds tragedy, a few key details were changed and the gothic backdrop shifted from North Carolina to Texas but the similarities to persons living—and dead—was hardly coincidental.

Although the 1935 Jean Harlow vehicle *Reckless* was loosely based on the Reynolds case, Production Code restrictions kept a franker dramatization off movie screens until the mid-1950s. By that time, Universal figured that the same American public that had devoured the Kinsey Reports was ready for the smorgasbord of degeneracy featured in *Written on the Wind*. George Zuckerman, who had written *Taza, Son of Cochise* for Sirk, was hired to adapt Wilder's bestseller. Despite countless changes mandated by the censors, Zuckerman somehow managed to retain the essence of Wilder's sordid narrative.

Stalwart, dependable geologist Mitch Wayne has been a faithful friend of multimillionaire oil tycoon Jasper Hadley and his family since childhood. The Hadley empire is so powerful and omnipresent that even the Texas town Jasper reigns over is named after him. Both of Hadley's adult children are spoiled, self-indulgent types, wallowing in their own depravity. Kyle is an impotent alcoholic while Marylee is an insatiable nymphomaniac, whose list of things to do includes the one man she hasn't already had . . . Mitch. "Marylee is like a sister to me" is Mitch's default response whenever it's suggested that he should make a decent woman out of her.

When Mitch meets demure secretary Lucy Moore, he is instantly smitten, believing he has finally found a woman as grounded and morally centered as he is ("Maybe we're two of a kind," he tells her.). Lucy, however, only has eyes for Kyle, who introduces the working girl to a world of plush, wall-to-wall luxury. After jetting off to a ritzy hotel in Kyle's private DC-3, Lucy immediately begins to have second thoughts. The designer gowns, expensive lingerie, and fancy perfumes seem like a down payment on her virtue. Once Lucy makes it clear that she's interested in Kyle for himself—and not for his extravagant lifestyle, the couple elopes . . . much to Mitch's dismay. However, the honeymoon is definitely over once Kyle and Lucy return to the Hadley homestead, where, in the best Sirkian tradition, pent-up longings and simmering tensions boil over into a highly stylized, psycho-sexual melodrama.

With its schizzy quartet of characters, *Written on the Wind* reflected just how conflicted postwar American society had become. In 1956, the year that the film was released, a traditional Biblical epic like *The Ten Commandments* dominated the box office while the tawdry *Peyton Place* became a runaway bestseller. For a culture in the throes of an identity crisis, *Written on the Wind* seemed to blurt out everything that had been left unspoken throughout the decade.

Given a choice of roles, what actor wouldn't want to sink his teeth into playing a maniacal alcoholic or a conniving nympho? As Rock was Universal's top-billed attraction, it was automatically assumed that the bravura role of Kyle Hadley had been reserved for him. As it turned out, nothing—not even the promise of an Oscar win—was allowed to tamper with Rock Hudson's virtuous, white knight image. "Rock Hudson would very much like to play the rich drunk, but his fans won't accept his doing anything shoddy," Universal's head of publicity, David A. Lipton, explained in a press release. "They like him because he's what they want their daughters to marry, or their children's father to be like. If we let him out of that sort of character, they'd howl."

If the ticket-buying public preferred Rock as noble, valiant, and eternally self-sacrificing, that's exactly what they would get. Hudson would play Mitch Wayne, the noble, valiant, and eternally self-sacrificing hero. The straight man, figuratively speaking. "As usual, I'm so pure, I am impossible," Rock told an interviewer.

Although Lauren Bacall would later confess that she loathed the story ("Soap opera beyond soap opera, a masterpiece of suds!"), she signed on to play Lucy Moore at the urging of her husband, Humphrey Bogart: "My career had not been flourishing, yet again, and when I told Bogie about it, he thought I should do it if the set-up seemed right. It had a big budget, a good cast. I'd never done anything quite like it before—a really straight leading lady, no jokes, so I said yes."

A decade earlier, a young beauty named Dorothy Malone had given Bacall some competition in the come-hither department when both appeared in the noir classic *The Big Sleep*. As a bespectacled bookstore clerk who seduces Humphrey Bogart one thundery afternoon, Malone made an indelible impression. Subsequently, she built a substantial career out of playing what Rex Reed described as "the classiest whores in Hollywood." Who better to play the town tramp cruising around in a ruby red sports car?

The plum role of Kyle would go to Robert Stack, on loan-out from 20th Century-Fox. Hudson and Stack had shared the screen in *Fighter Squadron* eight years earlier, only now their positions were reversed. Hudson was the major box office star, Stack the supporting player.* Despite his secondary role, Stack's scenery-chewing performance would dominate the picture. "He never said a word, not a peep," Stack would say of Hudson. "Since I was a loan-out actor and Universal was his home base, he could have used his influence to have the heart cut out of my part . . . I can't tell you how many others in this survival profession would have done this differently. He was in a position of power and didn't misuse it."

With *Written on the Wind*, Sirk presents his own unique brand of *Confidential*-style exposé. After introducing us to his mansion dwellers, who are as cosmetically perfect as their surroundings, the director reveals that behind closed doors, they are actually totally depraved lost souls. But Sirk doesn't stop there; he also seizes the opportunity to expose the dark underbelly of the American Dream. After all, he would later remark that *Written on the Wind* was "a film about failure."

"With *Written on the Wind*, Sirk is ready to get into the emotional underground of America in the 1950's," says film historian David Thomson. "He wants to explore some more radical ideas . . . Sirk was a very intelligent man but he went to great pains not to let

*One thing that hadn't changed since *Fighter Squadron* was the disparity between Rock Hudson's salary and Robert Stack's. As a Universal contract player, Hudson earned $27,000 for *Written on the Wind*, compared to Stack's $50,000. Of the leads, Lauren Bacall earned the most, taking home $100,000, even though she was billed below Hudson.

his intelligence show too much. He knew Hollywood well enough to know that displaying his intellectualism could be very alarming. So what he does is bring Rock Hudson in as his star because he knows Hudson can carry a big film like *Written on the Wind* and also deliver a large audience. Meanwhile, Sirk can examine these themes of family, class, unfulfilled sexuality."

From a contemporary perspective, the film contains more than a few insider nods to its leading man's real-life dilemma. In an early scene, Jasper Hadley says to Mitch, "It's about time you got hitched, isn't it?" To which Mitch responds, "No, I have trouble enough finding oil." It's almost an in-joke, a spoof of every *Photoplay* interview Rock Hudson ever gave. The cute, quick-witted dodge to that eternal marriage question.

In a later scene, Biff Miley (Grant Williams), the latest in a long line of brawny Marylee conquests, is dragged out of her room at the El Paraiso Motel and made to answer before Papa Hadley. After Jasper reprimands him for taking advantage of his daughter, Biff lays it on the line: "She picked me up . . . Your daughter's a tramp, mister." Although Marylee's promiscuity is hardly a closely guarded secret around town, Mitch cautions the young stud, "Let's keep this quiet." Here Hadley Oil could be the executive offices of Universal-International, doing their best to squelch rumors about their top star's homoerotic antics while hushing up the editors of *Confidential*. Is it any wonder that Hudson was the one actor that Sirk worked with more than any other? With a secret, sexually transgressive lifestyle imprisoned within a "normal," straight-acting, suitable-for-framing public persona, Rock Hudson is not only the star of a Douglas Sirk melodrama, he is one.

In *Written on the Wind*, Sirk's luxurious visual style and incisive commentary on American culture find their most exquisitely lurid outlet. In the film's most indelible sequence, a defiant Marylee cuts loose as "Temptation" blares on the soundtrack, providing the overture to what has been called "one of the most brilliant sequences of 1950s melodrama." Fired up by the frenzied music, Marylee flits about her bedroom while wearing a billowing chiffon negligee; she is a delirious, oversexed hummingbird. At one point, she dances with a framed photograph of Mitch, her unobtainable ideal.

Having just been told that his daughter has been keeping the El Paraiso Motel in business, Jasper Hadley starts up the stairs,* prepared to confront his wayward daughter. Halfway up, the long-suffering patriarch's heart gives out just as Marylee's dance of deliverance reaches a fever pitch. Jasper collapses, tumbles down the stairs, and dies. Both literally and figuratively, parent and child have destroyed one another.

Symbolic of the fact that he has sired a pair of narcissistic good-for-nothings, Jasper is mourned not by his biological offspring, who are otherwise engaged, but by his surrogate son and daughter—Mitch and Lucy. But Sirk doesn't let Jasper Hadley off the hook, either. While daddy was off drilling for profits and immersed in business deals, his children were psychically abandoned. Ironically, Kyle and Marylee, who have been given anything they could possibly want, are at the same time emotionally malnourished, having been weaned only on Hadley Oil.

Thanks largely to its laundry list of taboos, *Written on the Wind* grossed over $4 million when it was released in 1956 and the picture proved to be one of Rock's most popular films of the 1950s. Both Robert Stack and Dorothy Malone were nominated for Oscars, with Malone taking home the statuette for her peroxide blonde Iago. Over the years, filmmakers as diverse as Rainer Werner Fassbinder, Allison Anders, Todd Haynes, and Kathryn Bigelow have all paid tribute to the film's operatic intensity and its mesmerizing, dreamlike imagery. Oscar-winning Spanish director Pedro Almodóvar echoed the feelings of many when he said, "I

---

*The grand staircase prominently featured in *Written on the Wind* was known around the Universal lot as the "Stairway of the Stars." The most durable staircase in cinema history, it made its screen debut in the 1925 silent version of *The Phantom of the Opera* starring Lon Chaney. *Written on the Wind* marked its 320th film appearance.

have seen *Written on the Wind* a thousand times and I can't wait to see it again."

"THAT'S WHAT I was interested in—a man who kills *and* saves children," Douglas Sirk would say when asked why he wanted to make *Battle Hymn.* "This guy was an ambiguous character . . . in other words, highly interesting as a subject for drama."

Sirk's seventeenth film for Universal, *Battle Hymn*, was based on the extraordinary exploits of Colonel Dean Hess, the so-called "flying parson." A Cleveland-based minister, Hess had enlisted as an aviation cadet after the attack on Pearl Harbor. Church elders were stunned that such a devoutly religious man was determined to go into battle. Any attempts to talk him out of signing up proved futile. As Hess later said, "I felt that it would be morally wrong for me to say to others, 'I believe in your cause but you do the killing for me.'"

Dubbed a "one-man air force," Hess was involved in some 250 combat missions over Europe. During a bombing raid over a German railroad yard, Hess inadvertently destroyed an orphanage, killing thirty-seven children. "A little hole appeared in the wall from the penetration of the bomb casing," Hess wrote in his autobiography. "A moment later, the insides of the building spilled out . . . It seemed to stare at me like some malevolent eye. I wondered if beneath the piles of bricks a few small bodies still lay."

After the war, Hess returned to the ministry. Though in 1948, he was recalled and deployed to Korea to train fighter pilots. In his spare time, Hess and other airmen joined Korean social workers in rounding up orphans in Seoul. After evacuating and airlifting the children to an island off the South Korean coast, Hess and the others founded an orphanage, an act which many interpreted as atonement for the earlier tragedy.

With wartime heroics, a protagonist grappling with a guilt complex and adorable orphans all factored in, Hess's story practically demanded a Hollywood biopic. And it got it. When Universal suggested that Robert Mitchum should portray Hess on film, the flying preacher balked; he didn't want to be played by a "former jailbird" who had been arrested in 1948 for marijuana possession. But Hess couldn't have been more pleased with the studio's next choice—Rock Hudson. "He's the only man I know of who could do this part and keep it from being a war story," Hess told *The Hollywood Reporter.* "Hudson has great character and is so skillful in his portrayal, that I frequently felt that I was watching my alter ego."

Even if Hess felt that Hudson was the perfect actor to portray him and that Douglas Sirk had an excellent track record as a director, the Colonel wasn't about to leave anything to chance. Hired as a technical advisor on *Battle Hymn*, Hess became an inescapable presence on the set, even accompanying cast and crew when they headed off on location to Nogales, Arizona, which doubled for South Korea.

While setting up a shot with Rock at the International Airport just outside of Nogales, Sirk tumbled down an embankment and broke his leg. Wheelchair-bound throughout most of the shoot, the director found his technical advisor totally unavoidable. "I had a lot of problems because he was on the set, hanging around, supervising every scene," Sirk recalled. "I couldn't bring out the ambiguity of the character as I would have liked. There was a magnificent chance here to make a film about killing and flying."

In an effort to make the Rock Hudson version of Colonel Hess more layered and multidimensional, Sirk suggested that the character take up drinking. Hess would have none of it. "He was there on the set the whole time saying, 'I didn't drink' and all that, trying to make me stick to 'truth,'" Sirk recalled decades later.

When it came time to promote *Battle Hymn*, Edward Muhl, Universal's head of production (and one of Rock's staunchest supporters), urged the studio's advertising department to avoid any physical comparisons between Hudson and Colonel Hess: "There is a great lack of resemblance between them and any art showing them together would highlight this and accordingly hurt the picture in the mind of the audience."

On the other hand, Universal's publicity department made every effort to draw parallels between Hess's heroism and their star's own gallantry. Stories were planted in the press that suggested that Rock was considering adopting one of the twenty-five Korean war orphans that had been flown in to appear in *Battle Hymn* ("Is Hollywood's Handsomest Star Ready for Fatherhood?"). Another mentioned that Hudson was treating the entire group to a day at Disneyland—an outing the studio's public relations team had actually arranged.

Reviewing Hudson's latest effort in the *New York Times*, Bosley Crowther found it both routine and shrewdly calculated: "Perhaps the most candid comment to be made about Universal's *Battle Hymn* is also the most propitious, so far as its box office chances are concerned. That is to say, it is conventional. It follows religiously the line of mingled piety and pugnacity laid down for standard idealistic service films. What's more, it has Rock Hudson playing the big hero role."

In a more enthusiastic notice, *The Hollywood Reporter* noted that "Hudson has great natural warmth and growing maturity as an actor." In fact, in a deathbed vigil scene toward the end of the film, Rock is genuinely moving. As the gravely injured Captain Skidmore (Don DeFore) floats in and out of consciousness, Hess tells him that "death is just a gentle step from darkness to light." Moments later, after the captain succumbs, Hess breaks down. In need of his own consoling, he finds himself totally alone.

———

According to virtually all the fan magazines, Rock and Phyllis's marriage was a model of mutual devotion, understanding, and unwavering commitment. In reality, it was in shambles. While vacationing in Rome, Hudson and Gates encountered the young Italian actor that Rock had been involved with when he had last toured the city. The young man told the newlyweds that he was having lunch the following day with actress Anna Magnani. Would they care to come along? Rock eagerly accepted the invitation without consulting his wife. To Phyllis, it was obvious that her husband was completely captivated by the Italian. Capping a day of drinking, an argument ensued once the couple returned to the Grand Hotel.

Phyllis told Rock that she had no interest in getting together with the Italian. "Why don't you want to have lunch with him?" Hudson pressed. "Because he's a *silly little fruitcake*," Phyllis responded. Gates claimed that Rock hit her so forcefully that her necklace broke, causing pearls to scatter all over the hotel corridor. Then she began screaming. Bellboys rushed over and separated the couple. The next morning, a contrite Hudson apologized before bursting into tears.

The couple would reconcile, but Phyllis felt that the humble, good-natured, and down-to-earth man that she had married had let fame, and especially his Oscar nomination, go to his head. "He expected everything to be done for him, swiftly and in the best style," Gates recalled. "He had lost that boyish wonder that I had found so appealing in him." But some of Hudson's friends say that it was not the movie star but his wife who was all wrapped up in the five-star restaurants and front row seats.

A later companion of Hudson's, Tom Clark, remembered Rock saying of Phyllis, "The minute we got married and she became Mrs. Rock Hudson, everything changed. She did a complete about-face. She was very impressed by things like my stardom, by the money, by all the trappings of my name and all the glamour nonsense. You know I don't give a single damn for all that stuff, but she did."

Lee Garlington, another partner of Hudson's, remembers hearing similar stories: "I asked Rock, 'Why did you marry that woman?' And he said, 'You know, I thought I was in love with her, and when she moved in it was like somebody turned off the tap of a faucet. It changed overnight. She threw out my tan chinos. She threw out my Thom McAn moccasins. We were going to be big, rich movie stars and live the Hollywood way.' He also told me the entire marriage had been set up by Henry Willson. It always amazed me that Rock could be so easily talked into something. I mean, Phyllis was working on him. Henry Willson was working on him. *Confidential* was on his back for a while. I'm sure he felt they had to get married. Period."

"IT IS MY understanding that Rock Hudson's wife is to accompany him on the location . . ." read an interoffice memo from MGM's personnel director Bud Brown to logistics man Joe Finn. The studio was gearing up for its forthcoming production #1700. Along with Phyllis Gates, ten thousand pounds of camera equipment, two light green Shantung dresses, a snuff box, and six pairs of white boxer-type shorts (for Mr. Hudson) were all air shipped to Nairobi in July of 1956 for Metro's adaptation of *Something of Value*.

Robert C. Ruark's novel, published in 1955, detailed the brutal Mau Mau Uprising in what was then the British East African colony of Kenya. Peter McKenzie, the son of a white settler, has been best friends with native Kimani since their childhood days. After the death of Peter's mother, he and Kimani became virtual brothers as both are raised by the wife of a Kikuyu headman. Despite diverging communities and customs, Peter and Kimani maintain their close friendship over the years.

During a savage attack by the Mau Mau guerrillas, members of McKenzie's family are killed and some of Kimani's relatives are implicated. Ultimately, Peter and Kimani find themselves on opposing sides of the ongoing conflict, though both struggle with the personal and ethical ambiguities of their situation. At one point, when his loyalties are questioned, Peter responds, "You can't spend the first twenty years of your life with someone sharing bread and secrets and dreams and then one day say, 'Sorry, it's all over. We live in different worlds.'"

Prior to the publication of Ruark's novel, MGM had bought the movie rights to the book from Doubleday for $300,000. Once *Something of Value* reached the top of the bestseller list, the studio assigned producer Pandro Berman to bring the story to the screen. One of the producer's recent hits, *Blackboard Jungle*, had been directed by Richard Brooks, known for bringing an unflinching, pseudo-documentary style to his films. As well as an explosive temper to his sets.

Blackboard Jungle had not only provided a glimpse of an inner-city teacher's daily struggles at an interracial school, but it also offered some sharp-eyed social commentary on juvenile delinquency and racial strife. Though the film was controversial, it was also a hit. MGM hoped that Brooks could bring the same kind of bold, direct-from-the-headlines approach to *Something of Value*. Once Brooks signed on as director, he traveled to Kenya to scout locations and conduct research (which included consulting with Samadu Jackson, an actual African witch doctor). Meanwhile, Pandro Berman turned his attention to casting.

MGM had been grooming British leading man Bill Travers for stardom, pairing him on screen with the likes of Ava Gardner and Jennifer Jones. Travers was undeniably photogenic and came equipped with a British accent, making him a natural choice for the role of Peter McKenzie. However, studio executives were insistent that a powerful box office draw was needed to carry *Something of Value*. Suddenly, Travers was out and Berman was in negotiations with Universal to borrow their top star, Rock Hudson.

From the beginning, Berman had only one actor in mind to play the adult Kimani: Sidney Poitier. The twenty-nine-year-old had made an indelible impression as a rebellious student in *Blackboard Jungle*. Even though he had gained notice appearing in one of MGM's most profitable films, the actor still wasn't treated very respectfully. Beyond Berman's office, Poitier was referred to only as "the colored boy" in studio correspondence, which is both sad and ironic, considering the racial themes being explored in *Something of Value*. Not to mention the fact that the desegregation of America's schools was dominating headlines as the film went into production.

Once on location in Nairobi, the company encountered no end of challenges. The New Stanley Hotel, where the cast and crew were registered, would not permit Poitier to stay there. "Well, then, we have a problem," Rock informed his director. "Whatever you want to do, move or whatever, is all right with me." After learning how much Poitier typically earned to appear in films, the owners of the hotel suddenly changed their minds. As the manager told Brooks, "They have decided anyone who makes thirty thousand dollars for three months' work is not black."

With the issue of accommodations settled, it was time to embark on a field trip. Nearly forty years after the fact, Rock would recount this harrowing expedition in chilling detail: "One Sunday morning, the cameraman [Russell Harlan], the director, Sidney Poitier and myself, were taken out into this field with a white hunter," Hudson remembered. "We were told to stand and be quiet and not move, or we would be shot. When the Mau Mau found out that they were safe, they came out of the bushes and surrounded us. It was fucking *terrifying*! I never saw such hatred in the eyes . . . black, piercing eyes. They could look right through you and just sever you right in two. The white hunter introduced us as visitors from another country and said we wanted to meet them. I was a little self-conscious, to say the least. I offered my hand to shake hands. Finally, the leader decided to shake my hand and did. Now the tension's over. I started to put my hands in my pocket and he said, 'Don't put your hands in your pocket! You're wiping away the handshake!' Oh, Jesus Christ! It was a scary situation."

And it wasn't only the Mau Mau who were scary. Assistant director Robert Relyea recalled that director Brooks, a former Marine, "believed if he could make the actors hate him—make them want to kill him—it would come across on the screen as pure anger as it related to the story he was filming."

When a group of terrified extras was assembled before him, Brooks dispensed with pleasantries. "You'll be lucky if you're still alive after this is over!" he bellowed. The director welcomed Phyllis Gates to the Dark Continent with, "There isn't one thing here that won't kill you." And after leading lady Dana Wynter phoned her attorney boyfriend one afternoon, Brooks shouted to his assistant director, "Bob, do you think you can get that broad off the phone talking to her faggot boyfriend?" Relyea remembered that Brooks reserved most of his abuse for the film's leading man. "Because he felt Rock Hudson couldn't convey the anxiety and anger his character demanded without prodding, Brooks treated Rock badly, doing his best to make him miserable."

While Brooks's methods may have been brutal, at least in Rock's case, they appear to have been effective. Particularly in his scenes with Poitier, Hudson achieves an "in the moment" aliveness and intensity he ordinarily didn't display on-screen. In a climactic exchange, Peter and Kimani discuss how they've come to be on opposite sides of the battle. "What's happened to us? When did this hatred begin?" Kimani asks. "Before we were born, I think," Peter responds. In the film's most powerful scene, Hudson's weary resignation rings true.

As for the picture itself, *Something of Value* is extremely ambitious, occasionally riveting but not altogether successful. Director Brooks strives to achieve a kind of unsettling cinema verité experience. Some elements of the film readily lend themselves to this approach while others seem in direct opposition to it. In those moments when Kimani is anguished over being pulled in different directions by his conflicting allegiances, Poitier is extremely compelling. Overall, the sequences focused on the Mau Mau have an authenticity and power that the episodes on the McKenzie family farm do not.

Although Rock and company were halfway around the world from MGM, Hollywood was never too far away. After Brooks went to the trouble of transporting his cast and crew to Kenya, many of the scenes—even the exteriors—have a curiously artificial sound-stage look and feel about them. The Culver City influence is at its most intrusive in the scenes between Peter and Holly Keith, his "betrothed." Here Brooks's film is less like a Pathé newsreel and more like outtakes from *Mogambo*. It's obvious that the interludes with the young lovers exist only to satisfy the studio's mandatory quota of big-screen romance.

Though the reviewer for *Time* would cheekily dismiss *Something of Value* as "moments in bhwa-nality," other critics were far more impressed. In his *Commonweal* review, Philip T. Hartung called *Something of Value*, "forceful though hard-to-take . . . expertly played by Rock Hudson and Sidney Poitier . . . It covers too complex a subject and it depends too often for its effect on cruelty that is almost unbearable to watch."

The role of Peter McKenzie would prove to be one of the most physically demanding of Hudson's career. He later told friends that between the unrelenting African heat, his daily workouts on the set, and the stress caused by every Richard Brooks tantrum, he shed some fifteen pounds while the film was in production. Almost as taxed as her husband was, Phyllis was nervous and edgy during her weeks in Kenya. On one of Rock's rare days off, she made the mistake of broaching the subject of their troubled relationship. "I don't want to talk about it," was Hudson's terse reply. Before shooting wrapped, Phyllis flew back to Los Angeles alone.

————

One afternoon in 1957, Rock's secretary, Lois Rupert, rushed into his office with an urgent message. "Rock, there's a man on the phone and he says he's your father!" While Hudson had remained on good terms with his sister and cousins on either side of the family, Rupert understood that Rock's relationship with his father was strained.

"I was surprised when he took the call," Rupert said. "I got up from my desk and closed his office door to give him privacy. It was only a couple of minutes later that Rock opened the door and walked into my office. He did not look happy." Rupert would never forget Rock's heartbroken expression as he quietly said, "He didn't even ask how I was. He just wanted $5,000."

Rock explained that his father was a gambler and was frequently down on his luck. "I learned that he had called before from Las Vegas, saying he'd had a heart attack and needed money fast. But later Rock learned it was untrue. His father had been a heavy loser in the casinos and needed money to pay his debts," said Rupert. "Certainly for Mr. Scherer, it was nice to have a son who was a rich and famous movie star—at least when he needed money. Rock seemed to be nothing more than his father's banker. The debts were never repaid. Rock knew that his father thought he 'owed' it to him simply because his father's seed had given him life. Rock seemed to accept the 'guilt' and always gave him money whenever he asked for it. He was just the son that had been unloved by his father and over-loved by his mother."

CHAPTER 10
A FAREWELL TO ARMS

Director Charles Vidor, leading lady Jennifer Jones, and Rock on location
for David O. Selznick's troubled production of *A Farewell to Arms* (1957).
(Photo courtesy of Photofest*)*

rnest Hemingway would refer to it as "my long tale of trans-
alpine fornication." Published in 1929, *A Farewell to Arms* was
Hemingway's second novel and first widely acclaimed bestseller. Based on the writer's own experiences as a Red Cross
volunteer on the Italian front during World War I, *A Farewell to Arms* was hailed as "a high achievement in what might be
termed the new romanticism." The novel's unflinching depictions
of wartime atrocities are sharply contrasted with its tender though
ultimately ill-fated love story.

In 1918, Hemingway had been seriously wounded while serving as an ambulance driver in northern Italy. During his convalescence, the eighteen-year-old engaged in a short-lived dalliance with an older American nurse. Their fleeting relationship was reworked in *A Farewell to Arms* into a passionate *Romeo and Juliet*–style romance. In the novel, Lieutenant Frederic Henry, an American, falls for Catherine Barkley, a British nurse caring for him at a newly installed American hospital in Milan.

In 1932, *A Farewell to Arms* made its first trip to the screen in the form of an Oscar-winning Paramount production starring Gary Cooper and Helen Hayes. "There is too much sentiment and not enough strength in the pictorial conception of Ernest Hemingway's novel," declared the *New York Times*. Hemingway hated the arbitrary, studio-imposed happy ending. Even so, Depression-era audiences turned out in droves. Future mogul David O. Selznick always regretted that he hadn't produced the first film version of *A Farewell to Arms* himself. But by the time Paramount's adaptation was in theatres, Selznick had already resigned his post as executive assistant at the studio.

Fiercely ambitious and intensely driven, Selznick always envisioned bigger things for himself. Through his own Selznick International Pictures, he would produce what many considered Hollywood's finest achievement, a sweeping adaptation of Margaret Mitchell's "Story of the Old South." *Gone With the Wind* showcased all of Selznick's strengths as a producer: an ability to merge the literary and the cinematic, an obsessive attention to even the most microscopic details, and a genius for presentational showmanship.

Despite Selznick's extraordinary achievements, *A Farewell to Arms* remained elusive. Said Selznick, "It broke my heart that I was too young a producer to make it when it was first filmed. Through many long years, I tried to acquire it." In 1951, Warner Brothers—which now owned the rights to *A Farewell to Arms*—released *Force of Arms*. This version updated the action to World War II while reuniting the stars of *Sunset Boulevard*, William Holden and Nancy

Olson *("They Met Under Fire and Their Love Flamed!").* The picture was poorly received and in light of this, Selznick realized that his long-deferred dream of remaking *A Farewell to Arms* would probably never materialize.

However, just a few years later and through a strange turn of events, Selznick would finally get his way. Warner Brothers was about to release its highly anticipated musical remake of *A Star Is Born*, which represented an important comeback for Judy Garland. Seventeen years earlier, Selznick had produced the 1937 version of *A Star Is Born* and still owned the foreign distribution rights to that title. Ever the shrewd negotiator, Selznick brokered a deal with Warners. He would relinquish his foreign rights to *A Star Is Born* plus pay $25,000 in exchange for the remake rights to *A Farewell to Arms.* Backed into a corner, Warners agreed. Though it was another studio—20th Century-Fox—that consented to finance and distribute David O. Selznick's latest spectacular, which came complete with an Oscar-winning leading lady.

From the beginning, Selznick envisioned *A Farewell to Arms* as Jennifer Jones's finest hour. He was determined that his wife would surpass the strong performances she had given in *Madame Bovary* and *Carrie.* But while Jones had been temperamentally well suited to those roles, having her play a young nurse and one "full of bubbling energy" seemed something of a stretch. At thirty-eight, Jones was eighteen years older than Hemingway's heroine. Nevertheless, Selznick convinced himself that between her Academy Award–winning credentials and his own ingenuity, they could overcome any obstacles.

In terms of a director, *A Farewell to Arms* required the services of a master storyteller, one capable of marshaling the troops while not losing sight of the character-driven aspects of the love story. To many observers, the director's toughest challenge would involve any attempts to "collaborate" with his notoriously hands-on producer. "Most directors these days don't want to work with me,"

Selznick admitted. The producer's legendarily exhaustive memos were enough to scare away the faint of heart.

However, there was at least one member of the Directors Guild of America (DGA) who seemed capable of taking on both Hemingway and Selznick. A Renaissance man whose résumé included stints as a boxer, a portrait artist, and a Mexican cavalry rider, John Huston had directed everything from *The Maltese Falcon* to *Moulin Rouge*. What's more, he was responsible for two of Mrs. Selznick's finest efforts, *We Were Strangers* and the cult favorite *Beat the Devil*. And even before production had begun on *A Farewell to Arms*, Huston had managed to win over the ultimate tough customer—Hemingway himself. "Papa liked his ideas," said Huston's biographer, William Nolan. "Both men felt that the book would make a powerful film."

Despite the fact that the project seemed to be in very capable hands, there were not so subtle hints of the trouble to come in a 1956 memo from Selznick to Huston. At the time Selznick sent his wire, the director was shooting *Heaven Knows, Mr. Allison* in the British West Indies. For once, the typically long-winded producer cut right to the chase: "Could you concentrate wholly on *Farewell* until completion of photography, after which believe you would feel safe leaving post-production, including editing, entirely [in] my hands?"

A collaboration between Selznick and Huston may have sounded smart in theory, but in reality, these two strong-willed titans seemed destined to collide. If Huston was spontaneous and open to improvisational experimentation, Selznick left nothing to chance. Including the script. Selznick and screenwriter Ben Hecht would ultimately slog their way through no less than *nine* versions of the screenplay. With each new draft, Hemingway's anti-war story seemed to recede into the background while a romantic vehicle for Jennifer Jones shifted into sharper focus.

While Huston insisted on a more faithful adaptation, Selznick was convinced that lifting scenes directly from Hemingway's novel would result in a script that was "unplayable and undramatizable."

In another round of memos, the producer admonished Huston for treating Hemingway's novel as though it were "Holy Writ." As Huston continued "torturing" the script (as Selznick put it), the producer turned his attention to Lieutenant Henry. With the leading lady a foregone conclusion, this left the crucial casting of Hemingway's hero. "It's of utmost importance . . . that we have the ideal male lead," Selznick told 20th Century-Fox President Spyros Skouras. "And the ideal is Rock Hudson."

At thirty-one, Hudson was more than a few deployments too old for Lieutenant Henry, but his popularity and box office supremacy convinced Selznick that he was the perfect choice: "Rock Hudson is the first romantic idol since Gary Cooper and Clark Gable . . . He's got *it*—the thing that is indescribable. I was delighted we could get him. He's got a warm, likable quality that will last for years and years."

Rock was equally enthusiastic about headlining a $5 million prestige picture to be shot on location throughout Italy and Austria. And in CinemaScope and "the wonder of stereophonic sound," no less. In fact, Hudson was so certain of the film's blockbuster potential that he passed on playing the lead in Joshua Logan's *Sayonara* (which netted Marlon Brando another Oscar nomination) and Joseph L. Mankiewicz's *The Quiet American* (which Jean-Luc Godard would call the best movie of 1958). Let his fellow members in the Screen Actors Guild take on the Korean War or the geopolitics of Indochina . . . Rock Hudson had Hemingway.

Decades later, it would appear that at a pivotal moment in his career, Rock had made a questionable decision, but at the time, considering all of the elements involved, it seemed like a sure thing: "I did *A Farewell to Arms*. Why? A classic story produced by David O. Selznick, who made *Gone With the Wind*. You can't go wrong there. Directed by John Huston . . . can't go wrong there. And a hell of a good acting cast . . . Jennifer, Vittorio De Sica. So, I went with that. And little by little, things started chipping away. For example, Huston was fired the day before the picture began."

While on location in Italy's Dolomite mountains, push came to shove in the form of a vitriolic sixteen-page, single-spaced type-written memo that Selznick sent to Huston: "I should be less than candid with you if I didn't tell you that I am most desperately un-happy about the way things are going. It is an experience that I feel is going to lead us, not to a better picture, as you and I discussed but to a worse one—because it will represent neither what you think the picture should be, nor what I think it should be . . ." It was all downhill from there. Selznick capped his comments with, "I'm sure you are an honest enough man to prefer resignation." Later, Selznick would famously tell a reporter, "In Mr. Huston, I asked for a first violinist and instead got a conductor."

"And that was the end of John Huston," Rock would later say. "It was shot for a week or two without any director at all, though we had a second unit director."* Charles Vidor, the director hired to replace Huston, had hit his peak in the 1940s directing Rita Hayworth in *Gilda* and *Cover Girl*. Vidor had served in the Austro-Hungarian army, but even that seemed uneventful compared to the incredibly contentious set of *A Farewell to Arms*. "He was a very nervous man," remembered Oswald Morris, the British cine-matographer. "Bit his nails, twiddled his fingers. He told me they had given him a great party when he left California and his friends were going to give him another one in three weeks, after he'd been fired from the movie."

If Huston had been slavishly devoted to Hemingway's text, Vi-dor seemed only too willing to veer away from it. As Selznick put it, "I have had to go from the defender of changes from the book to the defender of the book!" The language barrier between the American cast and crew and their Italian counterparts wasn't the

*Andrew Marton, who had directed such action yarns as *King Solomon's Mines* (1950) and *Men of the Fighting Lady* (1954), shot some of the battle sequences for *A Farewell to Arms* but was uncredited. After principal photography was completed in August of 1957, Selznick's eldest son, Jeffrey, also captured some "atmospheric" footage with a second unit crew.

only communication challenge hindering the production. As Rock recalled, "I had these highly emotional scenes to do, crying and carrying on . . . and somebody who doesn't know how to direct anybody says, 'Okay, now . . . *cry.*'

"Well, it doesn't just happen, now does it?"

Although Vittorio De Sica was revered as Italy's great neorealist director (*Bicycle Thieves, Miracle in Milan*), he had been hired as an actor on *A Farewell to Arms*. De Sica would receive an Oscar nomination for portraying Major Alessandro Rinaldi, who suffers a breakdown after enduring one too many battlefront horrors. As Hudson remembered it, De Sica's directorial instincts kicked in at a moment when his guidance was desperately needed. "De Sica was a marvelous man and a hell of a director," Hudson said. "We were shooting in a little village up near the Austrian border, near the Alps. It's the last shot of the picture and I had to come out of a building sobbing, walking right past the camera. And De Sica saw that the director didn't know how to tell me what to do . . . We went into a dressing room and in his very limited English, talked to me. And he got me so grief stricken that I couldn't stop crying. I did the scene and that was that."

Hudson also clicked with Broadway legend Elaine Stritch, who made one of her rare film appearances as the wisecracking nurse Helen Ferguson. "I flipped over Rock Hudson," said Stritch, who at the time was involved with actor Ben Gazzara. "I was so knocked out by Rock Hudson that I'd do my hair and make-up in my hotel room, just in case I would bump into Rock Hudson at six in the morning on my way to hair and make-up at the studio. He liked me. Asked me out a lot. I was in heaven. I mean, just seeing Rock Hudson come down a winding staircase in the grand hotel in Rome, in a tux, to take me out to dinner. I mean, it was just too much. *Arrivederci, Ben Gazzara.* And we all know what a bum decision that turned out to be."

While Hudson bonded with his costars, everywhere else he turned, there was discord. After Charles Vidor received one too many Selznick memorandums, the director fired back: "The memo indicates that you think that you have on your hands a hopelessly inexperienced director. If you don't stop this nonsense, I will think that I am stuck with a totally inexperienced producer. Now, for heaven's sake, let me function or else come down and shoot it yourself."

After Selznick accused Oswald Morris of favoring Hudson over Jennifer Jones with his camera set-ups, the veteran cinematographer walked ("Mr. Morris and I personally were not seeing eye to eye on photographic style," Selznick told *Variety*.). Art director Stephen Grimes left after a blowout with production designer Alfred Junge. Then Selznick and associate producer Arthur Fellows reportedly came to blows while shooting a sequence in which Hudson and Jones, taking cover in a tiny rowboat, hide from a border patrol ship.

Although Selznick would say of his leading man, "I have never worked with a more cooperative actor than Rock," this didn't stop the producer from laying into him. "I do hope that Rock is going to work on his weight," Selznick told Henry Willson. The producer found the star "far too bloated looking for a man who had done rugged ambulance service in Alpine warfare." Selznick then advised one of the cinematographers, "Please keep your eye out for Rock Hudson's Adam's apple—which can be very unattractive pictorially and romantically, particularly if highlighted."

Convinced that some of Rock's nocturnal activities were affecting his on-screen appearance, Selznick issued a reprimand: "It would be in your own interests to cut down on the play and get more sleep until the picture is finished. It is all well and good for friends who don't have your kind of assignment to keep you up till all hours, but they are unknowingly being the worst kind of enemies to you when they do this."

She may have been half a world away, but Mrs. Hudson was another sticking point for Selznick. Hospitalized with a bout of hepatitis, Phyllis began badgering Rock to come home. Given the fact that Hudson was headlining a multimillion-dollar epic being shot in several remote locations, this didn't seem to be the most reasonable request. Not surprisingly, Selznick refused.

Once she was on the mend, Phyllis tried again. She made it clear to Henry Willson that she wanted Selznick to release Rock so that they could attend the Academy Awards ceremony as a couple. The producer vetoed this as well. Then Phyllis and Henry began hounding Rock over the fact that all of the overtime on *A Farewell to Arms* was eating into a contractually guaranteed vacation. Selznick was infuriated. Not only was the constant nagging "damagingly distracting" to his leading man, but the producer couldn't help but notice that Hudson seemed genuinely "frightened" of both his wife and his agent. Used to being controlled by both of them, Rock seemed incapable of making decisions himself.

In a telegram to his attorney, Barry Brannen, Selznick let it rip: "Try to make this obviously dim-witted woman understand that Hudson has literally knocked himself out for six months and that she's doing the worst conceivable disservice to him by keeping him in this upset frame [of] mind . . . Hudson has pitifully told me [of his] total inability to make his nonprofessional wife understand situation, but even more incredible is that Willson so stupid."

Years later, when asked to recall his long and disheartening days on *A Farewell to Arms*, Rock was unusually candid: "It wasn't a pleasant experience. The director and Jennifer didn't get along and there were lots of arguments . . . At the end, when you get into the tragedy of it in the hospital room and I had to start crying, what I was really crying about is that it was seven months of *misery*. I couldn't stop once I started."

Finally, in late 1957, it was all over. After five thousand Alpine troops had been put through their paces, two directors had come and gone, and the picture soared some $300,000 over budget, *A Farewell to Arms* was ready to be unveiled to the public.

In a movie season that included blockbusters like *Peyton Place* and *The Bridge on the River Kwai*, *A Farewell to Arms* (which

Selznick touted as "A Theatrical Event of the First Magnitude") was released on December 14, 1957. The reviews were not kind. "If there was a supreme Bad Taste Award for movies, *A Farewell to Arms* would win it hands down. This smutty version of Ernest Hemingway's novel will set thousands of stomachs to turning," said William K. Zinsser in his *New York Herald-Tribune* review. "Sweep and frankness alone don't make a great picture; and *Farewell* suffers from an overdose of both," said *Variety*.

As for Rock's work, *The Hollywood Reporter* (clearly unaware of all that had taken place during the protracted shoot) wrote, "Hudson is an actor who is exceptionally responsive to direction and under Charles Vidor he gives one of his best performances." The *New York Times*, however, wasn't sold on either of the leads. "The essential excitement of a violent love is strangely missing in the studied performances that Rock Hudson and Jennifer Jones give. The show of devotion between the two people is intensely acted, not realized. It is questionable, indeed, whether Mr. Hudson and Miss Jones have the right personalities for these roles."

Eventually, even David O. Selznick* conceded defeat: "I take credit for my pictures when they are good, so I must take the blame when they are disappointing . . . *A Farewell to Arms* is a job of which I am not especially proud." Looked at today, Selznick's *A Farewell to Arms*—as opposed to Hemingway's—is steadfastly determined to be Monumentally Impressive. Haunted by his early triumph with *Gone With the Wind*, the producer seems intent on recapturing its epic grandeur. It also doesn't help that Jones is far too mature for her role. In an early scene, when she mentions that

---

*Rock's secretary, Lois Rupert, remembered that when Hudson was shooting *Seconds*, "I received a call from [publicist] Rupert Allan with the news that David O. Selznick, for whom Rock had done *A Farewell to Arms*, had died. I told him. Rock fell very silent. I could see the director watching him, I'm sure he thought it had brought tears to his eyes. But the news did not. His first words were about Mr. Selznick's widow, Jennifer Jones, of whom Rock was most fond. He said, 'What a relief it must be for Jennifer. She hated him, you know.'"

she was engaged to a "boy" who was killed, it sounds strange rather than poignant.

In spite of the off-screen chaos he endured, Hudson manages a respectable performance throughout the picture. Toward the end of the film, he is superb in one scene in which a distraught Lieutenant Henry retreats to a café after being told that his newborn son has died. While muttering to himself about his experiences in the war, Henry subconsciously lines up a bunch of sugar cubes as though they are troops on the battlefield and then flattens them. This sequence, and Rock's final solemn walk through the deserted streets after learning that Catherine has died, were among the strongest scenes in the film. But as Hudson himself pointed out, was this really acting or simply emotional exhaustion blown up to Cinema-Scope proportions?

CHAPTER 11

THE TARNISHED ANGELS

"It got me so damn mad because I had to compromise,"
Rock would say of the studio interference he encountered while
making *The Tarnished Angels* (1958). Hudson had prepared to play
his seedy character exactly as described by William Faulkner but
Universal executives wouldn't stand for it.
(*Photo courtesy of* Photofest)

The producer wanted to call it *Sex in the Air.* The director considered the script well plotted but undramatic. The leading man was willing to cast aside his pretty boy image and go grunge, but the studio would have none of it. The Oscar-winning leading lady was shooting two films simultaneously and was understandably exhausted. And if all that wasn't enough, a stunt pilot was killed during production.

Despite the countless challenges involved in its making and the critical drubbing it received upon release, *The Tarnished Angels* would ultimately emerge as one of director Douglas Sirk's most revered efforts. The last of the Hudson and Sirk collaborations is also widely considered the finest screen adaptation of a William Faulkner novel—in this case, *Pylon*, published in 1935.

In Depression-era New Orleans, Burke Devlin, a boozy, disillusioned *Times-Picayune* reporter, is assigned to cover an unorthodox trio of barnstormers who regularly risk their lives performing at air shows across the country. The journalist befriends former World War I fighter pilot Roger Schumann, his parachutist wife, LaVerne (billed as "The Distaff Daredevil"), and their devoted mechanic, Jiggs. After Schumann's plane is damaged in a crash, he encourages LaVerne to seduce wealthy promoter Matt Ord in exchange for his rickety plane, which is so ill-equipped to compete in an air race that a devastating tragedy results.

After the commercial triumph of *Written on the Wind*, producer Albert Zugsmith seemed intent on not only recapturing its box-office success but also reassembling virtually the same cast for *The Tarnished Angels*. Rock would play the down-at-the-heels reporter, Robert Stack the air ace, and Dorothy Malone the much coveted LaVerne.

George Zuckerman, who had scripted *Written on the Wind*, was hired to adapt Faulkner's *Pylon*.* "They paid Faulkner fifty grand only after I had written a two-page memo on how I could get the script past censorship," Zuckerman said. The main concern for the Production Code office being the novel's suggestion of a ménage à trois involving Schumann, LaVerne, and Jiggs. There was also a problematic flashback sequence in which Schumann and Jiggs roll

---

*According to Douglas Sirk, it was a Universal "salesman" who came up with the film's title, *The Tarnished Angels*. "*Pylon* doesn't work as a title," Sirk told interviewer Jon Halliday. "I remember when I was taking it round, people kept saying, 'What is this title *Pylon*? It sounds like something to do with electricity.'"

the dice to determine who should claim responsibility for LaVerne's unborn child. That scene alone would inspire Francis Cardinal Spellman of the Catholic Legion of Decency to take to his pulpit.

Back in the director's chair, Douglas Sirk couldn't have been more excited about *The Tarnished Angels*. Ever since he had read a German translation of Faulkner's novel, he had longed to adapt it for the screen. Sirk was impressed with Zuckerman's initial efforts but did express one major reservation. "Strangely enough, the story does not speak to my heart," Sirk wrote in a letter to Al Zugsmith. "For reasons not yet quite clear to me, everything appears to take place on a very distant stage, very far removed from where we are . . . A plot full of possibilities for drama results in the present script in a minimum of drama."

As Sirk encouraged Zuckerman to show rather than tell in his rewrite, the leading man was already getting into character. Exhibiting the same sort of enthusiasm that he had during preproduction on *A Farewell to Arms*, Rock was eager to play Faulkner's cadaverous reporter, whom the author described as "like a scarecrow in a winter field," shabbily outfitted in "the raked disreputable hat, the suit that looked as if someone else had just finished sleeping in it." Rock sprang into action.

"I went down into the poorer section of Los Angeles and bought second, even third hand clothes—shirts with collars that were frayed, shoes with heels that were downtrodden . . . The studio executives saw the way I was dressed and they came down on the set in a fury. They said, 'What in the world are you doing? You can't play the part like that. *You're a star!* You have to be well dressed.' After that, we had to reshoot the whole thing. I even had to wear a fedora with 'Press' written in the hat band. It made Douglas so angry and me so angry, that I just said, 'The hell with it. Let's just get through this and get on to the next picture.'"

Years later, Sirk revealed that he actually had a hand in steering the characterization of Burke Devlin away from Faulkner's consumptive skeleton and back toward Rock Hudson's clean-cut image. In the end, the Universal-approved Burke Devlin was as neatly turned out as the Arrow Collar Man. And while there are hints that Devlin is leading a life of quiet desperation, a perfectly groomed Hudson looks like the toughest thing he's lived through is an especially long night at the Beverly Hills Polo Lounge. Although understandably frustrated by not being able to play the character the way he envisioned it, Rock not only maintained his professionalism but regularly treated his costars to characteristic displays of goodwill.

Dorothy Malone, who was shooting *Tip on a Dead Jockey* at the same time as *The Tarnished Angels*, remembered Hudson as "gallant" and a "tender type." The actress recalled that Rock patiently translated some of Sirk's more oblique directions for her. When an obnoxious drunk hassled Malone while the company was on location in San Diego, Hudson quietly and calmly intervened.

Expectant father Robert Stack also felt supported by his costar. In the midst of completing a scene with character actor Robert Middleton, Stack was stunned when an antique plane suddenly zoomed into view. A tattered banner trailing behind it announced: "It's A Girl." Hudson had arranged with the hospital to let him know when Stack's wife had given birth.

Rock was also instrumental in having twenty-one-year-old newcomer (and Henry Willson client) Troy Donahue cast as the ill-fated speed flier Frank Burnham. But was this another example of Hudson's professional generosity or, in this case, were there strings attached? "He saw me as a score," Donahue admitted years later. The actor would deny that he had been intimately involved with Hudson, but Mark Miller insisted that Troy had personally "auditioned" for Rock, which led to his casting in the film, thereby launching the career of yet another beefcake idol.

The seemingly endless procession of good-looking hunks that turned up in small roles in Rock's films—gas station attendants, traffic cops, bellboys—never ceased to amaze and amuse George Nader and Mark Miller. The minute some succulent blond turned up in Rock's latest movie, they instantly knew that it was probably not the young man's dramatic abilities that had landed him a speaking role in the film. Hudson's casting calls tended to claim whatever leisure time he could find, but once he was on the set he was all business.

"Even though he was the biggest star in the world at that time, Rock would never just coast on his stardom," said actor William Schallert, who played one of Hudson's newsroom colleagues. "When we were getting ready to shoot a scene, he'd be sitting by himself, studying his script. He wasn't admiring himself in the mirror or counting how many close-ups he had. He was focused on getting into character . . . It truly was a pleasant surprise for me to discover how dedicated he was. And I really thought Rock did some of his finest work in that picture . . . though at that point, I think people just took him for granted."

Not only would one of Rock's most committed performances of the 1950s go unnoticed, but critics at the time couldn't find much good to say about Sirk's movie in general: "*The Tarnished Angels* is a stumbling entry," wrote the reviewer for *Variety*. "Characters are mostly colorless, given static reading in drawn-out situations, and story line is lacking in punch."

The *New York Times*' Bosley Crowther liked it even less: "Mr. Faulkner's faded story does have some flavor of the old barnstorming tours . . . but there is preciously little of it in this film, which was badly, cheaply written and is abominably played by a hand-picked cast." Several decades after *The Tarnished Angels* was almost unanimously panned, contemporary critics would take a second look. Upon closer inspection, an underappreciated gem was found hiding beneath all of those raspberries. The praise—though belated—was so rapturous and sincere, one wonders if the critics who had initially blasted *The Tarnished Angels* had actually seen the same film.

Reviewing a reissue in the *Chicago Reader*, Dave Kehr raved about both the movie and its star: "Douglas Sirk took a vacation from Ross Hunter and Technicolor for this production, though he retained Rock Hudson, who turns in an astonishingly good performance as a journalist . . . The film betters the book in every way, from the quality of the characterization to the development of the dark, searing imagery."

So, is *The Tarnished Angels* a masterpiece or a misfire? The truth may lie somewhere in between. For every Sirkian masterstroke, there is a misstep. In an early scene in Devlin's apartment, when LaVerne recalls leaving her native Iowa after seeing a liberty bond poster with Roger's heroic image on it, this feels like Exposition 101, with backstory and character motivations doled out like heaps of lumpy mashed potatoes.

Yet, moments later, Sirk is at his most eloquent, though not a word is uttered. After LaVerne has fired up Devlin's imagination with tales of her flying and romantic exploits, Sirk captures his agonized expression in the shadowy half-light. The earthbound reporter is all too aware of everything he's been left out of, whether up in the air or in the bedroom. In the film's most brilliantly constructed sequence, Schumann takes to the skies in what will prove to be his final flight. On the ground, son Jack takes a spin in a "flying machine" carnival ride. Editor Russell Schoengarth's cuts come fast and furious as we see Schumann's plane spiraling out of control, the reactions of LaVerne and other horrified onlookers, and Jack, trapped inside his ride, helplessly watching his father's plane plummet toward the ocean.

———

"I was with a bunch of Explorer scouts in a bus heading to New Mexico to Philmont Scout ranch," remembers writer Armistead Maupin. "We stayed every night at army bases including Fort Campbell in Kentucky. Aside from the fact that I was constantly in a state of lust over the younger soldiers that were helping us out, I remember very distinctly going to the base movie that night and seeing *Twilight for the Gods* with Rock and Miss Cyd Charisse. The trailer for the movie was one of the campiest you've ever seen in your life . . . '*He was a man with a dark secret, she was a woman with thwarted love . . .*' And boy, do I remember Rock. I recall in one scene that his body was smeared with some kind of oil. Let's just say that it was a very impressionable moment and this was long before I ever met Rock in person." If only the movie had made that kind of indelible impression on everyone.

When Universal notified Hudson that his next picture would be an adaptation of the popular Ernest K. Gann novel *Twilight for the Gods*, his reaction was anything but enthusiastic. "I didn't think the story—that of a sea captain plagued by a past mistake, slowly going insane with bells in his head and all that jazz—was any world-beater," Rock later admitted. "But it was on the bestseller list . . . The script turned out worse than I feared."

Gann had adapted his novel for the screen and the all-too-familiar story, which concerned a boozy, court-martialed captain transporting a boatload of misfits from the South Sea Islands to Honolulu, seemed a bit too reminiscent of *Strange Cargo, Lifeboat*, and Gann's own earlier effort, *The High and the Mighty*—in that one, the most John Wayne had to contend with was an imperiled airliner. For *Twilight for the Gods*, Gann upped the ante by having Hudson's Captain David Bell grapple with a leaky brigantine, a mutinous crew, a conniving first mate, flashbacks to an earlier sea disaster, alcoholic binges, and the unrelenting advances of a tough-talking call girl on the lam. To lend some semblance of authenticity, most of *Twilight for the Gods* would be shot on location in Maui, where Mrs. Rock Hudson would join the company.

Universal's old standby, Joseph Pevney, was tapped to direct. Like Rock, Pevney immediately expressed his concerns that Hudson was too young to play the graying captain. Universal stood firm. "They just wanted Rock Hudson," Pevney recalled. "They didn't give a damn what movie he was in." Pevney surrounded Hudson with a first-rate supporting cast including Arthur Kennedy as the devious First Mate Ramsay, Leif Erickson as a theatrical agent, and Judith Evelyn (who had appeared as Elizabeth Taylor's mother in *Giant*) as Miss Ethel Peacock, a neurotic, past-her-prime opera singer.

A refugee from such MGM musicals as *The Band Wagon* and *Brigadoon*, Cyd Charisse is totally out of her element in *Twilight for the Gods*. The statuesque dancer that Fred Astaire dubbed "beautiful dynamite" is woefully miscast as Inez Leidstrom, the hard-as-nails "proven harlot" who finally conquers Captain Bell by giving him an erotically charged haircut. Whether she's pursuing the captain or fending off predatory deckhands, Charisse vogues her way through the film, at times almost en pointe, as though she's about to pirouette into a *Ziegfeld Follies* production number.

Hudson fares better as the beleaguered Captain Bell. In scenes that seem to encourage over the top histrionics, Rock is admirably restrained. He manages to be believable even as he delivers an impromptu sermon from the deck of the leaking *Cannibal*: "For peace of mind, there's no place like being at sea. You're just about as close as you can get to God out here. It's quite a church and the view from the front pew is pretty satisfying."

While he was contractually obligated to appear in any film the studio mandated, Hudson was correct to object to his own casting. As written, Captain David Bell is something of a second cousin to Humphrey Bogart's grizzled, gin-swilling Charlie Allnut in *The African Queen*. "It might have been perfect as an Edward G. Robinson role but not for me," Rock later commented. "It even presumed that I was a full-fledged captain at the age of 24, which was absurd. I didn't care about the character and apparently no one else did either."

Writing off *Twilight for the Gods* as "the absolute worst" movie of her career, Charisse blamed director Pevney for the film's failure. "He took a good book—a best-seller—and did not seem to know what to do with it." Charisse did acknowledge that the problems plaguing *Twilight for the Gods* weren't only confined to the director's chair. "Rock was then married to Phyllis Gates. All of us had a great time for a while. But one day Phyllis told me she was going home and, as it turned out, that was when she and Rock separated. That kind of put a pall on things."*

Thirty years after the fact, Gates remembered, "Whenever Rock had time off from the location, he went scuba diving instead of spending time with me. A couple of times, I asked him about seeing [a psychiatrist], and he cut me off immediately. I couldn't breach the barrier. He seemed depressed and yet he laughed much of the time, that deep laugh that entranced everyone. Only I could tell that it was hollow."

After the unhappy couple returned from Hawaii, Gates—feeling that she was having "one-sided conversations" with her increasingly remote husband—resumed therapy with her own psychiatrist. One afternoon, Phyllis returned home from an appointment to find a note from Rock—*I'm going to the Beverly Hills Hotel. Let's keep it quiet.*

The very next morning, Louella Parsons broke the silence by announcing the separation on the front page of the *Los Angeles Examiner*: "One of the biggest surprises to hit Hollywood in a long time came yesterday when Rock Hudson moved into The Beverly Hills Hotel under an assumed name. His wife remained at the family home. Neither intends to make an official statement, but there can be no denial of the fact that the Hudsons' marriage has hit a snag."

Of course, Parsons was not at all surprised by the news but at least she played along in print. Whereas Parsons's rival, Hedda Hopper, couldn't have been more brutally matter-of-fact. Wasting no time, she pitched an exclusive to Jack Podell, the editor of *Motion Picture* magazine: "Do you want me to do a special story for you on Phyllis

*On June 18, 1958, Universal's publicity director, Jack Diamond, sent production manager George Golitzin a memo regarding the fact that the ordinarily publicity friendly Rock Hudson had canceled plans for a personal appearance tour to promote *Twilight for the Gods*. It's unclear whether this was a result of the recent separation from Phyllis Gates or more of a reflection of how Hudson felt about his latest vehicle.

Hudson? She won't give it to anybody else. Of course, she won't say he is a fag and name his lover, but we can hint at that."

If Parsons was prepared to hint, Gates was not. "That would only harm Rock's career, and I'm not going to do that," Phyllis told her high-powered divorce attorney, Jerry Geisler. But she wasn't above secretly recording her estranged husband. "I needed some answers, and only Rock could give them," Gates says in her 1987 memoir. Although Phyllis informs readers that she summoned Hudson to their home to talk over their problems, she omits a crucial detail. While Gates invited Rock to bare his soul, an operative in the employ of private detective Fred Otash was not only listening in but taping every word of what would later be described as "Rock Hudson's Gay Confession." As Otash eventually revealed, "I was hired by his wife to get the goods on him to enhance her pending divorce negotiations."

Throughout the conversation, Phyllis coaxes one revelation after another out of an unsuspecting Hudson . . .

PHYLLIS: How long after we were married did you have your
    first homosexual affair?

ROCK: Oh, I don't know. The next day.

PHYLLIS: You told me you had an affair with your agent. How
    long did that last?

ROCK: No time at all. Do you think I would enjoy having an
    affair with him?

PHYLLIS: But you did it. Why?

ROCK: Because of naiveté, I guess.

PHYLLIS: Do you know how they refer to him in Palm Springs?
    As a bitch in heat.

ROCK: I feel a sense of loyalty to him, but I don't approve of his
    activities.

PHYLLIS: Who did you have an affair with in Italy?

ROCK: I saw Jean at the racquet club and she told me she had
    heard about some Italian actor I had an affair with in Italy

and then brought him back here. It's the biggest lie, for God's sake.

PHYLLIS: Can you deny that your pattern is that of a homosexual?

ROCK (CRYING): No, I can't deny it. But I never felt we were together on anything. I never felt you loved me.

Three months after the emotionally charged exchange was surreptitiously recorded, Gates filed for divorce, citing "extreme mental cruelty." On August 13, 1958, Rock and Phyllis attended the divorce hearing at the Santa Monica Superior Courthouse. Columnists noted that Henry Willson was also present, which was no surprise as he was the one who had tipped off the papers that he would be there. In addition to his customary self-promoting, Willson was regularly feeding the press stories about the divorce, doing everything possible to keep public sympathy firmly rooted in Rock's corner.

Gates told Judge Edward Brand that the Rock Hudson beloved by millions was terribly moody, seldom home, and uninterested in accompanying her to social events, unless they were business related. Gates testified that even after Hudson knew that she had been hospitalized with a bout of hepatitis, he had remained in Italy, continuing to work on *A Farewell to Arms*. Phyllis also told the judge that Rock had struck her twice, both times after he had been drinking heavily.

Judge Brand granted the divorce. In addition to $250 a week in alimony, Gates was awarded the Warbler Way house (worth an estimated $35,000), a Ford Thunderbird, virtually all of the couple's wedding presents, and 5 percent interest in Rock's production company, 7 Pictures Corporation. Phyllis would later say that she considered the settlement "paltry." Largely siding with Rock, the press criticized Gates for demanding more than her fair share. Radie Harris took the ex–Mrs. Hudson to task in *Photoplay*: "What has Phyllis contributed in her brief marriage that should penalize Rock with such a heavy financial responsibility to her, when she can't even fall back on the time-worn cliché, 'I've given you the best years of my life . . .'?" Despite the public reprimand, Gates returned to court and requested an increase in her alimony payments. Ultimately, Phyllis agreed to accept a cash settlement of $130,000.

But the payouts didn't end there. Contained in the archives of the Rock Hudson Estate Collection are a vast collection of receipts from pharmacies, gas stations, and department stores that Phyllis continued to forward along to Rock into the late 1960s—more than a decade after their divorce. Along with the receipts, Gates often enclosed brief notes—the most cryptic and possibly incriminating message reading: "Hi Hon—All's I need you for is $ $ $ $ and $ex $ex $ex Love, Phyl (Wifey)."

A number of Rock's friends and surviving partners have questioned whether Gates may have been extorting Hudson for money. Presumably, Phyllis would have had access to the recordings that Fred Otash's operative had made in January of 1958 in which Rock confessed to having had several gay affairs. And was it Phyllis that gossip columnist Liz Smith was referring to when she recalled helping Rock rid himself of an extortionist? "I was briefly involved in helping him ward off being blackmailed by a woman who swore she was going to the supermarket tabloids with her tales," Smith revealed in 2000.

At the time of his divorce, Rock would temporarily reside at The Voltaire, a luxury apartment in West Hollywood. But before moving into one of the units in this seven-story "chateau," Hudson would have the apartment swept for electronic listening devices. Rock also bought a three-bedroom house on stilts in Malibu, where he could retreat to whenever he wasn't working in Los Angeles.

In Malibu, Rock spent time with his longtime stuntman, George Robotham, who lived nearby. He went sailing and scuba diving with MGM contract player Don Burnett and his wife, actress Gia Scala. He believed that overexposure from his divorce would derail his career, even though his name still appeared at the top of exhibitor's polls and Universal had no less than five films in development with his name attached. It wasn't long before his days as a beachcomber abruptly ended; Rock was being summoned back to work.

More than two decades before the primetime soap *Falcon Crest* blew the lid off that hotbed of scandal and intrigue known as Napa Valley's wine-making country, there was *This Earth Is Mine*. Henry King, who had directed *Stella Dallas* and *The Song of Bernadette*, would oversee this CinemaScope adaptation of Alice Tisdale Hobart's novel, *The Cup and the Sword*, which had climbed to the top of the bestseller list in 1942.

As Universal was quick to point out in a steady stream of press releases they issued, the studio spared no expense in mounting an elaborate production that would be shot in dozens of vineyards and estates throughout California, including wineries owned by Paul Masson, Christian Brothers, and the Italian Swiss Colony.

Set in 1931, the story focused on the intertwining relationships of two very different generations of vintners. Heading an impressive cast, Rock would star as John Rambeau, the brash, power-obsessed manager of his family's vineyard, which has struggled through twelve years of Prohibition. While the young Rambeau thinks nothing of linking the family business to bootleggers and gangsters, his European-born grandfather Philippe (Claude Rains) worships the grape as "a holy fruit."

As this overripe saga begins, Philippe welcomes his granddaughter, a young Englishwoman named Elizabeth (Jean Simmons) to Napa Valley. Without Elizabeth's knowledge, Philippe has arranged for her to marry her cousin, Andre Swann (Francis Bethencourt), the heir to the rival Stag's Leap vineyard. If Elizabeth and Andre wed, Philippe will control all of the wineries in the Valley ("The grafting of vines is like a marriage," the young couple are repeatedly told.). The patriarch's plans are hindered by the fact that

Elizabeth falls in love with another cousin—John, who brings the transplanted English rose up to speed on the family's complicated back history. This includes the fact that John's Uncle Francis (Kent Smith) is really his father—an important part of the novel that is awkwardly introduced in the movie.

After a heated argument with Elizabeth, John temporarily turns his attentions to Buz Dietrick, a flirtatious vineyard worker. Later, Buz claims that she is pregnant with John's child and the announcement threatens to destroy the entire Rambeau dynasty. Billed as "Cindy Robbins," actress Cynthia Chenault made a memorable debut as "Buz" in *This Earth Is Mine* and she had Universal's top star to thank.

"Rock Hudson discovered me," says Chenault. "We were friends and he told me about this movie that was coming up and he thought I'd be good for it and he arranged to have me test with Henry King. It was a very emotional test. I cried. I laughed. It was probably the best acting that I've ever done. Afterwards, it turned out that Rock had been hiding underneath the camera. So, he had watched the whole thing and I had no idea that he was there. When it was over, he jumped up and he seemed so thrilled. I guess he felt responsible since he had suggested me. I did the movie with him and he was just fabulous."

Although Chenault says she considered herself Hudson's platonic "sidekick," the fan magazines had a very different take on their relationship. "In all the magazines in those days, they would mention my name and it would be followed by 'The Next Mrs. Rock Hudson . . .' He would get so upset about that. Though I was thinking, 'Gee, I don't mind if people say that . . .' And Rock would say, 'Well, I don't want people to think that you got this part only because you know me.'"

Chenault says that Hudson thoughtfully mentored her throughout the location shoot for *This Earth Is Mine*. "Rock got after me once. I was supposed to be packing grapes in a scene and he came over to me and said, 'Cindy, you get in there and you learn how to pack those grapes!' He wanted me to look like I really knew what I was doing. He made me work like a dog for a couple of hours before we ever did the scene but he was right. It needed to look believable."

All of that hard work would pay off. In reviewing *This Earth Is Mine*, the *New York Times* found only Cindy Robbins's performance, the cinematography, and the art direction worthy of praise. The overloaded narrative was faulted for its confusing and contradictory plot developments. As for the leading man, *Variety*'s critic noted, "Rock Hudson gives a sympathetic portrayal, but not a satisfying one because his characterization is riddled by inconsistencies."

CHAPTER 12

PILLOW TALK

The Winning Team: Rock, Doris Day, and Tony Randall in *Pillow Talk* (1959), the first of three blockbuster comedies for the trio.
(Courtesy of Universal Studios Licensing LLC)

N o one wanted to book it," remembered producer Ross Hunter. "The big movie chains all sadly told me, after seeing the picture that sophisticated comedies like *Pillow Talk* went out with William Powell. They also said that Doris and Rock were things of the past who had been overtaken by newer stars." In hindsight, it's hard to believe that the same Oscar-nominated *Pillow Talk* that grossed $7 million, unfastened Doris Day's cinematic chastity belt, and allowed Rock Hudson to play gay on-screen was considered hopelessly passé by America's theatre exhibitors.

And though it seems inconceivable now, after making more than forty feature films, Hudson had never once appeared in a bona fide comedy. After slogging his way through *A Farewell to Arms, Twilight for the Gods*, and *This Earth Is Mine*, Rock—like his devoted fan base—was desperately in need of a good laugh. Even so, when Hudson was first presented with a script entitled *Pillow Talk*,* he was apprehensive. Considering how hard he had worked to be taken seriously as an Oscar-nominated dramatic actor, would appearing in a suggestive sexcapade single-handedly negate years of time and effort? Then, too, what if he just wasn't funny? Hopefully, the script would be amusing enough so that nobody would notice.

The screenplay by Stanley Shapiro and Maurice Richlin concerned Brad Allen, an oversexed songwriter who woos assorted Eileens and Yvettes with romantic ditties he's custom-tailored especially for them. Brad's constant crooning over the phone incurs the wrath of Jan Morrow, the demure interior decorator with whom he shares a party line. As disembodied voices, they squabble ferociously, but once they meet in person there are sparks of a different kind.

The characters were ingratiating. The dialogue was clever. The farcical situations seemed reminiscent of Irene Dunne and Cary Grant at their best (*The Awful Truth, My Favorite Wife*).† And there were enough double entendres and risqué exchanges to keep it hot for 1959: "Mr. Allen, this may come as a shock to you but there are some men who don't end every sentence with a proposition."

---

*Although the screenplay was originally entitled *Pillow Talk*, the Production Code of America found this too suggestive and the script was retitled *Any Way the Wind Blows*. However, by August of 1959, producer Ross Hunter had managed to have the original title reinstated.

†While critics and audiences at the time didn't catch it, *Pillow Talk* was already a proven property. It's basically a redressed variation of the 1940 Jimmy Stewart–Margaret Sullavan comedy *The Shop Around the Corner*, which was musicalized in 1949 as *In the Good Old Summertime* for Judy Garland and Van Johnson. In both films, a feuding couple doesn't realize that they've already been communicating as secret pen pals.

If *Pillow Talk* was in some ways a throwback to an earlier era of cinema, in other ways it was looking straight ahead. Bubbling beneath the glossy sheen of the picture is a surprisingly sharp re-evaluation of gender roles and an exploration of the kind of themes that Betty Friedan would address in *The Feminine Mystique* only four years later. "One of the most interesting ways of looking at it is, it's both daring and nervous at the same time," says film historian David Thomson. "It takes a step forward and half a step back." What *Pillow Talk* needed and got was a leading lady who perfectly embodied the cultural shift from conservatism to liberation.

Doris Day had appeared in a succession of charming but steadfastly old-fashioned musicals. From *Romance on the High Seas* to *April in Paris*, the parade of wholesome, unfailingly sweet ingénues that Day had portrayed had cemented her screen image as a saintly but sexless Goody Two-shoes. "The World's Oldest Virgin" was the title she inherited from Borscht Belt comedians.

"I felt that it was essential for Doris to change her image if she was going to survive as a top star," producer Ross Hunter remarked. "No one realized that under all those dirndls lurked one of the wildest asses in Hollywood." Even so, Day was careful not to go too far in terms of retooling her girl-next-door image. "I liked those scripts about the man-woman game as long as they were done with style and wit and imagination. In my vocabulary, vulgarity begins when imagination succumbs to the explicit." How would audiences, who had grown accustomed to Day as America's singing sweetheart, accept her as a contemporary career woman decked out in slinky designer gowns courtesy of Jean Louis?

For his part, Rock realized that it was high time that he loosened up his image. Still, he remained hesitant about signing on, especially when he learned that his solemn, Maalox-chomping director typically made pictures with titles like *An Act of Murder* and *The Secret of Convict Lake*. What's more, Michael Gordon hadn't directed a feature film in nearly a decade. In 1951, he was blacklisted after he refused to name names when he appeared before the House Un-American Activities Committee. When Gordon appeared before the committee a second time in 1958, he informed. *Pillow Talk* was the director's ticket back to Hollywood. That is, if he could talk a certain leading man into cooperating.

"In Ross's office, I met the director," Hudson recalled. "Michael Gordon is a very intense guy . . . And I thought to myself, *That man is going to direct me in comedy . . . light, airy fairy comedy?* So, I said, 'Mr. Gordon, I am nervous about one thing. I have never played comedy. How do you play comedy?' 'Oh,' he said, 'Just treat it like the very most tragic story you've ever portrayed.'"

And so, Roy Scherer of Winnetka, Illinois, met Doris Kappelhoff of Cincinnati, Ohio. And in the tradition of Tracy and Hepburn, one of the screen's great romantic teams was born. As they got to know each other, Hudson began to refer to Day as either "Eunice Blotter," "Maude," or "Miss Adamant of 1959." She called him "Ernie." The made-up monikers were far more in league with the straightforward, down-to-earth types they both happened to be.

If their off-screen rapport was exceptional, their on-screen compatibility was even better. For starters, they looked terrific together. Day's sunshiny, platinum blond femininity contrasted perfectly with Hudson's dark, square-jawed virility. They were living, breathing Barbie and Ken dolls. As gleaming showroom models of traditional postwar gender ideals, Rock and Doris were famously described by *Time* as "a couple of 1960 Cadillacs that just happen to be parked in a suggestive position."

"The reason why they blended so well together was that it was this great ying-yang combination of her enormous energy and his detached bemusement," says film historian Thomas Santopietro. "He's this solid presence—a rock, as it were—and she's this pretty all-American girl, so they were the right melding of personae and personality. And, of course, the camera doesn't lie, and we all know they liked each other so much in real life, and that came through on the screen."

Every great screen couple needs a third wheel and Broadway's

Tony Randall would play Day's uptight suitor, the kind of never-gets-the-girl role usually inhabited by Ralph Bellamy or Gene Raymond. Before being cast in *Pillow Talk*, Randall had recently starred in both the stage and film versions of George Axelrod's satire, *Will Success Spoil Rock Hunter?* (which had originally been titled *Will Success Spoil Rock Hudson?* to Rock's great delight).

Whether she was starring in a dramatic biopic like *Love Me or Leave Me* or a musical extravaganza like *The Pajama Game*, Day was a skilled, versatile, and often underrated actress. Though her considerable talents were not lost on her costar. Hudson would later say that he learned all about comedic timing from his leading lady. "I honestly don't think I taught him anything he didn't already know after all his years in the business," says Day. "Between scenes, we'd walk and talk and laugh and I guess our comedic timing grew out of our friendship and how naturally funny we were together."

Tony Randall encouraged Hudson to watch the dailies of the first scenes they had shot with Day. After only a few minutes, Rock began to relax. "He discovered, with delight, that he had a real flair for comedy," said Randall. "He came alive in it. He couldn't contain his smile. He was bubbling. He began to have fun and the results are magical."

At one point in *Pillow Talk*, Rock's playboy composer, Brad Allen, masquerades as Rex Stetson, a Texas longhorn who seems more than a little light in the saddle. Telltale pinky extended, he sips his martini while revealing a mother fixation and more than a passing interest in Day's interior decorating. "It must be very exciting working with all them colors and fabrics," Rex enthuses, sounding like Bick Benedict's swishy second cousin.

In *Pillow Talk*, audiences were treated to the ultimate round of an illusion-on-an-illusion. With Rock Hudson in the lead, a predominantly gay man is playing a straight man who is impersonating a gay man. "I don't know how long I can get away with this act," Hudson's character says to himself at one point. Wink, wink.

Starting with *Pillow Talk*, a steady stream of what seem like self-reflexive in-jokes turn up in Hudson's films. They are so plentiful, in fact, that independent filmmaker Mark Rappaport would gather them all together in 1992 for his witty semidocumentary *Rock Hudson's Home Movies*. Though in 1959, when *Pillow Talk* was still in production, even these tongue-in-cheek asides were no laughing matter.

As film historian Richard Barrios has noted, "In the original script, the gay allusions in the Rex masquerade were fairly explicit until the Production Code Administration cautioned Universal against going into this prohibited area, an admonition which makes gayness sound a bit like a nuclear test site. In the film as released, Rex's assumed sexuality was alluded to coyly."

The Production Code Administration succeeded in toning down the Rex Stetson scene, but not another sequence that would emerge as *Pillow Talk*'s most iconic. In February of 1959, Geoffrey Shurlock cautioned the studio, "The entire sequence of Jan in her tub and Brad in his—employing the device of a trick screen—is unacceptable. The basic ingredient which we feel makes this sequence excessively sex suggestive is the fact that the two people seem to be facing each other in their separate tubs." Ross Hunter knew a brilliant sight gag when he saw one and the producer stood his ground. The tub scene not only remained in *Pillow Talk* but became a symbol of an entire era.*

When released in October of 1959, *Pillow Talk* broke box office attendance records and was endorsed by the Federation of Motion Picture Councils (which described the sex comedy as "a good, wholesome film, to which you can take your whole family"). The picture also brought its leading man some of the best reviews of his career.

---

*By this time, a precedent had already been set. In 1958's *Indiscreet*, a similar split screen device had been employed, making it appear that Cary Grant and Ingrid Bergman, who were in separate beds, appeared to be in bed together.

"The most exciting thing is that . . . Rock Hudson undergoes the metamorphosis from stock leading man to one of the best light comedians in the business," declared Jack Moffitt in *The Hollywood Reporter.* "He has acquired a playfulness reminiscent of Cary Grant with a puckish ability to handle droll double entendre gags equal to Gable's . . . his new found light touch should keep him at the top for years to come."

The *New York Times* named *Pillow Talk* one of the Ten Best Films of 1959 and it was nominated for five Oscars, winning for Best Original Screenplay. Despite Rock's outstanding personal notices, it was his costar who received an Academy Award nomination. "Being nominated for an Oscar for my role in *Pillow Talk* was a very pleasant surprise," says Day. "And, not only that, but there was this whole other wonderful reward, which was the great fun we had making that movie together. Most importantly, Rock and I became dear friends and that is something I will always cherish."

————

More than anything else, it was the need for privacy that motivated Rock to move from Malibu to Newport Beach in the summer of 1958. "Thank God, my beach home in Newport is not on the route of any of the tourist buses, whose driver points out the movie stars' homes," Hudson told Pete Martin of the *Saturday Evening Post.* "People down there pay no attention to me."

Of course, nothing could be further from the truth. Wherever he went, Rock inevitably became the center of attention and his new surroundings were no different. Almost immediately, Hudson became a charter member of Lido's super elite—a group of fun-loving, hard-drinking actors, directors, and writers that Rock's publicist, Roger Jones, dubbed "The Newport Bums." Among its principal players were a few high-ranking members of Hollywood royalty. This included one of Rock's idols, Tyrone Power, then in his early forties and married to his third wife, Deborah Minardos.

"Rock had a monstrous crush on Tyrone Power," says Lee Garlington, who would later become Hudson's partner. "He said that he idolized him as the epitome of a movie star. He wanted to be just like him . . . the whole nine yards."

"I don't know anybody who knew Ty who didn't love him," Hudson said. "I don't just mean like him—*love* him." For the rest of his life, Rock would express such reverence and affection for Power that several of Hudson's partners questioned whether the two men had actually been lovers. While some of Rock's friends were convinced that he had a brief but intense affair with Power, others dismissed the idea, insisting that the relationship was a close friendship and nothing more. Whatever the case, only a few months after Hudson had befriended him, Power suffered a major heart attack while filming *Solomon and Sheba* in Madrid. The actor's death, at age forty-four, made headlines around the world. Two months later, Power's third child and only son was born. Rock was asked to be Tyrone Power, Jr.'s godfather.

Another friendship that Hudson forged during his days in Newport Beach would prove to be more lasting. Rock felt an immediate rapport with legendary actress Claire Trevor and her husband, film producer Milton Bren. Trevor's career had peaked a decade earlier, when she won an Oscar for playing Gaye Dawn, the gin-soaked girlfriend of gangster Edward G. Robinson in *Key Largo*. Rock would always say that the scene in which Trevor agrees to warble her way through "Moanin' Low" in exchange for a drink, was one of his all-time favorite movie moments.

Hudson admired Trevor not only for her scene-stealing abilities but for her intelligence, humor, and innate sophistication. A dedicated art collector, Trevor herself had taken up painting. In fact, not long after meeting Rock, Claire began working on a large, surrealistic portrait of him, which would eventually be titled "The

Rock Hudson Story."* It depicted Hudson not as a dramatic actor but as the song and dance man that he had always longed to be.

According to Roger Jones, there was another actress—one he preferred not to name—who was so obsessed with Rock that she followed him to Newport Beach, hell-bent on becoming the next Mrs. Hudson. Renting a house only a couple of blocks from the one Rock had purchased on Via Mentone, the leading lady kept close tabs on her "intended." In a letter to Hudson, Jones recalled that across the gender lines, "The whole 'Newport Bums' crowd was after you, but *she* was determined to get you."

After it became obvious that Hudson was perfectly content with the male companionship that he had found on Lido, the actress packed up and moved out. As Jones would remind Hudson in his letter, "Later, when she moved back to town, she told people how much she disliked the ocean and ocean life, and was so glad to be back in Hollywood. What a wife she would have been to you, huh?"

As much as he cherished his time there, Rock's halcyon days in Newport Beach did not last. He was starting to be harassed. More than once, he thought he had heard gay slurs chanted when a group of teenagers passed by his house. He did his best to shake this off. But nothing could have prepared him for the very public humiliation he suffered when he was out sailing one afternoon.

Rock and his favorite shipmates, publicists Lynn Bowers and her partner, Pat Fitzgerald, were heading back to the mainland after a visit to Catalina Island. As they approached Newport Harbor, a group of teenagers partying on the shore spotted the *Khairuzan*, which they immediately recognized as Rock Hudson's boat.

---

*After Hudson's death, many of his possessions were auctioned off in April of 1986 by the William Doyle Galleries. Among the pieces up for sale was Trevor's portrait of Rock, which fetched $2,800. Also on the auction block was an unfinished wooden footstool inscribed in lavender ink by Elizabeth Taylor: *"E.T. stood here. She had to because she couldn't reach the sink. R.H. is a love, and I thank him always—even tho he is one foot taller. Your always friend, Elizabeth."* The high bidder on the footstool was a sixteen-year-old fan of Hudson's, who paid $1,400 for it.

Some of the young ladies began shrieking, excitedly waving their arms and calling out Rock's name. They couldn't believe that their heartthrob was in such close proximity. In response to this, the boys in the crowd became jealous of the "competition" from the handsome matinee idol. Suddenly, one male voice loudly yelled out, "Faggot!" It was as though the word had been shot across the bow of Hudson's boat, landing squarely at his feet. Soon, a group of teen-age boys were chanting *"Fag-got!"* Then it seemed like everyone on the beach had joined in. Within minutes, Rock's carefree outing had turned into an ugly scene. A kind of mass shaming. What hurt most of all was that Rock recognized some of his own neighbors in the crowd. They were shouting out "Faggot!" along with the others.

After that incident, it wasn't long before Rock left Newport Beach, turning the house on Via Mentone over to his mother, who would make her home there with her third husband, Joe Olsen.

———

Well before Rock's divorce had become final in August of 1958, the gossip columns and fan magazines had started devoting consider-able space to his rekindled "romance" with Universal script super-visor Betty Abbott. Even so, the authors of some of these articles felt obliged to inform the public that although Rock was "still sweet on Betty," he exercised the bachelor's prerogative by continuing to play the field.

Then in February of 1960, *Photoplay* trumped the other fan-zines by promising readers an exclusive—"Rock Hudson's Best Girl Reveals All." In a splashy four-page spread, the lady in question revealed that her favorite moments with Rock were spent at home. "There are times I curl up on the couch with my head in his lap, and he'll smoke and read and there won't be a word for an hour, just a sort of lazy closeness." Hudson's lady love turned out to be neither Betty Abbott nor Vera-Ellen but his dog, Tucker, who "told" her story to writer Jane Ardmore. So much for front-page exclusives. In reality, there was a new man in Rock's life.

"Rock was making *Pillow Talk* when I first became involved with him," says Bill Dawson, who was Hudson's boyfriend for a brief time in the late 1950s. "I remember he told me that his muscles ached from carrying Doris Day around all the time . . . It was in the early spring of '59 when Henry Willson's secretary, Pat Colby, called me and said, 'I want you to meet somebody . . .' I was teaching in those days and I said, 'I'm sorry, but I must be in bed by nine. I have to get up very early.' Pat said, 'Bill, if you pass this one up, I'll never forgive you.' They were looking for a safe, trustworthy companion for Rock and they figured I was a good candidate, I guess."

The son of a vaudeville performer, Dawson had been working as a teacher for several years. In 1955, Dawson applied for a teaching position with NATO and spent time working overseas in France and Germany. Upon his return to America, Dawson continued teaching but his daily workouts resulted in a successful sideline career as a beefcake model for publications like *Physique Pictorial*. Hudson liked what he saw.

"About a week after I met him, he would come and visit me and bring along a full bottle of Scotch and polish that off in one sitting," says Dawson. "At the time, he had just gotten divorced and he was living in West Hollywood, in a very modest little apartment on Cahuenga Boulevard. I had met Phyllis Gates at parties and she was not only a lesbian but a very butch lesbian and a clever one, too . . . When they divorced, Phyllis got everything."

At one point, Hudson introduced Dawson to Henry Willson. After sizing up the new man in Rock's life, Willson saw dollar signs. "I remember him saying during that initial meeting, 'You ought to quit teaching and let me manage you . . .'" Dawson recalls. "He was a very strange man and I'm glad that I didn't have to be dependent on him for work as Rock was. I can't imagine what some of Henry's boys went through . . . I remember there used to be this restaurant at the corner of Fountain and La Brea called Panza's Lazy Susan and Henry Willson was given carte blanche there for some reason. It's where he would take all of his new recruits—these gorgeous boys with the made up names. He would show them off like trophies."

More than sixty years after it took place, Dawson could still vividly recall the San Francisco premiere of *This Earth Is Mine*. "The night of the premiere, Rock and I had been playing around in the bedroom and really getting into it and we lost track of the time. I remember we jumped in the car and just made it to the theatre. I must say that I found it a very odd experience watching him passionately kiss Jean Simmons on screen and only an hour before, we had been doing . . . well, what we had been doing."

Dawson says that after only a few months into his involvement with Hudson, the relationship began unraveling. "By summer, I had started to lose interest. Rock had no formal education, so that really limited us in terms of conversation. Also, we were spending more time trying to keep him from being exposed than anything else. It was exhausting. At one point, I decided to head off to Fire Island without him. I said, 'Let's play it loose for a while . . .' and I think that really hurt him. That was pretty much the end of everything for us."

With *Pillow Talk* wrapped and his latest affair over, Rock was ready for a new challenge—it was called television. Hudson had already made a few tentative forays with appearances on *The Steve Allen Show* and an episode of *Climax!*, in which he played himself in "The Louella Parsons Story."

Now CBS wanted Rock to launch their new weekly series, *The Big Party by Revlon*. The premise was simple—a celebrity would host an "informal gathering" in their home and invite other stars over for some cocktail chatter and a sing-along around the piano. Forty years before the advent of the reality show, *The Big Party* would give viewers the feeling that they were eavesdropping on some fashionable soiree in Beverly Hills or crashing a chic gathering in a Manhattan penthouse. The show's sponsor, Revlon, believed that Hudson possessed the right mix of man-about-town suaveness and Midwestern innocence that would make him the perfect host.

In a way, *The Big Party* was an attempt to re-create the success of *The Big Show*, a popular radio program of the early 1950s, which featured a variety style format. The NBC radio broadcast had been hosted by the great lady of the American stage, the gravel-voiced and grand-mannered Tallulah Bankhead. Teamed with Hudson, could Bankhead do for television what she had done a decade earlier over the airwaves? For *The Big Party*, Rock and Tallulah would welcome an eclectic roster of guest stars ("alphabetically listed to avoid temperament") that included Sammy Davis, Jr., social satirist Mort Sahl, and the queen of MGM's aquatic spectaculars, Esther Williams.

The irreverent tone of *The Big Party* was set in the show's opening moments when Rock, installed in his "little room at the Waldorf," phones Tallulah and suggests grabbing a bite before the bash. "Shall we say dinner at the Colony?" Hudson asks. "Rock, that sounds wonderful. Should we dress, daahling?" To which Rock replies, "Of course, darling, it's not that kind of colony." *The New Yorker*'s John Lardner thought that Hudson gave "an interesting performance," and a convincing one, which managed to maintain the illusion that he was hosting an actual party. *Variety* left the party early, finding it "painfully contrived" while "Hudson's hosting left something to be desired. Certainly he didn't contribute toward easing the awkwardness when, on occasion, the going got rough and the party became tedious."

Rock couldn't have agreed more, telling the *Los Angeles Times*, "It sounded like a great idea, but it turned out awful." And after only a handful of episodes, the party was over.

———

Two to Make Hate, Death Is My Middle Name, and *My Gun, My Life!* were just a few of the preposterous titles that Universal's marketing department had proposed for the studio's adaptation of Howard Rigsby's western novel, *Sundown at Crazy Horse*. If the titles veered toward the outrageous, so did the plot.

Brendan O'Malley, a poetically inclined outlaw, is being pursued by Sheriff Dana Stribling, who has a warrant for O'Malley's arrest. Stribling's dogged pursuit isn't strictly business, as the young man O'Malley murdered happens to be the sheriff's brother-in-law. Both the lawman and the desperado end up at a Mexican ranch owned by Belle Breckenridge, an old flame O'Malley deserted some fifteen years earlier. Now married to a cattleman, Belle has a beautiful sixteen-year-old daughter named Missy. After O'Malley has an affair with Missy, he learns that he is actually the girl's father. In light of this revelation, O'Malley walks into a gunfight with Stribling, only his gun isn't loaded.

"Strange on the range" is how critic Leonard Maltin would describe the finished film, which was ultimately titled *The Last Sunset*. More than a decade before *Chinatown*, *The Last Sunset* featured an incestuous relationship as a climactic plot point. Though in the early 1960s, even the subtlest suggestion of incest flew in the face of everything the Motion Picture Production Code stood for. Despite the extremely controversial content, star Kirk Douglas was intrigued by Rigsby's story and determined to bring it to the screen through his own Bryna Productions.

Blacklisted screenwriter Dalton Trumbo, whom Douglas had hired to write the script for the still-to-be-released *Spartacus*, would write the screenplay. Douglas noticed early on that Trumbo seemed distracted by yet another assignment: Director Otto Preminger had promised Trumbo a screen credit on his Palestinian war epic, *Exodus*, something that the writer had been denied throughout the McCarthy era.

Trumbo's attention may have been divided, but he did his best to portray Brendan O'Malley's incestuous liaison as sensitively as possible. Even so, his script for *The Last Sunset* still raised eyebrows and the ire of Lauren Bacall, whom Douglas had hoped would play Belle. And she wasn't the only one.

If Rock had expressed concerns that *Pillow Talk* was a bit too risqué for his teeny-bopper fans, he was thoroughly revolted by *The Last Sunset*. Were his bosses at Universal kidding? They were not. After Douglas agreed to have Hudson's part beefed up so that Rock's top billing seemed justified, the studio announced that two of the biggest male stars in Hollywood would finally be teamed on the screen. After Bacall's turn-down, Douglas lobbied for Ava Gardner to play Belle, but eventually Oscar-winner Dorothy Malone was cast instead. Then the search was on for a director.

"I have to do your picture, and I have to do it better than any picture you have ever made before," director Robert Aldrich wrote in a letter to Douglas in late 1959. As Aldrich had proven that he could handle both Westerns (*Vera Cruz*) and melodramas (*Autumn Leaves*) with equal skill, Douglas invited him on board. Production began in Mexico in May of 1960. Most of the location shooting would take place in Aguascalientes, which literally translated means "hot waters," an entirely appropriate designation given all that was in store. Almost immediately, there were heated exchanges between Douglas and Aldrich.

"I was only a teenager at the time but I was old enough to understand that my father was under a great deal of pressure," says Adell Aldrich. "My understanding is that somebody—who shall remain nameless—didn't stick to the script . . . Somebody thought that another actor was getting better lines than he got. As my father had rehearsed with the entire cast for two to three weeks prior to going to one of the hottest, most godforsaken locations known to man, somebody could have expressed all of this back in Hollywood. But somebody did not."

According to Douglas, Aldrich showed up with a small platoon of screenwriters, with whom he was collaborating on various future projects. An enraged Douglas demanded that Aldrich's collaborators be sent packing. As far as the star was concerned, the script most in need of attention at that point was the one for the film they were about to shoot.

"Dalton Trumbo . . . quit his concentration on *The Last Sunset* to concentrate on the Preminger picture and by the time he came back to our film, it was too late to save it," Robert Aldrich recalled. Trumbo's biographer, Bruce Cook, described the final draft of the script as "uncharacteristically haphazard in conception and execution." If the half-baked screenplay and skirmishes between director and producer weren't already tipping the production toward disaster, there was an unusual uneasiness between the two stars.

"I had a problem working with Rock Hudson that I did not understand at the time," Kirk Douglas recalled. "He avoided any kind of direct contact with me. I was aware of how difficult it must have been for him—his costar also the producer, the boss. I tried everything I could to make him feel comfortable. But Rock always had a strange attitude toward me, never dealt with me directly . . . I'm glad I didn't know, until I read Rock's autobiography, that he was most attracted to blond, blue-eyed, rugged men."

But was it sexual tension or just plain tension? Some of Rock's lovers remember him saying that he hadn't exactly relished the experience of working with the quick-tempered Kirk Douglas. Off-screen, there couldn't have been two more diametrically opposed people—Douglas being all take-charge intensity, while Hudson was more laid back. On-screen, their acting styles also went in completely different directions. Douglas's showy, take-no-prisoners approach stands in sharp contrast to Hudson's quiet stoicism. There was no question whom director Robert Aldrich preferred: "Rock Hudson emerged more creditably from it than anyone. I found him to be terribly hard-working and dedicated and very serious; no nonsense, no 'I've got to look good.' Or 'Is this the right side?' If everybody in that picture, from producer to writer to other actors, had approached it with the same dedication, it would have been a lot better."

When it was released in June of 1961, *The Last Sunset* was found wanting. "A routine combination of Hollywood actors and Western film clichés is put forward in *The Last Sunset*," wrote Bosley

Crowther in the *New York Times*. "The actors all go through their assignments as if they were weary and bored. We don't wonder. After only an hour's exposure to them, we were weary and bored, too." In a review entitled "Ha, Ha, Ha," *Newsweek*'s critic noted, "This is not so much an adult Western as a smiling Western . . . Through gun duels, dust storms, quicksand, Indian fighting and cattle-rustling, everybody keeps smiling—except, sad to report, the audience."

In recent years, contemporary critics have reevaluated *Sunset* and drawn connections between it and the work of one of Hudson's favorite auteurs: "Aldrich's film is in some senses an attempt to transpose to the Western genre the elements of Sirkian melodrama—same studio, similar casting, and a plot about sexual neurosis," noted a reviewer for *Time Out London*.

The critical reassessment came too late for several of the film's principal players—none of whom remembered the picture fondly. "[It is] as frightful a piece of shit as one can imagine," said Dalton Trumbo. "I chant several excuses to myself each night before toppling off to sleep: I agreed to do it without the slightest idea my name would ever be on it; the script was shamelessly juggled during the course of shooting . . . it was distorted by entry into the cast of Rock Hudson. Even so, it wasn't a very good script to begin with, and the critics have dealt me some pretty harsh and wholly justified slaps."

In later years, whenever a reporter turned the topic of conversation toward his film career, Rock would speak at length about *Giant, Pillow Talk*, and even *A Farewell to Arms*, but if the subject of *The Last Sunset* was broached, he would clam up. When interviewer Ronald L. Davis asked about the movie in 1983, Hudson managed a few kind words for director Aldrich, before admitting, "That's a film that's kind of difficult for me to remember, because I didn't want to do it. I didn't like it, so I kind of conveniently put it out of my mind."

Henry Willson was holding court at the Mocambo one night when Rock suddenly turned to him and said, "Hey, there's your next big star. Right over there." Hudson's discovery was a fresh-faced, blue-eyed blond from Montana named Glenn Jacobson. If the young man's Nordic features and sturdy physique weren't enough to land him a bit part as an elevator operator in Rock's next comedy, Jacobson had yet another qualification to recommend him—he was a sailor. For Henry, it was like the Second Coming of Guy Madison. Even at first glance, Willson thought that Jacobson exuded an endearing, boy-next-door quality. If he seemed just-off-the-bus, that's because he was.

"That night, my navy buddy and I took a bus to Hollywood," Jacobson recalls. "We chose to go in our navy uniforms as we thought maybe people would be nice to us and buy us drinks. As it turned out, that's exactly what happened. We ended up at the Mocambo and I got the feeling that very few, if any, military guys ever went in there in uniform. You'd have thought that two giraffes had walked through the door or something from the way people stared."

Within minutes, a waiter appeared and told Jacobson and his friend that the pleasure of their company was being requested at one of the VIP tables. "I was a bit tipsy at that point and feeling kind of bold," says Jacobson. "So I told the waiter, 'Whoever it is, tell them to come over to us.' The next thing I know, Henry Willson is standing there saying, 'I'm having dinner with my client, Rock Hudson. Would you care to join us?' I didn't know who Henry Willson was but, of course, I knew Rock Hudson and I wasn't about to turn down that invitation."

Earlier in the evening, Mickey Rooney had bought Jacobson and his buddy drinks at Ciro's and thanked them for their service. Jacobson's newfound friends at the Mocambo were equally nice, but they seemed to appreciate a sailor in uniform for entirely different reasons than Rooney had. "Henry took me aside and told me that he thought I had something. Just from seeing me from across the room, he was convinced that I had this great potential as an actor. I had never given any thought to a movie career and wow, it was all being planted in my head one drunken night in the Mocambo."

True to his word, Henry made the rounds with his new recruit the very next day. Eventually, Willson landed Jacobson small roles in *Up Periscope* and *Operation Petticoat*. Robert Arthur, *Petticoat*'s producer, had promised Jacobson a more substantial role in his next picture, *Come September*, which starred Rock Hudson. All Jacobson needed to do to seal the deal was meet with the star. Privately.

"As I was walking over to Rock's house, I was thinking—man, if he tries to go too far in this meeting, this is not going to fly with me. I mean, Henry told me many times that I was the only client he handled that he didn't *handle* at the same time. He actually told me he admired me for that. But I was worried that Rock might be a different story. When I got to his place, he put a beer in my hand, which spooked me a bit . . . I really liked Rock and considered him a friend but I didn't want things to become awkward between us."

Instead, Jacobson said Hudson got right down to business: "Rock told me that he didn't think I would end up on the picture. I said, 'No, no. I'll expect that I'll be on it because the producer told me that he was looking forward to working with me in Rome.' Then Rock said, 'Gee, Glenn, we're very dear friends and I want to keep it that way but I think I know someone else who is better suited for this. We have another guy in mind.' He seemed to be testing me. Henry had already told me that Rock liked to have a playmate with him when he went on location. Someone of his own ilk. I got the picture and it really hurt. It hurt for a long time. I talked with Henry about it later and he said, 'Yeah, I know that Rock felt bad but that's the way these things work.'"

———

After a decade of nonstop hard work and single-minded determination, Rock Hudson had not only achieved his dream of becoming a star but he was now *the* star—the most popular, the most profitable, and the most celebrated. As the 1960s dawned, he had an Academy Award nomination to his credit along with a room full of Golden Globes, *Photoplay* Gold Medal Awards, and Bambi Awards (Germany's own Oscar). The Theatre Owners of America had named him "Actor of the Year" three times and he had already received his star on the Hollywood Walk of Fame.

As he was averaging three pictures a year, there was rarely a time when Rock wasn't working or preparing to work. Though whenever he managed to find some leisure time, he played just as hard as he worked. Despite the fact that Hudson, Henry Willson, and Universal did everything possible to protect their collective investment in "Rock Hudson," the star himself frequently threw caution to the wind and attended what the FBI characterized as "large-scale homosexual orgies," which the bureau and LAPD vice officers surreptitiously monitored.

Writer Robert Harmon attended a smaller scale, but no less memorable, gathering in 1960. "A friend and I were hitchhiking into Hollywood to see what kind of mischief we could get into," says Harmon. "This man who picked us up said, 'Would you like to go to a party?' And we said, 'Sure, why not?' We got to this place, which was like a frat house on the USC campus. When we walked in, it was obvious what was about to happen. I don't mean that everyone was naked. In fact, no one was but it just had that look about it. I just stood by the door as I was too paralyzed to leave, mainly because I saw so many movie stars. I was a movie-star-freaky kid, so this whole scene was completely overwhelming to me."

Harmon says that among the stars present was a clean-cut heartthrob who had married America's sweetheart just a few years earlier, a leading man with "supernaturally" blue eyes, and a lanky dancer who had appeared opposite Debbie Reynolds in a few lesser MGM musicals.

"The lights were turned off and when they were, I decided to make a hasty retreat," Harmon recalls. "But I picked the wrong door and ended up in the bathroom. I shut the door and then leaned my head against it. I was trying to regain my composure when I was groped. I had no idea that anybody else was in the bathroom. I was fumbling for the light switch when I realized I was in there with Rock Hudson."

While his friend became much better acquainted with the trio of stars in the living room, Harmon was granted a private audience with Hudson. "The bathroom had another door to it, which led to a bedroom that was apparently just for him. Everything about this set-up said that he was the king. I remember he put his hands behind his head as he leaned against the headboard and even that made me think, 'Here he is . . . the King of Hollywood.' The first thing we did was talk and the last thing we did was talk. The sexual portion was brief, not even memorable. I just trembled through it because I was so whacked-out being in his presence."

Even as the activity in the living room reached a fever pitch, Hudson and Harmon remained in the bedroom. "At one point, he got up and locked the door. We cuddled for a long time without it being sexual at all. I know that sounds pretty weird, but that's just the truth. We discovered that we actually had a few things in common. We were both born in Illinois, we both had the same initials and we both knew a lot about movies. There are a lot of actors who are in the business and yet they know nothing about movies but he did. We played this game called 'Who Am I?' where you have to figure out who a celebrity is based on clues. To this day, I remember he gave me Jessie Royce Landis. After I guessed her, he said, 'Oh my god, where else can I do this?' He was impressed by what I knew . . . he said he was excited about going to Italy and making a movie with Gina Lollobrigida and Sandra Dee. In the relatively short time that we spent together, I thought he was wonderful in a thousand ways."

"We were *Pillow Talk*—but with an Italian accent" is how actor Joel Grey would describe *Come September* more than fifty years after appearing in it. The frothy sex farce would be shot in CinemaScope and largely on location in picturesque Santa Margherita Ligure, a seaside resort along the Italian Riviera. Instead of the all-American Doris Day, Rock's costar this time would be the voluptuous beauty Gina Lollobrigida, described in Universal's publicity as "indispensably Italian as the Colosseum, as mouthwatering as spaghetti carbonara."

In his first screen teaming with "La Lollo," Rock would play Robert Talbot, an American tycoon so wrapped up in his business interests that he can only find time to visit his opulent Italian villa one month out of the year. Every September, the overworked executive unwinds in his hideaway while rekindling his romance with Roman girlfriend Lisa Fellini.

When he arrives unannounced two months ahead of schedule, Talbot discovers that members of his domestic staff have been renting out rooms in his home, which they have transformed into the hotel *La Dolce Vista*. The master of the house is unamused: "How would you feel if you find out Brutus was your majordomo, Lucrezia Borgia your cook and Benedict Arnold your upstairs maid?"

Talbot's uninvited guests include a group of rambunctious teenagers. Crooner Bobby Darin plays a medical student who breaks into song whenever he's not busy admiring Sandra Dee's "well-developed patellas." The casting of teeny-bopper icons Darin and Dee was a calculated move on the part of Universal.

Although Rock Hudson still reigned supreme as the studio's most important asset, he was now thirty-five years old. True, his name topped the exhibitor lists of the most popular stars in the world and, as more than one critic noted after seeing Hudson shirtless in *Come September*, he was remarkably well preserved. But even so,

Elvis, Fabian, and Troy Donahue were now claiming more space on magazine covers and in high school lockers. To the sock-hop crowd, Rock was starting to seem like an old-timer. Sure, his name could still fill seats but, just to play it safe, Universal execs knew that it was time to unleash the kids.

Anyone as career conscious as Hudson must have been unnerved by the fact that some of the younger heartthrobs were gaining on him. Even so, *Come September* made light of this. After Hudson's character wows Dee and her girlfriends with a killer mambo, Darin reassures his buddies, "Remember, the night is young and he's not . . . No man his age can defy the laws of medical science." Playing one of Darin's sidekicks was future Oscar-winner Joel Grey. Despite an immediate rapport with Rock, Grey says that their mutual confinement in the closet was never acknowledged, even when there was no one listening in.

"What's very interesting, looking back on it now, is that we went out to dinner without ever discussing anything having to do with what we knew about each other," says Grey. "There was this unspoken familiarity and trust and amusement that bonded us. Rock was this bright, playful, easygoing guy who had worked his way into this very powerful position. I really felt for him because I knew he was living that double life that was so scary at that time . . . I always had great sympathy and empathy for him but again, none of this was ever spoken aloud. That was just the way it was."

At least according to the film's leading lady, Hudson may have had nothing to hide. "I don't think he was gay then," says Gina Lollobrigida. "People can change. When we did our love scenes, he was quite . . . *normal*. He liked me very much. I felt something. It was more than a kiss." Whether this was the Rock Hudson version of Method acting or an authentic impulse, critics applauded the new screen team. Lollobrigida was hailed as "a superb comedienne" by the *New York Times* while *Variety* said that "Hudson comes through with an especially jovial performance, perhaps his best to date."

While audiences heartily approved of Hudson and Lollobrigida as a new screen couple, Universal had been inundated with requests for a reteaming of Rock and Doris Day. As 1961 came to a close, moviegoers got exactly what they wanted. In *Lover Come Back*, Hudson and Day play rival advertising executives squabbling over an account for a nonexistent product named "VIP." After a Nobel Prize—winning scientist is bribed to concoct something—*anything*—named VIP, he cooks up what he describes as "a triumph of advanced biochemistry," a flavorful mint laced with a hidden agenda—each sweet is the equivalent of a triple martini.

In a sense, VIP was manufactured from the same winning formula that made the Hudson-Day couplings so enormously popular. An irresistible bonbon done up in a glitzy Eastmancolor wrapper, VIP offers consumers "a good ten cent drunk" and "the kind of unspeakable fun your mother always warned you about." Like *Lover Come Back* itself, VIP is candy-coated sex.

As with *Pillow Talk*, Rock's character in *Lover Come Back* comes equipped with a sissified alter ego. In an attempt to seduce Day's straitlaced Carol Templeton, Rock's ne'er-do-well Jerry Webster poses as a presumably gay man. This time, he's Dr. Linus Tyler, a Greenwich Village—based scientist and "a confirmed woman hater." Try as she might, Day's character can't seem to bring Linus around. "Forget me, Carol," the antisocial doctor implores. "You deserve a man and not a mass of neurotic doubts." The self-parodying aspects of Rock's conflicted character meld perfectly with a storyline milking laughs from the consequences of false advertising.

"*Lover Come Back* is very sharp," says film historian Thomas Santopietro, who considers the picture the finest of the three Hudson-Day pairings. "We all know that the advertising world is built on deception and the act of deception is hugely important to their trio of films. Especially in those first two movies, Rock is always trying to deceive Doris . . . You also have this idea of a gay actor playing a straight man impersonating a possibly gay man, so it's like this house of mirrors. Also, in *Lover Come Back*, there's an ease in the way Rock and Doris play with each other. I think their rhythms are sharper. Because they are so comfortable together, the audience can just relax into the movie."

Rock and Tony Randall agreed that *Lover Come Back* was the most successful of their three vehicles. "*Pillow Talk* was such a success that we set out a year later to make it again," Randall said. "Practically the same script. Some of the lines were the same. Different director [Delbert Mann]. But believe it or not, the second time around, it turned out funnier."

The critics concurred. Even the notoriously difficult to please Bosley Crowther gave *Lover Come Back* a rave review in the *New York Times*: "A springy and spirited surprise, which is one of the brightest, most delightful satiric comedies since *It Happened One Night*." What's more, *Lover Come Back* clearly demonstrated why *Vanity Fair* critic James Wolcott pronounced Hudson and Day, "the best romantic-comedy team ever . . . the first couple of American pop."

———

"A strange romance" is how *Photoplay* would describe Rock's relationship with actress Marilyn Maxwell. Strange or not, the magazine's editors were so convinced that wedding bells were about to chime, they started hedging their bets in print: "Right now, five will get you ten in Hollywood that Rock Hudson and Marilyn Maxwell are about to get married. Right now, three will get you five that they will elope within the next six weeks."

After Rock and Marilyn attended a dinner for President Kennedy at The Beverly Hills Hotel in March of 1962, Maxwell was hounded by the press. Syndicated columnists and fanzine reporters demanded to know when she intended to march down the aisle with Rock. Sounding like several ladies before her who had been tagged "The Next Mrs. Hudson," Maxwell did her best to explain: "He's the very, very best friend I ever had. I adore him and he adores me. But it's just a friendship."

Maxwell was accustomed to being the subject of gossip and innuendo. The singer that the columnists had dubbed "The Darling Diva," was not only beautiful and talented but she had been romantically linked with stars Bob Hope and Frank Sinatra. "She's one of those girls who set a guy's pulse to racing by the merest glance in his direction," writer Damon Runyon once said of Maxwell.

A native of Clarinda, Iowa, Maxwell was only eighteen when she became a vocalist with the Buddy Rogers band and toured throughout the Midwest. At twenty, she was studying acting at the Pasadena Playhouse. By the following year, Maxwell was under contract to MGM. When she made her feature film debut in the wartime drama, *Stand by for Action*, the voluptuous Maxwell was proclaimed "one of the best sweater fillers in the country."

In 1949, Marilyn was working on the romantic comedy *Key to the City* with Clark Gable, when she was introduced to a struggling twenty-four-year-old actor named Rock Hudson. While there was an instant rapport, Maxwell was about to marry her second husband. Although that union proved to be short-lived, it wasn't until Maxwell was married to her third husband, writer-producer Jerry Davis, that she resumed her friendship with Rock, who was now at the top of his game in Hollywood.

Davis remembered that upon returning home from work, he would inevitably encounter "this handsome, six-foot-whatever man who was absolutely in tune with my wife. I felt a little like Woody Allen—'Hi, honey, I'm home . . .'" While Davis was aware of Rock's gay proclivities, at one point he felt compelled to question his wife about her closeness with Hudson. Davis found that "She would get quite defensive. She used to say, 'Are you paranoid? Do you actually think this man has any interest in me?'"

When Maxwell and Davis separated, Dorothy Kilgallen told readers of her syndicated column, "Marilyn Maxwell's estranged husband, screenwriter Jerry Davis, has been getting his kicks by telling friends he expects Marilyn to waltz down the aisle with Rock Hudson as soon as she gets the divorce . . . Marilyn says she has no such plans, she and Rock are just good friends, and she wishes Jerry would stop being such a wise guy with his wedding flashes."

However, when Maxwell and Davis divorced in 1960, her already close relationship with Rock only intensified. "She was in love with him," says Maxwell's longtime secretary Jean Greenberg. "She said he always told her he loved her but he wasn't *in love* with her . . . Though I know for a fact they were having an affair. Marilyn confided everything in me, and she talked about it in detail. They even talked marriage and about having children but Marilyn knew he would always be seeing other men . . . They continued to be lovers on and off and devoted friends."

"When you'd see pictures of Rock escorting all of these beautiful women to events, much of that was studio motivated," says Marilyn Maxwell's son, Matt Davis. "With my mom, I can honestly say that they truly loved each other but being with a woman wasn't really part of his true persuasion. I think they even talked about it and she said, 'I just can't deal with the boys running around.' She just couldn't cross that line. That was the only block to it. I really think they would have gotten married if it weren't for that. Though in every other way, they were as close as could be."

Sometimes the closeness turned clinging. According to Hudson's secretary, Lois Rupert, Maxwell often phoned her in desperation. "I could never count the times I answered the phone and heard, 'Where is he, Lois?' Never a 'Hello' or 'This is Max.' And thank God, for Rock's sake, I did know where he was, why he was late, or why he hadn't called her! Then she would gentle down, accept what I told her—which was the truth—and our conversation would end up much more pleasant than it had begun."

If Hudson was riding high as the king of the box office in the early 1960s, Maxwell's once-promising career had flatlined. At one point, the former star of MGM musicals was reduced to performing a "satiric striptease" in a New York burlesque house. Although Marilyn landed a supporting role on the television drama *Bus Stop*, this wasn't exactly the triumphant comeback she had envisioned.

Dropping out of the series after appearing in only thirteen episodes, Maxwell cracked, "There was nothing for me to do but pour a second cup of coffee and point the way to the men's room."

By the early 1970s, the actress once proclaimed "the big new star of tomorrow" was making occasional guest appearances on television and supplementing her income by selling household cleaning products. Maxwell turned to Hudson for support—financial as well as emotional.

"My mom went through a period that a lot of actresses in the industry do," says Matt Davis. "You hit forty and all of a sudden, you find yourself saying, 'Where's the work?' After she had me, she gained a lot of weight and had trouble coming back. At one point, things were really tight and Rock helped her through it. She owed him money and he just forgave the debt. He said, 'Just don't worry about it.' And that was very much who Rock was. He helped my mom through some of her toughest times."

As she closed in on fifty, Marilyn was not only overwhelmed by career pressures but she was plagued by health problems—high blood pressure, pulmonary ailments, and myopia. Finally, in the spring of 1972, there was a glimmer of hope. Maxwell was offered a nightclub engagement at the Regency Hotel in Chicago. It was while preparing for this that she suffered a fatal heart attack. Matt Davis, only fifteen at the time, discovered his mother's body.

"When I came home and found my mother dead in the closet, I just went into shock," Davis remembers. "Thank God, my mother's secretary called Rock and he rushed over. Then he took me up to his own house for a couple of days. My father was away in Acapulco at the time and it was going to take him awhile to get back . . . Once again, Rock stepped in and took care of everything for us."

A frightening spectre comes staggering out of the jungle. His clothes are shredded. His beard is matted and overgrown. He is wild-eyed and looks totally deranged. Suddenly, he catches sight of the first human being he has seen in months. Startled, he repeatedly shoots at the stranger until he realizes he's firing at his own reflection in a murky river . . .

After reading this sequence from the screenplay of *The Spiral Road*, Rock was confident that he had found his most compelling project since *Giant*. In this adaptation of Jan de Hartog's 1957 novel, Hudson would play Anton Drager, an atheistic intern who journeys into the jungles of Java and battles leprosy, a gin-soaked predecessor, a menacing witch doctor, and above all, his own lack of faith.

Taking his cue from the earnest tone of the story, Hudson told a reporter that his portrayal of the spiritually bereft physician would be one of his "most crucial" characterizations. "To me, it's like a screen test for a new actor. It's my most serious part. The deepest. This calls for a different type of concentration." When asked to compare *The Spiral Road* with some of his earlier efforts, Rock was positive that this picture would tower above them all: "*Magnificent Obsession* was a serious picture, but I now feel it was a surface one." He wrote off *A Farewell to Arms* as "just a love story." Although he didn't share his feelings with the press, Hudson told friends that *The Spiral Road* presented him with such an acting stretch, it virtually guaranteed him an Oscar nomination. Provided he survived the shoot.

In June of 1961, Hudson, actor Burl Ives, director Robert Mulligan, and a second unit crew flew to Paramaribo, Surinam. In a press release, Universal described the exotic location as one of the most dangerous ever visited by a film company and for once, no exaggeration was necessary.

As the primary location was only five degrees north of the equator, Hudson and company endured suffocating humidity, torrential rain, crocodiles, and a constant swarm of fungus-carrying mosquitoes. Though he managed to soldier on without complaint, Rock would ultimately be undone not by the extreme local color but by the film itself—the dramatic highpoints of which were swamped by a rambling narrative and a heavy-handed approach to the protagonist's God problem. Though Hudson couldn't see it, the redemptive theme of *The Spiral Road* was essentially a long-winded variation on *Magnificent Obsession*, minus Douglas Sirk, Jane Wyman, and any sense of proportion.

Lost in the long, drawn-out mix is a solid, occasionally inspired Rock Hudson performance. In a scene in which Drager recalls how his father's abuse first caused him to doubt the existence of God, Rock is genuinely moving: "My father would roar hell and damnation at me until he was hoarse . . . He'd beat me regularly trying to teach me to love God." At one point, his eyes well up and he wears an expression somewhere between barely contained rage and sorrow. He's equally superb in a climactic sequence in which the obstinate doctor is abandoned by his team and left for dead in a remote jungle post. Beneath the crazy man makeup, Hudson conveys a real sense of desperation, exhaustion, and paranoia.

Though he had fully committed to what he perceived to be a worthy endeavor, Hudson would not be rewarded for his efforts. Upon its release in August 1962, *The Spiral Road* was widely panned. "Interminable" was the word most critics used to describe the 145-minute drama. The cast was alternately dismissed as either "routine" or "wasted." Only *Boxoffice*—hardly an arbiter of cinematic excellence—considered Hudson's performance "his finest to date."

After completing *The Spiral Road*, director Robert Mulligan started working on a project that Rock desperately wanted to be a part of—the highly anticipated screen adaptation of Harper Lee's Pulitzer Prize–winning bestseller, *To Kill a Mockingbird*. After guiding Hudson through the grueling challenges of *The Spiral Road*, Mulligan believed that Rock could convincingly play Atticus Finch, a compassionate Alabama attorney defending a black man falsely accused of raping a white woman. Although Universal acquired the rights to *Mockingbird* with Hudson in mind, producer Alan J. Pakula wanted Gregory Peck, who ended up not only filling the role but winning an Oscar for his portrayal.

Another missed opportunity was a proposed collaboration between Hollywood's most-sought-after star and America's greatest playwright. "I had a producer friend, Paul Nathan, who was very interested in working with Rock," recalls actor Earl Holliman, who had appeared with Hudson in *Giant*. "When Rock was still married to Phyllis Gates, Paul sent him the script of *Summer and Smoke*, hoping that Rock might want to do it because it had been written by Tennessee Williams. They were also trying to get Kate Hepburn for the female lead. Most actors would have jumped at this but Rock read the play and he said, 'I didn't understand it.' I think Rock sometimes shortchanged himself. He was brighter than he would let on but that was one picture that he really shouldn't have let slip away."

––––––––

It seemed appropriate that Rock Hudson would end up living in a house once occupied by the High Lama of Shangri-La. When character actor Sam Jaffe, who played the Lama in the 1937 classic *Lost Horizon*, decided to move to London, his luxurious estate, which was situated on a steep ridge overlooking Beverly Hills, suddenly became available as a rental. The timing couldn't have been better. Rock was starting to have problems with some of his neighbors in Newport Beach, while Universal was starting to have problems with Hudson's long commute to the studio in Burbank. Jaffe's magnificent home seemed to be the answer to everything.

Initially, Universal intended to lease the house for Hudson for a year—that is until Rock decided he had to own it. Spread out over three and a half acres and enclosed by cliffs on three sides, the 5,000-square-foot home offered privacy, sanctuary, and spectacular views of the Pacific Ocean and the San Gabriel Mountains. Lacking the capital to purchase the property himself, Hudson and Universal's chief executives made a deal. If Rock agreed to renew his contract for another five years, the studio would buy the house for him. Several of his friends advised Hudson against this but he ultimately consented. After his bosses shelled out $167,000 to Sam Jaffe, Rock Hudson had his dream home.

Originally, Rock wanted to call the house "Whiskey Hill," but this didn't seem majestic enough for either the sprawling Spanish-style mansion or its occupant, who had now inherited Clark Gable's title as "The King of Hollywood." From the beginning, 9402 Beverly Crest Drive would be known as The Castle. Some friends say that it was George Nader who christened it this, while others remember that it was Hudson himself who first referred to it this way.* Whatever the case, after years of bouncing around from one address to another, The Castle would become Rock's primary home for the rest of his life.

Even though it was love at first sight, Hudson knew that the house desperately needed a makeover. Working closely with architect Edward Grenzbach and designer Peter Shore, Rock's extensive remodeling of The Castle would be conducted with great care and perseverance. In fact, renovations, both large and small, would continue on and off for the next twenty years. Rock's "vision" was that the house should blend the natural and the architectural while emulating the unaffected charm and clean, classically inspired lines of Spanish colonial architecture.

"I have to say that of all the houses that I've been in, anywhere in the world, Rock's house was my most favorite," says friend Ken Jillson. "It was the warmest, the most inviting. I remember it had just this one big wooden door. When you walked through it, you were in this magnificent Spanish hacienda. I mean, to this day, I could sketch out the floor plan from memory. That's the kind of impression this house made on you. Once you had been there, you never forgot it."

---

*In his 1990 memoir, *Rock Hudson: Friend of Mine*, Tom Clark—a former resident of Hudson's home—denied that it was ever referred to as The Castle: "I never in my life heard anyone call it by that name . . . It was a large house, yes, but not austere, not ostentatious." When a friend of Rock's read this passage in Clark's book, he commented, "Old Tom must have really been into his cups when he wrote that chapter. *Everybody* called it The Castle."

In keeping with Mediterranean tradition, the horseshoe-shaped house was built around a courtyard, which was almost entirely canopied by an enormous olive tree. Even before entering the house, with its red clay–tiled roof, visitors were dazzled by the vibrant gardens. Clarence Morimoto, Rock's Japanese gardener, had not only worked for Sam Jaffe but had also tended rose bushes for President Eisenhower and Charlie Chaplin.

"Oh, my god, that house . . . it was just so beautiful," says Cathy Hamblin, younger sister of Hudson's longtime companion, Jack Coates. "Rock loved flowers and they were everywhere. There were azaleas. There were gardenias. It was so lushly planted. If you stayed over, Clarence would leave a little sprig of night blooming jasmine by your bed. I remember that Gypsy Rose Lee lived down the hill and you could hear the peacocks screaming all the way from her property. All of these things just made you feel like you were in another world. I'd look around at how stunning the house and grounds were and I'd think, 'How do you live like this without having those gates locked? Where are your body guards?' But the house was just like him. It just felt so open and accessible and welcoming."

Behind its thick, stuccoed walls, The Castle's twenty-seven rooms had been furnished so that a Spanish Conquistador would feel right at home. "Over ninety percent of the furnishings in his house, he had shipped over from castles and churches in either Spain or Portugal," says Hudson's estate manager, Marty Flaherty. "I still have the receipts for things like 17th century andirons and 18th century torch holders. He had this thing about wrought iron. I won't say that it was a fetish but it came close. There was wrought iron everywhere . . . candelabras and wall sconces. There were even these oversized balcony chairs that he loved that were wrought iron."

There were two living rooms, one of which housed matching nine-foot-long couches that had been specially designed for *Pillow Talk* to accommodate Hudson's elongated frame. Once production wrapped, Rock asked Ross Hunter if he could keep them. "Everything in that house was big and rugged and manly," says Cathy Hamblin. "There was all of this massive, hand-carved, gorgeous furniture. I remember the floor in his bar was in this herringbone pattern and it had all been cut out of two-by-fours. He told me he had done all of the work himself."

It was this kind of rustic, ultra-masculine style that prompted a friend to dub The Castle's décor "early butch." In fact, the house's most obvious nod to showbiz glamour was its state-of-the-art movie theatre, which Rock slyly referred to as "The Playroom" (a tribute to the nocturnal activities that sometimes occurred there).

"I couldn't believe it when he showed me his incredible movie theatre, which blew me away," says Ken Jillson, who was occasionally recruited to serve as projectionist. "The theatre had a raised hardwood stage with electric title curtains. The projection booth was in another room and he had two 35mm projectors. He'd say to me, 'Hey, I'm having some friends over. I'm going to run two movies and serve dinner in between. Why don't you run one and I'll run the other one.' The friends turned out to be Carol Burnett, Liv Ullman, Roddy McDowall, and Nancy Walker . . . that's quite an audience."

For someone who never cared for the stage name assigned to him, Rock delighted in christening virtually every part of his estate. His own bedroom was "The Blue Room." The guest bedroom, boasting a color scheme best described as "bordello red," was known as "Tijuana." There was also "The Zsa Zsa Gabor Bathroom," so named because of its over-the-top furnishings and dressing-room lighting encircling the mirror. Outside, there was "Ferndale," which was often used as an outdoor urinal, and "Assignation Lane," a shadowy, romantically lit pathway that was perfect for illicit meetings.

On and off, Hudson would spend some twenty-three years turning The Castle into something very special—a place that reflected his tastes and uniqueness—a sanctuary where he could be himself. After years of roaming, Rock had finally found home.

CHAPTER 13

STRANGE BEDFELLOWS

Rock, Kathy Robinson, and Harvey Lee Yeary (the future Lee Majors)
in the early 1960s. "Do you think Hollywood will spoil their marriage?"
Hudson asked his secretary.

oward the end of their marriage, Phyllis Gates had said to
Rock, "You have worked eight hard years on your career, and
because of your abnormal sex drive, you are destroying yourself." While Hudson was loath to admit it, at least on this
score, his ex-wife probably had a point. "How do you resist a
temptation when it occurs?" Rock had innocently asked Phyllis.
"Paint, read, keep busy," she responded. After they divorced, Hudson did find a hobby but, not surprisingly, it didn't involve turning

out watercolors in the basement. Instead, Rock's hyperactive libido led him into one of the most outrageous and inexplicable episodes of his life. Provided that the rumors are true, of course.

As with all things Rock Hudson, there is no definitive version of the story. Different people tell different tales of his alleged participation in a gay sex scandal involving the 1962 Kentucky Wildcats football team. "If you want to talk about queer ambiguity, Rock Hudson in central Kentucky is a great example of it because there are so many different stories floating around," says Dr. Jonathan Coleman, an historian of sexuality at the University of Kentucky.

What prompted Hudson to make repeated visits to Lexington at the very height of his career is a mystery. Was it a sudden interest in thoroughbreds that drew a busy movie star to a city known as the "Horse Capital of the World"? "The most common thing you hear is that Rock was in Lexington because of horses," says Coleman. "The horse industry draws a lot of prominent folks to the area. Someone of Rock's stature being in Lexington for that reason wouldn't be that surprising."

Although Rock's mother was known to "play the ponies," Hudson himself is not remembered as an especially devoted horse fan. There is another frequently repeated (and socially acceptable) explanation for Rock Hudson's interest in the "Bluegrass State." While Elizabeth Taylor was on location in central Kentucky with MGM's Civil War saga *Raintree County*, Hudson paid her an extended visit. The movie was largely shot in Danville and Paducah, but Rock took the opportunity to explore other parts of the state whenever Taylor was before the cameras. While sightseeing, he drifted over to Lexington and found it to his liking.

The third and most plausible reason for Rock's connection to Lexington has only recently come to light. "The story that most people haven't heard is that Rock Hudson was friends with a gay couple from Chicago, John Hill and Estel Willson, and they opened

The Gilded Cage,* which was Lexington, Kentucky's first actual gay bar," says Jonathan Coleman.

"I knew a lot of the older queens in town and I heard that Rock Hudson was one of the owners of this gay bar," says Lexington historian Robert Morgan. "That was the rumor going around for many years. What's more likely is that he was close friends with the people who owned it. Probably their name was on the business but his fingerprints were in there somewhere with financing. Or, when he came to town, he laid a sizeable amount of money on the bar to basically make it his clubhouse while he was in town."

It may have been through his Gilded Cage connections that Rock became acquainted with James Barnett, who like Hudson, was a study in contradictions. A former wrestler turned professional wrestling promoter, Barnett was openly gay and remarkably successful in what was typically an uber-macho field. The Oklahoma native with rapier wit and dapper style had once been described as "the Noel Coward of the National Wrestling Alliance." Those who knew Barnett remember him as an unforgettable figure—a rare individual who could discuss headlocks and choke holds as knowledgeably as he could expound on Picasso and Mozart.

Barnett was well off, having been one of the pioneers of televised wrestling. Even so, he liked to give acquaintances the impression that he was even wealthier than one might have guessed. Whether he actually came from old money or not, Barnett—who was typically attired in a three-piece suit—exuded an air of "to the manor born." So what if the Rolls Royce he rode around in was borrowed or that the driver was some college boy hard up for cash?

---

*The Gilded Cage was located at 224 East Main Street in Lexington. "That space has a long queer history," says historian Jonathan Coleman. "In 1939, a bar opened there called The Mayfair. It was a notorious bookie joint but remembered as being gay friendly. After The Mayfair closes, that same space is then known as The Southern Cocktail Lounge from 1953 to 1962. It wasn't queer operated but remembered as cruisy. In 1963, it becomes The Gilded Cage and it's operated by a gay male couple, who were apparently friends with Rock Hudson."

After Barnett and his longtime companion, Lonnie Winter, moved into a luxurious residence on North Lakewood Drive in Lexington, it was not only open house but according to some, open season. The couple began inviting college football players, hoopsters, and other athletes over for parties.

"This is how the whole scheme began," says Shannon Ragland, who extensively researched the University of Kentucky scandal for his book, *The Thin Thirty*. "It didn't begin quite as sinisterly as one might think. Jim and Lonnie had these amazing parties. The best food, the best drink . . . why wouldn't you go? Initially, I don't think it was a quid pro quo situation. At first, it was about getting these athletes comfortable and dependent . . . Obviously, Jim and Lonnie were interested in the better players—the stars, if you will, but they took what they could get. At these parties, they kept an eye out for boys of meager means or ones that seemed . . . conflicted."

In addition to plying the young jocks with lobster, unlimited booze, and stag films, Jim and Lonnie showered their favorites—or at least the more obliging athletes—with expensive gifts: suede jackets, leather shoes from Milan. This was heady stuff for a poor boy from Louisville or Harlan. "Of course, Lonnie and Jim's interest in these footballers wasn't altruistic," says Ragland. "They wanted to have sex with these guys. And they were willing to spend from their considerable fortune to accomplish that goal." Some of the athletes enjoyed the free food and drinks without succumbing to the sexual advances of their hosts; other guests were more amenable.

At some point, the exchange of sexual favors for lavish gifts detoured into what Ragland describes as a "more pedestrian and base prostitution scheme," with respect to the more willing young men. Each year, new team members were invited to the house on Lakewood Drive in an effort to indoctrinate them. Amazingly, the entire scheme was anything but a carefully guarded secret. "Everybody knew about Jim and Lonnie," says Ragland. "It was well known among central Kentucky college athletes that this was going on. As crazy as it sounds, it was not a secret."

While not denying that the parties occurred, historian Robert Morgan and others take exception with the portrayal of Barnett and Winter as diabolical predators: "The way that the story has been presented is that these naïve young men accidentally fell in with this band of vicious homosexuals, who were exploiting them. I know people who were at these parties and that's not the way it was at all," says Morgan. Referring to the most receptive of the college guests, Morgan explains, "One not-so-old queen I know was at these parties and involved with a lot of the football players. People that were there have said that everybody was having fun and really enjoying the sex."

As incredible as it sounds, the number one box office attraction in the world may have joined the party in the early 1960s. Among the locals, it soon became common knowledge that Rock Hudson was a regular guest at the Lakewood Drive house.* A social climber without equal, Jim Barnett loved nothing more than to be able to announce to his athletes, "Rock will be joining us this weekend . . ." Whenever Hudson arrived at the Cincinnati Airport, Barnett would dispatch a Rolls Royce (borrowed from his commentator, Sam Menacker) to pick him up. While several University of Kentucky players have confirmed that Hudson regularly attended the parties, they have been reluctant to say more.

"I never had a player admit to me, 'I had sex with Rock Hudson . . .' although I never asked one either," Ragland says of his interviews with surviving members of the Kentucky Wildcats. "I had very credible people describe to me what was happening, though." Several players recalled that it wasn't a rare event for Hudson to

---

*According to the late Pat Colby, who was Henry Willson's assistant, it was actually during a weekend trip to San Francisco in March of 1962 that Willson introduced Rock Hudson to Jim Barnett. The starstruck promoter invited the actor to spend some time at his estate. "Rock didn't want to go," Colby remembered, "but Henry talked him into it . . . you can only imagine what kind of men a guy who promotes and brokers athletes might have roaming around his house!"

pay a late-night call to Wildcat Manor, as the team's dormitory was known. A shiny Cadillac would pull up, ready to whisk new recruits off to Lakewood Drive. "One of the key justifications that I heard repeatedly from athletes was what they did with him didn't make them 'queer,'" says Ragland. "In fact, they thought they were pulling something over on Rock. To these guys, getting together with him was just an opportunity to make some quick cash."

Some players went along for the ride, others did not. John Helmers, the team's handsome halfback from Owensboro, remembered that one night he was summoned to the dorm's communal phone. Rock Hudson was waiting. As Ragland puts it, "This would have been as unthinkable then as it would be today if a freshman footballer picked up the phone and Tom Cruise was on the line, asking him out on a date."

Hudson invited Helmers to a party at Barnett's house and the young man accepted. However, unlike some of his teammates, Helmers immediately clued into what was expected of him. After his sole visit, the halfback declined subsequent invitations to return to Lakewood Drive. Despite this, Helmers would hear from Hudson again. While at home during holiday break, he received a Christmas card from Rock: $200 in cash was enclosed. Along with the money was a note, requesting that Helmers call him when he had returned to Lexington.

It seems unfathomable that the same Rock Hudson who narrowly missed being exposed in the pages of *Confidential*, and who apparently married to ensure box office survival, would risk everything this way. Only a couple of years earlier, Phyllis Gates had warned Rock that his promiscuity was adversely impacting his career. "The whole town is talking about your activities," Gates warned. "I've heard that one of the major studios doesn't consider you a good risk anymore."

But that was in Hollywood. In Lexington, behind closed doors, Hudson obviously felt that he didn't have to be as discreet. After all, he was among friends—or so he thought. Though once again, Rock was in for a rude awakening. It seems that a professional athlete with whom Hudson had a brief weekend fling had stars in his eyes. "I got a call from him one day," recalled Henry Willson's secretary, Betty Butler. "He said he wanted to talk to Henry. I asked him why, thinking he was just another actor who wanted to sign with the agency. Instead, he told me that he had proof that Rock Hudson was a homosexual."

In exchange for burying any incriminating evidence (rumored to be photographic), the ambitious young hunk wanted what any guy blessed with leading man good looks and backwater sex appeal wanted. "He wanted to be a movie star," said Pat Colby, Willson's assistant. After sizing up the athlete, Henry Willson could only agree that this jock had definite potential. As usual, Rock had impeccable taste.

With Willson pulling strings behind the scenes, the would-be blackmailer would go on to make his uncredited screen debut in a campy B-film. And thanks to Henry's unique brand of damage control, Rock had dodged yet another bullet. Though at times, didn't it seem as though Hudson wanted to be caught, wanted to be exposed? Had he convinced himself that personal betrayals and extortion attempts were a small price to be paid for occasionally being himself . . . for being human?

———

The next project to come Hudson's way was a taut service drama originally titled *A Man's Castle*. The story, which was eventually renamed *A Gathering of Eagles*, was set during the Cold War and concerned the stern, uncompromising wing commander of a Strategic Air Command Base just outside of San Francisco. Among the responsibilities on the commander's "to-do" list is ensuring that all military personnel and equipment are prepared to go to war at any given moment. The psychological pressures that result from the commander constantly being in close proximity to "the red phone"—which connects him to base control—were examined in depth in Robert Pirosh's screenplay.

Rock's character, United States Air Force Colonel Jim Caldwell, is an exacting, hard-nosed taskmaster who believes that "nothing short of perfection is acceptable." The ultimate alpha male, Colonel Caldwell is such a toughie that when his second-in-command, Colonel Hollis Farr (Rod Taylor), abandons his post to save Caldwell's life, Farr receives a harsh reprimand and not so much as a thank-you.

On the domestic front, the constant strain that Caldwell is under begins to adversely affect his marriage to his British wife, Victoria (Mary Peach). The situation deteriorates even further after Caldwell makes the unpopular decision to force an aging, alcoholic colonel, Bill Fowler (Barry Sullivan) into involuntary retirement. After Fowler's botched suicide attempt, Caldwell barks at him, "I sure had you pegged . . . You couldn't even do a good job of blowing your brains out."

To moviegoers who had become accustomed to a light and breezy Rock Hudson trading witticisms with Doris Day, *A Gathering of Eagles* would offer an almost startling contrast and provide its leading man with an important change-of-pace portrayal. The role of Caldwell's long-suffering wife also marked a transition for British actress Mary Peach, who had recently appeared in comedies like *Follow That Horse!* and *A Pair of Briefs*.

"Brave wives are awfully dull and difficult to play, actually," says Peach. Though in the original version of Robert Pirosh's screenplay, Peach's character was not only more complex but she was having an affair with her husband's best friend. Once cameras started rolling, it gradually dawned on Universal executives that this meant that Rock Hudson was not, in fact, the ultimate object of desire. This could never do. As director Delbert Mann remembered, "As we got further into the shooting, the studio became concerned . . . so they mandated changes, which meant that it was the duty that was interfering in the marriage and not another man."

"I think they cast an English wife because they didn't think it would be right for an American to behave that way," says Peach, who remembers her leading man as "lovely but nervous." As production on *Eagles* progressed, Peach wondered why Rock's sociability was limited to the set. He may have playfully referred to her as "Peaches La Tour," but he left it to his secretary to take his costar on a tour of Nevada City. After a few weeks of shooting, she eventually discovered why he was so guarded about his private life.

"His dresser and my dresser were great friends," says Peach. "And I said to my dresser, 'Now just tell me if I've done something to offend him. He's so polite, he's so nice but I've only seen him when we're working together.' And the dresser said, 'Well, *you know . . .*' And I said, 'Don't I know what?' And he said, 'Well, you know, he's got boyfriends . . .' I said, 'Well, fine, I'm married. So what's the big deal?' But in those days, you just couldn't come out. Rock was genuine in every way but it was just this beastly thing that he had to pretend to be a heterosexual . . . He was just so stunningly beautiful and so, he had to pretend to be this great Romeo."

Screenwriter Robert Pirosh felt that the cordial yet remote relationship between Hudson and his leading lady found its way onto the screen: "It was a classic example of miscasting . . . Julie Andrews was going to play the part, but the director, Delbert Mann, decided that . . . Andrews couldn't act, she could just sing. And they brought in an actress from England whom nobody had ever heard of. Her name was Mary Peach. There was no rapport between her and Rock Hudson . . . Technically, it was a good film about the air force, and the relationships of the men were good. It was just the husband and wife's relationship that didn't work very well."

Universal spared no expense in terms of providing the production with an air of authenticity. Beale Air Force Base in Marysville, California, doubled for the film's fictional Carmody Base. The Air Force's then Chief of Staff, General Curtis Lemay, allowed director Delbert Mann complete access to several key SAC facilities.

Despite the scrupulous attention to detail and Rock's committed performance, *A Gathering of Eagles* came up short when it was released in June of 1963. Some critics noted more than a passing resemblance between Hudson's latest and the WWII classic, *Twelve O'Clock High*. *Eagles* was basically *Fighter Squadron* some fifteen years later, with Rock promoted from anxious flyboy to commanding officer. Only a year after the release of *Eagles*, it's straightfaced, earnest exploration of doomsday scenarios would be sent up in Stanley Kubrick's devastating satire, *Dr. Strangelove or: How I Learned to Stop Worrying and Love the Bomb*.

It was while he was on location for *A Gathering of Eagles* that Rock received word that a friend had died. As Lois Rupert recalled, "Rock met me at his front door with the news . . . 'Monroe is dead' is all he said."

Only five months earlier, Rock and Marilyn Monroe had posed for photographers at the annual Golden Globe ceremonies. In images captured of the event, Monroe, who was named World Film Favorite, is beaming as Hudson enfolds her into a protective embrace. With a shared history of abuse and exploitation, it was inevitable that these two should be drawn to each other. Recognizing that he posed no sexual threat to her, Monroe had latched on to Hudson and had lobbied for Rock to costar with her in *Let's Make Love* as well as her uncompleted final film, *Something's Got to Give*.

Lois Rupert remembered that in the early 1960s, Rock regularly received late-night distress calls from Monroe as well as another troubled superstar. "If it wasn't Marilyn Monroe crying on his shoulder, then it was Judy Garland," Rupert recalled. "It was almost like they took turns. Marilyn would call one night and Judy the next. He was always very patient, very understanding with both of them, even though he wasn't getting much sleep. I think he liked playing the big brother who comes to the rescue."

Within ten months of Monroe's death, 20th Century-Fox would release a hastily assembled documentary entitled *Marilyn*. Fox had initially approached Frank Sinatra about narrating, but when the studio wasn't able to come to terms with the singer Hudson stepped in. Rock not only provided poignant commentary—both on and off camera—he donated his salary to help establish the Marilyn Monroe Memorial Fund at the Actors Studio.

————

When Universal took a look at the disappointing box office returns on *A Gathering of Eagles*, it was right back to a battle-of-the-sexes comedy for Hudson. *Man's Favorite Sport?*, as Rock's next effort was entitled, had started life as "The Girl Who Almost Got Away," a short story that had appeared in *Cosmopolitan*.

Pat Frank's tale concerned Roger Willoughby, a renowned fishing "expert" with a secret. At Cadwalader & Peel, the sporting goods house where Willoughby is employed, he is revered as the high priest of rods, reels, and lures. Neither his bosses nor his customers suspect that Willoughby is a complete fraud—for the author of *The Compleat Angler* has never been fishing in his life. When his superiors invite him to compete in a big tournament, Willoughby is overwhelmed. After confessing his secret to the daughter of a lodge owner, she gives Willoughby a crash course in fly casting while reeling him in romantically.

Slight as it may have been, the story caught the eye of director Howard Hawks, who envisioned a screen treatment as the first feature in a proposed three-picture deal with Paramount. In his heyday, Hawks had directed some of Hollywood's finest comedies, including *Twentieth Century, His Girl Friday*, and *Gentlemen Prefer Blondes*. After a run of action films, Hawks was ready to return to his screwball roots. *Man's Favorite Sport?* would be closely modeled on the director's earlier masterpiece, *Bringing Up Baby*. In fact, Hawks hoped to reunite the stars of that picture—Cary Grant and Katharine Hepburn—for this quasi-remake.

After Grant passed, Hawks squabbled with Paramount over casting and the director's deal with the studio fell apart. Convinced that *Man's Favorite Sport?* was a hot property, Universal executives were only too eager to acquire it along with Hawks as both producer and director. Instead of Cary and Kate, the film would now star Rock and relative newcomer Paula Prentiss.

As this was yet another comedy in which Hudson's character was pretending to be someone he wasn't, it should have been business as usual for Rock. Only this time, the tables would be turned off-screen as well. While Hudson admired Hawks and affectionately referred to him as "a rogue," he was disappointed that the director seemed to be sleepwalking his way through their collaboration. "He made very many brilliant films," Hudson said. "But it was like he'd given up. And, therefore, it was quite disillusioning. All of the jokes and comedic sequences were repeats of things he'd done in his various other films . . . I think the director reaches a dangerous time in his life when he feels that anything he does is the best. Without trying."

Hawks had some misgivings of his own. Overlooking the fact that Rock had already headlined a string of hit comedies, the director decided that his leading man was, in fact, comedically challenged. Hawks didn't seem to be looking for a performance so much as a full-fledged Cary Grant impersonation: "Rock tried hard, and he worked hard, he did everything he could, but Rock is not a comedian. When you have visualized one person in it, and you're trying to get that, it's an awful tough job because you just don't come out right."

For the first time in his career, Hudson was handed an outline of scenes instead of a complete script. He found it difficult to adjust to the sort of freestyle ad-libbing that Hawks encouraged. If this wasn't unsettling enough, Hudson was also thrown by his leading lady. According to Rock's secretary, he liked Paula Prentiss but found some of her work habits a trifle bizarre.

"Before she was signed, we had heard about her madcap antics when shooting a film, and then saw her do it," Lois Rupert remembered. "She would walk into the shot, and just after the director yelled, 'Roll 'em!,' she'd jump up and down, make faces, and anything else she could think of—to let go of tension, I guess, but it threw Rock. He found himself flubbing his lines and having to shoot scenes over. To correct the problem, he did exactly the same thing to her. She was stunned. It was the end of her antics, at least on Rock's show."

Reviews of *Man's Favorite Sport?* were mixed with overlength being cited as the film's primary fault. A number of contemporary critics, such as the "devout Hawksian" Erich Kuersten, feel that *Man's Favorite Sport?*, with its sly exploration of sexual ambiguity, is deserving of a reevaluation.

"This is really a comedy about the failure of artifice," says Kuersten. "One comes away realizing that *Man's Favorite Sport?* shares more than just character and setting similarities to Shakespeare's plays. Like them, the superficial trappings and comedic elements of the story may be dated to the point of antiquity, but the underlying themes are still too progressive for most of society to recognize."

———

It was in 1962 that Rock first spotted Lee Garlington. Twenty-four at the time, Garlington was in Hudson's words, "a head turner." Tall, blond, and virile, Garlington possessed the kind of striking looks and commanding presence that typically translated into a seven-year contract with a major studio.

"I wanted to be a western movie actor because Randolph Scott was my childhood hero," Garlington says. "So, I landed in Hollywood in 1961 and realized that I was kind of pretty, which helped my chances but what I didn't realize was that I didn't have any talent. Not only that, but my family was slightly to the right of Adolf Hitler. I had been brought up ultra-conservative in Atlanta. So, when I hit Hollywood Boulevard, it scared the hell out of me. These people seemed so off the wall and avant-garde for 1961 that I really sort of freaked out. In those days, I was much too inhibited to become an actor but I wanted to get away from Atlanta and my domineering parents and strike out on my own. Because I loved westerns, Hollywood was the place I wanted to go."

Once there, Garlington discovered that "Hollywood in those days was quite gay. I mean, in West Hollywood there was practically a gay bar in every corner and several of them had been there for years by the time I hit town." Then, as now, a primary topic of conversation over cocktails was which movie stars were locked in the closet. "Rock Hudson certainly wasn't the only gay star in Hollywood in those days but he was the one that everybody seemed most interested in," Garlington says.

While working as an extra for the Universal television series *The Virginian*, Garlington heard more gossip about the studio's top star. "Around the lot, everyone either knew or strongly suspected that he was gay," says Garlington. "By that time, it was pretty much an open secret around town but because everybody loved Rock and they wanted to protect him, there was what I would describe as this conspiracy of silence going on. One of the reasons he wasn't outed was because on the set, he treated the lowest level gaffer or script girl with respect and kindness and friendship. And, trust me, most of the big stars couldn't be bothered."

Typically, movie stars and extras didn't interact unless a scene dictated it, but Garlington was determined to meet Universal's resident heartthrob. "Word kind of got out among us peons that Rock Hudson was on the lot making a movie," Garlington remembers. "The big stars had their own private cottages, so I decided I'd go hang out by his. I figured I'd check him out if he came in for lunch. And sure enough, he did. As he walked by, he never once looked in my direction, which was kind of depressing. But when he came back out . . . I remember he was walking away and he suddenly turned and looked back at me."

Rock liked what he saw. His interest piqued, Hudson did some checking. He asked around and found out who the handsome extra was—the one who had been loitering outside of his bungalow, pretending to be engrossed in *Variety*. When the word came back that Garlington was already involved with someone, Hudson held off in terms of pursuing him. "That was very much Rock," Garlington says. "Never pushy. Never pulled movie star rank. He was always thoughtful and a real gentleman."

The following year, Garlington gave up on acting and became a stockbroker. Around that time, there were also changes in his domestic situation. He broke up with the young man he had been living with and moved into his own apartment in West Hollywood. Once Hudson learned that Garlington was single, he came calling again.

"He invited me over and the first time I knocked on his door, I was terrified," Garlington recalls. "Nothing happened that night but he understood what was going on and why I was so nervous. He was very understanding. Very patient. Then he invited me back again and we just sort of fell into a relationship. From the beginning, it was understood that I could not move in. That would be too dangerous. We also could not be seen in public together. Being gay and working for a stock brokerage company—the squarest of the square in Beverly Hills—I was playing a double role myself."

Garlington remembers that on the rare occasions when he and Rock ventured out, everything had to be carefully choreographed. "If we wanted to go to a movie, Rock would call over to a theater in Westwood. He'd talk to the manager and they would reserve two seats on the very end, next to an exit door. They'd leave the exit door partially open and we'd slip in just as the house lights went down. After the movie was over, we'd have to jump up and run like hell. Otherwise, he would be mobbed by dozens of fans. They would circle around him, asking for his autograph. Then they would look over at me and say, 'Are you somebody?' And that used to piss me off. Once I answered, 'Yeah, I'm Troy Donahue . . .' and they believed it. For the first few weeks, all of the sneaking around and hiding we had to do was exciting but afterwards, it was hell."

Garlington says that at least during the period they were together, Rock did his best to avoid crowds and social gatherings. "We were not around very many gay boys, as I remember. We didn't have gay parties. For the sake of his career, he felt obligated to have one or two parties a year and invite all these Hollywood people and he hated it."

Usually, the world's most glamorous movie star could be found at home, outfitted in dungarees and a well-worn pair of Thom McAn moccasins. Rock and Lee would watch the news together or they would screen one of the movies Hudson had in his private collection. "I usually requested a western," Garlington says. Whenever Hudson's work schedule allowed, the quiet evenings at home alternated with road trips to secluded locations. "We took a trip to Puerto Vallarta," Garlington says. "It was just the two of us and it was one of our best times . . . There was this great house on the beach that Elizabeth Taylor always used whenever she was staying there. At that point in his career, Rock needed that kind of escape from all of the pressures he was under. I mean, it's a wonder that he didn't break more often than he did."

After an extended tour of Canada, Hudson and Garlington returned home and learned that a bizarre incident had taken place while they were away. "When we came back from a trip to Lake Louise, we discovered that a woman[*] had broken into his house and slept in his bed," Garlington recalls. Dorothy Jean Strashinsky, a thirty-two-year-old housewife from Anaheim, brought her five-year-old daughter, Deborah, along when she spent the night in Hudson's home. Strashinsky said that she was in love with Rock and admitted to sampling some of his liquor as well as helping herself to a few "souvenirs." Police found Hudson's passport, address books, and personal photos in her car. Although she had made a clean sweep of it, Strashinsky had somehow overlooked the motherlode.

[*]In January of 1964, Dorothy Jean Strashinsky told *Photoplay* why she felt compelled to break into Hudson's home. In an article titillatingly titled "I Slept in Rock Hudson's Bed," Strashinsky described events that led up to her being arrested and losing her job. Despite the controversy, Strashinsky didn't seem very remorseful: "In a way, it was worth it . . . I'm the only Rock Hudson fan in the world who's ever slept in his bed!"

"Inside a drawer in his bedside table, he kept all of these pictures of me without a shirt on," says Garlington. "In some of the shots, I may have had even less on. But she never found them. Just imagine if she had gotten a hold of those photos. That could have ended everything for him right there."

Despite the fact that Hudson would later refer to Lee as his "one true love," Garlington eventually decided to end his relationship with Rock, though they would remain friends into the early 1970s. Reflecting on their split, Garlington admits, "I am a very independent kind of guy and the fault was more mine than his . . . Before things came apart, I remember he went all the way to Atlanta and met my family. Rock particularly liked my father. He was always looking for a father figure and so was I. That was part of our problem. At least in the beginning, I thought that Rock was the only one that was big enough and strong enough to be the father image for me that my own father had not been. It turns out that he wasn't."

When Hudson found out that Garlington had started seeing other people, he was extremely upset. George Nader said that in all the years that he had known Rock, he had never seen him so distraught over a breakup. Fifty years after they went their separate ways, Lee says he didn't realize how much Rock had invested in their relationship: "He had a lot of boyfriends before me, and of course, a lot of boyfriends after me. I didn't necessarily think that I was just one of the mill but Rock was an actor. He was more than capable of acting like he was in love. At the time, I just took it all with a grain of salt . . . Rock never said what his feelings really were. If I had known how much he really cared, things might have been different for us. I'm not sure."

IT WASN'T ONLY obsessed fans who turned up at The Castle. Rising star Lee Majors occasionally visited. Hudson and Majors had met a few years earlier and quickly formed what columnists would term a "mysterious friendship." In fact, their association was shrouded in such mystery, that Majors's publicist, Paul Bloch, once denied that the two actors even knew each other. Shown photographic evidence to the contrary, Bloch resorted to the cornered publicist's default response: "No comment."

After Majors became a regular on the ABC series *The Big Valley*, one intrepid journalist was tasked with finding out how "the luckiest of blond young Hollywood gods" had risen through the show business ranks so swiftly. After all, just a couple of years before, Majors had been working for the Los Angeles County Parks & Recreation Department. "The truth of the matter is that Lee was first 'discovered' and helped along to sudden stardom by none other than Rock Hudson," a fan magazine reported in 1966.

Majors had grown up as Harvey Lee Yeary in Middleboro, Kentucky. According to one magazine profile, "Handsome, blond Lee, six feet tall and a football star, strolls into a restaurant in Richmond. A friend greets Lee. And with the friend is . . . Rock Hudson." Even while reporting this, the author of the profile admitted that it sounded like quintessential "Hollywood hyperbole."

In a more plausible account, a mutual friend—described as "a professor at Eastern State"—introduced Hudson and Yeary at a party. "That's basically the same story I heard," says Lee Garlington. "Rock occasionally visited some friend's house in Kentucky. After a few of these visits, he suddenly became a big fan of the Eastern Kentucky football team. Rock supposedly partied with some of the guys on the team . . . and Lee Majors was one of them."

Regardless of how Hudson and Yeary connected, once they had, Rock couldn't have been more attentive. Close friends believe that he was infatuated with Harvey Lee, who appealed not only to Rock's physical aesthetic but also to his sense of obligation. Yeary had lost both of his parents in separate accidents before the age of two. While playing college football, he suffered a spinal injury resulting in temporary paralysis. With his dreams of gridiron glory shattered, Harvey Lee turned his attention to the dramatic arts.

The help Hudson provided may have included financing Yeary's acting classes at the Pioneer Playhouse in Danville. Even if he didn't help Yeary financially, Rock regularly corresponded with the theatre's founder, Colonel Eben C. Henson, who provided glowing reports of Harvey Lee's progress: "I would say that your faith in him will be rewarded, for I predict if given the breaks he could achieve acclaim in the movie industry."

For a photogenic newcomer like Harvey Lee, relocating to the West Coast was essential. After all, star-struck hopefuls boarded buses bound for Los Angeles every day. Though they didn't usually have a family in tow. Harvey Lee not only had a pretty young wife named Kathy Robinson but at the tender age of twenty-three, the former football star had become a father for the first time. All three Yearys would become Rock's houseguests for a while. Rock's secretary would often babysit while Rock took Harvey Lee and Kathy out on the town. Lois Rupert remembered them as "an idyllic couple and so incredibly in love."

During this period, Hudson bankrolled Harvey Lee's appointments with doctors, dentists, and acting coaches. Hudson's old friend, the agent Dick Clayton, took the young man on as a client and before too long, it was goodbye, Harvey Lee Yeary. Hello, Lee Majors. At the time, Majors made no attempts to hide the fact that Rock Hudson was his mentor. In a magazine layout from early in Lee's career, one image shows him completing some household chores. Prominently displayed on the wall behind him is a framed photograph of Rock.

Shortly after Majors's Hollywood career was launched, rumors began circulating that Lee and Kathy, the most delightful couple to hit town in years, were getting ready to split. As Lois Rupert recalled, "Rock asked me one day, 'Do you think Hollywood will spoil their marriage?'" The question proved to be prescient. As Rupert recalled, "After Harvey Lee became Lee Majors, he and Kathy were divorced."

None of the domestic drama impeded Lee's progress, however.

Within a few years, Majors would be headlining his own hit series, *The Six Million Dollar Man*. In 1973, Lee wed Farrah Fawcett, resulting in a marriage made in pop culture heaven. By this time, any association with Rock may have started to feel too close for comfort. By the mid-1980s, Majors was still maintaining a high profile via another hit series, *The Fall Guy*, but he was conspicuously absent from Hudson's life at a time when his former benefactor could have really used some support. This was not lost on one columnist with an especially long memory:

"Rock Hudson put Lee Majors on the road to fame and fortune . . . but as the AIDS-stricken actor fought for his life, Majors was not among the celebrities—including Liz Taylor, Roddy McDowall and Nancy Walker—who were rushing to his bedside. As the superstar lay dying, his protégé was nowhere to be seen."

––––––––––

For once, Universal was in violation of its own "If it ain't broke, don't fix it" policy. The winning formula that had turned *Pillow Talk* and *Lover Come Back* into gigantic hits for the studio would be tampered with for the third and final Rock Hudson and Doris Day teaming.

Send Me No Flowers, which started shooting in December of 1963, was based on a Broadway fizzle of the same name by Norman Barasch and Carroll Moore. The stage version mustered only forty performances and garnered tepid reviews: "*Send Me No Flowers* is one of those popular comedies that hang a lot of baby jests around a papa joke, and that drive a rachitic bit of plot literally to the graveyard," said *Time*.

Despite the obvious red flags, *Send Me No Flowers* was judged the ideal vehicle to bring Hudson, Day, and Tony Randall back before the cameras. Norman Jewison had recently directed Day in *The Thrill of It All*, which had turned a tidy profit for Universal. As a thank-you, the studio entrusted him with their top stars for *Send Me No Flowers*.

Unlike *Pillow Talk* and *Lover Come Back*, which took place in a chic and glittering Manhattan, *Send Me No Flowers* is set in deepest suburbia, where the milkman keeps track of which customers are about to divorce. George Kimball, an electronics executive, is a highly neurotic hypochondriac who frequently mistakes indigestion for cardiac arrest. "Do you ever read the obituary page?" Kimball asks his long-suffering wife, Judy. "It's enough to scare you to death."

One afternoon, Kimball overhears his overburdened physician discussing another patient's terminal prognosis and assumes the bad news concerns his own defective ticker. Believing that he's only weeks away from his own expiration date, Kimball enlists the aid of his best friend in finding an able-bodied substitute husband for his wife: "I want a man who can afford to give Judy all the things I went into debt for."

When Kimball suddenly starts encouraging his wife to spend time with other men, a dismayed Judy suspects that he's having an affair. In another sharp detour from the previous Rock-Doris vehicles, *Send Me No Flowers* begins with the eternal bachelor and the perennial virgin already hitched. If much of the fun of the first two outings had been concerned with their game of cat and mouse, death hovers over the third installment from start to finish.

"*Send Me No Flowers* is so much weaker than the other two films they made together," says film historian Thomas Santopietro. "There is no chase. And all of Doris's great energy is gone. She simply has no task. She's just the helpmate listening to Rock, this guy we've always liked, who this time out spends two hours whining about his health. So, the underpinnings of the movie are all wrong, both in terms of what we've come to expect from them and for their personae."

About the only thing that works in *Send Me No Flowers* are the satellite characters orbiting about the weary leads. Clint Walker, the massive star of the Western series *Cheyenne*, appears midway through as Judy's college sweetheart, Bert Power. In one of the film's best sight gags, the six-foot-six Walker extricates himself from a sports car that redefines compact.

Paul Lynde is a hoot as Mr. Akins, the funeral director at Green Hills Mortuary ("Truly a Home Away from Home"). In their scenes together, Rock Hudson and Paul Lynde embody the flip sides of the homosexual male circa 1964. Hudson, the straightest acting gay man in the history of cinema, stands in sharp contrast to Lynde, the effeminate cream puff. In essence, both have their own drag show going on—Hudson as uber-butch Apollo, Lynde as snappy swish. Straight clone or sexless pansy. Take your pick, boys.

If *Pillow Talk* had introduced audiences to one of the great screen teams while hinting at even better things to come, *Lover Come Back* more than made good on that promise. Alas, *Send Me No Flowers* single-handedly broke the spell. While intermittently amusing, it loses steam long before the end credits appear. "For Rock Hudson and Doris Day, the third time is no charm," wrote the critic for *Cosmopolitan*. "*Send Me No Flowers* is very warmed over yesterday's mashed potatoes . . . the glamorous, highly paid box office bomb-shells can't even fall back on their much-vaunted physical charms in this film. He looks bored and flabby, and she has a genuine right to shoot her hairdresser and cameraman."

The reviews may not have been glowing, and while Rock made no bones about what he considered to be a distasteful comedy about death, this didn't seem to matter a wit to the ticket-buying public, who turned *Send Me No Flowers* into an even bigger hit than *Lover Come Back*.

AS *COME SEPTEMBER* had raked in millions for Universal, the studio wasted no time in reteaming Rock and Gina Lollobrigida in *Strange Bedfellows*, a comedy written, produced, and directed by Melvin Frank. With *The Reformer and the Redhead* and *The Facts of Life* to their credit, Frank and writing partner Norman Panama cornered the market writing lightweight, battle-of-the-sexes comedies featuring Hollywood's top stars.

Rock was cast as Carter Harrison, an American sales manager for the British division of Inter-Allied Petroleum Products. On his first day in London, Harrison is accidentally assaulted by Toni Vincente (Lollobrigida), part-time painter and full-time protestor. The couple impulsively marries but soon discovers that they are largely incompatible. They agree to go their separate ways and after a seven-year estrangement, they finally decide to divorce.

When Carter and Toni reunite in their divorce lawyer's office, sparks are rekindled and this leads to a passionate reconciliation. The afterglow quickly fades, and the couple is suddenly reminded that their marriage fell apart because they "agreed on nothing— politics, polygamy, peanut butter, Pushkin—you name it." Besides, Toni has a new man and fellow activist in her life, the free-thinking bohemian Harry Jones (Edward Judd). Both are charter members of the International Society for Freedom of Artistic Expression.

Strange Bedfellows is the kind of innocuous, old-fashioned romp in which characters still initiate a chase by hollering, "Follow that cab!" While it's the wispiest kind of fluff, the picture does offer a few fleeting compensations. In a sequence that reportedly cost $85,000, Lollobrigida paraded through Soho Square as Lady Godiva. Attempting to stop the exhibitionistic spectacle, Rock incites a riot. "Yankee Doodle Flips His Noodle," reads the resulting headline.

In another jaw-dropping scene (at least for 1965), Rock's character and Harry Jones wind up in bed together. Although played for laughs, actor Edward Judd is as masculine as Hudson is. When Rock and prissy Tony Randall end up in bed together in *Send Me No Flowers*, it's sitcom cute. When Hudson and another he-man hit the sheets, one wonders how they ever sneaked the sequence past the eagle-eyed Production Code.

Character actor Joseph Sirola, who was cast as the expressionist sculptor Petracini, recalls that on his first day of shooting, there was a gift basket and several bottles of vodka waiting for him in his dressing room.

"There was a note attached," remembers Sirola. "It said, *'Welcome aboard! What a pleasure to be working with a Broadway actor. I hope you will have as much fun as I know I will. Best Regards, Rock.'* . . . When we shot our first scene together, Rock said to me, 'Joe, listen, when you turn toward me, I'm blocking your light. So, step out so that you get the full light on you during your close-up.' Can you imagine? I mean, most stars like the fact that you've been left in the dark. The man was a class act in every way."

In sharp contrast, Sirola found that the film's leading lady lived up to her reputation as a temperamental beauty. When questioned by reporters about Lollobrigida's rumored peevishness, Hudson did his best to defend her: "We did two films . . . the second one was made away from her home in a foreign country. She speaks English quite well but she doesn't have a mastery . . . So, it was not as pleasant. She was uncomfortable here. But *Come September* was fun."

Almost unanimously, the critics concurred. Things weren't quite as wonderful the second time around. The *New York Times* dismissed *Strange Bedfellows* as a "generally labored and witless film . . . Gina Lollobrigida can't do much without a script. Mr. Hudson is likewise disadvantaged, but he seems to need direction more than lines. It's not easy to stand up there bravely and take pizzas, paint, and hot air in the face."

———

In 1964, Rock was introduced to Tom Clark, the man who would prove to be the most significant of all of his significant others. Within a few short years, Clark would become the most important individual in Hudson's life—personally and professionally. When the two first met, however, it didn't feel like an especially momentous occasion. As Clark later reported: "Rock Hudson . . . did not send icy fingers up and down my spine."

While there are bluer, bawdier accounts of how Rock and Tom first connected, the official version is a model of *Ladies' Home Journal* respectability. Publicist Pat Fitzgerald needed a fourth for bridge, so she called Clark. Midway through the game, Rock appeared unexpectedly. He had remained close to Fitzgerald and her partner, Lynn Bowers, since their sailing days in Newport Beach.

At first glance, the thirty-four-year-old Oklahoma native seemed the least likely candidate to fill the coveted position of Rock Hudson's longtime companion. Clark—though tall and pleasant-looking—was far from Rock's favorite flavor of blond Adonis. If Hudson's previous lovers had been rugged, outdoorsy types, Clark's natural habitat seemed to be the recreation deck of the *Queen Elizabeth II*, where he could be found sipping chilled martinis.

"Tom had this very 'Thurston Howell the Third' type personality," says friend Marty Flaherty. "Very grandiose. He would correct my speech, he would correct how I sat. Like if I was sitting with my legs too wide open . . . I remember Tom would say things like, 'Honestly, Martin, what are we going to do with you?' Then he would turn to Rock and say, 'We've really got to primp this bitch.'"

Equipped with a take-charge personality and take-no-prisoners directness, Clark wasn't known for holding his tongue, but in those rare instances when he did, he still managed to get his point across. "Uncle Tom's philosophy was . . . there's really nothing you can't say to someone, it's all in the way you say it," says niece Cindy Clark. "Once he said to me, 'Cindy, you must take after the Green's side of the family with your body structure.' That was his way of saying I was eating too much."

Tom's nephew, Ray Clark, remembers his uncle as "very stern and in a strange way, cruel with his words. He would hold nothing back to correct you." Though Ray also says that his uncle was "the backbone of the Clark family. I always felt that he was somewhat embarrassed by us, but I also knew that he loved us . . . He was the guy who got things done and kept track of everything. That's the way he was with us and after they got together, that's the way he was with Rock."

As Hudson and Clark got to know each other, they realized they had far more in common than either might have expected. Both had grown up during the Depression. Both had been in the service, though Clark's career in the Air Force was abruptly cut short when his superiors discovered that he was gay. Explicit letters that Clark had received from fellow officers and sergeants were confiscated and he was subjected to a humiliating psychiatric evaluation while stationed at Ellington Air Force Base.[*] After agreeing to an undesirable discharge, Clark was forced out of the Air Force in 1953. At one point, Clark, like Hudson, had caved to societal pressures and married.

More than anything else, Hudson and Clark shared an all-encompassing obsession with show business. Unlike Rock, Tom actually enjoyed some early success as an amateur thespian, winning a Maskers Award for his role in his senior class play. "He could have gone to the top," said Maybelle Conger, Clark's high school drama coach. However, once he was enrolled at the University of Oklahoma, Clark would shift his attention to literary pursuits, determining that "One day, I would write a novel that would sweep the world off its feet . . . the Great International Novel, never mind just American."

Like Hudson, Clark also had a penchant for self-invention. In his memoir, he claims that he graduated from the University of Oklahoma. In reality, he flunked out after a couple of years. Though after this, Clark did manage to land a writing job. But from the moment he started working as a rookie in the public relations department of the Union Oil Company in Houston, he felt trapped. Having spent the day waxing rhapsodic about the octane content of gasoline, the last thing Clark wanted to do was go home and pound

---

[*]On November 25, 1952, Arthur M. Sternberg, Ellington's psychiatric chief, conducted an evaluation of air cadet Tommy Clark and determined: "It is quite evident that this individual has certain homosexual impulses which have not been kept under control . . . It seems that his homosexual experiences may be construed more as evidence of his immaturity than as evidence of a homosexual adjustment." The following day, Clark agreed to accept an undesirable discharge.

out a novel. Bored and frustrated, Tom was relieved when his job was transferred to the West Coast. Hollywood—which had once seemed as unreachable as Oz—was now right in his own backyard.

Realizing that he wasn't destined for stardom, Clark settled for the next best thing. After swapping Union Oil for MGM, Tom diligently worked his way up from office boy to senior publicist. Whether he was escorting a legend like Greer Garson to a preview of *The Singing Nun* or ballyhooing a new discovery like Chad Everett, Clark was exactly where he wanted to be—among the beautiful people. "Stars—he loved the stars," recalled Clark's fellow publicist, Matthew West.

And now, on a rare evening off, Tom found himself shuffling the deck for the biggest star of them all—Rock Hudson. Everybody made a fuss over Rock. Clark would distinguish himself by playing it cool. As Tom knew, showing a star that you weren't the slightest bit interested in them was sometimes the surest way to get their attention. And despite his simulated disinterest, Clark was interested in Hudson—*very* interested.

Tom had heard all about Rock's steady diet of blond, blue-eyed stunners and how Hudson tended to devour them like potato chips. Gorgeous boys were a dime a dozen in L.A. and they didn't bother Tom as much as the fact that Hudson occasionally slipped and made reference to "Lee," who sounded neither like a quick fling nor a colleague in the industry. Was Rock living with someone? And then there was Clark's own domestic situation to consider—he also had a partner, a banking executive by the name of Pete DePalma.[*]

For the moment, Hudson was nothing more than Clark's bridge partner. Though if anyone knew how to turn a handshake into a contractual commitment, it was Tom. The fine print could all be

---

[*]A New York native, Peter DePalma served time in jail after he was convicted of embezzling from City National Bank. DePalma later became a personal assistant to a number of celebrities, including Rod McKuen, Brenda Vaccaro, and Michael Douglas. In 1967, DePalma worked for Rock Hudson in a similar capacity, having been given access to a number of Hudson's accounts.

worked out in time. Although Rock Hudson didn't know it yet, he had met his match in Tom Clark.

———————

After hitting the sheets with virtually the entire cast of *Strange Bedfellows*, Rock found himself right back in bed for yet another Universal sex comedy scripted by Stanley Shapiro. At this point, the studio's production team had the *Pillow Talk* formula down pat: Cast Hudson as an insatiable ladykiller who tangles with the modern-day equivalent of a vestal virgin. Make his prey undeniably attractive though frigid (the sort of uptight career woman who's been spending too much time in the boardroom and not enough in the bedroom). Then, in an effort to seduce the recalcitrant young lady, have an unquestionably virile Rock masquerade as a sexually defective nebbish in immediate need of fixing. Add a finicky Tony Randall type to the mix as the virgin's totally unsuitable suitor. Liberally sprinkle with one-liners and sight gags and then sit back and start tallying up the box office receipts.

In *A Very Special Favor*, Leslie Caron would play the kind of character Doris Day had practically patented. Caron's Dr. Lauren Boullard is a hypercritical psychotherapist whose mother-dominated, apron-wearing fiancé is a former hairdresser named Arnold Plum (Dick Shawn, assuming the Tony Randall role). Boullard's attorney father, Michel (Charles Boyer) begs his playboy pal Paul Chadwick (Hudson) to "save" his daughter from her forthcoming marriage to her effeminate intended. "Try the Red Cross . . . she sounds like a disaster area" is Chadwick's reply.

Eventually, Chadwick relents and becomes Caron's most demanding client. Describing himself as a "love toy," Chadwick reveals that he is wholly irresistible to sex-crazed women. It's to the point where he must barricade himself inside his apartment. "Hiding in closets isn't going to cure you," the good doctor tells Chadwick. "Your anxieties about women are reaching the psychotic stage." Within days, Chadwick has transitioned from his analyst's couch to her penthouse.

Playing to Lauren's savior complex, Chadwick attempts to reel her in by posing as a homosexual. Dr. Boullard will now have to "save" her patient from a motel rendezvous with his "boyfriend," who is really a female switchboard operator in drag.

What could Rock have possibly thought about these scenes while he was shooting them? The conflicts that he grappled with daily and the deadening silence he had to endure in order to maintain his position as Hollywood's most popular leading man were, in a sense, being played for laughs in *A Very Special Favor*. As inconceivable as it seems, Hudson's personal life had now been cannibalized by his own studio; his torment over his predicament had become the ultimate Hollywood in-joke. As Vito Russo noted in *The Celluloid Closet*, his landmark study of gays in movies: "[Rock's] masculinity is on trial throughout the film, its authenticity under constant scrutiny."

Throughout production, leading lady Leslie Caron was all too aware of Hudson's dilemma: "He offered a totally smooth surface, so that his sexual inclination couldn't be detected," Caron says. "The fact that he chain-smoked was indicative of the incredible stress caused by this dissimulation . . . he rubbed his thumbnails constantly, so that they were completely deformed, as if smashed by a hammer. He felt embarrassed, as if these nails could reveal his true leanings. He was grateful when I suggested that he glue on false ones for filming."

Before *A Very Special Favor* was released in the summer of 1965, Hudson asked director Michael Gordon to delete some of the racier sequences. This included one scene in which his swinging bachelor phones two girls simultaneously, promising both that he'll be over later. These antics prompt Charles Boyer's character to remark, "Even Napoleon wouldn't have attempted two invasions at once . . . you must have some French blood in you." The scene stayed and Rock wasn't happy. "What bothers me is that kids will see this movie," Hudson told the *New York Daily News*. "The idea of 11 and 12-year-olds sitting through two hours of bedroom talk doesn't appeal to me."

According to the *New York Times*, Rock had nothing to worry about: "It is hard to imagine who else could make a movie about sin and seduction that is as incredibly sexless and apple-pie moral as *A Very Special Favor*," wrote Richard F. Shepard in his mixed review. "A most contrived plot is not for children but is rather mild for grown-ups. As a sexy frolic, this one's about as debauched as an old Andy Hardy episode."

Even though *A Very Special Favor* opened strong and garnered its share of encouraging reviews, the picture left a sour aftertaste for its star: "The things I had to do to Leslie Caron were cruel. They weren't funny." Thankfully, Hudson's next picture offered a welcome change of pace from his string of sex comedies.

Thanks largely to the tremendous success of its 1964 Audrey Hepburn–Cary Grant caper film, *Charade*, Universal would release a spate of stylish 1960s thrillers that featured sinister goings-on, narrow escapes, and one word titles: *Mirage, Gambit, Arabesque, Blindfold*. The last of these being reserved for Rock Hudson, whom the studio decided, would look especially debonair in a spy spoof. As with the other Universal suspense films it closely resembled, *Blindfold* was Hitchcock Lite in tone. And like its predecessors, *Blindfold* featured an especially convoluted plot.

Dr. Bartholomew Snow, a Manhattan-based psychologist, is recruited by the CIA to assist in a top-secret military operation. While blindfolded, Snow is taken to "Base X," where he is asked to counsel neurotic scientist Arthur Vincenti (Alejandro Rey), keeper of state secrets. After discovering that his contacts are actually enemy agents, Snow sets out to rescue Vincenti. While fending off counterintelligence operatives and slinking through alligator-infested swamps, Snow is aided by Vincenti's sister, a "ballet dancer" employed at *Le Go Go*.

Tunisian beauty Claudia Cardinale was cast as Rock's fiery love interest, Vicki Vincenti. Before *Blindfold*, Cardinale had shared scenes with several Hollywood stars appearing in European productions, including Burt Lancaster, John Wayne, and David Niven.

While Cardinale enjoyed appearing alongside all of them, Rock Hudson would emerge as her favorite leading man.

"From the first day I met him, I knew we were going to be great friends," Cardinale says. "For me, Rock was just a fantastic man. Very sweet. Very intelligent. I did two movies with him and even when we weren't working, we were always together. When we did *Blindfold*, I had a house in California and he was always there. We'd have lunch or dinner together. Just the two of us. Talking and laughing. He really became one of my best friends . . . in so many ways, this was a man to treasure."

As *Blindfold* bounced between New York and central Florida, Hudson and Cardinale found plenty of time to bond during lengthy location shoots. While filming in Ocala's swamp region, Rock's leading lady attempted to get chummy with another of her costars—a thirteen-foot alligator that weighed over a thousand pounds. "I'm a bit crazy, huh? We were shooting the scene in the river and they were getting this big caiman ready to follow us. I bent down to kiss him and Rock went wild. He was really afraid and he pulled me aside and said, 'Claudia, are you out of your mind . . . what the hell are you doing?' But I like danger. When I made *Circus World*, I kissed all of the lions."

Like Vera-Ellen and Marilyn Maxwell before her, Cardinale would be touted as a potential "Mrs. Rock Hudson." Almost from the very moment they were introduced, the press started counting the days until a wedding date was set. Cardinale acknowledges that her relationship with Hudson was strictly platonic, though in the name of keeping up appearances and furthering Rock's career, she obediently assumed the role of La Beard.

"Of course, he was gay and during that period in America, that was just poison," Cardinale says. "We were always together as friends anyway, so we would just make believe that we were involved. I did it for him, to keep him going, because at that time, for a movie star to be gay, it was this really big scandal. Ridiculous.

Today, it's a different world but at that time, it was a terrible thing for him to have to deal with. I know it really weighed on him."

As usual, none of the strain showed on-screen. As a sort of second cousin to Cary Grant's Roger Thornhill in *North by Northwest*, Rock's Bartholomew Snow is thoroughly engaging. While Hudson handles the lightning fast changes from drama to comedy with great dexterity, several critics, like Robert Alden of the *New York Times*, were thrown by *Blindfold*'s frequent mood swings: "The team who fashioned this nominally suspenseful caper was technically knowledgeable but not quite certain whether it wanted to be mysterious or funny. Unfortunately, it never quite succeeds either way."

CHAPTER 14

SECONDS

"He identified with this guy," director John Frankenheimer said of Rock's reconstructed character in *Seconds* (1966). Here, Richard Anderson, Will Geer, and Hudson prepare for the big reveal.
(Photo courtesy of Photofest*)*

W e just don't know what to do with it," Paramount's publicity chief, Bob Goodfried, would say of *Seconds*. "It's a very interesting movie but the Rock Hudson in this movie isn't the Rock Hudson the public is used to seeing, or wants to see."

Following *The Manchurian Candidate* (1962) and *Seven Days in May* (1964), *Seconds* was the third and final installment in director John Frankenheimer's so called "paranoia trilogy," a genuinely unsettling trio of films that were released during a period when political assassinations and government cover-ups seemed to be occurring with alarming frequency.

Seconds started life as a novel by David Ely, whose work has been described as unusually prescient. "I would hesitate to characterize *Seconds* in terms of how our culture has proceeded in the last fifty years," Ely says. "Although I've written a lot of things as fiction that unfortunately, turned out to be true in political and social life." Ely's gripping narrative concerns a mysterious organization known only as The Company, which provides a unique service to graying, discontented clients eager to shed the skins of their unfulfilling lives: a stage-managed death, followed by a complete physical overhaul. Arthur Hamilton, a paunchy, conservative banker trapped in a soul-deadening existence in Scarsdale, signs on with The Company and is reborn as Antiochus—or Tony—Wilson, a playboy painter with a luxurious studio and a free-spirited mistress in Malibu.

With its highly original premise, *Seconds* caught Frankenheimer's eye. "He was fascinated by the book," recalled Evans Frankenheimer, the director's wife. "The story said that no matter what you do, you can't just go and be another person. You can't escape and start all over again." At the height of his *Seconds* obsession, Frankenheimer attended the theatre one evening in 1963. Before the performance was over, he knew that he had found a gifted writer capable of adapting David Ely's acclaimed novel into a film.

As screenwriter Lewis John Carlino recalls, "I had a play off-Broadway with Shelley Winters and Jack Warden, which dealt with identity. It was called *Epiphany*. Frankenheimer came to see this play, which is about a man who seeks to project his masculinity and control his wife. In a sudden reversal at the end of the play, he symbolically reveals himself as a homosexual. In a sense, I think the subject matter also led to the selection of Rock Hudson for *Seconds*."

However, the star of *Pillow Talk* was hardly anybody's first choice for such a dark dystopian exercise. Kirk Douglas had optioned the property through his Bryna Productions after Frankenheimer encouraged him to secure the rights. For Douglas, taking on a challenging dual role as a bottled-up banker and his repurposed younger self probably seemed like a direct route to his fourth Best Actor Oscar nomination. Though with *The Heroes of Telemark* and *Cast a Giant Shadow* waiting in the wings, Douglas's plate proved to be too full. Paramount Pictures then acquired the rights to *Seconds*.

As Frankenheimer and producer Edward Lewis originally conceived it, the same actor would be playing both the "before" and "after" versions of the character. Such a dramatic stretch would require the services of a highly skilled virtuoso. Someone like Laurence Olivier.* After Frankenheimer and Lewis flew to London and convinced Olivier that he was the only living actor who could effectively play both sides of the character, Paramount then decided that they needed a more bankable box office star to headline such a risky venture . . . somebody like Rock Hudson.

"Rock's performance in *Seconds* is really a credit to John Frankenheimer, who coerced him into taking the role," says Lewis John Carlino. "It was very dangerous for Rock to try that kind of role because there was such an audience identification with what he was and what he projected. Also, his fans had certain expectations about the kind of movies he usually appeared in."

Hudson convinced Frankenheimer that using two different performers would result in an even more startling contrast. To play the uptight banker in the first half of the film, Frankenheimer cast actor John Randolph, whose jowly, hangdog appearance is a complete 360 from Hudson's matinee idol suavity. To make the transition from one actor to another more believable, Hudson's hair

---

*David Ely, author of the novel *Seconds*, says that he was never consulted about any creative decisions related to the film, including casting. When interviewed for this book in 2015, Ely registered surprise that Rock Hudson had not been Frankenheimer's first choice for the lead. "Laurence Olivier? I never heard his name mentioned in connection with *Seconds*. My wife will be delighted to hear that story. Though, of course, she won't believe me."

was grayed and he was made up to look haggard and facially disfigured. "We wanted to beat him up as badly as possible, so that he didn't look too pretty" John Frankenheimer recalled. "To have Rock Hudson look badly at that time in his life was one of the great achievements in cinema, let me tell you."

In a fascinating post-surgery sequence, the banker's layers of bandages are removed and he sheds a tear as he gazes at his transformed reflection. Suddenly, it's Rock Hudson's face in the mirror—and in more ways than one. Those who worked on *Seconds* remembered that Rock was intensely focused on what he referred to as "the big reveal" sequence. Had there been an eerily similar moment like this when Roy Fitzgerald, a gay truck driver with an inferiority complex, was remodeled into Rock Hudson?

The carefully constructed star image that he and his keepers had created seemed to live inside of him, part alter ego, part parasite. Jokingly, he had even given it a name: Charlie Movie Star. The similarities between character and actor weren't lost on Frankenheimer: "If you look at it, he was kind of an invented personality, wasn't he? And he identified with this guy. If you destroy your past, then you're nothing. You can't function. And to become Rock Hudson, he had to destroy a great deal of his past."

In a party sequence in the latter half of the film, Tony gets drunk and becomes sloppy and unguarded. Rather than waiting around for Hudson to get inspired, Frankenheimer encouraged his star to get bombed. "I came up with the idea but Rock endorsed it," Frankenheimer revealed. As Tony belts back one after another, bits and pieces of his real identity begin to slip out. When he starts to reveal too much about his former life, other "reborns" in attendance close in and subdue him; the authentic self must never resurface. For in *Seconds*, as in Hollywood, if reality rears its ugly head, the game is over.

"Something happened to Rock there and it was a breakdown," says costar Salome Jens. "[Frankenheimer] got him drunk and he went into this crying jag that was very serious and it scared us all because we really didn't know what was going on. I was told at the end of the day that we would have to re-shoot that scene because none of it was usable . . . I didn't believe it when people told me he was gay . . . I'm sure that had to be very difficult for him because it was living some lie. The only thing we can't handle in life is a lie and it was there."

Playing this sci-fi variation on his own story, Hudson is more authentic than he has ever been on-screen. There are stretches with minimal dialogue where he is called upon to convey a wide range of emotions while suggesting the psychological entrapment of the character's fragmented self. In a scene in which the mysterious Nora Marcus (Salome Jens, haunting in the role) reads Tony's tea leaves, Frankenheimer's camera lingers on his star's intense, hawk-like expression. Actor and character are so aligned that the dividing line between the two is effectively blurred. As Tony reflects on abandoning his former life forever, there suddenly seem to be real thoughts—complicated and uncomfortable—going on behind Hudson's eyes.

In service to his character, Rock bravely attempts to unlock a more vulnerable side of himself. Considering that several of his confidants—including Mark Miller and George Nader—had advised him not to accept the role, it's all the more courageous that Rock decided to take the project on.

For *Seconds*, Frankenheimer wisely surrounded Hudson with a battalion of New York–trained actors, several of whom had been victims of the blacklist. The authenticity of their acting grounds the movie while infusing it with an irresistible air of black comedy. As a result, scenes are both horrifying and savagely funny at the same time. "Assuming that cost is not a decisive factor, death has many advantages," The Company's lawyer, Mr. Ruby, announces to a stunned Arthur Hamilton. As this model of diabolical efficiency, Jeff Corey has a field day, graphically describing "the careful obliteration of identifiable parts of the cadaver," while devouring a succulent chicken dinner.

Rock and Jane Wyman were "rapturously reunited" in Douglas Sirk's masterpiece, *All That Heaven Allows* (1955). *(Photo courtesy of* Photofest*)*

Rock on the set of *Giant*. *(Photo courtesy of Wally Cech)*

Rock's rival, James Dean, on location in Marfa, Texas, during the making of *Giant*. "It was like night and day with those two," costar Jane Withers remembered. *(Photo courtesy of Wally Cech)*

Rock found a soulmate in his *Giant* costar Elizabeth Taylor, seen here during a shooting break. *(Photo courtesy of Wally Cech)*

"Soap opera beyond soap opera, a masterpiece of suds!" is how Lauren Bacall would describe *Written on the Wind* (1956). *(Photo courtesy of* Photofest*)*

Hudson and Sidney Poitier in a scene from *Something of Value* (1957). Rock couldn't decide who was more terrifying—director Richard Brooks or the Mau Mau. *(Photo courtesy of* Photofest*)*

Doris Day and Rock in an iconic sequence from *Pillow Talk* (1959), which skirted Production Code censorship and became a symbol of an entire era. *(Photo courtesy of* Photofest*)*

Rock's boyfriend, William Dawson, in his *Physique Pictorial* days. *(Photo courtesy of Bill Dawson)*

Rock and Gina Lollobrigida starred in the hit comedy *Come September* (1961). "When we did our love scenes, he was quite . . . *normal*," said Lollobrigida. *(Photo courtesy of* Photofest*)*

LEFT: Lee Garlington, Emory University photo. *(Courtesy of Lee Garlington)*

BELOW: Rock and Marilyn Monroe attend the Golden Globe Awards in 1962. After her death, Hudson narrated the documentary *Marilyn* and donated his salary to help establish a memorial fund in Monroe's name at the Actors Studio. *(Photo courtesy of Photofest)*

Rock eyes partner Jack Coates, who would eventually leave Hudson for Dr. Frederick Whitam, at right. *(Photo courtesy of Cathy Hamblin)*

Rock and John Wayne were teamed for the first and only time in *The Undefeated* (1969). *(Photo courtesy of* Photofest*)*

Hudson had a fling with costar John David Carson during the making of the notorious *Pretty Maids All in a Row* (1971). *(Photo courtesy of* Photofest*)*

A beautiful friendship began when Rock guest-starred on Carol Burnett's variety special in 1966. When they teamed for the stage musical *I Do! I Do!*, they earned rave reviews and broke box office attendance records. *(Courtesy of Everett Collection)*

In 1975, Rock celebrated his fiftieth birthday by wearing a diaper. *(Photo courtesy of Diane Markert)*

Sherry Mathis (as Guenevere), Rock (as King Arthur), and Jerry Lanning (as Lancelot) in director Stockton Briggle's 1977 production of *Camelot*. *(Photo by Bob W. Smith)*

With Claire Trevor and Peter Kevoian backstage before a performance of *John Brown's Body* (1976). *(Photo courtesy of Peter Kevoian)*

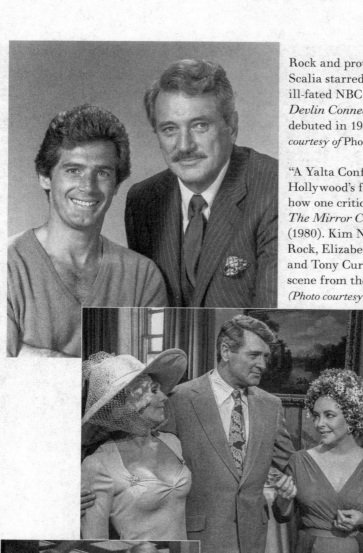

Rock and protégé Jack Scalia starred in the ill-fated NBC series *The Devlin Connection*, which debuted in 1982. *(Photo courtesy of* Photofest*)*

"A Yalta Conference of Hollywood's finest," is how one critic described *The Mirror Crack'd* (1980). Kim Novak, Rock, Elizabeth Taylor, and Tony Curtis in a scene from the film. *(Photo courtesy of* Photofest*)*

Rock and Gunther Fraulob enjoyed a Hawaiian getaway in 1984. *(Photo courtesy of Gunther Fraulob)*

As the President of The Company, Will Geer oozes all of the wholesome, mild-mannered charm of a country doctor, even as he shamelessly manipulates his client into abandoning his loved ones forever. "Isn't it easier to go forward when you know you can't go back?" Geer asks, as he nudges The Company's next victim to sign on the dotted line.

When Tony first meets Nora, she is outfitted in a dark hood and brooding on the beach, a refugee from Ingmar Bergman's *The Seventh Seal*. "Frankenheimer told me I was 'The Essence of Doom,'" Jens says. Rock's previous high-gloss pairings with Doris Day, Elizabeth Taylor, and Jane Wyman—as dreamy as they may have been—always seemed studio manufactured. In *Seconds*, Hudson's chemistry with Jens feels natural and genuinely intimate. Freed from his soundstage constraints, a new Rock Hudson emerges in *Seconds* and for once, he's breathing plenty of fresh air.

Frankenheimer wanted to include a scene in *Seconds* in which the character of Tony Wilson would finally shed any of the lingering inhibitions that he had inherited from his previous incarnation as Arthur Hamilton. He shot a sequence in which Tony joins dozens of naked revelers who are stomping grapes together while crammed into an overcrowded vat. "That was a ritual that I knew about that took place in Santa Barbara every year," says screenwriter Lewis John Carlino. "A lot of the people in that scene actually participated in that kind of wild bacchanal every year during the grape harvest."

The proceedings were so wild that Paramount insisted that Frankenheimer delete most of the grape-stomping sequence for the domestic release of the film. In 1966, the idea of a major Hollywood star like Rock Hudson observing a naked bacchanal—let alone having him strip down and join in—was totally unheard of—at least in the movies. Those present remember that Rock had been nervous about shooting a scene that most of his contemporaries would have flatly refused to appear in.

There was another aspect of the role that made Rock uncomfortable. "He had a very difficult time with one scene where they strapped him on a gurney," remembers Lewis John Carlino. "He became very agitated and Frankenheimer wouldn't allow them to release Rock. So, what you see in that scene is his real panic of being restrained and not being free to move as he wanted to. That's real stuff there. He was genuinely terrified."

In May of 1966, *Seconds* was screened as the official U.S. entry at the Cannes Film Festival. Rock Hudson's excursion into existentialism seemed like a natural for a largely European audience, but Lewis John Carlino remembers that Frankenheimer's thriller elicited a less-than-reverent reaction. "It was actually booed by the French audience," says Carlino. "There were whistles and cat calls. It was a great shock for all of us because we thought that we had something that the French would really love." When the audience was alerted to the fact that "Monsieur Rock Hudson" was in the house, the jeers quickly turned into a rapturous ovation.

Paramount's publicity campaign spoke volumes about how confused the studio was about promoting a film that wasn't easily categorized. Was it a sci-fi opus? A suspense pic? Could the romantic angle somehow be exploited? Finally, Paramount decided to pitch Frankenheimer's film as a conventional thriller.

In the end, nothing worked. *Seconds* grossed only $1.75 million domestically, considered an outright disaster by Rock Hudson standards (by comparison, *Send Me No Flowers*, released two years earlier, had raked in a then impressive $9 million). Even if the money wasn't there, Rock assumed that he could console himself with the reviews.

However, during its initial release, *Seconds* seemed to alternately confound and disturb critics. *Time*'s reviewer wrote, "Director John Frankenheimer and veteran photographer James Wong Howe manage to give the most implausible doings a look of credible horror. Once Rock appears though, the spell is shattered, and through no fault of his own. Instead of honestly exploring the ordeal of assuming a second identity, the script subsides for nearly an hour into conventional Hollywood fantasy."

Seconds would finally find its audience—the second time around. In honor of its thirtieth anniversary, *Seconds* was back in theatres, with its once-controversial grape-stomping sequence reinstated. The following year, the movie was finally released to the home-video market and its cult reputation continued to grow. Rock's performance was now being hailed as the finest of his career.

"The movie went from failure to classic without ever being a success," Frankenheimer would say three decades after the film's initial release. "When it first came out, those who wanted to see a Rock Hudson picture, didn't want to see Rock Hudson in this part. And those who wanted to see this kind of movie, didn't want to see Rock Hudson in it. As a result, that leaves an audience of five or six. This was literally a movie where you could call up the theatre owner and say, 'What time does *Seconds* go on?' and the guy would say, 'What time can you get here?' It was a terrible failure when it came out and now it's considered this great cult picture."

Mirroring the poignant identity crisis being explored in *Seconds* was the fact that Hudson was being forced to come to terms with his own box office mortality. After a long and successful reign as the king of Hollywood, there were undeniable signs that he would soon have to abdicate. Audiences had avoided several of his recent pictures; his Oscar nomination for *Giant* was a decade old. For years now, Rock had felt suffocated by his own screen image. Though when he tried to move in a new direction—as with *Seconds*—his fan base resisted.

While he was still undeniably photogenic and always exuded his own special brand of star charisma, there were newer, younger actors poised to take his place—Redford, Newman, Beatty. As well as a whole new breed of edgy, rebellious, countercultural icons— Nicholson, Hoffman, De Niro—who broke the typical movie star mold. One didn't have to look like Rock Hudson to make it in Hollywood anymore. In fact, it probably worked in your favor if you didn't.

On September 6, 1966, *Variety* announced that Rock Hudson

and Henry Willson had dissolved their eighteen-year professional association. Some say that it was Tom Clark who engineered the long overdue split, while others credit another member of Hudson's team with steering a new course.

"When Dale Olson took over as Rock's publicist, he told him the first thing he had to do was lose Henry Willson," says film critic Kevin Thomas, a close friend of Olson's. "Dale was incredibly firm about it because he felt that Henry Willson had become too big of a liability to him."

Over the years, Hudson had become increasingly resentful of Henry taking full credit for "creating" Rock Hudson—as though he were a box of cornflakes. The most egregious example of this being a *Look* magazine cover story. After interviewing Willson at length, writer Eleanor Harris concluded, "Rock Hudson is completely an invention of his agent. His name, his voice, his personality were all made up for him." Hudson fumed: "I don't think anybody has made me do something I didn't have what it took to do on my own. I must have had the drive, the desire, the brains, the guts—even if they were buried."

When the axe fell, Willson did not take the news lightly. After being dismissed by his most important client and prized "creation," the agent reportedly spewed a colorful stream of obscenities and threatened to expose Rock to the tabloids. And that wasn't even the worst of the threats. As Lee Garlington recalls, "Rock was complaining about Henry Willson one time and I said to him, 'Why don't you fire the sonofabitch?' And he said, 'I can't fire him because he threatened to have one of his boys throw acid in my face if I ever fired him, and I knew he would do it.'"

Rock would be spared the disfiguring makeover, even after a full-page ad appeared in *The Hollywood Reporter* announcing that John Foreman, cofounder of Creative Management Agency was assuming worldwide representation of Rock Hudson. When Foreman later segued into producing, Hudson would be represented by Flo Allen, a tennis pro turned talent agent. Striking-looking and as glamorous as the clients she represented, Allen was often photographed on Rock's arm. At one point, *Movie Mirror* reported that Allen was an example of how "Rock's choice of women is almost fantastically selective."

AFTER THE BOLD risk-taking of *Seconds*, it was right back to the kind of derring-do and narrow escapes that most Rock Hudson fans had come to expect. In *Tobruk*, Hudson's character is the same brand of strong-jawed commander he had played countless times before. On this crusade, Rock's stalwart hero would have to contend with hidden minefields, exploding fuel bunkers, and the obligatory web of Nazi spies. One of the film's early titles, *Hot Eye of Hell*, gives one a sense of the kind of hard-hitting, suspense-packed thriller that actor-turned-screenwriter Leo Gordon had in mind.

Set in North Africa during World War II, *Tobruk* was based (albeit very loosely) on an actual 1942 mission known as "Operation Agreement." A commando squadron comprised of German Jews masquerading as Nazis and British soldiers pretending to be prisoners of war set out for the port city of Tobruk with the intention of destroying the fuel supply of "The Desert Fox," Field Marshal Erwin Rommel.

While the real-life mission was a miserable failure, the cinematic rendition ended in a blaze of glory, complete with an array of Oscar-nominated special effects. In the film, the convoy is led by Canadian Major Donald Craig (Hudson), German-Jewish Captain Kurt Bergman (George Peppard), and British Colonel John Harker (Nigel Green). Considering that *Tobruk* was a period piece which involved several remote locations, a large international cast, and the services of no less than fifty-eight stunt men, the film's $6 million price tag was one of the heftiest in Universal's history. The movie would prove to be a daunting challenge for director Arthur Hiller, who would later specialize in more intimately scaled, character-driven dramas like *Love Story* and *The Hospital*.

Like George Stevens and Douglas Sirk before him, director

Hiller found Hudson not only completely cooperative but totally responsive. "Rock was just a pleasure to direct," Hiller says. "When the picture started, we were talking about his character—the major. I pointed out that to most people, Rock was 'Mr. Handsome,' and because of that dreamboat image, they probably thought of him as very soft. In our picture, he had to show great strength. And he did. He came through with the macho stuff and it was very believable. But I also said to him, 'Even when you're playing the strong side of the major, don't lose the caring.' And he didn't. Everything I asked for in terms of his performance was there. In fact, he often improved on whatever I had suggested. All of this made me realize that as an actor, Rock was capable of far more. I sensed that there was so much going on beneath the surface that never got used."

When *Tobruk* was released, the critics treated Hudson as an afterthought. Howard Thompson of the *New York Times* felt that George Peppard turned in his "best performance to date," while he found "the churning, cacophonous finale, excellently directed by Arthur Hiller, the best and least forgettable thing about the movie." As for the leading man, Thompson managed only a shrug: "Mr. Hudson does well enough in a limber but fairly standard role."

Tobruk would prove to be Rock Hudson's swan song as a Universal contract player. It seemed like the perfect time to make the break and leave home. Even if some of his recent films for Universal had earned big money, his most satisfying work experience, in *Seconds*, had happened at another studio. Uninspired by the majority of scripts that were coming his way, Rock decided it was best to retreat. "I had to make a decision, as expensive as it was, to do nothing," Hudson told the press. "The last four or five films I made were mediocre. I needed time to reevaluate myself."

———

One day, twenty-three-year-old Jack Coates's red Corvette broke down in front of The Castle. It was Bick Benedict to the rescue as

Rock came strolling out to lend a hand. Suddenly faced with the prospect of having to carry on a conversation with his favorite film star, Jack got scared, slammed the hood shut, got back in his car, and sped off. Despite this, Rock couldn't get the young man out of his mind. There was just something extraordinary about him. Starting with the obvious.

"Jack was very good-looking," says his younger sister Cathy Hamblin. "He had been a male model for a high-end men's store in Phoenix called Desert Squire. That's about the time my parents started figuring out he was maybe a little bit different but it wasn't a deal breaker for them. He moved to California kind of early on. He had hooked up with a rich Beverly Hills real estate developer and they were living together. But this wealthy guy was like, 'You will have a job.' So, Jack went to work at Standard Oil in his crisp little white uniform. One day, Rock Hudson pulled in and that was it . . . it was a full-service station, so to speak. The next thing I know, my brother was going out with him."

Though Hudson and Coates were immediately attracted to each other, there were a number of obstacles standing in their way. Jack had been living with the developer for a number of years and he was comfortable. Besides, friends had warned him that Rock would treat him as a sexual plaything and he'd be discarded once the initial thrill was over. And, then, Coates was steadfastly determined to obtain his college degree. At the time he met Rock, Jack was enrolled at UCLA and taking classes in anthropology. Not even a movie star was going to deter him from graduating.

A pattern was quickly established. Rock would pursue. Jack would evade. Rock would pursue. Jack would succumb. Though only temporarily. And on it went. Rock had confided to his closest friends that he thought Jack was really "the one." Finally, one afternoon over mint juleps, Rock won Jack over. Convinced that Hudson's feelings for him were genuine, Coates agreed to move into The Castle, stuffed koala in tow.

From the beginning, there was a playful, slapstick quality

to Hudson's relationship with Coates. If some of Rock's other romances had been too intense or fraught with conflicts, this one was far more Laurel and Hardy. They'd splash around in the pool with Nick the Dumb or one of Hudson's six other dogs. "Going out" meant root beer floats at Will Wright's or hot dogs at Pink's. Both excelled at what a mutual friend described as "conversational Scrabble"—highly competitive word games.

Unlike some of Hudson's other partners, Jack Coates seems to have been universally loved, both by the staff at The Castle and Hudson's longtime friends. "When I hear the name Jack Coates all I can do is smile," says Rock's friend Ken Jillson. "I mean, he was just a super charmer. Very sporty. Very masculine. A sparkling personality. And he just radiated sex from the moment you met him."

For a period of several years, Coates would spend Thursday evening through Monday morning with the movie star in Beverly Hills, while the rest of the time he was just another coed wandering around campus. "Jack couldn't quite decide on a degree," Cathy Hamblin says. "So, he ended up pursuing two degrees, which he never really used. He just had a lot of fun."

During the years that Coates was living with Hudson, Cathy Hamblin says that Rock became very close to her parents: "He came to dinner at our house a number of times. My mom would make a ton of chicken fried steak. That was the main meal for Mr. Rock Hudson. He came with his maid, Joy, who got rip-roaring drunk with my mother. Which was often the way it was when I stayed at Rock's house. Joy would have what were called 'eating days' and 'drinking days' and she didn't mix the two. On the eating days, we would all eat really well. On the drinking days, Rock would come home from work, see the condition Joy was in and say to us, 'Well, let's go to the Polo Lounge . . .' because he knew there wasn't going to be any dinner."

———

While it was totally out of character for Hudson to pursue a project that he hadn't been considered for, everything about *Ice Station Zebra* felt epic. This extravagantly budgeted espionage thriller would be shot in Cinerama, Super Panavision, and Metrocolor.

Alistair MacLean's bestselling novel followed the commander and crew of an atomic submarine as they attempt to rescue a meteorological team trapped in a remote weather station on the polar ice cap. Upon reaching the North Pole, the commander finds himself embroiled in an international incident involving a Soviet satellite. In adapting MacLean's nail-biter, MGM would spare no expense in terms of assembling a first-rate cast—which Rock Hudson couldn't help but notice didn't include him.

At first, several trade publications announced that Gregory Peck and David Niven, successfully teamed in *The Guns of Navarone* (based on another MacLean novel) would be reunited for *Ice Station Zebra*. John Sturges, who had turned *The Magnificent Seven* and *The Great Escape* into major hits, was signed to direct. Oscar-winner Paddy Chayefsky was hired to write the screenplay.

It should have been full steam ahead but instead, it was trouble at every turn. After reading Chayefsky's screenplay, Sturges was dumbfounded. Not only was a dramatically compelling third act missing but, worse, the character that Peck was slated to play had morphed from a cynical American agent into a *double* agent working for the Communists. "I have no objection to playing a Communist," Gregory Peck announced. "I've played an anti-Semite, an alcoholic, and Captain Ahab. But this is preposterous . . . I won't do it."

Peck wasn't the only one balking. The Department of Defense was threatening to withdraw its assistance to the producers, objecting to the way military life was depicted in several scenes in Chayefsky's screenplay, most notably a sequence in which a pornographic film was screened for officers aboard a submarine. The National Security Agency insisted that such an occurrence—involving enlisted men—was utterly inconceivable.

Director Sturges decided to start from scratch. A pair of new screenwriters were hired and warned not to follow Chayefsky's example—they went in the other direction. "A bunch of claptrap, patriotic bullshit" is how Sturges appraised their efforts. Another writer was brought on board for yet another rewrite. While the script was being overhauled, Gregory Peck, David Niven, George Segal, and other cast members bailed, citing scheduling conflicts.

With *Seconds* and four flop comedies casting doubts about his bankability, Rock Hudson's survival instincts kicked in. He desperately needed a hit. After being nudged by Tom Clark, Hudson made the unusual move of contacting producer Martin Ransohoff directly: "Marty, I'd like to be in *Ice Station Zebra* . . ." As uncomfortable as it was for Hudson, shooting from the hip worked. In February of 1967, the trades announced that Hudson had been cast as James Ferraday, commander of the USS *Tigerfish*.

It may have been the lead, but Hudson's role didn't present much of an acting challenge. When Charlton Heston had passed on playing Commander Ferraday, he had correctly observed that the part, while pivotal, wasn't a fully realized character. Rock's costars, Ernest Borgnine, Patrick McGoohan, and Jim Brown had the showier roles, the more memorable dialogue.

For a young actor named William Hillman, *Zebra* was a challenging experience. He waited hours to audition for director John Sturges, whom he remembered as "stern" and "kind of into himself." Then, after it was decided that the picture didn't require any comedic relief, virtually all of Hillman's scenes were excised from the release print. In the midst of all this drama, there was one bright spot—Rock Hudson, whom Hillman says not only "had a heart of gold" but was as heroic off-screen as on:

"We had shot until three o'clock in the morning and then I had to schlep out to the parking lot when everybody's gone. I had a Mustang convertible and somebody had slit all of my tires. I'm standing there, staring at my car with four flat tires and out of the blue, comes this Cadillac and it roars through the lot. The driver sees me, pulls over next to me. It's Hudson. And he says, 'What happened?' I tell him. He says, 'Stay right where you are. I'll be back.' I thought he was going to come back and give me a lift but instead, he drives off. I'm thinking, 'Oh, great, this movie star left me cold out here in the middle of the bloody lot.' About twenty minutes later, a truck pulls in and it has four brand new tires on it. This truck driver gets out and starts changing my tires. I said, 'What are you doing? I can't afford this . . .' And he said, 'It's all paid for, buddy.' Hudson bought me four tires, had them put on, asked the driver to bring a two-way ham radio so that I could talk to my wife—who was pregnant—and let her know that I was okay. That's the kind of guy Rock Hudson was."

The premiere of *Ice Station Zebra*, held at Hollywood's Cinerama Dome, should have been a celebratory occasion for Hudson, but it proved to be memorable for all the wrong reasons. "It was the last premiere he ever attended because they chanted 'faggot!' as he went up the red carpet," Mark Miller recalled. *Ice Station Zebra* went into wide release in the fall of 1968. In terms of the critical consensus, there was none; the reviews ran the gamut. While the *New York Times* summed it up as, "Another good, man's action movie to eat popcorn by," *The New Yorker*'s Pauline Kael was less impressed: "It's terrible in such a familiar way that at some level it's pleasant. We learn to settle for so little, we moviegoers."

One moviegoer not only settled but developed a full-scale obsession with *Ice Station Zebra*. While holed up in the penthouse of the Desert Inn in Las Vegas, reclusive billionaire Howard Hughes would phone television station KLAS—which he owned—and order them to air *Zebra*. Over and over again. Usually in the wee hours of the morning. At one point, per Hughes's instructions, the station was broadcasting the movie on a daily basis.

"IT TAKES A fine pair to do it like it's never been done before!" read the advertising copy for Rock's next picture, *A Fine Pair*. The provocative slogan appeared above an image of a masked Hudson, his arms enfolding a masked Claudia Cardinale. Were they lovers sharing a stolen moment or terrorists preparing to hijack the next plane out of Zurich?

If the promotional campaign for *A Fine Pair* reeked of exploitation, the producers* were willing to do whatever it took to recoup their $2 million investment. Taking note of the dismal response to preview screenings, National General Pictures (known for such dubious fare as *Tarzan's Jungle Rebellion*) decided to promote Rock's latest not as a lighthearted follow-up to *Blindfold* but as a kinky combination of *Bonnie and Clyde* and *I Am Curious (Yellow)*. At least in script form, the original story had seemed promising:

New York City police captain Mike Harmon is lured into a globe-trotting adventure by Esmeralda Marini, an Italian beauty who claims that she was an unwitting accomplice in a jewel heist. As Esmeralda's late father was an old friend, Harmon agrees to accompany her to Austria, with the intention of returning the stolen jewels to the luxurious Fairchild Estate. Once there, Esmeralda turns the tables—not only making Harmon her lover but also her partner in crime.

Though Tom Clark dutifully pointed out the many plot holes in the story, Rock seemed unfazed. *A Fine Pair* would not only re-team him with Claudia Cardinale, whom he adored, but the production also offered what was essentially a working vacation. "We worked in Rome, in New York, in Salzburg, in Paris," recalls Cardinale. "I mean, going around the world with Rock Hudson by your side, what could be more fantastic?"

Though shooting began in the fall of 1967, *A Fine Pair* wouldn't reach American movie screens until 1969, when it was relegated to the bottom half of a double bill, screening after the Elvis Presley Western *Charro!* After reading the reviews, Rock may have wished that his film had been permanently, rather than temporar-

---

*Claudia Cardinale's then husband, Franco Cristaldi, was the executive producer of *A Fine Pair*.

ily, shelved. In the *New York Times*, Roger Greenspun dismissed *A Fine Pair* as "a soggy caper twist . . . Rock Hudson appears forced, fragile and strangely listless in his role. While nothing in *A Fine Pair* is at any moment very clear, everything is at all times deadeningly familiar."

"WHY DON'T YOU hold your gun like that for the close shot?"
It was only the first day of principal photography on *The Undefeated* and already Rock was starting to think that John Wayne's constant suggestions were sounding an awful lot like commands. Although Andrew V. McLaglen was occupying the director's chair, there was no question that it was "The Duke" who was in charge. The fact that Hudson had over fifty films to his credit didn't seem to matter much. To Wayne—whose career stretched back to the silent era and included over a hundred movies—Rock Hudson was still the new kid on the block. And apparently, he needed all the help he could get.

"Why don't you turn your head this way?" Wayne asked Hudson. "That way your reaction isn't lost."

After shooting had wrapped for the day, Hudson had a sinking feeling: "I started thinking, am I going to be directed by this guy? Is he trying to establish dominance or something?" Before Wayne started giving him line readings, Rock decided that the Ringo Kid needed to be put in his place. With all due respect, of course.

The next day, Hudson turned the tables. "Duke, why don't you move over here when you finish speaking?" he asked Wayne while they were setting up a two shot.

Recognizing this as the payback that it was, Wayne pointed his finger at Hudson: "I like you." And from that day forward, there weren't quite so many "suggestions." Only an unspoken mutual respect between two hardworking professionals.

As a boy, Roy Scherer, Jr. of Winnetka had watched John Wayne single-handedly tame the Wild West during Saturday matinees at the Teatro del Lago. Now he was sharing the screen with one of his boyhood idols. This was both exciting and unnerving. Exciting—as Rock was appearing alongside an actor many considered to be the greatest movie star of them all. Unnerving—as Wayne was the prototypical male against whom all others were measured.

"You're soft! Won't anything make a man out of you?" Wayne's cattle rancher snarls at Montgomery Clift in *Red River*. It was essentially the same message that Hudson had received upon his arrival in Hollywood. As if keeping his sexual identity concealed behind a straight-acting façade wasn't bad enough, directors like Raoul Walsh and Anthony Mann had done their best to toughen him up and turn him into Universal's answer to John Wayne. Fortunately, Rock's innate gentleness and unassuming personality had defied these attempts.

In some ways, the two men couldn't have been more different, but to the company's collective surprise, Hudson and Wayne bonded. Between takes, they could be found playing chess; after shooting wrapped for the day, Wayne would invite Hudson to join one of his epic bridge games. When Rock retired for the evening, he took a member of the Los Angeles Rams to bed with him. Even this Wayne took in stride. "What Rock does in the privacy of his own room is his business. I don't care what they say; I think Rock's a hell of a guy." Later, when the subject of Hudson's sexuality was broached with Wayne, he reportedly shrugged it off. "It never bothered me. Life's too short. Who the hell cares if he's queer? The man plays great chess."

In their only screen teaming, both stars are trapped in an uninspired, by-the-numbers Western. A post–Civil War story about a Union officer (Wayne) joining forces with a Confederate colonel (Hudson) to battle Mexican bandits, *The Undefeated* had been kicking around Hollywood for years. As far back as 1961, there had been plans to bring Stanley L. Hough's original story to the screen. It had first been conceived as a vehicle for Hugh O'Brian—television's Wyatt Earp and Rock's old Universal rival. When O'Brian's *Undefeated* fell apart, a succession of studios and directors attempted but failed to revive the property with other actors attached.

By 1968, the project had finally landed at 20th Century-Fox. When John Wayne and Rock Hudson were signed within months of each other, this was considered a major casting coup. Having snared two of the most bankable stars in the business, Fox was virtually guaranteed a blockbuster, which the studio needed to recover the film's then impressive $7 million cost. The hefty price tag came as a result of Rock's salary, location shooting in Durango, Mexico, and an ambitious sequence that involved a stampede of 3,000 horses.

Though popular with fans of both stars, *The Undefeated* wasn't the smash that Fox had hoped for—that was *Butch Cassidy and the Sundance Kid*, released the month before. If studio accountants were surprised that the film was something of a disappointment, critics were not, especially given the fact that the film is directed, edited, and scored as though it were a TV movie of the week. There is a stilted, flat quality to most of the performances, and midway through the movie grinds to a halt to make way for an epic brawl.

For his part, Hudson manages to look good, even in Confederate gray and muttonchops. He also gets to deliver the film's best line. After taking a slug from a bottle, he quips, "If I can find the time, I'm gonna sit down and write the social history of bourbon."

Variety lamented the fact that although all of the necessary elements for a classic Western had been assembled, the end results were no better than "a rerun of the late, late show . . . neither Wayne nor Hudson seems to know whether they are in a light comedy or a serious drama. They are simply unbelievable."

"ONE OF THE most physically exhausting films I've ever done" is how Rock would describe *Hornet's Nest*. Set in Nazi-occupied Italy during World War II, the story focused on Captain Turner, an American demolitions expert on a mission to blow up the Della Norte Dam.

When Turner and his fellow army officers parachute into the village of Reanoto, they are ambushed by the Germans. Turner survives, though he is badly injured. A gang of young boys rescues the captain. They take him back to the enormous cave they've all been hiding out in since the Nazis slaughtered their parents. Aldo, the tough-talking leader of the orphans, tricks a German doctor named Bianca into returning to the hideout and caring for Turner. Once the captain has fully recovered, the boys demand that he teach them how to operate the ammunition that they have stockpiled. Their plan is to retaliate against the Nazis. Turner agrees but only under the condition that the pint-sized renegades help him destroy the dam.

Originally titled *Children at Their Games*, S. S. Schweitzer's story had made the rounds of all of the studios since the early 1960s. By the end of the decade, director Phil Karlson finally received a green light from United Artists to bring it to the screen, with Rock Hudson and Sophia Loren set to star. Shortly before production began, Loren withdrew from the project and she was replaced by Sylva Koscina, a Yugoslavian actress best known for the muscle-bound Steve Reeves epic *Hercules*. If Loren's name carried considerable clout at the box office, Koscina's did not. *Hornet's Nest* would now be riding on Hudson's name alone.

Cameras started rolling in May of 1969 in Northern Italy's Po Valley. As the four-month shoot wore on, the heat became oppressive as did the physical demands of Hudson's role. The character of the heroic paratrooper had been envisioned as an athletic twenty-five-year-old. Rock, now a slightly paunchy forty-four, was accustomed to puffing his way through three packs a day. At various points in the story, he would be required to scale walls, swim furiously, and drive a jeep with one hand while tossing grenades over his shoulder with the other.

According to Hudson's friend, Marty Flaherty, for the first and presumably only time in his career, Rock resorted to taking "whites"—better known as amphetamines—to enhance his performance. Popping a few uppers would help propel him through what was essentially a daily endurance test. The drugs would also help him keep pace with a largely prepubescent supporting cast.

Director Phil Karlson and producer Stanley Kanter had auditioned over 250 boys to fill the seventeen children's roles in the movie. One of their most important finds proved to be fourteen-year-old Mark Colleano,[*] who was cast as Aldo, the combative gang leader. Rock would describe Colleano as a "great natural talent" and confided to friends that the young actor was "stealing the picture right under my nose."

Colleano remembers that when he shot his first scene—which Hudson didn't appear in—Rock still made a point of being there to demonstrate his support. "I heard he was very impressed and that was really a tremendous compliment for me and encouraged me to work even harder," Colleano says. "Rock couldn't have been more generous . . . he always gave of his time, he rehearsed if you wanted to rehearse . . . I remember we had this very tense, dramatic scene where we're literally nose to nose. He looks up from tying his shoe and I get right in his face and say, 'You're not going anywhere because I've got the detonators hidden . . .' When he looked up at me, I started to laugh. The moment Rock saw that he just stopped me dead. He said, *'Don't do that!'* in this very powerful voice. That kind of shocked me because we were friends and he had always been so nice. So in all the takes after that, I was very serious. Looking back, he was trying to kill the giggles and boy, he succeeded."

Before *Hornet's Nest* was released in September of 1970, Rock told George Nader that he had no idea how the film would be received but he felt that Mark Colleano was deserving of a Best Supporting Actor Oscar nomination. However, once the picture opened, it would be ignored by the public and largely dismissed by critics—

[*]Mark's father, the acclaimed British actor Bonar Colleano, had played Stanley Kowalski to Vivien Leigh's Blanche DuBois in the 1949 London production of *A Streetcar Named Desire*. Mark's mother, the actress Susan Shaw, starred in the 1956 cult film *Fire Maidens from Outer Space*.

the *Los Angeles Times* called it "an overly long, routine action programmer." If Hudson had long ago learned to dust himself off and keep moving after a disappointment, his underage colleagues were hurt by the indifferent reception to the film.

"I was really sad because when the movie came out in England, it was on the second half of a bill with *They Call Me Mister Tibbs!*" Colleano remembers. "Our film didn't catch on at all, which was very disappointing because we all had such hopes. *Hornet's Nest* put a lot of pressure on me. I did feel a bit emotionally drawn after that experience and I'm sure that Rock did, too. When the Hollywood thing didn't happen for me, I kind of crashed a bit. One of my friends once said, 'You've been in some of the most prestigious flops ever made.'"

CHAPTER 15

WHISTLING AWAY THE DARK

"It's really too bad what happened with that movie," Robert Osborne
said of *Darling Lili* (1970). The production was plagued by bad weather
and bad press. Hudson had hoped to bond with leading lady
Julie Andrews but walked away disappointed.
(*Photo courtesy of* Photofest)

1970. It was the same year that Jack Nicholson became a star while
rebelling against pretty much everything in *Five Easy Pieces*. It
was also the same year that 20th Century-Fox presented Raquel
Welch as a subversive transsexual, hell-bent on "the destruction
of the American male in all its particulars" in *Myra Breckin-
ridge*. And Warner Brothers had one of their biggest hits that year
with the documentary *Woodstock*, which captured the ultimate
counterculture festival in all of its ganja-scented glory.

Over at Paramount Pictures, however, the studio seemed to be stuck in a culturally oblivious time warp. Their new catchphrase may have been "Paramount Is Where It's Happening," but that hardly seemed to be the case as a new decade dawned. Studio executives were rolling the dice on several old-fashioned, family friendly musicals, hoping to replicate the blockbuster success of such smashes as *The Sound of Music* and *Funny Girl*.

"I think that the people who were still in power in the movie business, by and large, did not understand the change in the sensibility of the times," says Peter Bart, who served as Paramount's vice president during the studio's turbulent years of transition. "Charles Bluhdorn, who had bought Gulf and Western and Paramount, was a very traditional European person and his favorite movie was *The Sound of Music*. That was his taste. So, he was totally ill-equipped to understand the American taste and the major changes taking place at that time."

Bluhdorn seemed obsessed with one star in particular: Julie Andrews. Paramount's president was hoping that Andrews could do for his studio what she had already done for Disney (*Mary Poppins*), Fox (*The Sound of Music*), and Universal (*Thoroughly Modern Millie*). For a time in the 1960s, it seemed that whatever Julie touched turned to gold. In fact, by mid-decade, Andrews was second only to John Wayne as the top-grossing film star in the world. Encouraged by the record-breaking box office receipts from Julie's string of hits, Bluhdorn was eager to have Andrews and her four-octave range grace a Paramount production the moment she became available. In order to sweeten the deal, the studio offered Andrews's soon-to-be husband, Blake Edwards, virtual carte blanche—the opportunity to write and direct whatever film she starred in.

Paramount's project was initially saddled with the lumbering title, *Darling Lili, or Where Were You the Night You Said You Shot Down Baron von Richtofen?* before it was shortened to the marquee-friendly *Darling Lili*. Screenwriter William Peter Blatty had collaborated with Edwards on his earlier comedies, *A Shot in the Dark* and *What Did You Do in the War, Daddy?* Still a couple of years away from publishing his landmark bestseller *The Exorcist*, Blatty was tapped to resurrect a pet project of Edwards's that had been languishing.

"Blake and I had worked together before and I admired him very much but there had already been problems in getting this new project off the ground," Blatty recalls. "Having failed to get Jack Lemmon interested in an idea he had for a World War I–era romantic comedy, Blake started dating Julie Andrews, and after a time asked me if I could come up with a way to make a female— namely Julie—the star of the film. I managed to do it overnight, the ultimate result being *Darling Lili*."

As it was set during World War I, *Darling Lili* was anything but up to the minute, though it would give Andrews an opportunity to play something other than an unflappable governess. She would portray Lili Schmidt, a German spy masquerading as adored English music hall entertainer Lili Smith.

With a score that included "It's a Long Way to Tipperary" and "Pack Up Your Troubles in Your Old Kit-Bag," the semi-musical didn't seem quite in tune with the era of The Beatles and Led Zeppelin. But who cared? Andrews was one of the most bankable names in the business. Whether her costars happened to be adorable Austrian moppets or animated penguins, Julie could be counted on to make anything work. What's more, Blake Edwards had a strong track record of his own, having directed such contemporary classics as *The Pink Panther* and *Breakfast at Tiffany's*.

Believing like everyone else that he was boarding a victory train bound for box-office glory, Rock agreed to play Major William Larrabee, the Allied squadron commander, who happens to be Lili's primary target; her assignment is to seduce the major and gain information concerning what the Allies have planned for the escalating air war. While attempting to extract privileged information from Larrabee, Lili falls in love with him.

With location shooting scheduled for Ireland, Belgium, and

France, *Darling Lili* would be one of the most elaborate productions of Hudson's career. *Lili* would prove to be so complex, in fact, that the mere one hundred days of shooting originally allotted to the production were soon a distant memory. More than two years would pass between *Darling Lili*'s first day of principal photography, March 18, 1968, and its theatrical release on June 24, 1970.

In the intervening twenty-eight months, major changes occurred on the world stage and in Hollywood. America's involvement in the Vietnam War dominated the headlines, making a World War I saga seem all the more out of touch. At the neighborhood movie house, extravagantly budgeted escapist fare had been overthrown in favor of grittier, antiestablishment character studies like *Midnight Cowboy* and *Easy Rider.* With a budget that started at $11 million and which eventually ballooned to an estimated $24 million, *Darling Lili* was one seriously overpriced antique.

But no fear. With two of the most likeable and charismatic stars in the business on board—the picture was a sure bet. At least until it became painfully obvious that Rock Hudson and Julie Andrews exhibited zero screen chemistry. "Their supposedly steamy love scenes had as much fizzle as day-old beer," remembered Peter Bart, who, as Paramount's junior executive, was required to screen the *Darling Lili* dailies. "Julie Andrews, totally believable as the faithful nanny in *Mary Poppins*, was never a threat to Marilyn Monroe as a sex goddess. As for Hudson, his predilection for men was becoming widely suspected in Hollywood . . . Their mutual disinterest, if not distaste, was abundantly visible in take after take as they embraced and kissed and then, when the director yelled 'cut,' they wiped their lips and breathed a sigh of relief."

It's often been said that the camera does not lie and in the case of *Darling Lili*, the strained atmosphere that existed on the set is almost palpable on-screen. From the beginning, Edwards's movie was plagued with bad luck and bad press. As the *International Herald Tribune* reported, most of the highly publicized delays were blamed on "waiting for the weather." "Sometimes we wait for days and days," Julie explained to a visitor. "And how do you pass the time?" the guest inquired. "We cry a lot," Miss Andrews said. It rained in Dublin. It rained in Paris. In Brussels, it not only rained but the company was greeted with a "U.S. Go Home!" banner. Union officials alleged that Paramount was infringing on Belgian labor laws.

In the *Los Angeles Times*, columnist Joyce Haber seemed to delight in reporting every misfortune that befell the beleaguered *Lili* team (such as when a shot involving 2,000 extras was postponed three times). While the film was still in production, Haber regularly took Andrews to task, suggesting that the actress, who was ordinarily the consummate professional, had suddenly gone diva. After Andrews canceled a few public appearances at the last minute, Haber began referring to her as "The 'Star' who is beginning to make Barbra Streisand seem like Goody Two Shoes." Typically, Haber would shoot straight from the hip and name names but, occasionally, she resorted to aliases when one of her blind items was especially salacious. In one notorious Haber column, she suggested that "Miss P and P" (the prim and proper Andrews), "Mr. X, the director" (Edwards), and "Mr. V.V." (the "Visually Virile" Hudson) were not only having a ménage à trois but were regularly spotted in San Francisco's hard-core leather bars, allegations that Andrews and Edwards heatedly denied. It was stories like this that prompted the classic Andrews rejoinder, "They should give Haber open-heart surgery and go in through the feet."

According to some of Rock's friends, he was genuinely unhappy throughout the drawn-out shoot, though he never brought his troubles to the set. "When he did the movie with Julie Andrews and Blake Edwards, he did not feel welcomed by them," says Hudson's *The Vegas Strip War* costar Dennis Holahan. "Other than speaking to him on the set, they never spoke to him. It's strange because anybody who worked with Blake usually adored him but I can tell you that Rock did not have a good experience working for them." Others recall that Hudson had hoped to bond with Andrews as he had with Elizabeth Taylor and Doris Day.

"It's really too bad what happened with that movie," says film historian Robert Osborne. "I know that the big disappointment for Rock on *Darling Lili* is that he was so looking forward to working with Julie Andrews and for some reason, I don't think he and Blake Edwards got along all that well . . . Julie is a total pro and a lovely lady but she also had a complicated husband that she adored . . . Rock tried his best, but the experience was not what he had expected."

Highly original and incredibly ambitious, *Darling Lili* seems to be in the throes of an identity crisis as it unreels. Is it a romantic comedy? An adventure yarn? A quasi-musical? With all of the intrigue involving wild chases through the streets of Paris, code books being stashed under mattresses, and aerial dogfights with the Red Baron—*Darling Lili* is overloaded with plot and spectacle.

Interestingly, the movie works best when the espionage takes a breather and makes way for a Julie Andrews ditty. Johnny Mercer and Henry Mancini's original songs, including the Oscar-nominated "Whistling Away the Dark," give Andrews an opportunity to display all of the colors in her wide-ranging musical repertoire. What's more, she looks ravishing in her Donald Brooks costumes and Edwards's camera is captivated by her every move. With Dame Julie commanding center stage, second-billed Rock Hudson is left to fend for himself. Given the fact that he isn't awarded nearly as much screen time as his leading lady, Hudson seems like just another handsome set piece—one that nearly gets lost amid the Chippendale breakfronts, crystal chandeliers, and other sumptuous bric-a-brac.

Screenwriter William Peter Blatty felt that the picture was also thrown off balance due to a few questionable decisions. "I loved and respected Blake, but I disagreed with his final cut of the film," says Blatty. "Our premise was that while Lili would sleep with a general or two to worm out secret battle plans, she in fact despises men to the point of wondering whether she's a lesbian. But there in reel one, we find Lili in a hot physical embrace with her German control. I know this stuff is typical writer nit-picking, but I really think it hurt the film."

The reviews ranged from the hostile ("Blake Edwards' attempted spoof of World War I spying emerges as infantile in every respect"—*New York* magazine) to the adoring ("The overall effect is surprisingly sweet"—*Saturday Review*). Though most critics, like Charles Champlin of the *Los Angeles Times*, found themselves of two minds: "It is certainly no effort to enjoy *Darling Lili* . . . yet it is painful to see so painstaking and fantastically costly an enterprise mounted on so flimsy and indeed questionable a story premise . . . the effect is of a skyscraper erected on Rice Krispies." In the *Village Voice*, Andrew Sarris saluted Rock's ability to maintain a straight face: "Hudson's performance in *Darling Lili* should be studied by all the off-off-Broadway phenoms as a model of straight behavioralism in even the zaniest context."

Upon its release, *Darling Lili* was branded "the $24 Million Valentine." As Paramount's head of production, Robert Evans, would later observe, "*Darling Lili* was Blake Edwards's wedding gift to his lady love and Paramount paid the bill. The film's losses were so exorbitant that, were it not for [Bluhdorn's] brilliant manipulation of the numbers, Paramount Pictures would have been changed to Paramount Cemetery."

As for Rock Hudson, the commercial failure of *Darling Lili* quickened his downhill slide at the box office and the production was not one that he would remember fondly. However, there was one endearing tie to the film that Hudson would never forget. Her name was "Veronique." Or at least that's how she would be referred to in the press. Described in *Photoplay* as "an 8-year-old ragamuffin from the slums of Paris," Veronique was one of twenty-five students enrolled in a day school for underprivileged children that the producers of *Darling Lili* recruited to appear in a musical sequence with Julie Andrews.

With her dark brown hair, huge hazel eyes, and winning disposition, Veronique captivated virtually everyone with whom she came in contact. Though no one was more enchanted than the film's leading man. He bought her ice cream, raced her through flower fields, and carried her around on his shoulders. She taught him French songs and nicknamed him *le gentil géant*. It wasn't long before Rock was envisioning himself as Veronique's legal guardian.

"One day, out of the blue, I asked myself, 'What if I adopted her? Took her home with me? I love her already, and she loves me. Why not?'" An unmarried movie star adopting a poor Parisian moppet? It sounded an awful lot like some shameless press agent's invention, but according to those close to Hudson, he couldn't have been more serious. "I thought long and hard. I thought how great it would be to have the child with me in my house because I really loved her so," Hudson told writer Henry Gris. "I've thought of adopting a child many times. If I haven't, it's mainly because, obviously, I'm single."

Rock's bachelorhood wasn't the only obstacle. Although Veronique was being cared for at what was essentially an orphanage, her parents were still very much alive, just not financially able to provide for her. Through an intermediary, Hudson broached the idea of legally adopting the child and raising her in America. "The message I received was a proud, 'No, you are very kind, Monsieur, and all that, but you can't have her.' It was quite a blow," Hudson later recalled. "They wouldn't give her up, but I could take her for one year. It was the most they would allow . . . But what would happen at the end of that year? After living in a big house like a little princess, she'd have to go back and face up to—what? It would have been utterly cruel."

Although Hudson's concern for Veronique's welfare seemed both characteristic and genuine, adopting a child in need certainly wouldn't hurt his public image. If Rock had married to keep his career afloat (as some firmly believed), was it out of the realm of possibility that he would adopt a child to boost his sagging box office?

Tom Clark, for one, believed that Hudson's intentions were strictly honorable. After *Darling Lili* wrapped, Clark recalled that

"Rock came home, still childless and unhappy because of it. He did donate a great deal of money to that orphanage and hoped that that enchanting little girl had something of a better life because of his largesse."

————

"Rock and Rod Join Forces" read the headline in the *Los Angeles Times*. Although Hudson and Rod McKuen had long discussed forming a production company together, the public announcement in January of 1970 finally made it official.

Under the banner of R & R Productions, the two would collaborate on feature films. Rock would star. Rod would direct, adding yet another job title to McKuen's seemingly endless list of hyphenates: poet-novelist-actor-singer-songwriter-record producer-gay rights pioneer. And movies were only the beginning. There would be television specials, a series of record albums, and a Broadway musical. Backed by McKuen, Rock Hudson would become a multimedia superstar, prepared to compete on the same playing field as Frank Sinatra, Barbra Streisand, and Elvis Presley. And with Rod McKuen's genius for cross promotion, Rock would be merchandised into pop culture infinity.

Even for a couple of overachieving workaholics, the plans sounded incredibly ambitious and many in the industry wondered if R & R Productions represented more than just a professional marriage. After all, their elaborate business plan virtually guaranteed that Hudson and McKuen would be together around the clock. And what had brought these two former Universal-International contract players together? The quick answer was Tom Clark, who was McKuen's publicist at the time. The more complex explanation involved mutual need.

A self-described "stringer of words," McKuen had sold over three million books of poetry by the early 1970s. As a singer-songwriter, McKuen's albums (*Listen to the Warm, In Search of Eros*) soared to the top of the charts and his gravelly voiced renditions of his own songs ("Jean," "I've Been to Town") were responsible for sold-out concerts around the world. Even if the critics had dubbed him the "King of Kitsch" and writer Nora Ephron had dismissed him as a "mush-huckster," McKuen had managed to tap into the popular consciousness while connecting with the highly coveted youth market. And McKuen had a thirty-room mansion in Beverly Hills to prove it.

The only realm that McKuen hadn't quite conquered by the early 1970s was Hollywood. Which is where Rock Hudson came in. By joining forces with one of the most recognizable stars in the industry, McKuen would gain entry. And by teaming up with McKuen, Hudson would be delivered to the doorstep of the American teenager, a key segment of the movie-going public that he needed to connect with in order to ensure career survival.

The first film planned by R & R Productions was *Chuck*, based on a novel that McKuen had published in 1969 under the pseudonym Carl Sterland. While it was critically savaged (*Kirkus Reviews* called it a "staggeringly awful confessional"), the story of a middle-aged man who discovers that he has an illegitimate son appealed to Rock. In the novel, father and son bond by getting high and visiting Tijuana brothels together. McKuen and Hudson believed that the protagonist's unconventional parenting skills would have strong countercultural appeal.

Since McKuen had never directed before, several of Rock's intimates feared that he was entrusting his film career to a man who, while phenomenally successful in his own right, seemed to be wading in over his head.

Tom Clark suggested testing the waters with a smaller-scale project first. Why not start with a record album? So, in March of 1970, Rock found himself recording fourteen Rod McKuen songs at Phillips & Chapel Studios in London.* He warbled his way through

---

*According to Hudson's longtime publicist, Roger Jones, Rock's LP project was largely self-financed. "You paid $80,000 to cut that record with Rod McKuen

"Gone With the Cowboys," "Happy Birthday to Me," and "Open the Window and See All the Clowns," among others. Photographer David Nutter was hired to snap images of Hudson and McKuen at work on their first joint effort.

"It was such a farce because I think Rod was madly in love with Rock," Nutter says. "When I went to the first session, it was ridiculous because here's Rod all dewy-eyed and everything and Rock Hudson couldn't have cared less. Then this good-looking younger man turned up to meet Rock and they left together. Poor Mr. McKuen wanted to commit suicide. He laid down in front of a 60-piece orchestra with his head in his hands and it was just pathetic. After this went on for a while, I dragged Rod down to the nearest pub and tried to talk him out of committing suicide . . . I mean, even on a good day, Rod was quite a drama queen, so you can imagine what this was like."

All too accustomed to having members of both sexes instantly fall for him, Rock seemed oblivious to McKuen's romantic interest. Hudson was single-mindedly determined to prove that he had what it took to realize his ambitions as a song and dance man. However, once all of the tracks of the recording sessions were mixed, the results proved to be decidedly *under*whelming. While his voice was pleasant enough, only occasionally did Rock's vocals border on thoroughly engaging. This was far from the embarrassing fiasco that some had predicted, though the finished album revealed that Hudson wouldn't be bumping Tony Bennett off the marquee at Caesar's Palace anytime soon. Nevertheless, Rock remained optimistic that he'd be as popular on turntables as he'd been in the movies.

"I'm 45 years old and that's a little bit late to start a singing career," Hudson admitted to reporter Toni Holt. "But I'd really rather sing than anything." Not only was Rod McKuen blinded by love but, apparently, he had gone deaf: "Let me put it this way; a lot of

---

in London," Jones wrote in a letter to Hudson. "I guess I better hang on to it, it might be a collectible."

people have sung some of these songs and nobody—*nobody*—ever sang them better than Rock does."

Titled *Rock, Gently*, Hudson's album came complete with a "Produced and Directed by Rod McKuen" credit, which seemed to suggest that the LP was a kind of precursor to their forthcoming cinematic collaborations. There was even a poster included that featured thirty-five images of Hollywood's new troubadour mugging it up in the recording studio. Where Rock's long-playing debut was concerned, everything was in place. Except a major record label.

Hudson expected that his album would be widely distributed through Warner Bros. Records, which had carried some of McKuen's own recordings. Instead, *Rock, Gently* was released through McKuen's own Stanyan Records label and available exclusively through mail order. With record stores bypassed and radio airplay forfeited, Rock's dreams of *Billboard* glory were dashed.

A year after Hudson's album was released, columnist Marilyn Beck reported that "thousands of copies of *Rock, Gently* are gently gathering dust in McKuen's warehouse . . . If you're interested in buying a copy, send a check to Rod's Stanyan Company. I'm sure he'd be delighted to unload some of the stock." After their first and only collaboration, Rock and Rod would go their separate ways. R & R Productions was immediately disbanded. *Chuck* was scrapped. Plans for a second feature film based on McKuen's best-selling poetry collection, *In Someone's Shadow*, were cancelled. As Tom Clark remembered, "Rock was about the angriest I ever saw him." And Hudson, when questioned about the album, flatly stated, "My first and last—it's awful."

———

Rock Hudson was ready to take on the sexual revolution. After appearing in *Darling Lili*—otherwise known as one of the most antiquated films of his career—Hudson was newly determined to show how cutting edge he could be. Managing a complete 180 from

Lili's gallant Major Larrabee, Rock would swing into the 1970s by playing the ultimate big bad wolf.

In *Pretty Maids All in a Row*, he would play Michael "Tiger" Mc-Drew, Oceanfront High School's assistant principal, football coach, part-time guidance counselor, and full-time Don Juan. When the neon "Testing" light is illuminated over the door of his constantly occupied office, it's understood that Tiger is busy scoring more than the latest batch of exams.

Fully dedicated to the student body—especially if it's ready, willing, and female—Tiger offers afterschool tutorials to the nubile young maids of the title. How strange, then, that so many of Tiger's students have a habit of turning up dead, with "So Long, Honey" notes pinned to their posteriors. "To me, he's a very intriguing character," Rock would say of Tiger McDrew. "A real schizo behind a Mr. Nice Guy façade."

In 1968, MGM announced that it was adapting Francis Pollini's darkly satirical novel, *Pretty Maids All in a Row*, for the screen. The black-comedy mystery would be directed by James B. Harris, who had produced *Lolita* for the studio, thereby proving that he had some experience with risqué projects involving underage eroticism. But by 1970, Harris was out and Roger Vadim was occupying the director's chair. *Pretty Maids* would mark the American feature debut for the French director. After Vadim showcased his first wife, Brigitte Bardot, as a voluptuous man teaser in *And God Created Woman*, he went on to present his third wife Jane Fonda, writhing in orgasmic ecstasy in the "Excessive Machine," in the sci-fi cult favorite *Barbarella*.

Now Vadim was prepared to take on the American teenager. "There is only one way to describe the story," Vadim told the press. "It is insolent, and I love insolence. But in no way am I making a critique of the American lifestyle or Americans. As a French director, I do not have that right." But critique he did. In Vadim's vision of southern California suburbia, everyone is simultaneously obsessed with sex and sporting events. Minutes into the investigation of the bizarre murder of a high school cheerleader, Keenan Wynn's dim-witted police chief seems infinitely more interested in the gridiron than the crime scene. "How do you think the team's going to do against Valley High?" he asks a student, with a newly discovered corpse lying only inches away.

Sexually inexperienced seventeen-year-old Ponce de Leon Harper (John David Carson) is constantly on the verge of an erection and overwhelmed by the steady stream of T and A coming at him before, during, and after class. Whether it's cold showers or completing the multiplication tables in his head, nothing seems to extinguish Ponce's eternal flame. Coach McDrew takes the young man under his wing and tutors him in the fine art of chick chasing. As though he's preparing a halfback for a scrimmage game, Tiger tells his protégé, "An animal body needs animal exercise."

Initially, Vadim hoped to cast all-American football pro Joe Namath as the lecherous coach. But MGM was insisting on an A-list actor for marquee insurance. Most established Hollywood stars would not relish playing a sleazeball heavy with next to no redeeming qualities. But after *Seconds*, Rock was hungry for an acting challenge that would allow him to break free from the confinement that came with being typecast as a romantic lead.

"It must be hard to switch from Doris Day to Roger Vadim," journalist Bob Colacello suggested to Hudson when they chatted for Andy Warhol's *Interview*. "That's the fun of it," Rock responded. "Ideally, I'd like to do a drama, a comedy, a western, a love story, a musical . . . I've tried every way I know to diversify."

For *Pretty Maids*, Vadim would surround Rock with an impressive supporting cast: Angie Dickinson played the sexually frustrated substitute teacher whom Tiger enlists to seduce Ponce (she revs things up by reciting Milton's *Paradise Lost*); Roddy McDowall portrayed Oceanfront's eternally befuddled principal ("I don't understand this," McDowall's character says when he encounters the corpse of a murdered student. "We've always kept our academic averages so high."); and two years before he started cracking cases as *Kojak*, Telly Savalas was the FBI agent intent on catching a homicidal Tiger by the tail.

Vadim interviewed dozens of young women in an extensive search for his miniskirted maids. Ultimately, only eight actresses were cast, including Diane Sherry Case, whom Vadim and writer-producer Gene Roddenberry spotted while she was on her way to an interview for an entirely different project.

"Rock Hudson was very sweet but what was really exciting was Roger Vadim," says Case. "He was fun to work with and it was kind of a wild set . . . I remember that Vadim and Jane Fonda got divorced around that time and it was probably partly because of that film. He had all these eighteen- to twenty-year-olds coming to their house in Malibu—testing—and some of them were disrobing or close to it. I just remember Fonda walking through at one point and I imagine she was rather disgruntled."

Barbara Leigh, who played Tiger's wife, remembered that the libidinous activity depicted in the film was matched by some of the behind-the-scenes goings-on. "Rock and John David Carson were having a little 'tete' at the time," says Leigh. "Everybody on the set knew. John David was bi and very cute. And during the film, I had a very brief affair with Vadim. It was brief mainly because my boyfriend at the time, Jim Aubrey, was the president of MGM and he was watching me like a hawk. In those days, I was very young and naïve and Vadim intrigued me, as I'm sure he did Bardot and Fonda. I liked Vadim and he had a good sense of humor but romantically, it didn't work for me. I didn't like his personal cleanliness habits. 'Hygiene,' I think is the word I'm looking for."

When studio executives screened Vadim's rough cut of *Pretty Maids All in a Row*, it was greeted with stunned silence. MGM, which had produced such family-friendly fare as *Lassie Come Home* and *National Velvet* in its fabled heyday, was now faced with the prospect of releasing its first X-rated picture. "Louis B. Mayer would have been rolling in his grave if MGM had released a picture with an X-rating," says publicist Germaine Szal. "Are you kidding? This was the same studio that had made the Andy Hardy series and all those Jeanette MacDonald and Nelson Eddy musicals."

To escape the Motion Picture Association of America's dreaded "X," *Pretty Maids* (which would eventually be branded as "one of the most politically incorrect films of all time") was subjected to a rigorous "reevaluation" process and substantial cuts were made. Tom Clark, for one, felt that this irreparably damaged the film: "The re-cutting ruined it and another great movie was sacrificed on the altar of studio politics and greed."

"MGM slashed it," Rock griped to *Playgirl*. "They became very moralistic, which was bullshit. They just wanted to make it more commercial. So they filmed a new ending, which gave them an R-rating." The R-rating was nowhere near as damning as an X, but it was still a first for a Rock Hudson movie. Even with some of the more risqué scenes removed, *Pretty Maids* managed to work some critics into a lather.

"Roger Vadim's first American film should have been incinerated before the print was dry," wrote Rex Reed in his scathing review. "Mostly it's just incompetent gibberish with scenes that seem to exist for the sole purpose of introducing a parade of Hollywood Deb Stars with overdeveloped mammaries and underdeveloped craniums." Kathleen Carroll's *New York Daily News* review was headlined "Sleazy, Crude, Lecherous Film," and it was all downhill from there: "As a sex satire-murder mystery, Vadim's film fails miserably . . . his vision of a grotesque Southern California is grotesque but lifeless."

Though two of the more influential critics seemed to have screened a completely different movie. Roger Greenspun of the *New York Times* found Hudson "remarkably good as the heavy" and he praised Vadim's satire as an "honorable work, intelligent where least expected and consistently fun to watch." In the *Los*

Angeles Times, Kevin Thomas[*] championed *Pretty Maids* as "a hilarious and outrageous dark satire of American morality with unflaggingly zesty dialogue . . . In a departure even farther out than *Seconds*, Rock Hudson . . . turns in one of the best performances of his career."

Depending on who you talked to, *Pretty Maids All in a Row* was either "one of the stupidest movies ever made" (according to Andrew Sarris in the *Village Voice*) or one of the ten best (per director Quentin Tarantino in *Sight & Sound*). Despite its defenders, *Pretty Maids All in a Row* bombed during its initial release, though eventually it would attract a devoted cult following.

———————

You are cordially invited to celebrate the wedding of
Mr. Rock Hudson and Mr. Jim Nabors
On Saturday afternoon, June 19, 1971

As practical jokes go, this one seemed harmless enough. Instead of a routine cocktail party, a gay couple in Huntington Beach[†] decided to gather their friends together for a far more momentous occasion . . . the wedding of two beloved celebrities, who would be joined in "holy matrimony." Guests were invited to attend the

---

[*] "Vadim was an outrageous guy," says veteran *Los Angeles Times* critic Kevin Thomas. "The last time I saw him, it was at a party for an upcoming [*sic*] French film director and he'd had a few. He looked me in the eye and he said the most wonderfully outrageous thing. He said, 'Kevin, I promise you that we will be lovers in the next life.' That's Vadim. I was very fond of him."

[†] Depending on which version of the rumor one heard, the gay couple that hosted the Rock Hudson–Jim Nabors "wedding" may have been from Huntington Beach, Manhattan Beach, Hermosa Beach, or Long Beach, where Rock had once lived with Ken Hodge. The location of the ceremony also changed and tended to become more exotic with each retelling: Tijuana, Vancouver, Las Vegas, Belgravia. "The truth is it didn't happen anywhere!" an exasperated Hudson told journalist Hy Gardner.

wedding of Rock Hudson and Jim Nabors, the star of the long-running CBS sitcom *Gomer Pyle, U.S.M.C.*

Whether the hosts could claim some sort of insider knowledge concerning the closeted homosexuality of both stars or whether their prank had been inspired purely by gossip, it is unclear. What is clear is that the nuptials were not at all meant to be taken seriously. The tongue-in-cheek tone of the "ceremony" was evident from the beginning, starting with the most obvious joke. Once Rock Hudson married Gomer Pyle, he would officially be known as "Rock Pyle." With Truman Capote officiating and Liberace providing "musical accompaniment," this should have been enough of a tip-off that the wedding was a lark, an irreverent gay fantasia.

"All of this was started by a bunch of silly-assed faggots and I'm allowed to say that because I am a faggot," says Hudson's former partner, Tony Melia. "I don't think they were being vicious. They were just stupid and not realizing what they were doing. I don't know if whoever printed the fake invitations sent them to people or if somebody knew somebody who got it to the press but they certainly ran with it."

What started as a bit of backyard camp would soon become the stuff of urban legend: *Rock Hudson married Jim Nabors.* Although Hudson and Nabors were friends and Rock had guest-starred on an episode of *The Jim Nabors Hour* in 1970, the two were never romantically involved. Besides, same-sex marriage was nowhere near a reality in the United States in the early 1970s.

In the face of all contrary evidence, the marriage rumors refused to die, spreading like wildfire. In November of 1971, the story landed on the front page of the *National Examiner.* After claiming that "perversion in Hollywood is more rampant than ever," the *Examiner* was quick to assure readers, "But Rock Hudson and Jim Nabors are not among those who indulge." The article also quoted an unidentified "former girlfriend of Hudson's," who vouched for his red-blooded heterosexuality: "He's rugged, really rugged. Believe me, he is all man. There's nothing queer about Rock."

For two decades, Hudson had played it straight to prevent being exposed by the press. Now the press was insisting that the same Rock Hudson that they knew to be gay was actually . . . straight. And the grandest irony of all—the public debate over Hudson's sexuality had been prompted not by one of his actual same-sex relationships but by an imaginary one.

Even though the Hudson-Nabors wedding was pure fantasy, the rumors surrounding it ended up causing some very real damage: CBS canceled *The Jim Nabors Hour* in 1971. While it's been suggested that Nabors's highly rated program fell victim to the network's "rural purge," many believe that the backlash from the gay marriage story doomed the show. Then there was the Rock Hudson version of damage control. "I'll tell you one thing that makes me sad about this, and that's that Jim Nabors and I are no longer friends. We can't be seen together," Hudson told a reporter in the early 1970s. Though even after the rumors had subsided, Hudson chose not to resume his friendship with Nabors.

"When Roy was finished with a relationship, and that includes the friendship he had with Jim Nabors, he'd have nothing to do with that person," says Tony Melia. "That was a pattern with him and that's the way it went with Jim. And believe me, Jim Nabors is just a great, wonderful guy and he never deserved that. It wasn't Jim's fault, after all. But that whole scandal really damaged Roy's public image because people believed it."

Even Rock's mother felt the full impact of the rumors, says Craig Muckler, producer of the cult hit *Microwave Massacre*. Growing up, Muckler was a surrogate grandson to Kay Olsen. Craig and his family would spend summers at their cabin in Lake Vermilion in Minnesota. And they could always count on an extended visit from Kay.

"I remember the summer we picked Kay up at the Duluth airport," Muckler says. "The first thing out of her mouth to my mom was, 'You probably heard that awful rumor about Rock.' My mother said, 'Yeah, we've heard that bullshit.' For some reason, people not only believed that Rock Hudson had married Jim Nabors but they also thought they were honeymooning in our cabin. There were all these gawkers wandering around our cabin day and night. We even had people calling us and asking, 'Are Rock and Jim there?' It was a very disconcerting time for Kay. I'm pretty sure that Rock being gay kind of killed her in a way. She always tried to hide that fact from us but it would come out in other ways. Once, Kay and my family and I were having dinner at a café and this very effeminate gay guy walked by our table. He was wearing rouge and eye shadow. I recall Kay saying, 'Do you mean you've even got them up here?' It's almost like she went out of her way to say that she disapproved."

Meanwhile, the real man in Hudson's life, Jack Coates, had come to the painful decision that it was time to move on. Some friends remember that Coates felt that his own identity had been sacrificed the moment he had assumed the role of "Mrs. Rock Hudson." Others say that Jack had finally had his fill of all of the machinations and manipulation that were part of daily life at The Castle. "I wish I'd been more sophisticated at chess playing because I couldn't take the intrigue in that house. It was brutal," Coates recalled.

Jack was also interested in someone new. Dr. Frederick Whitam was an Arizona State University professor. A sociologist who studied homosexuality from a cross-cultural perspective, Whitam had published a number of books on the subject. Here was an accomplished and esteemed professional who didn't come with all of the baggage that an internationally famous movie star did.

"I was so mad at Jack for a while," recalls Coates's sister, Cathy Hamblin. "It was like Rock was breaking up with me. Jack said, 'No, he really wants me to be happy. He wants this for me.' Jack had only the kindest thoughts about their time together . . . so who was I to be upset? But I was."

CHAPTER 16
MCMILLAN & WIFE

The Generation Gap personified:
Rock and Susan Saint James drew huge ratings
when they starred as *McMillan & Wife*.
(*Courtesy of* Photofest)

From *Get Smart* to *Supermarket Sweep*, producer Leonard B. Stern was the man responsible for some of the best dumb fun on television. In the late 1960s, Stern had created a string of fondly remembered though not terribly successful sitcoms (*The Hero, He & She, The Governor and J.J.*). By the early 1970s, Stern was badly in need of a hit. It finally arrived in the form of a script for a television movie entitled *Once Upon a Dead Man*. Stern and cowriter Chester Krumholz came up with a story that seemed simultaneously classic and contemporary.

Once Upon a Dead Man read like a modern version of MGM's *Thin Man* series, which dated back to the 1930s. In Stern's updating, Stewart McMillan, a San Francisco–based police commissioner, investigates the disappearance of an ancient Egyptian sarcophagus. McMillan cracks the case with the assistance of his impetuous younger wife, Sally. Their snappy repartee seemed closely patterned on that of Nick and Nora Charles, the martini-swilling sleuths who bantered their way through six *Thin Man* movies.

It may have been derivative, lighthearted fluff but *Once Upon a Dead Man* also seemed like the ideal vehicle to help facilitate Rock Hudson's transition from movie to television star (even if he dismissively referred to the tube as "illustrated radio"). The much-publicized two-hour movie would serve as the pilot for a new NBC series called *McMillan & Wife*.

"Rock and his agent, Flo Allen, liked the idea of a classy TV series," says producer Paul Mason. "Leonard Stern had pitched it to them as a stylistic *Thin Man* type mystery program . . . It would take deep pockets for this kind of series. I liked the idea and took it to Sid Sheinberg, who was president of Universal TV and he suggested that we make one two-hour movie and see what kind of reaction we got from the network. NBC bought it after they saw three days of dailies."

If Commissioner McMillan was the stalwart center of every show, his free-spirited spouse would be a kind of Lucy Ricardo in bell bottoms—forever attempting to get in on the investigative act. The role required an actress who could convincingly play the upscale sophisticate and the wide-eyed kook. Rock's first choice to play his television wife was his friend, Stefanie Powers. Hudson believed that Powers had the right kind of flair for the role, but by the early 1970s she was committed to a pilot of her own. Leonard Stern then lobbied for Barbara Feldon, best known as Agent 99 on *Get Smart*, which Stern had executive produced.

Feldon was a strong contender, but as she was closing in on forty, Universal executives pushed for Hudson to be paired with a younger costar. Future Oscar winners Diane Keaton and Jill Clayburgh were among the finalists that Rock and Leonard Stern met with during a succession of lunches. At the last of these meetings, Rock was introduced to a twenty-five-year-old contract player.

If Hudson was known as the most tight-lipped star in Hollywood, Susan Saint James had been dubbed "Instant Mouth" by one of her directors. She was outspoken, opinionated, and a champion of countless progressive causes. Rock, a die-hard chain-smoker who was in the habit of knocking back several Scotches with his steak dinners, suddenly found himself in the company of a health-conscious vegetarian who made her own clothes and soybean soup.

It was immediately clear that they were the Generation Gap personified, though Rock instinctively knew that their polar-opposite personalities would only enhance their on-screen rapport. As producer Paul Mason remembers it, "We presented Rock with a variety of leading ladies, some of whom he knew quite well, but he picked Susie. It turned out to be a very shrewd choice." What's more, Saint James had a sterling track record as a Universal contract player. In 1969, she had won an Emmy Award for her role in NBC's *The Name of the Game.*

Once Hudson and Saint James were on board, the producers then hired two experienced character actors to round out the principal cast. Pint-sized comedienne Nancy Walker would play the McMillans' acerbic, boozy housekeeper, Mildred. John Schuck was Stern's first and only choice to play Sergeant Charles Enright, Commissioner McMillan's oafish sidekick.

A few weeks before production launched, Schuck happened to spot the show's leading man wandering around the streets of San Francisco. "I was in North Beach and I look up and there's Rock Hudson across the street, looking very movie star," Schuck says. "That was my first impression of him—*This man is a movie star.* Tall, broadshouldered, handsome as all get-out and quite animated. He had a big smile on his face and was obviously enjoying the day . . . When we started working together, I discovered that on a surface level, he was always warm and very available. But you could tell there was only so far you could go and he would shut off or shut down . . . So, he was a good friend but at the same time, very private."

McMillan & Wife would air on *The NBC Mystery Movie* in a monthly rotation with two other programs produced by Universal Television: Peter Falk's *Columbo* and *McCloud*, which starred Dennis Weaver. When it aired in September of 1971, Hudson's pilot earned respectable ratings and largely positive reviews ("a nifty blend of cop meller and intrigue," said *Variety*). Betting everything on Rock's drawing power, NBC executives remained hopeful that *McMillan & Wife* would become a semi-regular series.

"Our first season, we were not particularly successful," remembers John Schuck. "We rode into the second season on Peter Falk's coattails as *Columbo*. It was really in the second season, I think, that our audience found us and we found our audience, which was great." Now that he was regularly appearing in millions of living rooms, Rock started receiving fan mail from a younger generation of admirers. Many of them hadn't been around to witness the ascension of Rock Hudson during the *Magnificent Obsession* era.

"Television brought Rock back to life. It introduced him to a whole new audience," says publicist Germaine Szal. "Most of the letters he got were from teenaged girls or lonely housewives. But some of it was from young men. They either wanted career advice or to take him to bed or both. In some cases, they would send photos of themselves. When I was sorting through all of this, it occurred to me that Rock had this unique magnetism . . . an ability to appeal to just about everyone. Even though he was pushing fifty . . . He still had it."

Despite the twenty-one-year age difference between them, Hudson and Saint James proved to be a winning combination on-screen. In fact, many fans felt that Rock hadn't been as well matched with a costar since teaming with Doris Day a decade earlier.

"There was real chemistry on screen. You can't fake that," says costar John Schuck. Off camera, Rock was thrown by his costar's attempts to inject some originality and spontaneity into scripts that sometimes seemed hackneyed.

"She taxed him," recalled director Bob Finkel. "She would come to a scene with such enthusiasm and such preproduction work—and this was a shock to Rock because now he had to change what was planned. He would have to go to work . . . Susan tried to bring some creativity to the set and Rock couldn't deal with it. He just liked to do his little number and go right back to the trailer." As Paul Mason remembers it, "On screen, they were wonderful. Off screen, not too wonderful. Susie fell in love with her make-up man and married him. He did not like Rock. It was strained but we managed to work around it."

During the six-year run of the show, the McMillans investigated Satanic cults, mob bosses, and gold smugglers. Along the way, an impressive collection of guest stars appeared. The roster included a mix of old pros and promising newcomers, including: Tab Hunter, Roddy McDowall, Joan Van Ark, Keir Dullea, Van Johnson, Tyne Daly, Jackie Coogan, Barry Sullivan, Donna Mills, Shirley Jones, and José Feliciano. Several of Hudson's former leading ladies also turned up, including Julie Adams, Dana Wynter, and Salome Jens.

Actress Carole Cook, who had a recurring role on *McMillan & Wife* as society maven Carole Crenshaw, recalls an especially memorable lunch she had with Hudson: "We didn't go to the commissary. He always had lunch brought to his dressing room . . . I remember Susan Saint James, who is a darling girl, was going through a hippie period and she'd just had a child named Sunshine. Rock and I were sitting together talking and she was back on the set after having had time off for maternity leave. She said, 'Oh, do you want to see a picture of the baby?' Rock said, 'Of course.' And she whipped out a picture and it was one of the baby still in the birth channel. I'm telling you, Rock fled the fucking scene. I laughed my ass off. I mean, I was screaming with laughter but Mr. Hudson was having none of it. He just left. And I think I made some sort of smart remark like, 'Well, it looks just like Gabby Hayes.'"

DURING THE EARLY days of *McMillan & Wife*, Rock developed what members of his entourage had come to refer to as yet another intense infatuation. "I think it was probably around 1972 when we met in Miami," says Kenneth Griggs. "I was about 24 years old. It was right after the sexual revolution and everything. I mean . . . I was *busy*."

In those days, Griggs was working in one of Miami's showrooms, where interior designers would come to purchase high-end furniture. Virtually all of Griggs's colleagues were young gay men. "When one of the older showroom owners would have a party, we'd all be invited," Griggs recalls. "At one of these parties, Rock happened to be there. He was smoking and I remember turning to a friend and I said, 'Quick, give me a cigarette.' I went over and asked him for a light . . . That's how everything got started."

Griggs seemed to meet all of Rock's basic requirements—he was blond, butch, and ruggedly handsome. "I do remember us kidding one another that we had matching mustaches," says Griggs. "I also remember him telling me that I was totally his type."

At the time, Griggs was in what he describes as "a real back and forth relationship" with a live-in boyfriend, though he continued to see Rock over a period of six months. With Hudson's commitment to *McMillan & Wife* keeping him on the West Coast, Griggs realized that the relationship was "just one of those things. I guess a part of me was thinking, 'This will never go anywhere.' And once Danny, my on-and-off boyfriend, knew that I had been seeing Rock Hudson, he became a lot nicer to me and we got back together. Years later, when I moved out to L.A., I didn't even know how to get in touch with Rock as so much time had passed. Looking back, I'm sorry that we didn't continue a friendship of sorts because we had this great connection for a while."

While *McMillan & Wife* consistently ranked high in the Nielsen ratings, Rock's movie career continued to founder. Hudson's next film, a character-driven Western entitled *Showdown*, would do nothing to revive his flagging box office appeal. The buddy picture aspects of Theodore Taylor's screenplay seemed vaguely reminiscent of *Butch Cassidy and the Sundance Kid.*

Originally titled *Once Upon a River, Showdown* was set in the late 1890s. Chuck Jarvis (Hudson), the sheriff of lonesome Cumbres, New Mexico, finds himself in the awkward position of pursuing his lifelong friend turned outlaw, Billy Massey (Dean Martin), who has been involved in a train robbery. While the two have been pals since childhood, flashbacks reveal that Chuck has always followed the straight and narrow while the more adventurous Billy has evolved from charming con man to wanted outlaw. Over the years, there's also been an ongoing rivalry for the affections of a feisty café owner named Kate (Susan Clark). While Billy finds her "as pretty to look at as four aces" and does his best to win her over, the pragmatic Kate ultimately marries Chuck.

Showdown would be the final film for sixty-one-year-old George Seaton, who had directed such classics as *Miracle on 34th Street* and *The Proud and the Profane.* In sharp contrast to his earlier hits, Seaton's *Showdown* is sluggishly paced, saved only by the playful exchanges between Rock and costar Dean Martin. In fact, events that took place during the making of *Showdown* were far more intriguing than anything that ended up on-screen.

"He wasn't awfully fond of Rock," Susan Clark says of Dean Martin, who seemed miserable throughout the location shoot in remote Chama, New Mexico. Martin was so unhappy, in fact, that he walked off the film only twenty-four days after production had started. The desolate location; the death of his favorite film horse, Tops; and his aversion to Hudson all seemed to push Dino over the edge. Universal chief Lew Wasserman ordered the production shut down and the studio filed a $6 million lawsuit against Dean Martin.

Two weeks later, Martin returned to Chama and Universal

withdrew its lawsuit. Production resumed but not for long. Several days later, Hudson was filming a scene that required him to be behind the wheel of an antique locomobile. When Rock swerved to avoid a truck, the locomobile overturned. Hudson emerged with a number of broken bones and a concussion.

While Rock recovered, his longtime double, George Robotham, completed some stunts and long-distance shots. Hudson's colleagues were stunned to find him back before the cameras even though his fractures hadn't completely healed. Despite everything Rock had endured on *Showdown*, unkind reviews would be waiting at the finish line. "A tale that . . . simply stresses phlegmatic performances," said *New York Times* critic A. H. Weiler. "Unfortunately, the people and problems in *Showdown* are a letdown."

BY THE TIME Rock returned for the next season of *McMillan & Wife*, there was a new man in his life. A graduate of the University of Nebraska and an insurance salesman, Anthony Melia came equipped with chiseled features, enormous charm, and what George Nader once described as "the full movie star aura." It was Rock's second favorite pastime that would bring them together.

"There was, at one time, a whole bunch of gay guys in southern California who played bridge on an ongoing basis," Melia says. "I was in some of those bridge groups and often Roy would be there. Tom Clark and Pete DePalma, who were partners at the time, were also there . . . After I got to know Roy through our bridge playing, we then started to see each other. Then we became lovers." Unlike some of Rock's previous partnerships, which he had entered into gradually and cautiously, things with Melia progressed very quickly.

"I had a house at that time up on Sunset Plaza. He would come up at various times, sometimes practically unannounced and spend a lot of time with me . . . After seeing each other for some time, he asked if I would move in. And so I did." When he first moved into

The Castle, Melia says that Rock was at his carefree, fun-loving best. "He was a terrific gentleman with a wonderful sense of humor and a twinkle of mischief. He was very generous. Very smart. He loved word games. When it came to things like Scrabble, he was just amazing. We had a lot of fun together in the beginning." Despite a promising start, Melia says that his relationship with Hudson soon deteriorated, almost as quickly as it had begun.

"For one thing, he was delusional in the fact that he felt that no one in the world really knew he was gay. He would warn me not to tell anybody that we were together because he knew that I was out and proud and didn't care who knew it. I never flaunted the fact that I was gay but I also wasn't going to spend my life hiding and being in the closet . . . One day, George Cukor, the director, was coming over to the house. Now I knew George and had attended several Sunday afternoon pool parties that he had hosted. I remember Roy saying to me, 'I have to talk business with George Cukor and you can't be here.' I said, 'Well, I know George.' He said, 'I don't care. I don't want you here.' And I was really upset about that. I mean, come on, I'm thirty-nine years old, for God's sake, and a businessman. I'm not a little child that you send to his room."

Drinking was another issue for Melia, who describes himself as "a comparative lightweight." As it happened, Melia's residency at The Castle coincided with a period in which Hudson's alcohol intake increased. "I think it was starting to get a bit out of hand then. I remember his maid, Joy, was very devoted to him but she was as much of an alcoholic as he was."

Melia says that the tipping point came when they decided to spend Thanksgiving with Hudson's mother. "Kay and I had an incredibly good rapport," says Melia. "She was from Illinois. I was from Nebraska. We were both sort of non-sophisticated people in our own way. Roy adored his mother and he gave her lots of deference. He did whatever she asked of him and he was very protective of her. When Roy saw his mother and I getting close, he was very jealous of that and felt it was almost an invasion . . . He could be very proprietary about some of the people in his life but especially his mother."

By early December, it was clear that it was all over. "I remember one day, Mark Miller pulled me aside and said that Roy wanted me to move my things out of the house. And I said, 'Well, let him tell me himself.' But he didn't. I thought, 'Little Tony Melia, you don't want to stay where somebody doesn't want you . . . leave.' And that's exactly what I did."

———

"Have you heard the one about Prince Rainier and Tennessee Ernie Ford?" Rock would often ask a new acquaintance. Among Hudson's inner circle of close friends, comedienne Carol Burnett was one of his favorites, and an anecdote concerning her very regrettable brush with royalty would become a fixture in Rock's repertoire.

In August of 1967, Hudson had invited 400 Hollywood luminaries, including Lucille Ball, Henry Fonda, Debbie Reynolds, and Groucho Marx to an "informal" Mexican-themed party at his home. The lavish soiree was in honor of Carol Burnett. "He just said, 'Well, you're going to be doing your [CBS] variety show soon, so let me throw you a big old bash . . .' And that's what he did," Burnett says.

While Burnett was the evening's sole honoree, many of the show business elite had also turned out to welcome Princess Grace and Prince Rainier of Monaco, who were visiting Los Angeles. For Burnett, who had grown up a starstruck kid addicted to double features, the party was heady stuff. "Of course, I was just a wreck," Burnett says. Although the arrival of Her Serene Highness and Prince Rainier had been signaled with a traditional bullfight processional played by the Guadalajara Kings, Burnett had somehow missed their grand entrance.

"Princess Grace and Prince Rainier still hadn't arrived yet to my knowledge, so I went up to the bar to get a glass of wine. There was this gentleman standing there and I said, 'Hey, you Ol' Pea Picker, you!' because that's what you always called Tennessee Ernie Ford. It was his catchphrase. Well, it turns out that it was really Prince Rainier standing there. He didn't know what to say and he just stared at me like I was . . . *something else*. I was so embarrassed. When I told Rock, he howled. He absolutely howled."

Hudson had first worked with Burnett in 1966 on her CBS variety special, *Carol and Company* and they instantly clicked. "I remember thinking . . . not only is he wonderful to look at but he's also got some good comedy chops," says Burnett. "He was just a lot of fun to be with, which is why we kept inviting him back when we were doing the weekly show."

In 1973, Burnett was approached about headlining a West Coast production of the Tony Award–winning Broadway musical *I Do! I Do!* Based on Jan de Hartog's play, *The Fourposter,* the show revisited fifty years in the lives of a married couple.

"Gower Champion wanted me to do it," Burnett recalls. "Right away, I said, 'Let's get Rock Hudson!'" As the husband and wife were the only characters in *I Do! I Do!*, Hudson and Burnett would be on stage continuously. Rock had several challenging solo numbers to sing, including "I Love My Wife" and "The Father of the Bride" and, at one point, Hudson even had to execute a soft-shoe while barefoot. All of this, not to mention holding his own opposite Burnett, who, in addition to being the first lady of television comedy, had won raves for her Broadway debut in *Once Upon a Mattress.* Despite Hudson's initial trepidation about performing live, Burnett says that Rock quickly got over his stage fright.

"Well, right from the beginning, he took to it like a duck to water . . . It was hard work but we had so much fun rehearsing. There were times when Gower had to sit on us because we'd look at each other, especially during the opening song, where they walk toward each other singing and we'd crack up. It became like giggling in church."

During a week of tryouts in San Bernardino, the show not only sold out every performance but both stars garnered encouraging reviews. From there, it was on to opening night in Los Angeles, complete with a who's who of Hollywood occupying nearly every seat in the orchestra section. Including Doris Day in the front row.

"When we first opened, Rock could be a bit of a devil," Burnett remembers. "After we'd do the opening number, the curtain would come in and we had to get into bed. While we were waiting for the lights to come back up, he'd say, 'You'll never guess who's in the audience tonight. You just won't believe it.' And I would scream at him before the lights came up, 'Don't you dare tell me!' He loved to know who was in the audience. The last thing I wanted to know was that some big star was sitting out there but he just loved to tease me."

The four-week run of *I Do! I Do!* would break box office and attendance records for the Huntington Hartford and the reviews were uniformly outstanding. A year later, in the summer of 1974, Hudson and Burnett kicked off a national tour of *I Do! I Do!* at the Dallas Music Hall. This was followed by performances at the Kennedy Center in Washington and the St. Louis Municipal Opera Theatre.

"In St. Louis, there was an audience of about 20,000 people," Burnett says. "What was weird about that one is that we were playing in an outdoor theater. Rock and I had to change the scenery during the blackout and, of course, in the summertime it doesn't get dark until after nine o'clock at night. So, the entire audience was watching us run around like crazy people while we were arranging the scenery and bumping into each other. But I guess the audience was used to that. They really made us feel welcome. It seemed like everyplace we went that summer, it was just terrific. And Rock was like nobody else."

———

"I have this unforgettable image of Tom Clark in my mind," says Armistead Maupin. "He's in The Castle's master bedroom, sitting up in this enormous four-poster bed with his silk sleep shade up over his forehead while he's watching his requisite morning episode of *The $10,000 Pyramid* . . . It was like Mrs. Vanderbilt reclining in her boudoir."

It was 1973. Tom Clark had officially taken up residence at 9402 Beverly Crest. For better or for worse, Clark would become the central figure in Rock Hudson's life for the next decade. Tom was now on board as both domestic and business partner to Rock, while also acting as his traveling companion, closest confidant, and full-time drinking buddy.

Now that he was out of Henry Willson's clutches and free from his contractual enslavement to Universal, Hudson felt it was best to keep his management team close to home. After hiring longtime pal Mark Miller as his secretary, Hudson then appointed Clark as an officer of his production company, Mammoth Films. Several intimates registered surprise that Hudson, who had always carefully compartmentalized every aspect of his life, now seemed to be indiscriminately mixing the personal and the professional.

"Rock always had this weak personality. He was easily swayed, easily influenced," says Lee Garlington. "Mark Miller was his friend, then he becomes his secretary. I mean, I liked Mark—but *please.* Then Tom Clark moves in on him and starts taking over. Next thing you know, he's Rock's lover. Now, if there's any one person that is not Rock's type, it was Tom Clark."

Once he was ensconced in The Castle, Tom wasted no time in ascending the throne and ordering a top to bottom renovation of Rock Hudson's life. Like Phyllis Gates before him, Clark felt that Rock's lifestyle was too laid-back, too ordinary, too middle-class. *"You're a movie star, goddamn it! Will you act like one"* was to become a familiar refrain echoing down the halls.

Under Clark's watchful eye, rooms were remodeled, furniture rearranged, buckets of Kentucky Fried Chicken confiscated. Although it embarrassed Hudson, a vintage Rolls-Royce would now be at his partner's disposal. "It didn't bother me at all," Clark would say with a shrug, "but I was to the manor born." If Hudson and Mark Miller had once sat down to informal lunches with the household staff, those days were over. "Tom is obviously rankled by the 'servants' being at the same table," George Nader noted in his diary. "He is a real study. He is beginning to use 'our' in all his sentences. Tom believes he is Queen of The Castle."

Although he could be high-handed and sometimes condescending, it was Clark who would arrange for all of Hudson's employees to receive a substantial (and long overdue) raise, along with a generous bonus. Before Tom arrived, Rock had been completely hands off with the staff—so much so that it was easy to forget that he was the head of the household.

"He never questioned anybody," says Marty Flaherty, who worked at The Castle for over a decade. "You could say or do anything you wanted. I mean, Rock was so laid back that he answered his own front door. Then Tom came in and things changed. Tom was the 'wife' that Rock needed in his life. He took care of all of the details a big star like Rock didn't have the time, the interest, or the knowledge to do." Because Hudson was so easygoing and non-confrontational, he could never bring himself to reprimand anyone.

Tom, on the other hand, had no problem laying down the law. If an issue came up involving a staffer, it would now fall to Clark to do the heavy lifting—as in the case of Hudson's longtime housekeeper. Leatrice Lowe, whom everyone called "Joy," had worked at The Castle for years and Rock considered her family. They had been through a lot together, including a harrowing episode in 1965 during the Watts Riots.

As the south side of Los Angeles erupted into violence after an altercation between an African American motorist and the police, Joy expressed concern about a friend of hers named Peggy, who lived in war-torn Watts. Fearing for her life, Peggy had barricaded herself inside her home. Rock sprang into action. Getting behind the wheel of his new Town & Country station wagon, Hudson embarked on a dangerous rescue mission with Joy, her young son, and a menacing-looking German shepherd named Fritz in tow.

Making their way past police barricades and rioters armed with Molotov cocktails, Rock and company finally reached Peggy's front door. After the terrified woman climbed aboard, they raced back to Beverly Hills. As Joy later recalled, "We drank a lot that night, and laughed. When you finish something like that, you feel your nerves."

Nearly a decade later, there was still a lot of drinking going on, to the point that Joy would disappear into her room for days, leaving her domestic duties unattended. Accustomed to overlooking his housekeeper's chronic benders, Rock never said a word about the unmade beds or overflowing ashtrays. Never one to remain silent, Tom angrily confronted Joy, who responded by hurling a container of cottage cheese across the room. It wasn't long after this episode that Rock made the painful, though inevitable, decision to let Joy go.

Other cast changes at The Castle followed. Before Tom arrived on the scene, Rock had palled around with his stuntman, George Robotham, wardrobe man Pete Saldutti, and makeup artist Mark Reedall. Clark decided it was time to upgrade the invitation list. Among the new regulars would be producer Ross Hunter and his partner, art director Jacque Mapes; Danny Kaye and his wife, Sylvia Fine; Nancy Walker and her husband, singing teacher David Craig. Instead of a stuntman, Rock now found himself seated beside Olive Behrendt, an elegant Los Angeles socialite and patron of the arts.

Roddy McDowall, who had appeared with Rock in *Pretty Maids All in a Row*, would also become a familiar face around The Castle. Although he had been spared Henry Willson's special brand of star-making, McDowall had endured the same kind of heterosexualizing in the press that Hudson had. "Calling All Girls" was the title of a 1950s fan magazine photo spread that depicted Roddy and

Tab Hunter as "eligible bachelors" scouring their little black books in search of female companionship.

In reality, McDowall was even more deeply closeted than Hudson. Discreet and unfailingly professional in public, Roddy could finally relax and let his guard down at The Castle, where his encyclopedic knowledge of films—both classic and campy—would be fully appreciated. McDowall would also find love at The Castle. Rock had hired a young man named Jimmy Gagner to transfer his film collection to videotape. Shortly after McDowall and Gagner were introduced, an affair developed and Jimmy would end up moving in with Roddy.

As for his own domestic partnership, Rock seemed convinced that in Tom Clark he had finally found the deeper emotional bond he had long been searching for. As Hudson told George Nader, "I've always been looking for a Mark," referring to the long-term, mutually satisfying relationship Nader shared with Mark Miller. "I've never found it, and I hope I can with Tom."

Friends of the couple weren't so sure. Rock's former roommate, Bob Preble, gave Tom Clark a mixed review: "He took control of Rock but he also got Rock drinking very heavily, as he was an alcoholic." Others, like actress Elaine Stritch, were initially on the fence about Clark but eventually warmed to him: "At first I wasn't quite sure of Tom, but then I got to know him. I think he was genuinely very, very attached to Rock and really loved him."

Broadway star Judy Kaye, who would befriend both Hudson and Clark, recalled that Tom was a constant in Rock's life. "You better believe he was completely present," says Kaye. "You didn't get Rock without Tom . . . Sometimes they battled hugely, but even so you could tell that they really cared about each other a great deal. Of course, this was before things really went south later on."

Over time, as both Hudson and Clark's alcohol intake increased, some of the darker undercurrents in the relationship became more readily apparent to others. Instead of being a supportive partner to Rock, Tom sometimes came off like an abusive parent. "In the early days of their relationship, I think Rock saw the value of having somebody around like Tom, who was two steps ahead of him," says Armistead Maupin. "That's always the value but that's always the danger—that someone you trust can take over your life and suddenly be in charge of you. Tom could be awfully unpleasant and publicly nasty to Rock. He'd call him 'the matinee idol.' He would do this in front of Rock and the whole point of it was to stress that Rock wasn't a matinee idol anymore."

Just as Hudson had named his own alter ego "Charlie Movie Star," he would give Clark's brutally honest, boozed-up evil twin a not-so-affectionate nickname: "Little Tommy Truth." Fueled by one too many Scotches, Little Tommy would unload on Rock, venting all of the bitterness and resentment that he had been stockpiling over the years. And if Tom would never be Rock Hudson, he would make certain that Roy Fitzgerald fully understood that *he* would never be Rock Hudson again either. The emotional complexities involved in having a partner who was best friend, fallen idol, and punching bag all rolled into one were enough to keep Clark's glass perpetually full. And the put-downs spewing forth.

"I would say that mentally, it was really an abusive relationship," says Hudson's friend, Ken Maley. "Tom was really high maintenance. Very volatile. You really didn't want to engage him if he had been drinking . . . Most of the time, it wasn't what other people would think of as a happy, compatible relationship, but compatibility can mean a lot of things. In their case, I think it was this explosive relationship, which to Rock, may have been better than nothing."

One of Rock and Tom's most memorable stand-up, knock-down arguments occurred while they were in the midst of preparing for Hudson's fiftieth birthday party in 1975. Guests were asked to come in costume, and Tom and the entire staff at The Castle worked overtime transforming several rooms in the house for a grand celebration. The larger of the two living rooms was converted into an elegant dining room, with silver candelabras topping eight tables. The smaller living room became a 1920s speakeasy, complete with a dance floor. Rock hadn't been consulted about the preparations and this led to an epic screaming match with Tom, capped by an angry exchange of fuck yous.

All seemed to be forgotten by the time the guests arrived, however. Carol Burnett and husband Joe Hamilton were flappers; Mark Miller, Buddy Hackett, and publicist Rupert Allan were a trio of Arabs straight out of Hudson's clunker *The Desert Hawk*. As a band launched into the opening strains of "You Must Have Been a Beautiful Baby," Rock descended the staircase wearing an oversized diaper, to the delight of everyone present. After greeting his guests and mingling for a while, Hudson disappeared upstairs. When he returned, he was wearing Tom's birthday present: a T-shirt bearing a special message that paid tribute to their latest blowout. In bold letters, it read: "Rock Is a Prick."

Before embarking on a fifth season of *McMillan & Wife*, Rock would spend his hiatus working on a new movie. Entitled *Embryo*, the thriller marked Hudson's return to the science fiction genre, which he had last visited with *Seconds* a decade earlier. Rock's character, Dr. Paul Holliston, is a recently widowed medical researcher and a modern-day version of Doctor Frankenstein. After developing a revolutionary growth hormone that rapidly accelerates the maturation process, Holliston begins experimenting on a fourteen-week-old human fetus. Within a matter of weeks, the infant has evolved into a profoundly intelligent and stunningly beautiful woman, whom Holliston names Victoria.

Unaware of her sinister side, Holliston proudly introduces Victoria to his coworkers and friends, passing her off as his new research assistant. The mysterious beauty with the Mensa-level IQ impresses everyone except Holliston's very suspicious sister-in-law, Martha, who finds his superhuman assistant too good to be true. When Martha starts asking too many questions, Victoria injects her with an experimental drug, triggering a fatal heart attack.

Victoria seduces Holliston but afterward is racked with pain. Realizing that she has become addicted to one of Holliston's experimental drugs, Victoria discovers that she will die without the antidote—pituitary gland extract from a newborn fetus. Which is where Holliston's expectant daughter-in-law comes in.

When Rock's participation in *Embryo* was announced in the trades, even the staunchest members of his fan club began wondering if his judgment had somehow been impaired. "I put Rock into *Embryo* . . . it turned out to be terrible," Tom Clark admitted. Though there had been warning signs from the beginning. *Embryo* would be produced not by Universal or MGM but by Cine Artists, responsible for such four-star schlock as *To the Devil a Daughter* and *Lex, the Wonder Dog*.

Gone were the days of A-list costars like Elizabeth Taylor. The supporting cast, which included Nicaraguan fashion model Barbara Carrera, Roddy McDowall, Diane Ladd, and Dr. Joyce Brothers, may have redefined eclectic, but it was clear that the producers of *Embryo* were wholly dependent on Hudson's waning star power to carry the production.

When the producers trumpeted the fact that Rock had agreed to shoot his first nude scene for the film, the announcement seemed like pure publicity gimmick. Fans who had watched the boy next door grow up on-screen were aghast. Rock did his best to explain that the total exposure was all in service to the story. "When a scene demands it, that's that," Hudson told the press, which also registered its disapproval. Upon hearing that Hudson intended to bare more than his sparkling teeth in *Embryo*, one of his former boyfriends cracked that if Rock did indeed go full frontal, the movie would have to be shot in CinemaScope.

Kevin Thomas of the *Los Angeles Times*, who could always be counted on to champion Hudson's work on the screen, didn't disappoint: "In the most demanding part since the not dissimilar *Seconds*, Hudson sustains the film in a far-ranging, demanding role." Even though *Embryo* had its supporters, the shoestring quality of the film and its failure at the box office made it clear that although Rock Hudson was still an enormous draw on television, he could no longer be considered a bankable movie star.

Rock had now appeared in an unbroken string of flops. Could everything be blamed on weak scripts, washed-up directors, or difficult costars? Or had Hudson simply overstayed his welcome on the big screen?

By the mid-1970s, most stars of Rock's generation had been reduced to headlining sitcoms or appearing on the dinner theatre circuit. Jimmy Stewart was pitching Firestone Tires while Henry Fonda was plugging Life Savers. Other screen legends simply retreated altogether. Cary Grant, recognizing that he could no longer convincingly play the romantic lead opposite actresses half his age, had retired from films at age sixty-two. But not Rock. Alongside his other addictions, he was an inexhaustible workaholic. But as his film career continued to deteriorate, it became clear that in terms of job security, there were only two viable options: television, where he could maintain his popularity, or the stage, where he could maintain some semblance of creativity.

When he wasn't counting the days until his contractual obligations to *McMillan & Wife* would be fulfilled, Rock kept busy by searching for a new theatrical venture. The tour of *I Do! I Do!* had been so rewarding that Hudson was eager to recapture the excitement of performing live. It just so happened that publicist turned producer James Fitzgerald was intent on staging a dramatization of Stephen Vincent Benét's *John Brown's Body*.

Published in 1928, Benét's Pulitzer Prize—winning epic poem explored many aspects of life during the Civil War. In 1953, Fitzgerald had been part of an acclaimed staged reading of *John Brown's Body*, which had toured the United States. That production had starred the Rock Hudson of an earlier generation, Tyrone Power. While still working his way up through the ranks at Universal, Rock had attended a performance with roommate Bob Preble. Both the show and its star made an indelible impression. The thought of following in the footsteps of an idol like Power was irresistibly appealing.

As 1976 was America's Bicentennial year, James Fitzgerald was convinced that a national tour of *John Brown's Body* headlined by Rock would be a commercially viable undertaking. As Independence Day approached, patriotism would be reaching a fever pitch and the tour would capitalize on all of the flag-waving and fireworks. As the production was essentially a live history lesson, college campuses topped the list of performance venues.

When Fitzgerald initially pitched the idea of a twenty-city tour from San Diego to Miami, Tom Clark was enthusiastic. Not only would the production afford Rock the opportunity to prove himself as a legitimate dramatic actor, but he would be directed by John Houseman, legendary cofounder of Orson Welles's Mercury Theatre. To support Rock, Fitzgerald had already tapped two actors that Hudson admired—Joseph Cotten and Colleen Dewhurst.

Although Houseman was indeed on board as director, it turned out that Fitzgerald hadn't actually secured commitments from either Cotten or Dewhurst. Ultimately, Leif Erickson (who had appeared opposite Rock in *Twilight for the Gods*) was hired to enact roles ranging from Abraham Lincoln to a slave named Cudjo. This left the one female role to be cast. Rock suggested his friend Claire Trevor. Although she was an Oscar-winner with an impressive list of credits, Trevor hadn't appeared in a feature film in nearly a decade and her last Broadway production dated back to 1947. Even so, Trevor was thrilled: "As soon as they said that Rock Hudson wanted me, I jumped at it."

Reviewing an early performance, *The Hollywood Reporter*'s Ron Pennington sounded hopeful: "Trevor and Hudson—who has developed considerable stage presence and agility—have many excellent moments." But it was Bill Edwards's *Variety* review of a well-attended Pasadena performance that Hudson would never forget. When his agent, Flo Allen, read the notice to him over the phone, Rock was practically levitating: "Hudson proves himself a fine actor, revealing a strong side to his dramatic talent that has seldom been explored by films. Making his dramatic stage debut, Hudson acquits himself admirably and should now be able to take his place in the ranks of exceptional stage performers." *McMillan & Wife* producer Jon Epstein had the review framed and it became one of Rock's prized possessions.

In addition to the three leads, *John Brown's Body* also featured a sixteen-member chorus (eight boys, eight girls), which provided a cappella accompaniment throughout the show. "I was in the chorus and I had this beautiful solo and I think that's kind of how I got Rock's attention," says actress Florence Lacey. "We became good friends through that tour. Rock was really great about making us all equal and all together and all fun—even we lowly chorus members. The entire chorus would travel by bus from one venue to the next and Rock actually got jealous of the time that we spent on the bus. He even bought us a guitar to play on the bus. It was so sweet."

While the reviews of *John Brown's Body* had been almost uniformly outstanding, attendance was a different story. Often the company played to half empty houses or the show was staged in locations that were far from ideal. By summer, most college campuses were deserted. For the random students hanging around the dorm, *John Brown's Body* didn't seem especially enticing.

Despite solid reviews and strong box office during a two-week run in Florida, the tour of *John Brown's Body* began to fall apart. "When we finished in Florida, they told us the rest of the tour was cancelled," chorus member Peter Kevoian remembers. "We were all forlorn. At the airport, when it was time for all of us to fly home, you could see that Rock was having these pangs of 'I'm never going to see these people again . . .' So, he said to all of us, 'There's a party at my place. Come on over when we get back to California.' We all gathered again at Rock's house. Juliet Prowse was there and just a couple of other people in his life that he cared for. We had a great time. Then it came time for people to go home and Rock wouldn't let us leave. I stayed for three days, and on the third day I said,

'Rock, I have to go home and change my underwear.' After that, it was a summer of parties that Rock and Tom kept inviting us to."

JACK COATES, WHO was still drifting in and out of Rock's life by the mid-1970s, would introduce Hudson to Armistead Maupin after a performance of *John Brown's Body* at the San Bernardino Playhouse. "The moment he extended his hand to me in a handshake, the lights went out. I recall saying, 'Well, this is the chance of a lifetime.' Rock laughed and was a totally good sport about it. Subsequently, he came to San Francisco and invited a whole bunch of guys, including myself, out to lunch on Nob Hill. I had bragged to him that I had a story that was going to start running in the *Chronicle* the next morning."

The story turned out to be the first installment of Maupin's highly addictive serial *Tales of the City*, which would perfectly capture the major cultural shifts taking place in America during the swinging 1970s. Readers would experience the sexual revolution through the wide eyes of Mary Ann Singleton, a refugee from Cleveland, Ohio, who impulsively moves to San Francisco.

"The very first episode of *Tales of the City* appeared on May 24th, 1976," Maupin recalls. "Rock, unbeknownst to me, went to the desk clerk at the Fairmont Hotel and got the bulldog edition of the *Chronicle*. Once we were all assembled upstairs, Rock got up and gave a very sweet, if slightly wobbly reading of the first chapter. It was astonishing to hear him reading Mrs. Singleton's words to her runaway daughter—*'I was just watching* McMillan & Wife, *and there was this terrifying story about San Francisco . . .'* and there was McMillan himself doing the reading. It never stops reverberating with me. It was a huge moment in my life."

Coinciding with Maupin's literary breakthrough was a long-awaited moment of truth—coming out to everyone, including his mother: "I couldn't help but think if she knew that Rock Hudson was a friend of mine, everything would be all right because there were no reference points for heroic gay males at that time," says

Maupin. "When Rock and Tom Clark invited me to dinner in the Tenderloin, I told them that I had just come out and that my life was so much richer. I also said that it was probably time for Rock to do the same thing. Very cheeky on my part, but what the hell. I said, 'You should write a book. Come out that way. I can help you because I know how to approach the subject matter.' Tom said, 'Not until my mother dies.' I remember thinking if I were fucking Rock Hudson, I would have no problem at all telling my mother.'"*

Rock Hudson's coming out confessional would never materialize. "He was surrounded by people who wanted to keep making money, and that meant protecting his image at all costs," Maupin says. Despite all of the years he had been confined to the closet, Rock had never missed out on anything. In fact, he had always been way ahead of the curve, sexually speaking. And by the 1970s, the entire culture had finally caught up with him.

It was the era of *Deep Throat*, *Shampoo*, and *The Joy of Sex*. If the birth control pill had emancipated straight society, the Stonewall Riots and the Gay Liberation movement had helped queer culture become more visible and mainstream than ever before. In New York, out and proud gays could visit Fire Island, the Continental Baths, and the Crisco Disco. San Francisco's enticements included the Castro, the Purple Pickle, and an after-hours dance club known as Trocadero Transfer. No matter where the party was, Rock wanted to be there. The Bay Area above all, as it reigned supreme as a kind of pansexual Disneyland.

"Rock thought San Francisco was his playground," says friend Ken Maley. "He just dove right into the action. I remember when Rock and Tom were visiting San Francisco, I took them to one of the gay sex clubs called The Glory Hole.† You paid a modest en-

---

*A 2001 miniseries adaptation of Armistead Maupin's 1982 novel *Further Tales of The City* features a character named Cage Tyler, an amiable though closeted movie star reportedly based on Rock Hudson.

†The Glory Hole, formally known as the South of Market Club, was located at 225 6th Street in San Francisco.

trance fee and you got a membership card. You then had to sign the card and I remember when Rock started filling his out, Tom Clark said, 'Oh my god, he's signing his real name!' Rock didn't seem self-conscious about this at all but of course, he and Tom were well cocktailed at that point."

Dimly lit, popper-scented, and frequented by libidinous males of every description, the club consisted of two parallel rows of cubicles—or buddy booths—that faced one another. Above this was a mezzanine level where patrons could look out over the whole room. For the voyeuristically inclined, this was about far more than getting a bird's-eye view. As there were no ceilings on the booths, one could see all of the illicit activity taking place inside the cubicles.

"I remember standing on the balcony with Rock and he was surveying the whole scene," Ken Maley recalls. "Occasionally, one of the guys in the booths below us would look up from whatever he was doing and there would be this exclamation, '*Oh my god, it's Rock Hudson!*' He got a huge kick out of it. In fact, one of the guys there was a major fan of Rock's but had never met him. I knew which booth this guy was in and I took Rock over, knocked on the door and pushed Rock inside. The guy nearly fainted. He was suddenly in a four-by-four space with Rock Hudson. It was probably one of the great moments in his life. Looking back, it was a grand adventure for all of us. In fact, I still have Rock's Glory Hole membership card."

While San Francisco's gay scene could never truly be replicated, Rock would make a valiant attempt back in Los Angeles. "The word would go out that there was going to be a party at The Castle and a select group would be invited to attend," says Ken Maley. "Rock had this propensity for boy parties. If he had been out on the road or away, he would call Mark Miller, major domo at The Castle, and say, 'Let's have a boy party . . .'"

At that point, Miller would call the well-connected optometrist Wes Wheadon, who would go to work. "I knew a lot of folks in the community," says Wheadon. "If you're going to have a pool party with a bunch of young men, you'd want to bring out the nicest eye candy that you can find and a lot of my friends were very handsome guys . . . I would call up whoever I could get my hands on and say, 'Here's the deal. Here's the address. Just show up. You can have a nice day swimming and carrying on and you'll get to meet Rock." By the time Hudson was back in town, everything would be in place. "At the appropriate day and time, the whole courtyard and around the pool would be chock-a-block with these stunning boys," says Ken Maley.

The parties would become the stuff of legend. It was assumed that the guests would consider The Castle "a closed set" and not discuss anything that occurred behind its walls. If a knockout blond was invited to stay over, he would be esteemed as much for his discretion, composure, and good manners as for his physical attributes. To make certain that everyone remained on their best behavior, there would not only be one host presiding over the party but *four*.

"The main hosts were Rock and Tom, though by the time the party was underway, they were pretty well cocktailed, because that's the way the day started," recalls Ken Maley. "Then there was Mark, who was the gatekeeper and overseer. George Nader would be there, but he always kept a very regal distance, seated in a throne-like chair. Very aloof. You never knew what George thought about the whole thing."

Accounts differ regarding how wild the parties really were. "In a way, Rock was very proper," says Wes Wheadon. "I never saw him get so drunk that he got sloppy or aggressive with guests . . . It wasn't like he was there picking up people and stuff." Mark Tillman-Briggle attended parties at The Castle with his partner, director Stockton Briggle, and doesn't remember witnessing anything untoward: "I don't think Rock was ever as promiscuous as some people have made him out to be. I mean, I was at a lot of those parties in the 80's and I never saw the kinds of things that some people have said took place. Though I do remember asking,

'Why does everybody leave Rock's parties so early?' and somebody said, 'Well, if you don't leave early, it probably means that you're an unemployed actor.'"

Upon being apprised of some of the goings-on at one of Rock's "blond Bacchanalias," George Nader began self-deprecatingly referring to himself as "a fuddy-duddy . . . the straitlaced country cousin." Though Nader wasn't the only one who was taken aback. Since they had appeared together in *Written on the Wind*, Lauren Bacall had only seen Hudson occasionally. When they were reunited, Bacall thought she sensed something different about her former leading man:

"It's funny, I guess as he became more involved in the homosexual scene—maybe he wasn't that involved with it in the beginning, I don't know—but he changed. I remember he came backstage when I was playing *Woman of the Year* at the Ahmanson [Theater] in L.A. He had a mustache and he looked quite different. He was a great big, friendly, sweet guy who had a secret life. Boy, he sure kept it secret—but he sure had it. [I] found out that he used to have daisy chains and gangbangs and God knows what!"

IN 1976, AFTER five successful seasons, *McMillan & Wife* was revamped as *McMillan*. At this point, Susan Saint James and Nancy Walker—both of whom had been nominated multiple times for Emmy Awards during the run of the show—exited the series. Saint James moved on to feature films with *Outlaw Blues*. Walker divided her time between her own short-lived series and playing Valerie Harper's domineering mother on *Rhoda*. John Schuck became a semi-regular on *McMillan* after he was offered his own ABC series, *Holmes & Yoyo*, in which he played a crime-fighting android.

"Believe it or not but I don't think any of those changes really affected Rock," says Tony Kiser, who became an associate producer on the show at age twenty-four. "This was a job to him. I don't think he thought he was making great art. He wasn't doing *Giant* all over again. This wasn't some role of a lifetime . . . When he'd finish a scene, he would go back to his trailer and work on his needlepoint. I mean, he was just the sweetest, friendliest guy but also completely private."

With most of the principals gone and the format retooled, there was much speculation about whether *McMillan* would be able to maintain its footing at the top of the Nielsen ratings. Universal's television division remained confident that as long as they had Rock (at $125,000 an episode), they would be fine.

In an attempt to breathe some new life into the series, Martha Raye came on board as Commissioner McMillan's housekeeper, Agatha—sister to Nancy Walker's Mildred. Network executives initially resisted the idea of casting the sixty-year-old Raye but Hudson insisted.

Also hired at Hudson's urging was Peter Kevoian, the young actor whom Rock had befriended during the tour of *John Brown's Body*. "Rock was an amazing gentleman," says Kevoian. "But a little sad by the time I worked with him. It was like his career had peaked and *McMillan* was coming to an end. He drank a little too much and smoked too much for his own good but he was a true friend . . . I auditioned for the role of a young officer on *McMillan* but didn't get it. Rock called me and said, 'You didn't get the part but I asked them to give you an episode. We'll write you into the show. We'll get you your SAG card. I want you to come on the set and learn as much as you can. That's what I can make happen for you.' And he did everything that he promised."

By the time the final episode of *McMillan* aired in 1977, Rock had more than had his fill of the network series game. In interviews, the ordinarily reserved Hudson was surprisingly candid about the fact that his interest in the show was largely financial. "I don't like doing the series at all," Rock admitted to one reporter. "I'm pleased people like it, but I wish the shows were better. I only do it for the money."

Hudson was equally frank about his bosses at NBC, telling one interviewer, "The networks get scared if two people write a letter objecting to something. There would be a big meeting about it. For example, the McMillans had a martini every evening before dinner. They'd sit down and talk about who killed who and there was this ritual of making a martini. Well, suddenly, there was to be no more drinking. So, they wrote a scene where I come through the door and say, 'Boy, I'm bushed . . . I need a glass of . . . milk.' *What?* Mind you, I should have done it but I didn't. I said, 'Oh, fuck that, for Christ's sake. Let's go over to the bar and I'll make a fucking martini . . .' You know, it's that stupid . . . I'll never do another series because there is no time to do good work. You have to exist in mediocrity."

As Rock was in the midst of the final season of *McMillan*, it fell to Tom Clark to have an initial meeting with a persistent young man from Dallas named Stockton Briggle, who was determined to direct Hudson in a forthcoming production of pretty much *anything*. Briggle had already directed stars like Gloria Swanson and Ann Miller in several well-reviewed regional theatre productions, but he had set his cap at working with Rock, one of his boyhood idols.

Clark met with Briggle and William Ross. The latter was not only the artistic director for the Cape Cod Melody Tent but also the producer of very profitable tours of *Fiddler on the Roof* and *No, No, Nanette*. They pitched the idea of Rock as Nathan Detroit in a new staging of *Guys and Dolls*. Clark's face fell. Hudson had been invited to tour in that role before and the idea simply didn't appeal to him. While Rock admired the score, he felt that he wasn't well suited for the character of the fast-talking gambler.

Ross then proposed an updating of *Camelot*, with Rock starring as King Arthur. In director Stockton Briggle's hands, this would be anything but your typical bus-and-truck tour of *Camelot*. Feeling that the original Broadway version from 1960 had been "an empty hit," Briggle was prepared to overhaul what he perceived to be the show's weakest link—its problematic book. As Briggle told Hudson, he was striving for something more cutting edge and in tune with the swinging 1970s. For the young director, the show was really about a "homoerotic three-person relationship." King Arthur and Lancelot may both be in love with the alluring Guinevere, but they are also in love with each other. Revisiting the Arthurian legend and giving it some resonance for audiences in the post-Stonewall era would be a daunting task, to say the least. Briggle knew that he and his star would have to work long and hard to make their revisionist *Camelot* work.

Befitting the provocative subtext of the show, even the marathon planning sessions that Hudson and Briggle shared were erotically charged. "It was almost a sexual thing," Briggle later admitted. "Rock emanated such power when he was thinking and working. I've always believed a director has to seduce an actor into falling in love with him . . . But with Rock, it was the opposite. I fell in love with him."

Hudson had been so thoroughly engrossed in his epic-length conferences with Briggle, he had managed to overlook the fact that he should be terrified. Teaming up with Carol Burnett was one thing, but wouldn't the critics crucify him for having the unmitigated gall to take on one of the most beloved roles in the American musical theatre? King Arthur had already been indelibly played, both on stage (Richard Burton) and screen (Richard Harris). And what about the demanding score? For their final Broadway collaboration, Alan Jay Lerner and Frederick Loewe had written some of their finest songs, including the title tune, which had become an unofficial anthem of the Kennedy administration. Would Rock's pleasant but largely untrained voice be able to do Lerner and Loewe's songs justice? Adding to Hudson's anxiety was the fact that the tour included a stop at New York's Lincoln Center. His performance as King Arthur would be reviewed by some of the most influential critics in the country.

"From the beginning, he was very concerned about whether he was delivering," says actor Robert Ousley, who played Sir Dinadan in the touring company of Rock's *Camelot*. "He wanted so much to be good in this particular role. As I've done a lot of classical theatre, he would ask me if I would watch his act one closing monologue. He asked me to give him notes and tell him what I thought of his performance. He was someone that wanted to be his best and prove that he was able to do it and that he wasn't just this handsome movie star. I have the greatest respect for him because he just tried and tried." Members of Hudson's *Camelot* company found that Rock brought a unique quality to his interpretation of King Arthur.

"I had never really experienced what true star quality was but I experienced it with Rock," says actor John Leslie Wolfe, who played Sir Castor of Cornwall. "The cast would have a party and he'd walk into the room and literally, the room would just sort of stop . . . And on top of that, he turned out to be the nicest, most genuine person that I ever met that was a star."

Michael Licata, who would go on to become a prolific stage director, started his career as an actor. In *Camelot*, Licata played a page. "That's French for third tree from the left," Licata says. "At the time, I was twenty-three and I was kind of intimidated by the whole scene. Rock was always going to be 'Mr. Hudson' to me, even though he was very friendly . . . You know, he may not have been the finest King Arthur. He may not have been as highly skilled as some of the other actors that had done the role. He may not have had the best voice . . . but I'll bet he was the best loved of all of them. There was just something about him that audiences couldn't get enough of. It was the 'It' factor in spades."

While the Lincoln Center engagement was canceled (as plans were underway for a Broadway revival to open the following season), *Camelot* was successfully staged everywhere from Dallas to D.C. Although audiences across the country seemed to love Rock's quietly commanding King Arthur, Robert Ousley remembers that no matter how beloved Hudson was by the public, one especially cutting critical barb could devastate the star. "It affected him deeply. He wasn't used to that kind of attack," says Ousley. "He was quite hurt by some of the viciousness that would be produced by some of these little small-town critics, that had absolutely no right or qualifications for being a critic in the first place. He was a sweet, sweet man and he would take every review—good or bad—very seriously."

————

Late one evening in October of 1977, Claire Trevor, who lived only a few doors away from Rock's mother, called Hudson with some devastating news: "Your mother's had a stroke." Although Rock and Tom were both under the influence, they somehow made it to Newport Beach without incident. While they had completed the trip in record time, it was still too late. Kay had died before they arrived. In the last six months of her life, Hudson had refused to see her. He told George and Mark that he preferred to remember his mother as the fiercely independent dynamo she had been in her younger years. Recently, she had been bedridden, battling recurring bouts of the flu and a number of other ailments, including Parkinson's Disease.

Just as he had always indulged his mother, Rock made sure that Kay had everything that she needed during her final days. Hudson asked Claire Trevor to check in on her regularly. Every two weeks, Mark Miller would drive in and replenish the groceries and make sure the bills had been paid. Miller became well practiced at inventing excuses when Kay would inevitably ask, "Why won't my son come?" First it was the final season of *McMillan* that was keeping Rock away, then it was rehearsals for a new miniseries.

For as long as either could remember, it had been Rock and Kay against the world. So, how could he accept that his mother, the one constant in his life, was dying? How could he bear to watch her slip away? He couldn't. He withdrew to protect himself.

"Stoic" was the word that friends used to describe Rock in the days following Kay's death. There were no displays of emotion and he reported to the set of his latest project even though the producers had invited him to take a few days off. "When Katherine died, all of the holidays lost much of their luster for Rock," Tom Clark remembered. Gone were the lavish Christmas dinners that Hudson had hosted in the past. Gift-giving, which had always been one of Rock's greatest joys, suddenly didn't hold quite the same interest for him.

Unless someone brought Kay up, Rock rarely spoke of her, though she was very much on his mind when he was interviewed by the *New York Daily News* a year after her death. Ostensibly, the interview was an opportunity for Hudson to promote his latest television project. Instead, he began reminiscing about two of the most important women in his life, Marilyn Maxwell and his mother. Of Kay, he would say, "I was an only child, so I had to be a big brother to my mother. She was Irish and had quite a temper. I remember when I was seventeen years old and wanted to take the car on Saturday nights, I'd have to get her mad first. Then I'd throw both arms around her and hold her so she couldn't move and say, 'Now what are you going to do?' She'd break up laughing and give me the keys to the car."

CHAPTER 17

BLUE SNOW

Rock Bottom: Hudson's screen career reached its nadir
as he battled "six million tons of icy terror" in producer
Roger Corman's disaster epic *Avalanche* (1978).
(Photo courtesy of the Rock Hudson Estate Collection)

or a disaster film produced by "The Pope of Pop Cinema," Roger
Corman, and exploitatively promoted as "six million tons of icy
terror!" *Avalanche* would manage to attract some top-drawer
talent, both in front of the cameras and behind the scenes.

Screenwriter Gavin Lambert was hired to write the script.
As Lambert had received an Oscar nomination for adapting D. H.
Lawrence's *Sons and Lovers* for the screen, it was hoped that he
would bring some literary gravitas to the disaster genre, which was

known for shameless overacting, unintentional hilarity, and lining up an assortment of Hollywood stars well past their prime to take on some horrifying apocalypse.

While it was obvious that *Avalanche* didn't aspire to be much more than your typical by-the-numbers disaster film, Lambert felt that it was important to present believable characters that audiences could care about before the inevitable catastrophe struck. As such, his script for *Avalanche* emphasized the love triangle at the center of the story. Fiercely driven developer David Shelby invites his ex-wife, Caroline Brace, to his new multimillion-dollar Colorado ski resort in the hopes that they can reconcile.

Once there, Caroline meets eco-friendly photographer Nick Thorne, who has been adamantly opposed to the construction of Shelby's lodge. Thorne is convinced that Shelby's reckless development has wreaked havoc with the awesome balance of nature ("Things aren't normal. There's a heaviness and it's growing. I can feel it!") Meanwhile, Caroline is torn between Shelby's commanding, take-charge personality and Thorne's more laid-back free-spiritedness. If Shelby's complicated love life and the opening of his controversial resort weren't enough to keep him occupied, one of his planes crashes into a mountain during a snowstorm, setting off a devastating avalanche.

As it had been modeled after *The Poseidon Adventure* and *The Towering Inferno* (two all-star productions from "Master of Disaster" producer Irwin Allen), *Avalanche* was in immediate need of some big-name actors to justify its budget of $6.5 million. Considering this, Corman's New World Pictures aimed high in terms of casting. Charlton Heston, who had battled a buckling San Andreas fault in 1974's *Earthquake*, was first approached to play David Shelby but he declined. Screen legend Ann Sothern was offered the role of Shelby's vivacious mother, but she passed as well.

On December 19, 1977, *Daily Variety* announced a "names only" casting call for the three leads. A week later, *The Hollywood Reporter* noted that Rock Hudson and William Holden (who years earlier had competed for the role of Bick Benedict in *Giant*) were "virtually set." When Holden decided that *Avalanche* didn't belong on the same shelf with *Sunset Boulevard*—or even *The Towering Inferno*—Robert Forster was cast as the nature-loving photographer. Mia Farrow, still several years away from the career resurgence she'd experience through her collaborations with Woody Allen, agreed to play the romantically challenged Caroline.

Gavin Lambert's character-driven screenplay attempted to put people ahead of special effects, but actor-turned-director Corey Allen apparently saw things differently. Lambert told Patricia Goldstone of the *Los Angeles Times* that Allen "dewrote" his script—quashing most of the character development and making the avalanche itself the star.

"Sounds awful," was Tom Clark's brutally honest reaction when Rock recited the plot of *Avalanche*. "But he was absolutely determined to do it; feeling that disaster films were hot," Clark remembered. "I told him that this happened to be a very poor one . . . but he had to do it and he did it, and it was a *disaster* all right." As for big, hulking Rock Hudson being teamed with fragile, waiflike Mia Farrow, Clark pronounced their pairing "about as right as Whoopi Goldberg and Charles Boyer."

After assembling cast and crew at the Tamarron Resort in scenic Durango, Colorado, in the winter of 1978, "King of the B's" Roger Corman decided that the budget required some wholesale trimming.* "The only thing that I have to say about Roger Corman is that he would have been an enormous success if he had managed a discount house because he was that kind of frugal," says actor Jerry Douglas, who played mountie Phil Prentiss. "He was a very nice guy but boy, did he know how to save a dime . . . With both Rock and Mia Farrow, he probably paid them half of what they

---

*The first film that Roger Corman produced, *Monster from the Ocean Floor* (1954) was shot over a six-day period and at a total cost of only $12,000. From there, it was on to such comparatively big-budgeted New World releases as *Boxcar Bertha*, *Night of the Cobra Woman*, and *I Escaped from Devil's Island*.

usually earned but this was a period when they weren't busy, so they grabbed it."

While on location, director Corey Allen was under pressure to bring *Avalanche* in weeks ahead of schedule. The turbocharged pace of the production didn't seem to bother Rock, who was accustomed to the breakneck speed involved in turning out *McMillan* episodes. According to those who worked on *Avalanche*, Hudson was an unruffled model of professionalism throughout an incredibly brisk shoot. This despite the fact that he was well aware that the movie was essentially the death knell for his feature film career.

Even though Hudson had found his cinematic nadir in *Avalanche*, Jerry Douglas says that Rock never seemed anything other than grateful to still be in front of the cameras. "He was a total pro, even though he was a heavy, heavy drinker at that time," Douglas says. "I remember when we were done for the day, he liked to hang around the bar. He was not a snob star at all. He used to talk to everybody. He really loved people and people loved him . . . He would get a few drinks in him at night and he would get a little flirtatious. After he had three or four scotches, he'd come over to me and say, 'Well, Jerry, are we going to dance tonight?' I'd say, 'You're a lousy dancer and I know a few guys prettier than you. I'll see you around.' And he'd laugh his ass off."

The release of *Star Wars* the year before had introduced moviegoers to state-of-the-art computer-generated imagery. Now audiences would expect a disaster film to feature spectacular and thoroughly convincing special effects. With *Avalanche*, what viewers got was so amateurish-looking that by comparison, George Méliès's *A Trip to the Moon*, released in 1902, looked cutting edge. After Corman objected to the red snow supplied by his effects team, they managed a slightly less offensive blue.

As journalist Patricia Goldstone noted, "Roger Corman appears to have indulged a pathological urge to cut corners . . . The avalanche scene itself virtually disappeared, so it's like a disaster film without a disaster." According to Tom Clark, what remained of the icy cataclysm "looked like it was shot through tapioca pudding." As Corman's budget wouldn't allow for any Industrial Light & Magic wizardry, the *Avalanche* crew frequently had to conjure up not-so-special effects from whatever raw materials they could find, which seemed to have been retrieved from the back of a truck.

As Jerry Douglas remembers: "We had some bad weather in the middle of the shoot and by 'bad,' I mean it got warm. Well, we had this scene to do where Rock and I are digging through a snow tunnel, trying to reach his mother, who is trapped inside the resort . . . We're in this fake tunnel that's got white crap all over it that's supposed to look like snow but it wasn't very convincing . . . Now imagine, Rock and I were laying in this thing for hours face-to-face and only about four inches apart. I said, 'Rock, if you do what I think you're thinking of doing, I'm going to kick your ass.' I said, 'I don't like your breath right now. I think you need some mouthwash, so don't you dare kiss me . . .' He got a big kick out of it. This was our way of getting through all of this. I always enjoyed his sense of humor . . . He was, without a doubt, one of the most agreeable people I ever worked with."

Even before *Avalanche* was released, some of the key participants began distancing themselves from the movie. "It was so bungled and rewritten by the director that I had my name removed from the credits," said screenwriter Gavin Lambert.

In July of 1978—only six months after shooting had commenced—the movie was given a well-publicized world premiere in Denver. Although both Hudson and Farrow attended the festivities, the celebratory mood didn't last long. The *Washington Post* capped its devastating, thumbs-down review with: "After theatre managers add up the receipts, *Quarantine* may seem a more appropriate title for *Avalanche*, an inept disaster melodrama now at several obliging, unlucky locations. This fizzled brainstorm from New World looks like a cinch for the first supplement to *The 50 Worst Films of All Time*."

While virtually all of the reviews were jeers, one of Rock's champions paid tribute to his efforts. *The Hollywood Reporter*'s Robert Osborne wrote that "Hudson makes a good yell-into-the-telephone tycoon, and his presence adds an importance to the project it otherwise wouldn't have had." Despite the show of support, the writing was on the wall. Twenty years earlier, Rock Hudson had been an Oscar-nominated leading man, headlining a prestige picture like *Giant*. Now he had been relegated to a low-budget disaster film in which he was sharing the screen with a leading lady twenty years his junior and blue snow.

Avalanche was released and immediately vanished from theatres. Depression set in and Hudson's drinking increased to such a degree that a few close friends suggested that both Rock and Tom Clark might benefit from checking into a rehabilitation facility. All of this well-intentioned advice would not be heeded. Instead, Rock did what he always did, which was to seek refuge in his work. Even if the movies didn't want him anymore, television certainly did.

JUST AS THERE had been several failed attempts to reunite Rock Hudson and Doris Day on-screen, a small battalion of producers, directors, and screenwriters had been batting around ideas for projects that would bring Rock and Elizabeth Taylor back together. For a brief moment, it looked as though Robert F. O'Neill, who had won an Emmy for producing *Columbo*, had succeeded.

O'Neill had Hudson and Taylor in mind for a sweeping ten-hour NBC miniseries based on Arthur Hailey's 1971 bestseller, *Wheels*. The *New York Times* had described the novel as both "an exposé, and a salute to the auto industry." In the tradition of Hailey's *Airport* and *Hotel*, *Wheels* was also an intricately plotted soap opera. This time around, the setting was 1960s Detroit, which the author characterized as "more of a gambling center than Las Vegas, with higher stakes."

Adam Trenton, a senior executive at National Motors, is totally immersed in the development of "The Hawk," the "miracle of a modern automobile," which comes complete with such revolutionary innovations as out-of-view engineering and an onboard computer. Feeling ignored by her workaholic husband, Trenton's beautiful wife, Erica, carries on a torrid affair with a debonair young race car driver. Meanwhile, the Trentons' youngest son, Greg, becomes embroiled in a blackmail scandal before volunteering for active duty in Vietnam.

"Not on your life!" was Rock's initial response when *Wheels* was offered to him. After six seasons of *McMillan*, the last thing Hudson wanted to do was to shackle himself to an elaborate television production—and for the same network that he had just escaped from. After Tom Clark went to work on him, Rock eventually changed his mind and signed on.

While they had succeeded in snagging Rock Hudson, the producers weren't as fortunate with Elizabeth Taylor. Even after dangling a $1 million payday in front of her, Taylor passed. While she loved Hudson, the protracted shooting schedule for a miniseries didn't appeal to her. Lee Remick, whom Hudson had long wanted to work with, agreed to step in as Erica Trenton. Future Broadway star Howard McGillin, twenty-four at the time, was cast as Rock's troubled son. Despite the fact that he was nearly six foot three, McGillin was handed a pair of high-top Converse sneakers specially outfitted with wedges so that he'd appear even taller and more believable as Hudson's son.

At the time he was cast in *Wheels*, McGillin was in the same kind of Universal stock training program that Hudson had been enrolled in nearly thirty years earlier. "I remember Rock told me that when he was loaned out to do *Giant*, he was making $300 a week as a contract player. So, he had been down that road, too," McGillin says. "In the first scene we shot together, I remember we had to walk around and talk and there I was in my platform Converse sneakers and I just remember how incredibly kind Rock was. He did everything he could to make me feel comfortable."

Sixty-one different locations throughout southern California doubled for Detroit. There would be a few days of shooting in

South L.A. before the company packed up and moved on to Hancock Park. McGillin recalls that during a rare moment of relaxation, he had an opportunity to spend time with not only one Rock Hudson but two:

"I remember one day, we were sitting in his trailer, waiting for them to set lights for a scene. And what turns up on the TV in his trailer but *Pillow Talk*. It was surreal for me and also kind of thrilling as I was watching him watch his younger self. When it cut to a commercial, Rock said, 'Do you think it still holds up?' And I just thought that was both sweet and revealing. I guess every actor is insecure but he just wanted to know that the stuff he had done really mattered and that it stood the test of time. Which it certainly did."

When it aired in May of 1978, *Wheels* pulled in huge ratings and generally favorable reviews, including Howard Rosenberg's in the *Los Angeles Times*: "It takes a while for *Wheels* to get rolling, but once it does, what wonderful rubbish, the kind of stupid and trashy stuff that's fun to watch if you don't take it all seriously."

ROCK MAY HAVE charmed audiences in *I Do! I Do!* and received some of the best reviews of his entire career for *John Brown's Body*, but he knew there was still a major mountain left to climb: Broadway. Was he ready? Robert Fryer thought so. The producer, who had given "The Great White Way" some of its biggest hits, including *Auntie Mame* and *Chicago*, invited Hudson to audition for his latest Broadway-bound musical, *On the Twentieth Century*. Fryer's offer almost seemed too good to be true. If cast, Rock Hudson—otherwise known as "Joe Movie Star"—would now be working with some of Broadway's most acclaimed artists.

Hal Prince, who was responsible for such landmark American musicals as *Cabaret*, *Company*, and *Follies*, would be directing. Cy Coleman, who had *Sweet Charity* under his belt, had written the score. Betty Comden and Adolph Green, who had racked up countless stage and screen credits, including *Singin' in the Rain*, had supplied both book and lyrics. Rock was, of course, elated to be included in such magnificent company, but that exhilaration quickly turned to despair when John Cullum, a seasoned veteran of many Broadway productions, was cast instead.

As a consolation prize, Hudson was offered the national tour. While he wouldn't be making his Broadway debut, he'd be head-lining performances everywhere from Detroit to San Francisco. True, *On the Twentieth Century* wasn't nearly as well-known as *Camelot*, but Rock would be starring in a musical with an unde-niably classy pedigree that had recently won five Tony Awards. Really, how could he lose?

Before fully committing to the tour, Hudson thought he should see what he was getting himself into. Tom Clark told Fryer that he and Rock wanted to attend a performance of *On the Twentieth Century*, which had opened to mixed reviews in February of 1978. Unlike the critics, Hudson was completely sold on the show. He was in awe of John Cullum, impressed with rising star Judy Kaye, and especially taken with Imogene Coca's scene stealing turn as the lovable religious fanatic Letitia Primrose.

Tom Clark, on the other hand, was nowhere near as enchanted. At intermission, he didn't hold back when he delivered his charac-teristically blunt assessment: "It's terrible, Rock. And it's definitely not for you." Despite Clark's disapproval, Hudson had already made up his mind. He may have been denied the opportunity to make a splashy Broadway debut, but he wasn't going to miss out on touring with a Hal Prince show.

While initially intimidated by his latest undertaking, Hudson decided that the best way to get through the tour was to view the show as "a 2½ hour Carol Burnett sketch." That approach helped ease his anxiety, as did fully immersing himself in the preparation process. "I had the luxury of having the script for a long time be-forehand," Hudson said. "I kept reading it over and over. I didn't learn it; I absorbed it." At a press conference, he told the assembled reporters that he considered Comden and Green's book, "Damned near perfect . . . They took one of the best backstage comedies of all time and gave it a whole new spin. It's no wonder this story has had so many lives."

On the Twentieth Century had started life as an unproduced play entitled *Napoleon of Broadway*, which in turn formed the basis for Ben Hecht and Charles MacArthur's own 1932 Broadway hit, *Twentieth Century*. The riotous comedy concerned a megalomaniacal producer named Oscar Jaffe, who has suffered a string of flops and is now in dire need of a hit. Having transformed lingerie model Mildred Plotka into screen goddess Lily Garland, Jaffe hopes her star power will turn his new production of *The Passion of Mary Magdalene* into a smash.

The down-on-his-luck impresario relentlessly pursues his "Hoboken Cinderella" with contract in hand. Jaffe's hot pursuit isn't strictly business as Garland is not only a former protégée but also an old flame. When both board the luxurious locomotive of the title, Oscar uses all of his wiles (and other people's money) to entice his "baby Bernhardt" into starring as "the wickedest woman of her age."

Two years after its initial Broadway run, *Twentieth Century* was transferred to the screen by director Howard Hawks and it became one of Hollywood's finest screwball comedies. John Barrymore had a field day playing Oscar Jaffe. The hammy showman proved to be the perfect role for the actor known as "The Great Profile." In the shadow of Barrymore, could Rock Hudson pull off his own Oscar Jaffe?

"I salute him for taking it on," says Hudson's *Twentieth Century* costar, Judy Kaye. "It was hard for him. A big musical wasn't his bailiwick by any manner or means, although the acting part certainly was. But a show like that is very demanding and I've never seen anybody work as hard as Rock did. He took it on with both fists and really committed himself."

Hudson could barely contain his enthusiasm when he learned that he had landed the tour. "I was excited as hell. Dizzy as a matter of fact," Rock told journalist Michael J. Bandler. "I can't wait to get to the theatre . . . I'm like a child with a new toy. [It's] a little gift-wrapped present, and I treat it as such—with reverence."

Judy Kaye, who replaced star Madeline Kahn when she left the Broadway production early in the run, was also excited, though for entirely different reasons. "When I heard that Rock Hudson was going to take John Cullum's part for the tour, I thought, 'I'm doing this for all the women in America.' . . . Seriously though, it's nice to find out, after admiring him from afar, how talented, honest, and giving he is. It's a lovely discovery."

If Tom Clark had immediately expressed his concerns about Rock's involvement, all of his fears seemed to be coming true once rehearsals started. The production team had assured Hudson that changes would be made to tailor the role to his personality and that the songs (which Rock termed "killers") would be carefully rearranged to suit his limited range. According to Clark, none of these changes were made.

What's more, the stormy Svengali-Trilby dynamic of the story seemed to be replayed in the early rehearsals Hal Prince had with Hudson. "[Hal] was very difficult and hard on him," recalled actress Leslie Easterbrook, who understudied leading lady Judy Kaye. "Hal's not a particularly easy person to work with, and he was giving Rock very harsh instructions." According to Easterbrook, there were never any retaliatory displays of temperament or star tantrums. Rock just sucked it up and pressed on. "He never showed any kind of anger or pouting, things that actors—especially stars—will do when a director really takes them to task," Easterbrook says. "My main reaction was, boy, he's a real actor. He really wanted to learn, to work hard."

Judy Kaye recalled the working relationship between director and star altogether differently: "I never saw Hal give Rock a really hard time and Hal certainly could have if he had wanted to. Actually, I thought Hal Prince was very supportive because he really wanted that tour to happen. That tour was not going to happen if Rock wasn't there . . . so they both knew that they needed one another to get that show on the road."

As Prince was getting ready to take on *Sweeney Todd*, his rehearsal time with Hudson was limited. The *Twentieth Century* tour would actually be overseen by Prince's longtime associate, Ruth Mitchell, of whom Tallulah Bankhead once said, she would have been "the most perfect person in the world if she could only play bridge."

Tom Clark may have been a boozy, pampered prima donna at times, but even so, he was still Rock's most perceptive career advisor. Early on, Clark recognized that *On the Twentieth Century*, with its operetta-inspired score, rapid-fire dialogue, and screwball pacing, played away from most of Rock's strengths. Sure, Hudson had managed a respectable King Arthur in *Camelot*, but the very grandiose Oscar Jaffe was so far removed from his own low-key personality, that he may as well have been playing the alien transvestite Dr. Frank-N-Furter in *The Rocky Horror Picture Show*.

The *Twentieth Century* tour got underway in June of 1979. In Chicago, there were raves for the female leads: "Judy Kaye is the life and Imogene Coca the spice," pronounced J. Linn Allen in the *Chicago Reader.* The leading man, meanwhile, was paid the ultimate left-handed compliment: "Rock Hudson is not as bad as you would expect, which seems to be his fate in life: he never is. He has no natural talent for singing, dancing, or comedy, but, that accepted, he does remarkably well."

As the tour moved on, Rock was continually reminded that he had been miscast. "Hudson is the most likable fellow on earth, but he's about as flamboyant as Jell-O pudding," wrote Dan Sullivan in his *Los Angeles Times* review. "As for his songs, he carries them— just. Weep for Hudson's tameness. He couldn't be wronger." While Tom Clark could have easily gloated and said, "I told you so," he instead told veteran reporter Dick Kleiner, "The critics were actually kinder to him than I expected but the reviews were still poor. For once, I felt the critics were justified in these raps."

A FEW DAYS after the release of the first *Star Wars* movie, producer Charles Fries and his business associate, Malcolm Stuart, found themselves in a meeting at NBC with the network's development director, Deanne Barkley. "We talked about the impact of *Star Wars* and sci-fi projects," Fries recalls. "Then, we looked at each other and said in chorus, '*Ray Bradbury's The Martian Chronicles!*' Deanne said, 'I'll have to get approval but I'm recommending a six-hour mini-series on the project.' And that was it."

The first important challenge fell to scriptwriter Richard Matheson. Could he establish a sense of narrative continuity that could somehow link Bradbury's episodic tales? "You had to find a central character like Rock Hudson's to run through the material and pull it all together so that there was something unifying the three episodes," Fries says. To that end, Matheson beefed up the character of Colonel John Wilder. The expanded role would not only provide the necessary connective thread but also justify the reported $750,000 the producers were paying Hudson. The large supporting cast included Roddy McDowall, Bernadette Peters, and Fritz Weaver.

After determining that a thoroughly convincing Mars could not be created on a soundstage, the search was on to find a location that could double for "the Red Planet." "Malta was perfect because the island was treeless, just like Mars," Fries says. "They also had the largest water moat, to my knowledge, in existence at that time. So we built the Martian community over the moat."

When *The Martian Chronicles* aired over three consecutive nights in January of 1980, the ratings were high and reviews were mixed. In *The Hollywood Reporter*, Gail Williams said that NBC's miniseries "could use a lot more Martians and a lot less ignorant human beings," though she gave director Michael Anderson high marks for "managing to convey a sense of wonder" in the opening scenes on Mars. Producer Fries agrees that in terms of the completed *Chronicles*, there are some plusses and minuses to be considered: "On the one hand, I was very pleased that we were able to accomplish this very difficult feat. On the other hand, a feeling of 'could we have done more?' existed."

It may not have been Rock Hudson's most important movie, but *The Mirror Crack'd* was certainly one of his most entertaining efforts. Based on Agatha Christie's 1962 mystery, *The Mirror Crack'd from Side to Side*, director Guy Hamilton's adaptation concerned a Hollywood film company invading the quaint English village of St. Mary Mead. While shooting a remake of the creaky costume drama, *Mary, Queen of Scots*, the film's stars bring glamour, intrigue, and murder to town.

When a local woman is poisoned, several members of the company become prime suspects, including director Jason Rudd (Hudson), the fifth and final husband of the pill-popping Marina Gregg (Elizabeth Taylor), a fading screen queen desperate to make a comeback; the crass, flask-toting producer Martin N. Fenn (Tony Curtis); and Marina's nemesis, the vulgar starlet Lola Brewster (Kim Novak). Scotland Yard assigns their best man, Inspector Dermot Craddock (Edward Fox), to the case. Craddock in turn consults with his elderly aunt, Miss Jane Marple (Angela Lansbury), an amateur sleuth who has "an uncanny knack of being always right."

Producers Richard Goodwin and John Brabourne graced *The Mirror Crack'd* with the kind of chic stylishness and all-star sparkle that was in short supply in movie theatres by the 1980s, a cinematic era dominated by *Ghostbusters*, *Rambo*, and Molly Ringwald.

Screenwriter Barry Sandler, who would stir things up a couple of years later with his screenplay for the gay-themed *Making Love*, not only "Americanized" Agatha Christie's dialogue but he supplied *The Mirror Crack'd* with some of the bitchiest zingers this side of *All About Eve*. "Chin up, darling. Both of them," Novak's Lola chirps to Taylor's Marina. The kind of fierce rivals known to grind glass in one another's cold cream, Marina and Lola trade put-downs as freely as air kisses.[*]

An inveterate movie buff, Sandler was thrilled to be working with a cast composed of screen legends. One of which he had already seen up close. "I had known Rock socially a bit," says Sandler. "Jon Epstein, who was a producer at Universal and a close friend of Rock's, was notorious as a party giver. They were all gay parties. A mix of producers and executives and twenty-one-year-old boys. Nothing orgiastic but it was typical gay Hollywood. Rock would always show up and was always very friendly and the life of the party. He'd have a few drinks and get very flirtatious with everybody. He was just very out and open. There was nothing closeted or repressed about him at these parties. He was very friendly, let me put it that way."

Initially, Natalie Wood, who had appeared with Rock in *One Desire*, was set to play Marina. "I was a huge Natalie Wood fan growing up," Sandler says. "My god, she's iconic and I jumped at the chance . . . Then one day I got a phone call from Richard Goodwin and he said, 'Natalie just left the movie.' I was crushed. She and Guy Hamilton didn't get along. They argued and she didn't feel she could work with him. I was very downhearted. Then he said, 'Don't you want to hear the good news? We just signed Elizabeth Taylor.'"

Taylor was then in her post–Richard Burton caftan-wearing period and eager to get back to work. "At that point in her career, she was married to John Warner, the senator, and as it turned out, not thrilled with living in Washington," says Sandler. "She liked the part, she liked the movie but I think more importantly, she

---

[*] "When we were casting *The Mirror Crack'd*, and before they signed Kim Novak, I had suggested Debbie Reynolds for Lola," says screenwriter Barry Sandler. "It would have made sense for those who remember the whole Eddie Fisher scandal, but the producers thought that it would be too much of a gimmick and it would have detracted from the mystery. It would have also turned the whole movie into a camp thing . . . not that it wasn't already."

wanted to get away from Washington and she wanted to be with Rock." Twenty-five years after *Giant*, Hudson and Taylor were together again. Their on-screen reunion inspired a few clever jokes. In one scene, a weary Marina gazes at her reflection in the mirror and murmurs, "Bags, bags, go away . . . Come right back on Doris Day . . ." prompting a priceless double take from Rock.

"A Yalta Conference of Hollywood's finest" is how film critic Gerald Peary described the press junket for *The Mirror Crack'd* that he attended in early 1981. "I was part of a roundtable of journalists at a New York hotel, with several of the stars circulating from table to table," Peary recalls. "From across the room, I heard Liz Taylor squawking, telling off a journalist who asked about her weight. We had Rock Hudson for twenty minutes. He was gentlemanly, friendly, and told us how much he enjoyed riding the subways in New York. Suddenly, some journalist at my table blurted out, 'Mr. Hudson, is it true that you used to live with Jim Nabors?' Hudson was taken aback. The journalist repeated the question, trying to sound like a tough-guy reporter. Hudson said, 'No, that is not true.' The rest of us sat stunned. We realized that question really meant, 'Are you a homosexual?' and that was a tasteless, irrelevant thing to ask. Those like me who were big Rock Hudson fans felt ashamed."

After *The Mirror Crack'd*, Rock agreed to play the lead in a made-for-TV movie for NBC entitled *The Star Maker*. Hudson's character, movie mogul Danny Youngblood, presides over the busiest casting couch in show business. Even though director Lou Antonio considered the project "total sleaze," he persuaded Rock to sign on, promising that the script would be improved. "It just wasn't very good when you read it," says Antonio. "But I thought Rock could bring something human and real to it. There were quite a few dramatic scenes and I thought he might be able to use some of his own experiences, his own emotions and we could work on it and turn it into something that wasn't pure dreck."

Antonio had directed several episodes of *McMillan & Wife* and

Hudson respected him. What's more, the supporting cast was appealing: Suzanne Pleshette, Brenda Vaccaro, and Melanie Griffith. Also on board was a newcomer whom sharp-eyed viewers may have recognized as the "Jordache Jeans Man," a good-looking model turned actor named Jack Scalia. A few years later, Scalia would work with Hudson again. And in time, Rock would come to refer to the charismatic young man from Brooklyn as "my son."

With no promising feature film scripts coming his way, Rock wasn't in a position to turn down work. However, when he was initially offered a four-hour made-for-TV movie entitled *World War III*, he passed. Although he would be playing an American president attempting to avert a nuclear holocaust, Hudson found the doomsday scenario off-putting and exploitative. "When I first read it, I thought it shouldn't be made," Rock said. "Then, when I had given it more thought, I realized—absolutely, it must be made to make us human beings realize what idiots we are."

AFTER THE LONG run of *McMillan & Wife*, Rock had sworn off series television as he found everything about the network game unsatisfying—except, of course, his salary. However, NBC executives were so anxious to have Hudson headlining another hit show, they made him an offer that he couldn't refuse: his name included in the title, approval over his costars, and best of all, complete creative control (Rock's own Mammoth Films would coproduce with Viacom).

"I said I'd never do another TV show. But I think as you get older, you learn to keep your mouth shut more because you never know how badly you're going to embarrass yourself later," Hudson admitted to *People*. When asked why he had agreed to star in another mystery series, Rock's answer came quickly, "I like to work."

As developed by John Wilder, the concept for this new outing—which was initially titled *The Rock Hudson Show*—was familiar with a twist: Brian Devlin, a former military intelligence officer, is now the director of L.A.'s Performing Arts Center. In his off hours,

Devlin goes sleuthing with Nick Corsello, a racquetball pro turned private detective. As it turns out, Corsello is also the son that Devlin never knew he had. While father is suave and cultured, son is brash and street smart. Before even a single episode aired, critics joked that the show should have been called *McMillan & Son*.

"NBC asked me to come up with a concept for Rock," remembers John Wilder. "They favored an action-drama detective show but with the depth of character I had delivered on *The Streets of San Francisco*. As I've always loved father-son stories, I thought it would be great for Rock to have a son, someone as physically imposing and attractive as he was. But I wanted rough edges to oppose the polish Rock's character had acquired. I hoped that I could find that actor!"

Jack Scalia, who had appeared with Hudson in *The Star Maker*, was cast as Nick. The show's father-son dynamic spilled over into real life as Rock immediately took his costar under his wing. "Events happen in people's lives and Rock Hudson was an event for me," says Scalia. "When I was growing up in Brooklyn, if one of the guys in the neighborhood was feeling their oats and chasing after a couple of girls, we'd say, 'Who do you think you are . . . *Rock Hudson?*' Now, suddenly, here I am working with the same guy and he couldn't have been a better mentor. He brought me into this whole new world and said, 'Here it is, kid. It's all for you . . .'"

Hudson suggested a meeting in New York, where Scalia was living at the time. "He was so genuine and funny that I kind of forgot about the whole star thing," Scalia says. "So, we're walking along Central Park West and all of a sudden, this crowd of people started running after him and asking for his autograph. I stood back and just watched this unfold. He signed every single autograph and everybody walked away with a smile. I said, 'Doesn't that bother you?' And he said, 'It'll bother me when it stops.' I learned so much just from observing him. In fact, Rock never gave me advice. All he ever said to me was, 'Stick around, kid.' And what that 'stick around' meant was watch, listen, and learn."

If star and costar immediately hit it off, their show—which was retitled *The Devlin Connection*—was never on the same sure footing. From the beginning, the series was hampered by one important challenge after another. Says John Wilder, "On the very first day of location shooting, the crew discovered a car with a dead body in it. A man had committed suicide in his car . . . In retrospect, that probably wasn't a good omen."

In the spring of 1981, a Writers Guild strike halted production on dozens of television shows, including *The Devlin Connection*. No sooner was the strike resolved than the show was plunged into another crisis. "I won't say that I had a nervous breakdown but boy, I must have been close," says Wilder. "My whole world blew up. I was blindsided when my ex-wife sued me for divorce. My four young children were suddenly a hundred miles north of my workplace. I tried my damnedest to focus on work but it was impossible." While teetering on the brink of a breakdown, Wilder was forced to crank out scripts. As a result, the quality Rock had hoped for wasn't there and, according to Tom Clark, "There was chaos on the set."

Then, during the second month of taping, there was another important setback. "I was working when I started getting these chest pains," Hudson recalled. "I couldn't catch my breath. I was being my usual compulsive self, too wrapped up in my work, worrying, overeating, smoking, and drinking too much . . . I was over 50 and ripe for trouble."

Nearly a decade earlier, Susan Saint James had warned Rock that his frequent Scotches and three-packs-a-day habit virtually guaranteed a visit to the emergency room. And now here it was. After being admitted to Cedars-Sinai Medical Center in L.A., doctors discovered that Hudson had severe coronary artery blockage. They would have to perform a quintuple bypass operation immediately. Rock fought this, insisting that he had to return to work and at least finish the episode in progress. "I didn't want to be bothered by trouble," Hudson later said. "We'd already shut down production with the writers' strike. Enough already." Rock's medical team insisted. Postponing the surgery—even for a few days—could cost him his life. It was only after he learned how high the stakes were that Hudson finally relented.

During the six-hour quintuple rerouting, blood vessels from Rock's leg were used to bypass the damaged arteries. The surgery proved to be successful. Even so, Hudson found it impossible to break some bad habits.

"I went to see him in the hospital and I remember he really downplayed the whole operation," Jack Scalia says. "He was supposed to be taking it easy but right away, he says to me, 'Do me a favor and look inside that drawer.' I opened it up and there's a package of cigarettes in there. He says, 'Give me one of those cigarettes. After everything I've been through, I really need one.' I said, 'I'm not giving you one. I'm going to go tell Tom.' He got angry and said, 'Go tell Tom. See what I care.' Then he starts opening up his gown and he says, 'So, Jack, have I shown you my scar?' This was in the old days when they just cracked you open and you were left with this massive scar. I said, 'I really don't want to look at that, Rock.' He says, 'Okay. Deal. I won't make you look at it if you give me a lousy cigarette.' That was the kind of character he was."

A brief stay in intensive care was followed by a Caribbean cruise. Throughout the trip, Tom Clark and Claire Trevor alternated duties as Hudson's well-oiled but highly attentive nursemaids. Although Rock's doctor, Rex Kennamer, had advised him to go easy and forget about his professional obligations for a while, Hudson didn't waste a minute of his twenty-four-day vacation. Instead of kicking back, Rock began poring over some of the new *Devlin Connection* scripts, which only succeeded in raising his blood pressure. "We read them with dismay," Tom Clark recalled. "It seemed to both of us they were absolutely unplayable . . . It wasn't the show we had set out to do."

Suddenly, John Wilder was out as producer and Jerry Thorpe (*The Untouchables*) was in. This followed a similar shake-up, which had already taken place in NBC's executive offices. Network president

Fred Silverman, who had greenlighted *The Devlin Connection*, resigned and was replaced by Brandon Tartikoff, who agreed with Hudson that the series needed to be retooled.

"None of what went on with the show changed anything between Rock and I," says Jack Scalia. "Our friendship shifted to a deeper level. There was a lot more openness. He was still funny but now there was a sense of vulnerability as he was dealing with his own mortality. We were talking once about his childhood and he started getting emotional. He started tearing up and I said, 'What's that all about, Rock?' And I looked over and his eyes just instantly cleared up. Allowing someone to see his pain, even for a minute, must have been hard. He didn't let many people in."

A full year after it had been slated to debut, *The Devlin Connection* finally premiered in October of 1982. Despite the chemistry between Hudson and Scalia, all of the false starts and bad breaks the series had weathered resulted in a show that was, at best, mediocre. *The Devlin Connection* debuted at a dismal number sixty-two in the Nielsen ratings and it was downhill from there. With only thirteen episodes in the can, NBC pulled the plug. The cancellation didn't seem to faze Hudson, who was not only enjoying his new lease on life but publicly admitting that he felt "rather smug about the new me."

If Hudson was "exhilarated" by his own *Seconds*-style reboot, others felt that the new Rock was a complete stranger. Hudson's physician had warned Tom Clark that after a heart bypass operation, patients often underwent a distinct personality change, though the effects were usually temporary. "It is very difficult to describe the change or, rather, those changes, because it wasn't just one thing, but several," Clark remembered. "He behaved in ways he never behaved in the past. He said things he never would have said before the operation . . . I thought, well, this too will pass—but it never did pass. Rock was a different man from the time of his surgery until his death."

According to Mark Miller, the changes that Clark described

were a result of Hudson giving up the bottle and finally emerging from a decade-long alcoholic fog. Clear-eyed and completely sober for the first time in years, Hudson realized it was time to make some drastic changes.

"When Rock came out of the heart by-pass surgery in 1982 and stopped drinking, he said to me, 'My God, I'm living with a drunk . . . ,'" Mark Miller remembered. Hudson decided that in order to maintain his sobriety, Clark would have to go. "Ship him to New York, to my apartment until we can figure out what to do next," Hudson told Miller. As Claire Trevor was preparing to fly back to New York on business, it was decided that Clark would accompany her. Once they landed, Trevor would check into her suite at the St. Regis while Clark would move into the Beresford, Rock's six-room luxury apartment on Central Park West.

Although everything had been meticulously planned, all did not go well. "Claire called me the next day to report that it was the worst flight of her life," Miller remembered. "Tom got drunk on the plane and caused a scene Claire would never forget. He gave every first-class passenger an earful about his affair with Rock Hudson and how he had been kicked out of 9402 Beverly Crest in Beverly Hills and was now going to live in Rock's fabulous apartment."

In Tom Clark's version of events, he decided—without any promptings from others—that it was time to go. Fed up with a postsurgical Rock Hudson who was brooding, petulant, and wholly unlikable, Clark determined that he needed a change of scenery. As he remembered it, Hudson made every attempt to persuade him to stay but his mind was made up: "I felt an overpowering need to get away by myself for a while."

Regardless of which rendition is correct, Hudson really cleaned house. This included the dismissal of Flo Allen, Hudson's longtime agent at the William Morris Agency. Putting his personal feelings for Flo aside, Rock signed with Marty Baum at Creative Artists Agency. The first order of business to be addressed was the fact that Rock Hudson—one of Hollywood's most beloved stars—had not appeared in a feature film since *The Mirror Crack'd* had been released in 1980.

"Did you have a nice Easter?"

This was Rock Hudson's highly original opening line to Michael Kearns. It was the Monday after the holiday. 1983. The two actors could have been chatting on the set between takes. Only they weren't. They were sitting across from one another, wearing nothing but towels, in the sauna at Brooks Baths.

"It was this reputedly legit bathhouse on Beverly Boulevard in L.A.," says Kearns. "It was just across the street from CBS. Brooks Baths had been there for years but its big claim to fame was that Rock Hudson was known to hang out there . . . literally."

Then in his early thirties, Kearns was one of the few openly gay actors in Hollywood, and his shades-up policy regarding his sexuality almost certainly impeded a promising screen career. While he had won acclaim for his stage performances, that success didn't translate into starring roles in feature films (he's billed as "Man in Shower" in *The Kentucky Fried Movie*). As Kearns had learned, in Hollywood there was such a thing as being too honest. The movie star sitting across from him fully understood this, too.

"When I found myself alone in the sauna with Rock Hudson and it was clear that he was interested, I realized I was suddenly living every gay man's fantasy," says Kearns. "But what's interesting is there was nothing lascivious or lurid about it. He seemed sad to me and sad is not sexy. If I ever saw an aura around someone, it was then. And it was dark. Rock seemed kind of desperate to me . . . as it turned out, it wasn't just a sexual experience we shared, it was a human experience. This was about connecting with a lonely human being, who I then felt empathetic towards. He was stripped down, as it were, both literally and figuratively. I could feel his pain then, though it wears on me more today. I'm older now and have a better understanding of what he was struggling with."

Kearns was so moved by his fleeting encounter with Hudson that in 1991 he wrote *Rock*, a provocative theatre piece in which four characters explore their connections to Hudson, either real or imagined. In one sequence, a distraught Hudson confides in Marilyn Monroe: "There's a little girl in me that I just trample to death." Norma Jeane Baker sympathizes with Roy Fitzgerald and sees them as two halves of an iconographic whole: "I put on 'Marilyn Monroe' like a pair of earrings. Roy put on 'Rock Hudson' like a jockstrap."

In the course of writing his play, Kearns came to the realization that "Rock was a brilliant actor, though not necessarily on the screen. His most brilliant performance was playing 'Rock Hudson' all his life. I think the acting he did off screen required more work, more transformation. Then you start to wonder . . . Who would he have really been if Roy Fitzgerald had been allowed to exist? What would he have really talked like? I mean, from the very beginning of his life, this is someone who had to act just to *survive*."

CHAPTER 18

CHRISTIAN

Taller, blonder, sexier. "Marc Christian was
Rock Hudson's dream man," says Hudson's friend Ken Maley.
"Well . . . at least in the beginning he was."
*(Photo courtesy of the Associated Press;
Photographer: Lennox McLendon)*

B y the fall of 1983, Tom Clark had vacated The Castle and a
new man, thirty-year-old Marc Christian,* was suddenly on
the scene. From the moment Rock first encountered Marc he
was hooked. "Physically, he fit Rock's type perfectly," says
Hudson's friend Ken Maley. "It was like a paper doll cut-out.

*Marc Christian was born Marc Christian MacGinnis on June 23, 1953. At the
time of his birth, his parents, Miles and Jeanne, were living in Manhattan

You couldn't have found a taller, blonder, sexier guy. In every way, this was Rock's dream man. Well, at least in the beginning he was."

If Christian's physical attributes weren't already enough to win him scores of admirers, this beauty also came equipped with brains. Marc could converse intelligently about politics, sports, history, the arts. During their initial meeting, Marc told Rock about *Decades*, a proposed radio documentary that he hoped to produce. The project sounded both ambitious and vague. It involved "putting together a history of popular music from the time the phonograph was invented."

This segued into a discussion concerning Rock's vast collection of 78 RPM records. According to Christian, Hudson expressed interest in having the discs transferred to tape, with scratches and crackles minimized. A self-described "musicologist," Marc assured Rock that one of his specialties was sound restoration. Christian gave Hudson his number. Not long after, Rock hired Marc. "To start doing his records," as Christian put it.

As for how he morphed from Rock Hudson's sound engineer to his bedmate, Christian described this as "a very slow and evolutionary thing." In fact, by Marc's estimation, he met with Rock seventy to eighty times before any sort of sexual intimacy occurred. But according to one of Hudson's closest friends, a physical relationship began not long after the two met. "They got right down to business," Mark Miller said. "They didn't go steady or talk it over for a few months."

After enduring more than a decade of Tom Clark as ruler of the roost, some staffers at The Castle felt that the coolly detached Christian was a breath of fresh air. Though, in time, things would deteriorate so dramatically that George Nader would eventually say of Christian: "Like a snake enters the garden, that young man entered this house." According to some of Rock's former employees,

---

Beach in Los Angeles, though they would later raise Marc and his younger sister, Susan, in Villa Park, a small city in Orange County.

there were signs of trouble almost from the moment that Marc moved in.

"Rock was going out of town to do *The Ambassador* with Robert Mitchum in Tel Aviv," remembers estate manager Marty Flaherty. "I'm there with Rock the night before. Christian's supposed to be there but he isn't. Rock and I are having cocktails, getting drunk. It's getting later and Christian still hasn't shown up. I ended up spending the night at Rock's house and Christian never came home. That was one of the only times I ever saw Rock cry. When the limo came to pick him up, I could see that Rock was upset but he gave me this big hug before he took off. Right after the limo pulls away, Christian shows up. Only he's not alone. He's having a party with all of his friends. They'd been up all night. It was obvious that the last thing that Christian had on his mind was saying goodbye to Rock."

––––––––

In 1975, Israeli mini-moguls Menahem Golan and Yoran Globus, who specialized in producing low-budget exploitation films, acquired the screen rights to *Fifty-Two Pickup*, a suspense novel set in Detroit by the master of crime fiction, Elmore Leonard. Nearly a decade would pass before cameras actually rolled. Retitled *The Ambassador*, the script that Golan and Globus green-lighted bore only the vaguest resemblance to the plotline of Leonard's novel.

In terms of the setting, Detroit was out and Tel Aviv was in. Leonard's protagonist, manufacturing executive Harry Mitchell had been transformed into Peter Hacker, the U.S. Ambassador to Israel, who is attempting to bring peace to the Middle East during the Israeli-Palestinian conflict. In *Fifty-Two Pickup*, the married Harry Mitchell finds himself negotiating with blackmailers who have filmed him having sex with his twenty-one-year-old mistress. In *The Ambassador*, the diplomat's wife has a steamy tryst with a P.L.O. leader that is secretly filmed by the Israeli Intelligence Agency. They want $1 million for the negative. Unable to pay, the ambassador orders his security advisor to retrieve the incriminating footage, no matter what.

From the beginning, several of Rock's closest confidants did their best to dissuade him from appearing in *The Ambassador.* Tom Clark went first. Although they were no longer living together, Rock still turned to Tom for professional advice regarding which of the scripts submitted to him looked promising. *The Ambassador* did not. "Rock, I read that and it's a dreadful script," Clark told Hudson. "I rejected it for you a couple of years ago . . . Don't do that one. It's a bomb waiting to go off."

But Rock was so desperate to appear in a theatrical feature that he was willing to accept third billing as well as a role that Telly Savalas had backed out of at the last minute. Filling in for Lieutenant Kojak and playing the supporting part of the security advisor may have been humbling enough, but what really smarted was that for the first time in decades Hudson was not playing the lead.

While veteran director J. Lee Thompson was happy to have Rock Hudson in his movie, he, too, tried to talk Hudson out of it. "I didn't think the part was really big enough for him. It was a subsidiary part," Thompson said. "Right from the start, he implied we would have to do something with the part, to make it stronger and better. We did our best, which was unfortunately, not really good enough." If Hudson's role was far from satisfactory, at least he would be in some fine company, with Robert Mitchum assuming the title role and Oscar-winner Ellen Burstyn playing the diplomat's adulterous wife.

Back in L.A., Rock had wanted nothing more than to go back to work. But once he arrived on location in Israel, he sank into what his director described as "a very great depression." Everything seemed wrong. Gone were the days when Rock Hudson occupied the plushest bungalow on the Universal lot. He had now been relegated to a fly-infested trailer in the Negev Desert. Although he didn't complain, it was obvious that he was miserable. The heat was unbearable, the food wretched, the movie subpar.

While shooting in the occupied West Bank, cast and crew were watched over by armed patrols meant to ward off terrorist attacks. Their presence made an already anxious Hudson even more agitated. In fact, the only thing that distracted Rock from his assortment of agonies was smoking—something he did constantly even though it had been forbidden by his doctors.

If Rock had hoped to bond with the film's leading man—whose legendary career predated his own—he was disappointed. "I don't think Mitchum cared for him, or he for Mitchum," Thompson remembered. While *The Ambassador*'s director did everything possible to make Rock feel welcome, Hudson couldn't help but think of himself as a third wheel. After all, Mitchum and Thompson had already collaborated on two earlier films. They had developed a closeness and a shorthand style of working together.

Producer Menahem Golan was respectful and obliging of Hudson throughout production. In the few scenes she shared with Rock, Ellen Burstyn did her best to be encouraging and supportive. Nevertheless, it seemed as though nothing could bring Hudson out of his depressive funk. Even when the entire company surprised Rock with a cake in honor of his fifty-eighth birthday, it required some serious effort on his part to look overjoyed. *What the hell was there to celebrate anyway?* Try as he might, he couldn't shake the feeling that his movie career—which meant more to him than anything else—was essentially over. If the size of his role didn't confirm this, the size of his trailer certainly did.

WITH HIS WORK completed on *The Ambassador*, Rock returned to Los Angeles in early January of 1984. Marc Christian welcomed Hudson home by meeting him at the airport. From the moment they reunited, Marc noticed that Rock's physical appearance had changed considerably in just the two months that he had been out of the country. "When I moved into the house, he was about ten pounds overweight," Christian recalled. "When he got back, he was about ten pounds lighter. He told me that he took the weight off because he didn't like the food." Hudson's once radiant complexion had turned to a dull, ashen gray.

Back at The Castle, Hudson's changed appearance was mentioned by others but not dwelled upon. After all, this was supposed to be a happy homecoming. Christmas was Rock's favorite time of year, and shortly before his return, Christian had hosted a tree-decorating party. Hudson was moved by the pictures and holiday messages that Marc and his friends had displayed amid the ornaments. So began what Christian would later refer to as a "golden period" in his relationship with Rock.

Those who cast a cynical eye toward Christian's association with Hudson say that the only reason Marc recalled the months following Rock's return with such fondness was because he was treated royally. "At the beginning of the relationship, it was basically shopping sprees for Marc Christian," says Hudson's estate manager, Marty Flaherty. "Marc wanted to get into acting, so he was given acting lessons by the best coaches. Marc wanted a new portfolio, so he was sent to the top photographers, who took head shots. He wanted a Mercedes Benz. He wanted new ski outfits. He wanted presents bought for him and his friends. Rock was so giddy and smitten over him, that he just did it. Rock was getting older and now he had scored this hot, young trophy boyfriend. But for Rock, it was even more than that. He really thought he was in love. And he thought that this was the person."

Whenever he was accused of being an overindulged boy toy, Marc Christian stood firm. People had simply gotten the wrong impression. True, Rock may have added Marc to the Mammoth Films payroll at $400 a month, but that was only so Christian could receive health insurance. Besides, Marc claimed that three of the four hundred he was handed each month was immediately turned over to his parents. If Hudson chose to foot the bill for Christian's dental work, gym membership, and personal trainer, he had done so voluntarily. The full-scale restoration of a 1959 Chevy Nomad belonging to Christian's father, which totaled $20,000—was something

Rock took it upon himself to arrange. Miles MacGinnis was dying of lung cancer and Hudson hoped that seeing his car returned to its original splendor would boost his spirits.

Even though he had been outfitted with the ultimate Beverly Hills accessory—a celebrity drama coach, Christian didn't display a fraction of the ambition that the young Rock Hudson had in terms of pursuing his career. Among the staff at The Castle, Marc was known as "The Sleeping Prince." As they recalled, he tended to awaken midmorning. After visiting the gym, he would forgo meeting with casting directors and instead return home to catch up on *Days of our Lives*. Who had time to brush up on Stanislavski when your schedule might include meetings with Michael Jackson or dinners at Spago with Belinda Carlisle? Not to mention frequent excursions to San Francisco and Santa Barbara.

While Rock's houseman, John Dobbs, took to Christian ("I liked Marc. He was intelligent and he treated me as an equal"), most of Hudson's friends did not. "I was afraid for Rock when I met him," says actress Florence Lacey. "From the beginning, it was awkward because I had been such good friends with Rock and Tom as a couple. I tried to be social with the new guy. I tried to like him. But I have to say it was very uncomfortable."

"I met Marc Christian a couple of times and he was certainly not as attractive as Jack Coates had been, nor anywhere near as fun and engaging," says Rock's friend Ken Jillson. "He was just very quiet. I didn't think that he had much going on."

Rock's *Camelot* director, Stockton Briggle, also found it challenging to warm up to Hudson's new companion: "Marc Christian—I don't think, in my own personal opinion, ever cared anything about Rock any more than the fact that he was a big movie star . . . I tried hard to like him, but I found him cold and calculating. Nobody knew his real past."

According to some of Hudson's intimates, it was sordid tales of Christian's past that finally turned the tide in the relationship. While Rock had been out of the country, stories had started to circulate among staffers at The Castle that Christian "was very well known around town"—the implication being that Marc had worked as a paid escort. Mark Miller claimed that just after Rock returned from Israel, Christian came clean, allegedly telling Hudson: "I want you to know that I have taken money for sex from men . . . when I was down and out, and only when I did not have a bartending job. I did not do it all the time, but I don't want you to hear it from your rich friends."

There were also rumors concerning Marc's relationship with his closest confidante. At the time he met Hudson, Christian had been sharing a one-bedroom apartment in Hollywood with a former studio publicist named Liberty Martin. Christian would typically refer to her as his "best friend," unbothered by the fact that Martin was more than thirty years older than he was. "Liberty Martin was a wild character," says attorney Robert Parker Mills. "She was Gloria Swanson straight out of *Sunset Boulevard*. She was extremely theatrical and had the whole 1930s Hollywood thing going on. She wore these big, wide-brimmed hats, which not only gave her this grand aura, but also hid the ravages of time."

Even in the freewheeling 1970s, Marc Christian and Liberty Martin's long-term cohabitation raised eyebrows. As Liberty put it, "We don't understand ourselves. How could anyone else?" Christian frequently found himself attempting to explain his unorthodox relationship with Martin. "I asked him about her at one point," recalls Rock's friend, Gunther Fraulob. "Marc said, 'She is my mentor and best friend.' So then I asked him, 'Are you two sexually together or something?' And he said, 'No, she's more like my mom.' Though I wouldn't be at all surprised if he was getting money out of her."

In several later interviews, Christian denied that he had ever been paid for sex. As for confessing to Rock that he had been forced into a life of prostitution, Marc insisted that conversation never took place. Nevertheless, within a couple of months of Hudson's return to The Castle, it became obvious that his relationship with

Christian had changed. Rock's friends believe that after Marc revealed that he had been a hustler, Hudson knew that he could never again be seen with Christian publicly. What if one of Marc's clients spotted Hudson and Christian together somewhere? This would make Rock more vulnerable than ever. If the tabloids got wind of his affair with a male "courtesan" (as Mark Miller referred to Christian), it would be even worse than *Confidential*'s insinuations, more damaging than the Jim Nabors rumors. Rock Hudson would be over.

In only a matter of months, Marc Christian had gone from golden boy to damaged goods. There was an uncomfortable distance between Hudson and Christian when they visited Nader and Miller in Palm Springs. "You'd have thought they were two strangers stranded together for the weekend," Nader observed. Rock's butler, James Wright, noted that "there was no warmth or caring" between the two once they returned from the desert. By the end of March, Wright noticed that in Hudson's bedroom, there was a mattress on the floor, to the right side of the bed. Mark Miller would later recall that not long after this, Christian was deported to "Tijuana," as the six-shades-of-red guest room was known.

Only a few months earlier, Hudson had gushed about Christian to his *On the Twentieth Century* costar, Dean Dittman. Now Rock found himself venting all of his miseries. "You've got to get rid of him because you're suffering," Dittman told Hudson. "Does he have something on you? Is that why he's still in the house?" While Rock waved away Dittman's concerns, there were four "letters of affection" that he had sent to Christian while he was in Israel. If the letters somehow fell into the wrong hands, the loving sentiments expressed therein could now be used to expose him.

Rock's publicist, Rupert Allan, didn't mince words in describing Hudson's relationship with Christian, characterizing it as "A brief affair turned vicious. Rock was terrified of him because Marc Christian had told him that he knew the heads of the *Enquirer* and that they had offered him a lot of money for a story that Christian could give them about Rock being a homosexual and therefore Rock would never work again as a lead in a film and Rock was terrified of that."

By the spring of 1984, Hudson seemed to want only one thing from Christian—distance. Which doesn't mean that they parted company. Characteristically, Rock did not order Marc out of the house or even suggest that he should start packing his bags. Instead, Hudson resorted to passive-aggressive tactics that had achieved the desired results in the past. It may have taken years to disentangle himself from Tom Clark, but once Rock decided that their time together was over, he simply froze Tom out. The silent treatment had also worked with Tony Melia and countless others. But Marc Christian was different from all the others. He did not leave. After consulting with a high-profile attorney, he decided to stay put. Eventually, Marc would move out of the main part of Hudson's home and into the screening room.

Around the same time that Hudson's relationship with Christian began unraveling, problems also started to surface regarding Rock's most significant partnership. In February of 1984, the editors of two British tabloids, the *Daily Express* and the *Daily Star*, contacted Mark Miller. Was there any truth to the rumors that a disgruntled Tom Clark planned to file a multimillion-dollar palimony suit against Hudson?

"The fat hit the fire," George Nader noted in his diary. Hudson instructed Miller to get in touch with Emily Torchia. Widely regarded as one of the most resourceful publicists in Hollywood, Torchia worked for Rock's P.R. man, Rupert Allan. Torchia went to work. Calls were made, strings were pulled, and the rumor was squelched. "I'm not the suing type," Clark announced to the relief of everyone involved. Besides, Tom still held out hope that he and Hudson would eventually reconcile—this despite the fact that Marc Christian was still in residence at The Castle.

Tired of wrangling with both Christian and Clark, Hudson decided it was time to explore some new options. Since 1983, Rock had been working with a physical trainer named Ron Channell, whom he had met at the Sports Connection, a fitness center in West Hollywood. Channell was originally from Tampa, Florida, and like Marc Christian, had been flirting with a career in show business. With his muscular build and three days' worth of facial hair, Channell reminded some of his clients of "Bluto," the burly antagonist from the *Popeye* cartoon series. When Channell first met Hudson, the once svelte leading man was paunchy and easily winded. Embarrassed by this and not wanting to be recognized at the gym, Hudson asked Channell if he could work him out at home.

It wasn't long before Rock started referring to Ron as his "best friend." Channell made it clear from the beginning that he considered himself "straight" and that a close friendship was all that he was prepared to offer. This may have been a deal-breaker for most gay men closing in on sixty but not Rock Hudson. The Hollywood legend enjoyed helping the aspiring actor with his career pursuits. If Channell was nervous about an upcoming audition, Hudson would help him select a monologue and run through it with him. However, more often than not after a workout, the two would spend the afternoon just "goofing off." As Ron dabbled in songwriting, he might try out one of his compositions, just doodling on the piano. Rock would then take over, ripping through a Boogie-Woogie tune.

Of course, Marc Christian didn't relish the thought of being replaced by an aerobics instructor. "Ron talked like a hayseed and had no chin," Christian would say of Hudson's new best friend. Feeling betrayed by Christian and frustrated by the fact that his relationship with Channell hadn't progressed beyond the buddy stage, Rock turned his attention to another young man who seemed like a promising new companion. Gunther Fraulob was twenty-nine years old and bore an uncanny resemblance to the young Lee Garlington. Hudson and fellow actor Dean Dittman met Fraulob at The Silver Fox, a gay bar in Long Beach.

As usual, Rock fell hard and fast. Though this time he made a conscious decision to not bring Fraulob to The Castle, where the presence of yet another young hunk was bound to stir things up. "Whenever we met, it was away from Hollywood," Fraulob says. "At the time, I was living in a rental place in Long Beach and he would visit me there. Basically, his M.O. was he'd come over and we'd talk for a while. Usually, I would tell him what was going on in my life—the latest break-up or whatever and he would tell me about all of the drama going on at his house with Marc Christian."

From the beginning, Fraulob says that he was aware that Hudson was interested in more than just conversation. "During one of our talks, he confessed that he felt a very strong attachment to me," says Fraulob. "He wanted to take our friendship to another level. But I loved him in a different way. I said, 'You know, you're like a big brother to me,' which is probably not what he wanted to hear. I mean, at the time, Rock was almost sixty and I was in my twenties. I was dating guys who were 24 or 25. Rock was at a very different place in his life . . . I did my best to try to let him down gently."

While they agreed to be friends, Fraulob recalls that at least once, things went a bit further: "I had just broken up with this guy that I thought I was in love with. I remember saying to Rock, 'I'm never going to be able to find love in this crazy gay world.' I was going on a bit, to be honest. Rock grabbed me and kissed me and said, 'You wouldn't know love if it were staring you right in the face.' When I pulled myself together, I said, 'Rock, what are we talking about here?' He said, 'I think you know.' Nobody ran off that night. In fact, I think we had an even stronger bond after that whole episode."

Hudson confided in Fraulob, telling him how distraught he was over the situation with Christian. Fraulob thought that getting away from it all might be the answer for Hudson: "It was getting close to Easter and I talked him into coming with me and spending a week at my parents' place in Hawaii . . . My parents were one hundred percent German, which I know was part of Rock's ancestry. My dad spoke English like he was just off the boat. My mom was a bit more Americanized, though they were both very simple people. My parents lived in the middle of nowhere. We had an acre of land with an ocean view."

Rock's weeklong Hawaiian idyll in the spring of 1984 would prove to be the calm before the storm. Upon Hudson's return to The Castle, Mark Miller and others expressed their concern about Rock's rapid weight loss. He was in for more of the same when he attended a state dinner at the White House in honor of Mexico's president, Miguel de la Madrid. First Lady Nancy Reagan cornered Rock and told him that he was in need of fattening up. He responded with, "You're thin, also."

Two weeks later, photos taken by the official White House photographer arrived at The Castle. Along with an image of Hudson posing with the Reagans, there was a profile shot of Rock enclosed. With this picture, the First Lady had attached a note advising him to have the pimple on his neck checked. Not only was it visible in the photo but Rock admitted that it had been there for about a year and seemed to be getting larger. Only when Marty Flaherty told Rock that if the cyst wasn't removed in a timely manner, it could leave a scar did Hudson agree to see his doctor. When all else failed, appealing to the movie star's vanity usually did the trick.

MARK MILLER WOULD later refer to June 5, 1984, as "the beginning of where the walls came tumbling down on all of our lives—forever." As Miller remembered it, that was the day Rock joined him in his office and delivered some devastating news: He had AIDS. Maybe cancer, too. Miller would later say that while attempting to absorb all of this, he had to fight the urge to bolt from the room: "An inner voice said, 'Do not desert. Don't get out of the chair . . .' Somehow, I held myself in that chair, but I was in utter panic."

The diagnosis was both horrifying and overwhelming. Though Miller later admitted that at least part of Hudson's admission was not entirely shocking. According to Mark, as far back as 1975, Rock had been tested at the Kelsey-Seybold Clinic in Houston, where he was diagnosed as having the onset of liver cancer. At that time, he had been ordered to slow down and stop drinking but the professional advice had gone unheeded. Now it was too late.

While terrifying, cancer was at least familiar. AIDS was something else again. As Miller put it, "I thought it was a disease that fairies on Santa Monica Boulevard got." Not Rock Hudson. In 1981, one of the first headlines concerning the epidemic appeared in the *New York Times*. It read: "Rare Cancer Seen in 41 Homosexuals." Three years later, the mysterious disease had been given a clinical sounding name—Acquired Immune Deficiency Syndrome—and researchers had identified a probable cause, but there were still countless unanswered questions. How was the virus transmitted? Could something as seemingly innocuous as a hug or a handshake be responsible for spreading the disease?

Hudson told Miller that he had been crying for a week, having received his AIDS diagnosis from a Beverly Hills dermatologist who had biopsied the lesion on his neck and identified it as Kaposi's sarcoma. Until now, Rock had kept everything to himself, telling no one. But now Hudson was no longer holding back. He admitted to Miller that he felt "so filthy" that he had AIDS. After decades of being confined to the closet and keeping his mouth shut, the lesions and sores that had started to sprout on his body were the most hideous kind of public declaration imaginable. Why bother denying the truth when every part of your anatomy was screaming it out for you?

Hudson asked Miller to accompany him to an appointment he had scheduled a few days later with Dr. Rex Kennamer, his personal physician, and Dr. Michael Gottlieb, an AIDS specialist from UCLA. Following his quintuple bypass, Rock believed that he suffered from "white coat syndrome." He found that after meeting with one of his doctors, he couldn't remember a single word that had been said.

During the appointment, Hudson asked Dr. Gottlieb if AIDS was necessarily a fatal diagnosis. After a measured pause, Gottlieb suggested that it would be wise if Rock got his affairs in order. The doctor then asked Hudson if he had a lover. Rock responded that he didn't currently have one, although a former companion was still living with him. According to Miller, Hudson then added that he and his lingering ex had not engaged in any sexual activity for several months.

Dr. Gottlieb explained to Rock that there was no telling how someone might react when informed that a partner—whether current or former—had AIDS. Some lovers were understanding and supportive. Others bolted, never to be heard from again. There is some dispute regarding whether Dr. Gottlieb advised Hudson to tell his former partner of his AIDS diagnosis. In one version of Mark Miller's recounting of events, Gottlieb told Rock, "You are a famous man and there will be headlines when this is announced, so it is up to you whether to tell your former lover or not." In another, Gottlieb told Rock, "I'm going to leave it up to you how to handle telling your former lover."

On the ride home, Hudson and Miller discussed who should—and should not—be told about Rock's AIDS diagnosis. When the subject of Christian was broached, Miller claimed that Hudson said, "He—[Hudson]—could have gotten AIDS from Marc and he wanted him out of the house by five o'clock that afternoon."

Miller said that he talked Hudson out of this. What if Christian had been exposed? After all, he was dependent on Rock's production company, Mammoth Films, for health insurance. If Marc was booted from The Castle, he'd be back on the couch at Liberty Martin's place. Besides, throwing him out could have dire consequences. If Christian had already threatened to fill the *Enquirer* in on his gay affair with Rock Hudson—as several of Rock's friends and employees maintained—what might he do with this new information? Making an alleged blackmailer aware of an AIDS diagnosis would be equivalent to handing the enemy surplus ammunition.

"You're absolutely right," Hudson responded. "Marc Christian and Liberty Martin will destroy me in five minutes if they have this news." It was decided that Christian would remain in Rock's house, at least for the time being, but he would not be told of Hudson's diagnosis.

Besides Miller, only a handful of people in Rock's inner circle would be made aware of his diagnosis, including George Nader, Dean Dittman, butler James Wright, and, eventually, Hudson's business manager, Wallace Sheft. Rock also insisted on sending anonymous letters to four individuals he had sexual encounters with prior to receiving his AIDS diagnosis. George Nader mailed the letters from Palm Springs so that the recipients wouldn't immediately connect the dots as to who the sender was. The letters were brief and to the point . . .

> *We recently had sex together and I have been informed by my doctor that I may have AIDS. Please go to your doctor and have a check-up.*

According to Mark Miller, "Only one person ever responded . . ." A twenty-two-year-old that Hudson had a fling with immediately guessed the identity of his correspondent. "He was a young man from New York, who found out the next day he had AIDS. He sold his story to one of the tabloids for $10,000. He died six months later. His story was not published for a year and a half after Rock died. His name was Tony."

At the height of his health crisis, Rock received a number of important job offers—including one that he found irresistible. Stockton Briggle wanted him to headline a London production of the Tony Award–winning musical *La Cage aux Folles*.[*] Hudson would

---

[*]Producer Allan Carr wanted Rock to replace star Gene Barry in the original Broadway production of *La Cage aux Folles*. "Rock intimated that he wanted to play the part," recalled agent Marty Baum. "It didn't bother him to consider playing a homosexual on Broadway." However, Hudson's deteriorating health prevented him from accepting the role and Van Johnson ended up replacing Barry.

be playing Georges, the gay owner of a drag nightclub whose partner, Albin, is the club's star attraction. The couple agree to play it straight for the sake of Georges's son, who is bringing home his straitlaced fiancée and her conservative parents. Hudson asked Nader and Miller what they thought. They advised him to turn it down—not because the story hit too close to home but because the physical demands of a three-month engagement would exhaust him. "Not in your condition," Miller said. "The London press is the worst in the world. They will destroy you." Hudson passed on *La Cage* but instantly regretted it.

Then there was a project that had been simmering on the back burner for over a year. Actor turned producer Jimmy Hawkins (who had appeared with Hudson in *Winchester '73*) had come up with an idea that would reunite Rock and Doris Day on-screen. After Hawkins outlined his *Pillow Talk II* premise, Oscar-winner Delbert Mann was sold and he set up a meeting with Hudson.

"The next week, we were sitting in Rock's living room—the writer, myself, and Delbert," Hawkins recalls. "The writer pitched him our story [in which Doris and Rock are divorced but back in contact as their daughter plans to marry Tony Randall's son]. When the pitch was over, Rock said, 'You know, people have been pitching ideas for *Pillow Talk II* for twenty-five years and this is the single greatest idea I've ever heard.' He said, 'I speak for me and I speak for Doris. We're in. This is really great.' Then, he went over to the telephone and he called Doris Day and told her all about it."

Both Day and an executive for Universal Cable were as enthusiastic as Hudson had been, though Hawkins remembers the executive asking a lot of questions: "He loved the pitch but then he said, 'How is Rock? The rumor is that he's very thin and there's something wrong with him.'" Although *Pillow Talk II* sounded promising to all involved, the gravity of Hudson's condition would ultimately derail the project.

Whether it was complete denial or an acute awareness of what little time he had left, Rock became more work-focused than ever before. He ordered his agent, Marty Baum, to scour the shelves in search of a property that would allow him to stretch as an actor. At this point, it really didn't matter if the project was a feature film, a miniseries, or a television show. All that Hudson wanted was to appear in a production that exuded class, sophistication, and intelligence. What he got was a made-for-TV movie entitled *The Vegas Strip War.**

As rumor had it, *Vegas Strip* was based on casino magnate Steve Wynn's remarkable comeback in the "Capital of Second Chances." Whether or not this was true, the story seemed awfully familiar. Neil Chaine, owner of the Desert Inn, is forced out of ownership by his double-dealing partners. Determined to make it on his own, Chaine pours everything he has into revitalizing the Tropicana, a neighboring hotel that's teetering on the verge of bankruptcy.

"From the beginning, Rock had an enthusiastic and vivid interest in the subject," said writer-director George Englund. "He didn't know much about the hotel business, didn't know much about gambling. He had a lot of questions, intelligent questions . . . Through the whole production, he was earnestly trying to work on the part, kept exploring it, refining it. He was a joy to work with."

To surround Hudson, Englund assembled an eclectic supporting cast composed of equal parts veterans and newcomers: James Earl Jones (sending up boxing promoter Don King), *The Karate Kid*'s Pat Morita, and future superstar Sharon Stone—whom Rock went out of his way to help. "He'd call me in the morning and say, 'Order me some breakfast. I'm coming over and we're running the lines . . .'" Stone says. "He literally taught me every day how to do my job because I didn't know how to do my job."

When he wasn't bringing Stone up to speed, Hudson found time to bond with actor Madison Mason, who played one of Chaine's

---

*The title of the movie changed continuously throughout its production and even after it aired. Actor Madison Mason remembered that it was initially entitled *The Vegas Hotel Wars* before NBC changed the title to *The Vegas Strip War.* The home video version was retitled yet again as *The Vegas Casino War.*

backstabbing partners. "We became close friends and he was a kind, loving, considerate man," Mason says. "I knew he was sick when I signed on to the picture. Nobody else knew but his doctor had just diagnosed him with AIDS. I was close friends with his nurse's son, who said to me, 'Listen, nobody knows much about this disease, but watch out because he's got it.' Even so, he was right there for everyone and always giving of himself."

"The hottest ticket in town" is how Rock described another *Vegas Strip* costar, Dennis Holahan, to Mark Miller. Hudson wasn't only impressed with the young actor's striking looks but also his pedigree. A Yale graduate and Vietnam veteran, Holahan became an attorney before leaving his practice to pursue an acting career.

"I was married to the actress Loretta Swit around the time Rock and I used to go out to dinner," Holahan recalls. "I remember he said, 'How do you manage to get out?' Meaning, how come I could go out and have dinner with him without my wife. I said, 'That's not a problem.' Here's what the sad part was to me—he was surprised that I would allow myself to be seen having dinner with him in a restaurant. He somehow thought that would be bad for my career. That rumors might start. He was thinking of me and I was very touched by that."

During their dinners, Hudson confided in Holahan that things weren't going well on the home front: "He didn't want to be nasty about it, but he was hoping that Marc Christian would move out. He was really upset about it . . . I mean, can you imagine Bette Davis or Joan Crawford under those circumstances? It would have been '*Get the fuck out of my house!*' as a vase goes flying across the room. But not Rock."

The mixed reviews for *Vegas Strip* didn't claim nearly as much column space as Hudson's dramatic weight loss. After the subject was broached by one interviewer too many, the star became increasingly annoyed: "Everybody asks about my health. All the damned time. Is there some kind of damn conspiracy going on here? 'You've lost weight . . .' they say. Of course I've lost weight. I've tried to lose weight since I was 24. I'm now at the weight I should be—198. I've been 220 most of my career and trying to hold in my stomach is a bore."

AT ONE POINT during the *Vegas Strip* shoot, Hudson had suffered a bout of laryngitis and had to contact a specialist to help him regain his voice. Then he started having difficulty remembering his lines. One scene had called for him to recite reams of dialogue while dealing cards. After flubbing his lines a few times, Rock became upset. He told George Nader that he was finding it difficult to concentrate for extended periods of time.

While Rock was still in Las Vegas, Dean Dittman had learned of an experimental new drug, HPA-23, which had been developed by scientists at the Institut Pasteur in France. The drug had shown some signs of preventing the replication of the AIDS virus in the bloodstream—at least immediately after it was administered. Although HPA-23 was already being touted as a "miracle cure" by some, its long-term effectiveness had not yet been demonstrated. Further tests were being conducted in Paris. There were legitimate concerns about the toxic side effects as HPA-23 had caused damage to the blood system or liver in some patients. Nevertheless, it now seemed like Rock's only hope. Arrangements were made for Hudson to fly to Paris and start receiving HPA-23.

Both Nader and Miller felt that Hudson was in denial regarding the severity of his condition. At one point, Rock had snapped and said, "I don't have AIDS! If I'm dying, it's from liver cancer. I've known I've had it for ten years, for Christ's sake! What is all this AIDS shit?"

Whether it was a refusal to face facts or a concerted effort to live life to the fullest, Rock decided that his trip to Europe was going to be about far more than an infusion of HPA-23. As he would be in France at the same time that the Deauville Film Festival was honoring George Stevens, Rock planned to attend the event and pay tribute to the *Giant* director. Hudson's publicist, Dale Olson, also booked him on a London-based talk show.

In early August, Mark Miller reserved a two-bedroom suite for Rock and Ron Channell at the Ritz Hotel in Paris. They were booked for a month. As Ron had been kept in the dark regarding Hudson's AIDS diagnosis, he would not be made aware of the experimental drug testing. In any conversations between Hudson and Miller that Channell might overhear, "story conferences" would become code for HPA-23 treatments. Several days before they departed for Paris, Hudson stopped off in New York, where he met with his business manager, Wallace Sheft, and his attorney, Paul Sherman.

After having conversations with Nader and Miller regarding "devising and bequeathing," Rock decided to make significant changes to his will, which had been executed in August of 1981. In a codicil, Rock revoked an earlier bequest to Tom Clark, who was to have received all of Hudson's personal and household furnishings as well as his automobiles, film library, and other tangible effects. The codicil would also override another section of the will, which authorized Clark to distribute items among friends of Hudson's as well as any charitable organizations Clark deemed appropriate.

Other changes were made. Rock's friend and former agent, Flo Allen, who had originally been named as another beneficiary, was removed from the will. Hudson disinherited any heir (namely his twelve cousins) who might be living at the time of his death. No provision was made for Rock's adoptive sister, Alice Scherer Waier. George Nader was named the primary beneficiary of a trust Hudson established in 1974, with Mark Miller the next in line. Although Miller had hoped to have been named the executor of the will, that role would be assumed by Sheft, the head of a Manhattan-based accounting firm, who was also named trustee of the trust fund.

As Nader and Miller had been Hudson's closest friends and confidants for over thirty years, to most observers it made sense that they would come first, especially since Rock and Tom Clark had gone their separate ways. And in the years since Sheft had taken over as Hudson's business manager, he reportedly built up Rock's estate to the point that it was worth an estimated $27 million, including some valuable real estate holdings. As the executor had to be an individual with the experience and expertise to handle such a complex estate, Sheft seemed like a logical choice. It all looked right on paper, but some of Rock's other friends have expressed their doubts.

"I think they manipulated his will," says film historian Robert Osborne, who had befriended Hudson years earlier. Osborne appeared to lay the blame on Miller, Nader, and Sheft. "I very much think so. That one group took over, because there was nobody around to call the shots on it. I mean, Tom Clark had left and it weakened his position. When he did come back, I think he only came back under conditions that were set for him to come back under. But there was nobody around to blow the whistle or protect Rock in any way. It's heartbreaking because he was somebody that deserved to have protection. He never did anything mean—I don't think—in his life. He wasn't built that way."

At least publicly, Tom Clark didn't seem bothered by the fact that he had been shut out: "When Sheft told me that Rock had written a new will, eliminating me as his beneficiary, I shrugged it off. I was surprised but not devastated." Clark even had a theory as to why Hudson had removed him. "I think that, because he believed Marc Christian was making threats, he anticipated that his estate would be the subject of litigation and by writing me out of the will, he was sparing me the hassle and ugliness he knew would be coming."

As far as Marc Christian was concerned, this was yet another fantastic notion of Tom Clark's. Even though staffers at The Castle remembered that Rock and Marc were barely communicating by this time, Christian said that not only were they talking but they had even discussed revisions to Hudson's will: "I remember when Rock went to New York to do it. He said, 'I'm going to go to New

York. I'm going to change my will and get Tom out, because I could have a car accident and he'd get everything, and I hate the son of a bitch now.'"

Christian assumed that his name would replace Tom Clark's in the amended will, even though Rock had never expressly said that would be the case: "He never sat me down and said, 'I'm going to put you in my will,'* because he never talked about his money."

In late August, Mark Miller wished Rock and Ron Channell a "successful business trip" before they boarded the Concorde to Paris. The day after landing, Rock had his first meeting with Dr. Dominique Dormont, one of the specialists at the Institut Pasteur, a biomedical clinic then at the forefront of AIDS research. Despite the fact that he had initially been told that he would have to receive injections at his hotel, Hudson instead met with Dr. Dormont at the Percy Military Hospital. After conducting a thorough physical, Dormont concluded that Rock was in the "middle stages of AIDS," with a badly compromised immune system and Kaposi's sarcoma lesions.

In order for the HPA-23 treatment to be completely effective, daily infusions were recommended. This would mean that Hudson would have to remain in Paris for approximately three months. Rock resisted this idea, citing professional commitments, but he did agree to a shorter course of treatment. "If Rock had agreed to stay in Paris for a long-term course, probably the disease would have stabilized," says Dormont. "But he felt the work in films was more important. My impression was, he was thinking Rock Hudson couldn't be killed by this virus."

After he consulted with Dr. Dormont, Hudson's UCLA specialist, Dr. Michael Gottlieb, phoned Mark Miller to say that he

---

*During his 1989 trial and while under oath, Christian seemed to contradict himself when cross examined by defense attorney Robert Parker Mills. "Q: Did you have any reason to believe that you were named in Hudson's will? A: Yes, I did. Q: What reason was that? A: Rock Hudson told me he was going to put me in his will. Q: When did he tell you that? A: At least half a dozen times."

was "guardedly optimistic" about the possibility of delaying or arresting Rock's condition once additional infusions had been administered. Though Rock reported that the treatments made him nauseated, by early September he had actually gained six pounds. He was surprised to find that he had plenty of energy and his spirits were given a lift as he showed Ron Channell around Paris, where he also happened to run into some old friends.

"I was on the street in Paris with a friend of mine named Toni Kaye, a dancer on *The Carol Burnett Show*," Robert Osborne recalled. "We were walking around and ran into Rock. Now, Paris is not a small town, so to run into someone you knew struck me as the strangest thing in the world. I didn't know this then, but he was actually marking time because he had appointments in Paris. This was a year before it came out that he had AIDS. So, he said, 'What's going on?' We told him we were out buying food for a Mexican dinner. We were going to see Tom Jones, a publicist for Disney who was over there on a vacation with his wife. Rock said, 'Oh my god, I haven't seen Tom Jones for years. All my friends that I thought I'd be seeing here are not in town. I'd love to come to your dinner.' And so he did. It turns out Olivia de Havilland came as well. The dinner went on for all hours, because it was quite a drinking group. We laughed and he had the best time. When I found out later he was over there on this very serious matter, it struck me even more about what a complicated time in his life that was and how good for him it was to have that evening with old friends. Because after that, things were pretty grim for Rock Hudson."

In late September, Rock phoned Mark Miller from Paris. Hudson brought his old friend up to date on his recent adventures with Ron Channell. Miller then inquired how Hudson was feeling. "Oh, so so . . ." Rock had attempted to sound upbeat and untroubled, but his tone clearly said otherwise. After they hung up, Miller began sobbing uncontrollably. When James Wright, who was working nearby, asked what the trouble was, Miller blurted out, "Rock has AIDS. The boss is gonna die." James comforted Mark and pledged to tell no one about Hudson's diagnosis. Wright then assured Miller that he would stay on and help in any way that he might be needed.

After Rock had received several HPA-23 treatments, Dr. Dormont informed him that tests revealed that the AIDS virus was no longer present in his blood. Dormont stressed that although the virus had been temporarily sidelined, Hudson still had the disease. Nevertheless, Rock seemed to hear only what he wanted to—that the virus was no longer present. Hudson may have misinterpreted this as having been given a clean bill of health. "He was a little too optimistic," recalled Dr. Dormont. "He did not feel AIDS would be fatal to him. If he had taken his disease seriously, he would have stayed longer in Paris, but he didn't want to . . . He was not afraid of dying. Perhaps for him it was not so important to prolong his life, I don't know. He never talked about life and death."

––––––––

If, by the early 1980s, America was experiencing the worst recession since the Great Depression and nine million people were unemployed, Aaron Spelling was having none of it. The producer's primetime soap opera, *Dynasty*, which launched in 1981, attempted to heal the national psyche by peddling luxury porn to the masses. Featuring a main title sequence in which oil flowed as freely as vintage champagne, *Dynasty* may have been totally divorced from reality, yet at the same time it was perfectly in sync with the Reagan-era 1980s. At the White House, a first lady outfitted in Galanos ball gowns was hosting lavish state dinners served on Lenox china, which reportedly cost $1,000 per setting.

On the set of *Dynasty*, things were no less deluxe. "There was no such thing as a plastic flower on that show," says assistant director John Poer. "If you ever saw flowers on the set of *Dynasty*, they were real. Aaron Spelling insisted on this. It was his opinion that if Joan Collins was playing a scene in a room filled with the best crystal and china, it would all feel real—to her, to the crew, to the audience." *Real* being a relative term, of course.

As created by Richard and Esther Shapiro, *Dynasty*'s storylines were brimming over with such melodramatic excess—extortion plots, catfights, murder trials, Moldavian massacres—that the show frequently bordered on self-parody. But just try to look away. By the mid-1980s, *Dynasty* occupied the number one spot in the Nielsen ratings, with over twenty million homes tuning in to witness the travails of oil tycoon Blake Carrington (John Forsythe), his beautiful but long-suffering wife, Krystle (Linda Evans), and Blake's ex-wife, a fur-draped master manipulator named Alexis (Joan Collins).

The three leads were supported not only by several photogenic newcomers but also a bevy of guest stars—one-time A-listers like Ali MacGraw, George Hamilton, and Diahann Carroll—whose careers were in need of resuscitation. However, Spelling had set his sights on the one star who could do as much for *Dynasty* as the show could do for him—Rock Hudson.

With the series heading into its fifth season, it seemed the perfect time to spice things up by giving Krystle Carrington an extramarital love interest. This would keep viewers hooked while the presence of a legendary leading man would bring some Golden Age glamour to primetime. There was only one problem. The legend in question couldn't be bothered.

Spelling used all of his wiles to get Hudson to commit to at least a dozen appearances—there were power lunches, discussions about a spin-off series, and promises of countless star perks. Much to the producer's dismay, Rock seemed neither interested nor impressed. For once, the workaholic star had more on his mind than his career. Nevertheless, while Hudson was in Paris, starting his HPA-23 treatments, Spelling and his collaborators continued to pursue him. *Dynasty* creator Esther Shapiro had no idea why Rock was in France, though she followed him over, intent on persuading him to join the cast of her show.

Shapiro said, "Please don't feel pressured because I've flown all this way. I've heard no before." Finally, Hudson flashed his megawatt smile in Shapiro's direction. "What the hell, maybe I'll just do it." Aaron Spelling sweetened the deal when he agreed to pay Rock $100,000 per episode. Even so, Hudson would only agree to appear in seven shows and not the twelve that the producers had been pushing for.

In the fall of 1984, the trades announced that Hudson had been cast as wealthy rancher Daniel Reece. One episode called for Reece to kiss Krystle Carrington during a passionate embrace. Upon reading the script, Rock was horrified. At the time, it hadn't yet been determined if the HIV virus could be transmitted through open-mouth kissing. With the welfare of actress Linda Evans in mind, Hudson tried to think of ways to "work around" the kiss.

On the day the sequence was shot, Rock's restraint seemed to backfire. "I remember that the director at the time was concerned that he wasn't kissing Linda Evans forcefully enough," says assistant director John Poer. "There was a conversation about whether he should attempt the kiss again, only with much greater enthusiasm."

Though the producers insisted on reshooting the sequence, Hudson still held back. "In retrospect, it was incredibly touching how hard he tried to protect me," says Linda Evans. "No matter how much the director and producers pressed, he refused to put me at risk."

When Rock's *Dynasty* debut aired in December of 1984, the dramatic change in Hudson's appearance was startling to the millions who tuned in to see him mix it up with the Carringtons and the Colbys. Painfully thin and prematurely aged, Hudson looked haggard and depressed in his scenes. "I asked him if the cameraman was mad at him because he looked so awful on screen," Marc Christian recalled. "He looked like a walking cadaver . . . He said other than having the flu, he was fine and he was satisfied with the way he looked."

The notorious kissing sequence, which aired a couple of months later, was also cause for concern. "Perhaps it's my imagination, but Linda Evans looked terrified under a cement mask of placid resignation," observed George Nader. In the version of the scene that was broadcast, Hudson's discomfort is palpable as he chastely grazes Evans's lips. "Room-temperature passion," is how columnist Michael Musto termed the most noncommittal kiss in screen history.

———

What do I do? The voice on Mark Miller's answering machine sounded frantic. It was Ron Channell, calling from Paris, desperately seeking Miller's advice. Channell had accompanied Rock to Paris in late July of 1985. Initially, the plan was for Hudson to resume HPA-23 treatments but even prior to landing, it became clear that Rock was beyond experimental testing. During the harrowing transatlantic flight, a ravaged and exhausted Hudson slipped in and out of consciousness. Once Channell managed to check them into the Ritz Hotel, Rock collapsed. This prompted the call to Miller, who in turn called Hudson's Los Angeles–based physician. Channell was instructed to rush Hudson to the American Hospital. Within days, conflicting statements were issued regarding his condition.

"My official statement is that Rock Hudson is in the American Hospital in Paris, where his doctors have diagnosed that he has cancer of the liver and that it is not operable," publicist Dale Olson announced. A day later, Bruce Redor, spokesman for the American Hospital, denied this: "As far as we know, that report is false, and it certainly wasn't given by the doctors at the American Hospital in Paris." Olson then told the Associated Press, "What I know is what I said before. I'm trying to reach the people in Paris to find out what's going on."

As the speculation surrounding the real nature of Rock's illness continued, network news shows and cable channels continuously aired images from a July 16 press conference, where Hudson joined Doris Day to announce the launch of *Doris Day's Best Friends*, a pro-animal series which was to begin airing on the Christian Broadcasting Network. At that point, Hudson was in no condition to be making public appearances and everyone around him, including Dale Olson, advised against it. "I said, 'Rock, you look terrible,'" Olson remembered. "He said, 'I need to do this for Doris.'" Even in his debilitated state, Hudson wasn't about to let down his beloved costar.

As media interest in Rock's condition intensified, Mark Miller arrived in Paris. When he first saw Hudson in his hospital bed, Miller was devastated. "When I entered the room, I knew he was going to die. Before Paris, I thought he could turn it around, but when I saw him in that room, I knew." Rock asked, "Where's Ron?" Though it was difficult, Miller told him the truth, "I shipped him home on the Concorde this morning to New York." There were concerns that if Channell remained in Paris, he would be falsely tagged "the last lover" by the tabloids. A despondent Rock muttered, "I knew he'd desert me when the chips were down." After a few moments of silent reflection, Hudson then told Miller, "It's going to be a real mess and I'm sorry. You're going to be put through hell and I apologize."

Mark began to cry, but he managed to hide this from Rock by walking over to the window and pulling the shades partially closed. When he was able to speak, Miller said, "There are photographers on the roof trying to get a shot of you."

"MR. ROCK HUDSON has Acquired Immune Deficiency Syndrome," Rock's friend and French publicist Yanou Collart announced to the press corps gathered outside the American Hospital of Paris on July 25. "He came to Paris to consult with a specialist in this disease. Prior to meeting the specialist, he became very ill at the Ritz Hotel." As cameras flashed and clicked away, Collart confirmed that Hudson had been diagnosed as having the disease a year earlier.

Reporters badgered her for additional details, shouting out questions simultaneously. Collart then made a statement that seemed to contradict her earlier announcement: "The last test made in America before he came here showed that he was not having any trace of

AIDS, any virus." When questioned further, Collart was quoted as saying, "But he has been cured."

Later, Collart insisted that she had been misquoted. Once the press conference concluded and the hordes of reporters had dispersed, Mark Miller went to check on Rock. "Did you throw it to the dogs?" Hudson asked. "Yes," Miller answered. Rock said quietly, "God, what a way to end a life."

The night before Collart read her statement, President Reagan had phoned in his support to Hudson's hospital room. Friends and former costars, like Elizabeth Taylor and Angie Dickinson, called to encourage Rock and wish him well. As the news of Hudson's diagnosis—and the tacit admission of sexual identity that accompanied it—ricocheted around the world, Rock's coworkers, friends, and relatives were stunned.

"I just remember having my breath knocked out of me," says Howard McGillin. The actor who had played Hudson's son in *Wheels* was now on the verge of Broadway stardom. "I had just moved to New York and I was in rehearsals for *La Bohème* with Linda Ronstadt. I remember passing a newspaper kiosk in Greenwich Village and saw the headline on the *Daily News* proclaiming 'Rock Hudson Has AIDS.' I felt so many things—shock, sadness for Rock and real terror for myself. I knew I had to come to terms with my sexuality. I was married with two small children at the time and had been locked in a real struggle over the knowledge I was gay. I had to leave Los Angeles for the same reasons Rock had felt it necessary to hide his own sexuality all those years—the homophobia of Hollywood and the culture at large . . . Now, the man who had symbolized virility and Hollywood glamour was not only dying of 'gay cancer' but was being forced to bare the secret he had worked so long to conceal from the world. I don't think I fully realized it at the time, but it was undeniably a turning point in my life."

Marc Christian claimed that the first time he learned that Rock Hudson had AIDS was at the same time the rest of the world was made aware of it: "I'm watching the television and Yanou Collart, who was the French press secretary for him, came on and said he has AIDS. And my first reaction was, 'They just discovered this?' But then she said, later on, 'Which was diagnosed a year ago in the United States . . .' And then I knew I had been lied to." Christian maintained that after enduring Hudson's night sweats, he had asked him if he had been tested for AIDS. According to Marc, Rock became angry and responded sharply, "I was checked out for everything, including AIDS, and I don't have it."

When Christian heard about Hudson's AIDS diagnosis, he said that he was completely stunned: "I thought I was a dead man. At first, I didn't believe what I was hearing. Then I began to sweat. Then I blacked out. Afterward, I vomited. I got chills and became extremely depressed."

However, Marty Flaherty and others believe that Christian had known about Rock's diagnosis long before it made international headlines. "Marc Christian knew Rock had AIDS before anybody, so he set this whole thing up," says Flaherty. "I remember when I was enrolled in this acting studio, the Van Mar Academy and one of the guys in the class comes up to me and says, 'I hear Rock Hudson has AIDS.' I'm going, *'What?'* It turned out he was the cousin to the nurse that did the blood extraction on Rock . . . the nurse told Christian, 'Stop having sex with [Rock].' Christian knew before anybody, even before Rock knew himself and that's the truth."

CHAPTER 19

THIS IS YOUR LIFE

Rock's star on the Hollywood Walk of Fame.

After returning to America in a chartered 747, Rock was admitted to UCLA Medical Center for treatment. In late August, just before being released, Hudson announced that he wanted Tom Clark to return to The Castle with him. George Nader, for one, questioned whether this was such a brilliant idea. As he wrote in his journal: "I tell Tom he is two people—okay sober and a monster when drunk." Even so, it was decided that bringing Tom back to The Castle—even in his semi-glazed condition—might offer Rock some comfort and reassurance in his final days.

After he was given the green light to return, Tom wasted no

time in regaining control of all things Rock Hudson. He made certain that Hudson took his pain pills exactly when he was supposed to. He fretted over whether a permanent I.V. tube should be implanted in Rock's chest. He strategized ways to fatten Hudson up, fantasizing that at some point, the man of the house would be well enough to host star-studded dinner parties again.

Just as Tom was settling back into The Castle, another former companion resurfaced. Jack Coates returned and spent a few hours quietly reminiscing with Rock. They shared a long laugh when Coates offered to make Hudson his favorite snack, a sandwich that was half peanut butter and jelly, half ham and cheese, piled on white bread and topped off with Miracle Whip. The easygoing, irreverent tone of this meeting was markedly different from Hudson's final confrontation with Marc Christian.

When Rock had been admitted to the hospital, two lists had been compiled—one included the names of individuals that he wanted to see (with Elizabeth Taylor, Juliet Prowse, Marty Flaherty, and Ron Channell among the chosen), while another list displayed the names of would-be visitors that should be turned away. Marc Christian's name appeared on the "do not allow" list. "I tried to visit him at the UCLA Medical Center. But I was barred and even threatened with arrest," Christian claimed. "Finally, I snuck in. It was very emotional. I asked him, 'Why didn't you tell me?' And he said, 'When you have this disease, you're alone.' I told him, 'You're only alone if you want to be.'"

Tom Clark, Mark Miller, and Hudson's private nurse, Tammy Neu, all confirmed that Marc Christian visited Rock in the hospital. However, they all insisted that the visit was supervised and that the meeting with Hudson did not square with how Christian later described it. Everyone present remembered that the only reason the meeting took place was because Christian had insisted on it. He adamantly refused to leave The Castle unless his marching orders came directly from Rock.

Hoping to finally resolve the tenancy issue, Mark Miller drove

Christian to UCLA and Hudson spoke with him, though very briefly. Those present recall that there was no heart to heart, no teary mea culpa. Clark remembered that when Christian emerged from Hudson's hospital room, he announced: "Well, Rock asked me to move out, so I'm moving out." Everyone within earshot breathed a sigh of relief. But after meeting with a high-powered attorney, Christian suddenly changed his mind. "When Marc met with the lawyer, Marvin Mitchelson, he probably said something like, 'It may help your case to stay in the house . . .'" says Christian's last partner, Brent Beckwith. "So, I tend to think that he was following the advice of his attorney when he didn't actually leave Rock's place."

Although Mitchelson had pioneered the concept of palimony and referred to it as "marriage with no rings attached," Christian said that he had not broached the subject of palimony laws with the Beverly Hills attorney. Marc also maintained that at no point during his initial meeting with Mitchelson did they discuss what might transpire if Christian was not named as a beneficiary in Hudson's will. According to Christian, the only reason he met with Mitchelson was to discuss the fact that he had been asked to vacate Rock's home.

After Mark Miller learned that Christian had met with a lawyer, he attempted to dissuade him from meeting with Mitchelson again. "Trust me, you'll be taken care of in some way," Miller assured Christian. "Don't take this to court. It will hurt Rock and hurt you." Christian would later testify that he told Miller, "I have no intention of going to court. I just want to know what my rights are." Christian then alleged that Miller threatened him in no uncertain terms: "If you go to court, I'll smear you . . . We are going to call you a male hustler, a street hooker . . . If we allege it, it will go all over the world and it will be believed. If that doesn't work, we'll call you a drug addict."

Miller denied that he threatened to smear Christian. In a conciliatory gesture, he agreed to allow Christian to remain on Hudson's property. As Marty Flaherty recalls, "[Miller] said, 'Why don't we just move Marc Christian into the theatre? It's not connected to the house, so he can come in through the garage instead of the front door. That way, we'll never see him. Rock's secretary was not known for his good ideas. I mean, if you're handing Christian everything—his own pad, money, food, garage, and access to many of Rock's valuables—why on earth would he ever want to leave? It just didn't make sense." To Miller, this new strategy may have been about keeping one's enemies close while doing everything possible to circumvent a lawsuit.

With two of Hudson's former companions now residing (more or less) under the same roof, it didn't seem possible that the atmosphere at The Castle could become any more intense, but there was yet another act waiting in the wings. In early September, Hudson's lawyer, Paul Sherman, appeared and handed his nearly bedridden client a bunch of contracts. Rock eyed the stack of papers with interest. Sherman explained that these were the contracts for Hudson's autobiography. In late August, Mark Miller had flown to New York and met with executives from William Morrow. After entertaining them with anecdotes concerning his thirty-five-year friendship with Hudson, Miller had secured a lucrative book deal. Rock Hudson was going to tell all in what the trades would not-so-tactfully describe as a "deathbed memoir."*

Hudson was told that he would be "collaborating" with Sara Davidson, a soft-spoken forty-two-year-old journalist who had authored the bestseller *Loose Change*. But even before they started working, a number of important challenges almost derailed the

---

*After Hudson's death, questions arose regarding how coherent he had been while his autobiography was being prepared. Attorney Paul Sherman told the *Washington Post* that when he met with Rock a month before he died, they discussed legal matters related to the memoir. "I had a perfectly lucid conversation," Sherman said. "[Hudson] signed a contract turning over his share of the money from his book—every cent of those monies and all the subsidiary rights to the Rock Hudson AIDS Research Foundation."

project. For starters, George Nader and Mark Miller felt that Tom Clark was doing his best to "sabotage" the book. Early on, Clark told Davidson that he would only discuss his role in Hudson's career; he didn't feel comfortable talking about their personal relationship.

Davidson had expressed some of her contagion concerns to Dr. Michael Gottlieb, Hudson's AIDS specialist from UCLA, who did his best to allay her fears. After being reassured, Davidson visited The Castle and conducted three forty-five-minute interviews with Rock, who made every effort to cooperate, although he sometimes found it difficult to concentrate and tired easily. As Davidson would later tell the *Washington Post*, "He had good days—the first day I met him, he was downstairs talking to people, telling jokes . . . up to the end, he'd have a great day and then a terrible day." After the initial sessions, Davidson traveled to Palm Desert, where she would meet with Nader and Miller, who would supply many of the anecdotes included in *Rock Hudson: His Story*.

Meanwhile, Tom Clark noticed that the same Rock Hudson who had been guardedly optimistic about his condition just a few months earlier now seemed resigned to the fact that he was dying. Part of that realization may have had something to do with the fact that he suddenly had plenty of time to think.

"People deserted him when he was sick," says Marty Flaherty, who recalled that many friends came to see Hudson when he was in the hospital but there were far fewer visitors once he returned home. But several diehards—George Nader, Elizabeth Taylor, Roddy McDowall, Jack Scalia, and Betty Abbott—continued to make pilgrimages to The Castle. Depending on the day one visited, Rock might either be clearheaded and focused or disoriented and inattentive. As Flaherty recalls, "You never knew which Rock you were going to get."

Some visitors were instantly recognized. "It's Dean!" Hudson exclaimed when Dean Dittman paid a visit one afternoon. However, things were altogether different when Jean Simmons, Hudson's costar from *This Earth Is Mine*, dropped in. Although Simmons had been to The Castle on countless occasions, Rock no longer recognized her. She left in tears.

Others attempted to reach out but claimed they were shut out. Hudson's sister, Alice Waier, was living in Oregon and hadn't seen Rock since their father had passed away a couple of years earlier. The images of a gravely ill Hudson that had saturated the airwaves alarmed her. "When I saw my brother on the news, it reminded me of when my grandfather was very ill," says Waier. "I tried contacting my brother but the whole entourage was terrible. They deliberately kept me away from him. It was a very sad situation and I'll never get over it."

If some family members, friends, and hordes of reporters were turned away during Hudson's final days, one really big name was granted an all-access pass: Jesus. Although Rock may have been baptized as a Catholic, he had never been particularly religious.* As it became clear that Hudson's condition was rapidly deteriorating, Tom Clark felt that Rock needed to connect with what he termed "a spiritual higher power." Enter actress and born-again Christian Susan Stafford, who predated Vanna White as a letter-turning hostess on the game show *Wheel of Fortune*.

Stafford had just returned from India, where she had been working alongside Surgeon General C. Everett Koop, caring for leprosy patients. As Stafford had experience comforting people who had been ostracized because of their disease, Clark hoped that she might be able to bring some of the same compassion to the world's most high-profile AIDS patient. "Do you realize that people would

---

*According to family lore, Rock's maternal grandmother had secretly taken him to be baptized as a Catholic at Sacred Heart Church in Winnetka while his mother was out working. However, by the time Hudson was in the service, he seems to have switched affiliations. When he completed a military questionnaire, he penciled in "Protestant" in response to an inquiry regarding "My Religious Belief." By the 1980s, Hudson seemed to have changed his mind yet again. According to Marc Christian, "Rock had always said that he was an atheist."

not even go into his house because they were afraid that maybe it'd be contagious?" said Stafford. "There were some that wouldn't even call him, thinking that they might get AIDS over the phone."

According to Stafford, other born-again members of the show business community began visiting Rock voluntarily, without any encouragement from her. The group included pop singer Pat Boone and his wife, Shirley, as well as Gavin MacLeod (*The Love Boat*'s own Captain Merrill Stubing) and his wife, Patti. Shirley Boone, who had been a devoted Rock Hudson fan for years, went on an eight-day fast in the hopes of manifesting a miraculous recovery; she would eventually be joined by twenty others. When the fast ended, the group asked if they could come to The Castle and pray for Rock.

Marc Christian, for one, was appalled, recalling "Shirley Boone... racing in with her Bible ablaze and doing her voodoo rites over his body," while Mark Miller was grateful: "One has to imagine the generosity of these faithful people, coming to pray with and for Rock." Elizabeth Taylor happened to be visiting one day when Boone's prayer group returned. "Truly a sight to behold," George Nader remarked. "Cleopatra among the holy rollers." Several of the faithful stayed as far away from the sickbed as possible. Taking note of what appeared to be Rock's rejected expression, Taylor said, "Oh, for goodness sake!" With that, she hopped in bed with him and cradled Hudson's body, rocking him gently as she did. The prayer vigil concluded and everyone quietly filed out of the room.

By the end of September, Rock was spiraling downward. Unable to express himself in complete sentences, he would either murmur a few syllables or make grunting noises. He slept much of the time, sometimes twelve hours a day. Hudson's nurse, Tammy Neu, felt that her patient, who was now down to ninety-seven pounds, couldn't hold on much longer.

Clark, Nader, and Miller began preparing for the inevitable. Calls were made to Rock's closest friends, asking if they would be willing to speak at a memorial service. Claire Trevor was at the top of the list. "She is most cordial, calm, and realistic," Nader noted, though Trevor doubted that she could make it through a tribute without breaking down. Roddy McDowall not only agreed to speak but suggested reaching out to Elizabeth Taylor, who immediately said yes.

A week earlier, Taylor and Shirley MacLaine had cosponsored a benefit for AIDS Project L.A., which was billed as a "Commitment to Life." The gala event took place at the Bonaventure Hotel and featured performances by Carol Burnett, Sammy Davis, Jr., and Bette Midler. The most powerful part of the event came toward the end of the evening. In a move that the press termed "graceful," Linda Evans appeared and introduced Burt Lancaster, who read a statement from Rock Hudson:

"People have told me that the disclosure that I have been diagnosed as having Acquired Immune Deficiency Syndrome helped to make this evening an immediate sellout, and that it will raise some one million dollars to help the battle against AIDS. I have also been told the media coverage of my own situation has brought enormous attention to the gravity of this disease in all areas of humanity, and is leading to more research, more contribution of funds, and a better understanding of this disease than ever before. I am not happy that I have AIDS. But if that is helping others, I can at least know that my own misfortune has had some positive worth. Thank you, Elizabeth. Thank you to all my friends who are attending this evening, and to the thousands who have sent their prayers, thoughts, love, wishes, and support."

Clips of Lancaster reading Hudson's words were broadcast around the world. Rock's message was both an eloquently phrased expression of gratitude as well as a rallying cry. The feeling behind the words was characteristically Rock Hudson—the chips may be down but, even so, it's your duty to reach out and help others. The sentiment seemed to be pure Rock, even if the words were not. A controversy erupted when some of Hudson's associates suggested that he wasn't coherent enough to have written the statement attributed to him. Were words being put into his mouth?

"Rock Hudson never, never publicly acknowledged he had AIDS," an irate Ross Hunter told the *Los Angeles Daily News*. "All those statements made in his name were lies. He knew nothing about any of them. He fought all his life to stay out of the limelight, and the last thing he would have wanted was to have been thrust into it the way he was." Hunter charged "that 95% of the time, he wasn't lucid. He could recognize his friends when he was shaken into consciousness—but that was all. Then he'd drift off again."

When questioned about this, Tom Clark admitted, "The statement was not written by Rock. But can't we just say they were his thoughts? Those words have been so encouraging to so many millions. Let him have those words as his legacy."

Dr. Michael Gottlieb responded to Hunter's charges in an interview with Rona Barrett: "There is no truth to the notion that Rock Hudson was unaware of his diagnosis and unaware of his role in bringing this to public attention. He was aware and fully participatory in the process of founding an organization that will carry on research into AIDS and help all of us as a result. And it damages that cause to make allegations of that kind."

Despite all of the backstage drama, the Commitment to Life Gala had been a great triumph, raising $1 million and attracting plenty of press attention. It was pioneering AIDS activist Bill Misenheimer and L.A. catering mogul Bill Jones who had persuaded Elizabeth Taylor to become the fundraiser's chairperson; the star was eager to get involved. "Elizabeth was just so angry that people were not believing how serious AIDS was," says Rock's friend, Wes Wheadon. "She had two assistants, both gay men that died of AIDS. One had it and killed himself, which devastated her. The other guy died without any warning because in those days, you got diagnosed and you were dead in a month. So, she was really becoming very militant about this cause."

Galvanized by the success of the Commitment to Life event, Taylor and company decided to establish an AIDS foundation, which would raise funds for clinical research as well as providing primary care for patients. The result was the L.A.–based National AIDS Research Foundation, which Taylor and Michael Gottlieb created. This organization would eventually merge with the Manhattan-based AIDS Medical Foundation.

The newly formed amfAR (American Foundation for AIDS Research) would be jump-started with a $250,000 donation from Rock Hudson. Though even this goodwill gesture was questioned by the press: Was the same Rock Hudson who had recently been hospitalized in full command of his faculties as well as his bank account? The actor's business manager, Wallace Sheft, assured reporters that Hudson "agreed wholeheartedly with the gift I advised. We discussed it, and he agreed with it . . . There were other people in the room. He knew what was going on. He liked the idea of helping."

As other donations started pouring in to amfAR, Bill Misenheimer would credit Hudson's public disclosure with turning the tide: "It was the single most important thing that happened to open people's minds and to help us raise funds." If the nonprofit organization he helped found was off to an encouraging start, Hudson himself was struggling. Rock was not responding well to some of his recent blood transfusions, which were followed by extended periods of thrashing and twitching. Despairing over Hudson's grave condition and exhausted from caretaking, Tom Clark was at his lowest ebb when an unexpected visitor appeared at The Castle one afternoon.

Clutching a Bible in one hand and a map to the movie stars' homes in the other, "Eleanor" informed Tom that she had received an important message from God for Rock Hudson. She had to see him. "I said to myself, oh-oh, *one of those*," Clark recalled. "I said, 'It is impossible. He is very sick and there are no visitors allowed.'" But Eleanor would not be deterred. "I know I will see him because Jesus told me I would."

Impressed with the woman's tenacity and noting that Eleanor bore a vague resemblance to Rock's late mother, Clark relented and ushered her upstairs to Hudson's bedroom. The woman informed Rock that he had an important "final ministry" to fulfill. One that would have a more powerful and lasting impact than his film career. Rock listened attentively as she spoke. "Jesus told me to tell you that he has great plans for you."

This surprise visit was followed by a scheduled one with Father Terrance A. Sweeney, who was not only a Catholic priest but a five-time Emmy Award–winning producer. Susan Stafford had summoned Father Sweeney, who anointed Hudson, gave him communion, and then got creative in terms of taking confession, as Rock was almost completely nonverbal at that point. Even after Father Sweeney's departure, Hudson kept things to the point. "Thanks for that" is all Rock said to Tom.

Back in 1952, a televised tribute to Roy Fitzgerald on *This Is Your Life* had concluded with friends and family gathered around him, everyone expressing their affection and support. More than thirty years later, the sentiments were still the same, but now the guest of honor was fighting for his life . . .

As dying was a serious business, Rock tried not to smile whenever he overheard one visitor whispering to another that his mind was gone. Maybe it was, but he still knew that was nobody but Doris singing "Sentimental Journey" over the loudspeakers as he shipped out on another tour of duty . . . *Gonna take a sentimental journey, gonna set my heart at ease, Gonna make a sentimental journey to renew old memories* . . .

Rock felt a weight on his chest as Pat Boone placed a Bible there. He was no longer the "Beefcake King" and it was heavy . . . Then the bed started shaking as Tom slipped under the covers on one side of him and Elizabeth Taylor on the other. "Liz, what would the *Enquirer* say about this?" he heard Tom say. "Don't call me Liz," Elizabeth answered.

Then, George Nader and Mark Miller sauntered into the room, linked arm in arm, singing "Mockin' Bird Hill." They had some serious competition as the mysterious "Eleanor" was kneeling on the floor, clutching a map of the movie stars' homes and speaking in tongues.

Now someone was talking softly in one ear, encouraging him to forgive his father for abandoning him, while in the other, he was being asked to accept the Lord Jesus Christ as his personal savior. It was a lot to think about, especially when your mind was gone. Or at least elsewhere. He was mesmerized. His boyhood idol, Jon Hall, was preparing to take the plunge. Only now Hall wasn't swan-diving into a shimmering lagoon as he had in *The Hurricane* but into Rock's forty-foot pool, which was filled with a dozen young men, each one a stunning blue-eyed blond. Suddenly, Tom announced, "I'm going downstairs and get another cup of coffee. How about you . . . another cup?" It took every last bit of effort that he had left to speak, but Rock heard himself say, "No, I don't believe so." Then it was all over.

ROCK HAD WANTED to be cremated with his ashes scattered in the ocean. This request would be fulfilled, but another of his wishes—that there be no memorial service—would be overruled. If anything, Hudson would have liked his friends to gather on a yacht, sip champagne, and swap a few funny stories. But a yacht seemed impractical, given the number of people involved. Alternative plans were discussed among the members of Rock's inner circle and, initially, a very traditional Hollywood ceremony started to come together.

"I got a call from Mark Miller, who said, 'Can you help me make the funeral arrangements?'" says Ken Jillson. "We called Forest Lawn and they rolled out the red carpet for us. Then, Elizabeth Taylor calls Mark and she's furious and says, 'I don't want to go to Forest Lawn. We'll have a memorial at The Castle. We'll have margaritas and mariachi music and a few speakers. We'll do it the way Rock would have wanted it.' She turned out to be right. Having it at The Castle excluded it from a public forum, which was really smart."

The day before the memorial, a grand white tent went up in the backyard at The Castle. Beneath this, a hundred white chairs were arranged, fifty on either side of a center aisle. The gardener, Clarence Morimoto, and Marty Flaherty were busy planting masses of pink and white flowers—"Elizabeth Taylor style." Director Stockton Briggle and his partner, Mark Tillman-Briggle, created an elegant memorial program that reflected the dual nature of Rock's personality, as it included a serious quote from poet Kahlil Gibran and a nonsensical one from *Taza, Son of Cochise*.

The day of the service, Doris Day telephoned Mark Miller and told him she wanted to attend but wouldn't be able to handle it. The other notable no-show would be George Nader: "I didn't go to the service because Ross Hunter and Jacque Mapes were supposed to be there. If I went and saw them there, I would have thrown them in the pool." Rumor had it that Hunter was now referring to Nader and Miller as "Greed and Avarice." Miller was unruffled ("I get to be avarice!"), but Nader was not amused.

Everyone else would be there, though, as the press was well aware. The guest list had been leaked ahead of time and it read like a who's who of Hollywood: Carol Burnett, Angie Dickinson, Robert Wagner, Lee Remick, Susan Saint James, Roddy McDowall, Stefanie Powers, Nancy Walker, Connie Stevens, Martha Raye, Ricardo Montalban, and "optometrist to the stars," Wes Wheadon. Rock's old friend, the actor Craig Hill, flew in all the way from Barcelona. MGM's "million dollar mermaid," Esther Williams, crashed the event. At 5:15 p.m., the "informal" tribute—which Nader referred to as "The Elizabeth Taylor Quaker Memorial Service," began. Father Sweeney spoke, as did Burnett and Dickinson. John Schuck and Constance Towers performed a medley from *I Do! I Do!* Then Taylor closed by saying, "Rock would have wanted us to be happy. Let's raise a glass to him."

With so many celebrities in attendance, Hudson's young friend Gunther Fraulob stood out simply because he was one of the few people present who wasn't instantly recognizable. At the memorial, Fraulob met Marc Christian for the first time. "He wanted to know what I had to do with Rock," says Fraulob. "I said, 'Well, he went to Hawaii with me and spent a week with my parents.' Christian looked shocked. I should have connected the dots right there and asked myself why he was so interested. Then he called me a couple of days later and I was very surprised. He started in by saying, 'This guy, Tom Clark, has jumped in here and he says he's Rock's spouse. I'm Mrs. Hudson. Not this guy.' We talked for hours. Basically, Christian had me convinced that he was the victim in all of this. As I started to get to know him, I couldn't believe this was the same guy that Rock had said was blackmailing him."

Despite everything Hudson had told him about Christian, Fraulob found that he was not only sympathetic to his handsome new friend but attracted to him. "He was very charming and after all of our long talks, I felt this connection to him," Fraulob says. "One thing led to another and we ended up in bed. Of course, we had safe sex but I remember him saying that he was the safest person on the planet and there was no need to worry. He said, 'I've been tested by every expert in the book and I'm clean.' Christian and I had only been together a month but I thought we had this genuine connection. Then, the next thing I hear is that he's hired Marvin Mitchelson and he's suing Rock's estate.* His whole lawsuit was based on the premise that 'I have this terrible fear that I'm going to come down with AIDS. I can never have sex again in my life.'

---

*Four months after Marc Christian filed his lawsuit, the estate of Rock Hudson fired back with a $2,072,000 countersuit, alleging that Christian had blackmailed Hudson, had sex for money in Hudson's home (while Rock was on location in Israel for *The Ambassador*), and stolen $60,000 worth of Hudson's possessions. After the suit was filed by Wallace Sheft, Hudson's executor, Christian denied the charges and accused Sheft and others of attempting to "blackmail and coerce" him into dropping his own suit against the estate.

He was telling the world he was celibate and yet, he had sex with me twice.* I was watching him on the news and I was shocked. He wouldn't answer my calls. Then I realized that I had been taken. I'll admit I was stupid. I thought we had been bonding but all along, he was trying to get all of the information that he could out of me. I was starting to have feelings for him and it really hurt to find out that I had been played."

Before his case went to trial, Christian attempted to arrange an out-of-court settlement with Hudson's estate, but he was rebuffed. "Marc asked for $300,000 to be put in a trust, so that if he came down with AIDS, that money would be available for medical care," says Christian's partner, Brent Beckwith. "Marc said that they essentially told him, 'Screw you. We're not going to do that and if you try anything, no faggot is going to win in court' . . . Marc was the kind of person that you didn't fuck with. And he had a revenge factor. I think a big part of this case was a big 'Fuck You' to Mark Miller and George Nader. They were the beneficiaries of the estate and they were really pulling the strings when Rock was so sick."

In 1989, after Marc Christian won his suit against the estate, defense attorneys sought to overturn the $21.75 million jury award by presenting new evidence—in the form of a sworn statement—that directly contradicted Christian's testimony on the critical issue of fear. The statement had been provided by Gunther Fraulob.

When asked why he didn't come forward during the trial, Fraulob told a reporter, "I didn't want to drag my name through the mud. I didn't think my involvement would help the case in any way." Thirty years later, Fraulob hasn't changed his mind: "Who knows what would have happened if I had spoken up earlier? I just didn't want to drag my friends and family into the courtroom and have them become part of the whole circus . . . I finally had to

---

*"Marc, have you been with someone else since Rock?" an audience member asked Christian when he made a second appearance on *Donahue* in February of 1989. "No," Christian answered. "It's not an unimportant question," host Phil Donahue remarked.

speak up, though, because I knew that what Christian said was a blatant lie."

According to one source, some physical evidence exists that completely discredits Christian's testimony. "After the trial was over and the judgment came in, I got a call from an individual whom I had attempted to interview prior to the trial," says private investigator Paul Cohen, who was hired by Robert Parker Mills, the attorney representing Hudson's estate. "This individual showed me a video of him and Christian having sex. What was important about that video was that the television was on in the background and it showed the date and time of the broadcast, which was exactly when Christian said he was celibate. That was the basis of the remittitur action for the judgment and it was successful."[*]

Gunther Fraulob says that when he thinks back to the day of Hudson's memorial, there is sadness but there is also anger: "Everyone at the service was wonderful but where were all of these wonderful people when that whole nightmare of a trial was going on and Rock's good name was being tarnished? Why didn't anyone come to Rock's defense after he was gone and couldn't speak for himself? I didn't speak up for the money. I didn't do it for publicity. I just did it because I wanted to do the right thing and stand up for Rock."

SUNDAY, OCTOBER 20, 1985.
The Warehouse Restaurant in Marina Del Rey.

"ELIZABETH TAYLOR AND Stockton had talked about the spreading of the ashes," says Stockton Briggle's partner, Mark Tillman-Briggle. "They wanted to make sure that the press wasn't going

[*]In 1989, a superior court judge reduced Christian's jury award to $5 million. Two years later, Christian settled out of court for an undisclosed sum, which defense attorney Robert Parker Mills says was "nowhere near the $5 million compensatory damage award."

to be all over it. So, that morning, we all went to breakfast down near the docks. After that, Elizabeth got in a car and drove away and all of the reporters and paparazzi followed her. She was the decoy. They went chasing after her while the rest of us walked down and got on the boat. I thought that was very big of her because she was allowing everyone else to have this private moment with the spreading of the ashes."

Around 11:30, a group of thirty-five boarded a small yacht called *Tasia II*, which Warehouse owner Burt Hixson, a friend of Hudson's, had located last minute. Among those making the three-mile journey toward Catalina Channel were Tom Clark, Stockton Briggle, Jack Coates, Dean Dittman, Susan Stafford, Mark Miller, Ken Jillson and his partner, Al Roberts, and four of Rock's cousins from his mother's side of the family. Marc Christian not only attended—which surprised a number of the other passengers—but he even brought his friend Liberty Martin.

If the mood en route was high-spirited, it would turn solemn by the time the boat reached its destination. The group gathered on the starboard side and Susan Stafford began reading the Twenty-third Psalm. Then there was some discussion about whether Jack Coates, Tom Clark, and Marc Christian—representing Rock's companions at different stages of his life—should all hold the brown plastic box containing Hudson's ashes. Wouldn't it be a beautiful symbolic gesture if they all scattered Rock's ashes together? It quickly became apparent that Clark didn't think so. This was something he preferred to do alone.

"Tom Clark took the ashes and spread them out into the water," Stockton Briggle remembered. "And when he did that, the most amazing thing happened. This huge rainbow appeared all around the area where he had spread Rock's ashes. This is the truth. We all just stood there and tried to comprehend that such a thing could have happened. So, Rock's ashes went out to sea, surrounded by a huge rainbow. That was finally how he was put at peace."

As the passengers said a final farewell, the mood was mournful and contemplative. Then, as George Nader recalled, seemingly out of nowhere, "A lonely seagull flew over the yacht . . . and shat on Mark's beautiful cashmere sweater Susan had given him for his birthday the year before. Mark looked up at the seagull, laughed and said, 'Rock had the last laugh.'" In a split second, the feeling on the boat had changed from sadness to hilarity and as his friends all agreed, that is exactly the way Rock would have wanted it.

Although he wasn't present for the memorial events, actor Peter Kevoian, whose appearances on *McMillan* had been arranged by Hudson, couldn't stop thinking about the man he referred to as his mentor: "After he died, the one memory I kept returning to was this day when I was at Rock's house. We were lying by the pool and I said, 'Can you give me any advice? I'm new to this business and I don't know . . . I just don't think I'm special enough to succeed. How did you come to decide that all of this was right for you?' And Rock said, 'I had a dream once when I was young. I dreamt that I was in a room and there were these lights circling 360 degrees around the room. The lights were pin-spotted in the center of the room on a perfectly cut diamond. I saw myself as that diamond. The lights all around the room and all around the world were focused on me. And I was filled with the most brilliant light. That was when I truly believed that I was destined to be something special . . . a star, if you will.'"

ACKNOWLEDGMENTS

ASSISTANCE AND CORRESPONDENCE

Woolsey Ackerman, Alida Aldrich, Cassandra Babbitt, Chris Bacon, Miranda Barry, Brent Beckwith, Tane Beecham (Winnetka Historical Society), Michelle Bercon, Rachel Bernstein (Margaret Herrick Library), Cassie Blake (Public Access Coordinator, Academy of Motion Picture Arts and Sciences Film Archive), Peter Brodeur, Mary Ellen Budney (Beinecke Rare Book and Manuscript Library, Yale University), Willard Carroll, Anita Clearfield, Nancy Coleman, (The Oracle Known as) Edward Sykes Comstock (USC Cinematic Arts Library), Len Cortigiano, Laura Craig, Patrick Cristaldi, Mitchell Danton, Douglas Davenport, Neil Davin, Wendy Davis, Kay de Toledo, Nicole Ziegler Dizon (Director of Communications and Alumni Relations, New Trier Township High School District), Denise Dubravec (Principal, New Trier High School, Winnetka Campus), Linda Evans, Martin Flaherty (Rock Hudson Estate Collection), Alexa Foreman (Turner Classic Movies), Cullen Gallagher, Dr. Sandra Garcia-Myers (USC), Lee Garlington, Paul Garlington, Ellen Geiger (Frances Goldin Literary Agency), Allan Glaser, Jodi Goldberg, Heather Greene, Martin Griffin, Ken Gross (Walsh History Center, Camden Public Library), Alan Helms, Darcy Hettrich, Steve Hodel, Suzanne L. Hoffman (Wilmette Illinois Family History Center), Jorgen Joergensen, Molly Kennedy (Illinois Genealogical Research), Tami Kennedy, Ginny L. Kilander, Jane Klain (Manager, Research Services, The Paley Center for Media), Lotti

Pharriss Knowles, Kristine Krueger, Nicci Leamon, Ann Leifeste, Nancy Leman, Paul MacDougall, Boyd Magers, Diane Markert, Quinn McGuire, Jane McKnight, Cristina Meisner, Dee Michel, Craig Miller, Cal Morgan, Lynn West Mullen, Maura Murphy, Gary Natkin, Russell B. Needham, Keary Nichols, David Orr (Cook County Clerk, Bureau of Vital Records), Gerald Peary, Heidi Perkins, David M. Perry, Howard Prouty, Mark Quigley (Archive Research and Study Center, UCLA), Beverly Radell, Karen Richards, Cynthia Richardson, Jaydon Riendeau, Joanne Riendeau, Ryan Riendeau, Lily Robinson, Donna Roginski (Wilmette Illinois Family History Center), Jenny Romero (Research Archivist, Margaret Herrick Library), Peter Royle, Bree Russell (USC Cinematic Arts Library), Laura Russo (Howard Gotlieb Archival Research Center), Steve Sauer, Jerry Scherer, Liz Scherer, Dr. Lanny Seese, Brett Service (Curator, Warner Brothers Archives), Robert Sigurdson, Charles Silver, Rick Speer (Lewiston Public Library), Eric Spilker (for screening his print of *The Lawless Breed* for me), Robert Spindler (Archivist, Arizona State University), Justin Spring, Claudia Squitieri, Kim Stankiewicz (Chicago Ancestry), David Stenn (for his invaluable assistance in reference to the Marc Christian trial transcripts), Anna Steuber (Florianfilm GmbH), Seth Stewart, Kevin Stoehr, Chris Sweet, Ashley Swinnerton (Film Study Center, Museum of Modern Art), Germaine Szal, Sean F. Taylor (SAG-AFTRA), Bertrand Tessier, Brian Tessier (Peter Jones Productions), Heather Thomas (Library of Congress), Lou Valentino, Patti Van Cleave (Winnetka Historical Society), Melissa Veilleux, Larry Verbit (Vice President, Business Affairs & Legal, Ralph Edwards Productions), John R. Waggener (American Heritage Center, University of Wyoming), Robert Wagner, Phet Walker, John Walters-Johnston (Moving Image Division—Library of Congress), Kirby Warnock, Tom Weaver, Jack Webster, Steve L. Wilson (Curator, Harry Ransom Center, The University of Texas at Austin), Rebecca Wolf (Winnetka-Northfield Public Library), Hailey Woodall (Photo Assistant, American Heritage Center), Dan Works (Maine

Public Broadcasting Network), Prince Zaporoschenko, Abigail Zelz (University of Maine Alumni Association), Laurie Zuckerman.

For the guidance and support this project received, special thanks to the following: Academy of Motion Picture Arts and Sciences; American Heritage Center at the University of Wyoming; Arizona State University; Beinecke Rare Book & Manuscript Library at Yale University; Harry Ransom Center, University of Texas at Austin; Howard Gotlieb Archival Research Center at Boston University; Lewiston Public Library; Museum of Modern Art Film Study Center; New Trier High School (Winnetka Campus); Rock Hudson Estate Collection; University of California, Los Angeles; University of Southern California Cinematic Arts Library; Wilmette Illinois Family History Center; Winneconne Public Library (Winneconne, Wisconsin); Winnetka Historical Society; Winnetka-Northfield Public Library.

SPECIAL THANKS . . .

A life with the cinematic scope and complexity of Rock Hudson's requires long and careful examination, and I'm very grateful that I didn't have to go exploring alone. I am forever indebted to those extraordinarily resourceful members of "Team Rock," who provided an overwhelmed author with unparalleled support and invaluable assistance over the course of four delirious years: Alexa Foreman (of Turner Classic Movies)—whether it was chauffeuring me all over greater Illinois or rounding up an impressive list of the famous, infamous, and notoriously tight-lipped for me to interview, you were the consummate professional and the ultimate Dr. Watson. As Bette Davis says to the unfailingly efficient nurse played by Mary Wickes in *Now, Voyager*: "Dora, I suspect you're a treasure."

Diane Markert—you are, quite simply, a walking encyclopedia of all things Rock Hudson. You may have been half a world away in Omro, Wisconsin, but you were always *right there* with whatever I needed. I think your crowning achievement was unearthing a nearly sixty-year-old letter from G. D. Buccola Investment Co., which detailed when the water was turned on in Rock's Newport Beach Home (February of 1959). You somehow found it all—from Nielsen numbers for the debut of *The Devlin Connection* to a *Scarlet Angel* costar stashed away in Copenhagen (and in your "spare time," you managed to pore over the finer points of the California Health & Safety Code, Section #103526). Bravo from start to finish.

Kim Stankiewicz (of Chicago Ancestry and Genlighten.com)— Without your extraordinary efforts, we would not have been able to uncover all of those priceless artifacts, from the Cook County Archives and beyond . . . including the original version of Rock's birth certificate, Katherine Wood's marriage certificates, and the transcripts from her divorce hearings. If all that weren't enough, you located the military files for Seaman Roy Fitzgerald as well as Tommy H. Clark and Wallace E. Fitzgerald. All of this information not only sets the record straight but really helps bring Rock's early years to life.

My gratitude to Karen Richards, who compiled some helpful genealogical information concerning both sides of Rock's family tree. Kudos as well to proxy researcher Ann Leifeste, who carefully combed through mountains of material related to *A Farewell to Arms* during a series of visits to the Harry Ransom Center, which archives the voluminous Selznick Collection.

Jerry and Liz Scherer very graciously welcomed myself and Ms. Foreman into their home in Decatur and in addition to good-naturedly putting up with our barrage of questions, shared rare family photos, correspondence, and many memories with us. Sincere appreciation to Lee and Paul Garlington for allowing me to spend time with them at their beautiful estate in Carmel and for providing me with a batch of rare images documenting the Hudson-Garlington partnership. My El Paso pen pal, Wally Cech, worked as a caterer on the set of *Giant* back in the summer of 1955. To complement her photographic memory, Wally has a scrapbook filled with snapshots she took of Rock, Liz, and Jimmy, which she didn't hesitate to share with me.

After our formal interview, Alice Waier followed up with additional calls and letters, and I appreciate her taking the time to tell me everything she remembered about her beloved brother. Martin Flaherty of The Rock Hudson Estate Collection not only sat for two extensive interviews but also helped me contact other important interview subjects; Marty provided me with access to some private correspondence and journals, and more than a few photographs in this book come courtesy of his one-of-a-kind archive. Ken Maley, San Francisco–based media consultant extraordinaire, also furnished me with some unpublished material that he very kindly let me hold on to for far too long. Thank you to Craig Miller and Robert Sigurdson for arranging my interview with the late Mark Miller.

Fellow biographer David Stenn made me aware of the fact that the complete transcripts from the Marc Christian trial are contained in his own collection, which is archived at the Margaret Herrick Library, where I was also ably assisted by Jenny Romero, Rachel Bernstein, Kristine Krueger, Howard Prouty, Faye Thompson, and Lea Whittington. Grateful thanks to Phet Walker, for reading through reams of material relating to the Christian trial and for streamlining it all for me.

Glance through the acknowledgments section of virtually any showbiz biography or book about Hollywood and inevitably you'll come to the paragraph where Ned Comstock of the USC Cinematic Arts Library is showered with praise. I can assure you that all of the accolades are well deserved as Ned is the Wayne Gretzky of all librarians: the smartest and most skillful player in the history of the game.

Dan Works and Chris Sweet of Maine Public Broadcasting dedicated themselves to the arduous and time-consuming task of transferring the audiotapes of over one hundred interviews into digital files. Once this process was complete, Nicci Leamon and Maura Murphy painstakingly transcribed the interviews and shared their impressions and insights. Keary Nichols, graphic designer without equal, thank you for archiving, scanning, and restoring hundreds of images of the Rock known as Hudson.

Heartfelt thanks to Cal Morgan, the initial editor on this project, for getting me started and to my current editor, Gail Winston, for her patience and faith. My agent, Ellen Geiger, deserves a round of applause for her unflagging support and encouragement.

NOTES

Introduction

xvi "Mr. Rock Hudson has": *New York Times*, July 26, 1985.

xvi Myra Hall: "Hudson's Neighbor Offers Press 'Lawn Seats' for Private 'Tribute' at His House," by Jeff Gottlieb, *Los Angeles Herald Examiner*, October 19, 1985.

xvii "He is the center": From "Dear Rock" by Roger Jones (unpublished manuscript) from the Roger W. Jones Papers (Collection #12621), archived at the University of Wyoming/American Heritage Center.

xvii "straight goodness of heart and uncomplicated directness": Halliday, *Sirk on Sirk*.

xvii "the single most influential AIDS patient ever": "The Untold Story: Rock Hudson's Final Days" by Elizabeth McNeil, *People* magazine, April 27, 2015, p. 71.

xvii "He accepted it like it was measles": "Actor's Illness Helped Reagan to Grasp AIDS, Doctor Says," *New York Times*, September 2, 1989, p. 8.

xviii "If Rock Hudson can have it": *People* magazine, vol. 24, no. 7, August 12, 1985.

xviii "in his most paradoxical role": "Rock Hudson's Most Paradoxical Role" by Anne Taylor Fleming, *New York Times*, February 15, 1989.

xix "I hear Rock's being drugged": Mark Miller, *Trio of Forever Friends* (unpublished memoir completed in 2007), pp. 277–78; George Nader's diary entries regarding the phone call from Ross Hunter are dated July 5–6, 1985.

xix "Tom Clark has turned": Miller, *Trio of Forever Friends*, p. 351; George Nader's diary entry regarding Clark is dated October 15, 1985.

xx "I was kept out of the loop": Alice Waier, interview with author, January 2015.

xx "unduly influenced" . . . "forced him into": "Oregon Woman Sues Rock Hudson Estate; Says she's half-sister," *The Spokesman Review*, May 3, 1986, p. 13.

xx "If you have AIDS": "Between Rock and a Hard Place: Marc Christian, Hudson's Ex-Lover, Tells All" by Barry Adkins, *New York Native*, Issue 140, December 23–29, 1985, pp. 21–24.

xxi "routine and perfunctory" . . . "dark moods": Gates and Thomas, *My Husband, Rock Hudson*, p. 153.

xxii "Remember that movie": Alice Waier, interview with author, January 2015.

Chapter 1: Winnetka

1 "If one must live in Chicago": The quote from A. W. Stevens is referenced in the 2009 documentary, *Winnetka Story*, directed by John Newcombe and produced by the Winnetka Historical Society (www.winnetkastory .com).

2 "In order to have": Judge Joseph Burke is quoted in the *Chicago Daily Tribune*, March 18, 1937, p. 10.

2 "I was right there when": Pearl Scherer's comments are taken from *This Is Your Life: Rock Hudson*, which was originally broadcast on NBC on December 17, 1952.

3 "He told me that he had difficulties": Diane Ladd's comments are taken from an episode of *Larry King Live*, which was originally broadcast on CNN on October 1, 2003.

3 "true life told in" . . . "honeymoon apartment": *Star Stories: Rock Hudson* by Jane Ardmore, p. 1.

3 "a handsome, dark-haired woman": "The Rock Hudson Story" by Joe Hyams, *Photoplay*, February 1957, p. 90.

4 "Your father loved the gaming tables": from "Dear Rock" by Roger Jones, from the Roger W. Jones Papers (Collection #12621), archived at the University of Wyoming/American Heritage Center.

4 "Rock's grandfather, Theodore, was a farmer": Jerry Scherer, interview with author, April 2015.

4 "One day, my grandmother": Alice Waier, interview with author, March 2016.

5 "He got away with murder": Hudson and Davidson, *Rock Hudson: His Story*, p. 17.

6 "I was home from school": Dorothy Kimble's comments are taken from the documentary, *Rock Hudson: Acting the Part*, which was originally broadcast on the A&E Network on March 7, 1999 (Peter Jones Productions).

7 "he packed his things" (footnote): Divorce Decree, Katherine Scherer vs. Roy H. Scherer, the Circuit Court of Cook County, December 6, 1932.

7 "There was family gossip": Oppenheimer and Vitek, *Idol: Rock Hudson*, p. 4.

7 "You don't understand, Kay": *Star Stories: Rock Hudson* by Jane Ardmore, p. 5.

8 "I was on an airplane with Rock's mother": Mark Miller, *Trio of Forever Friends* (unpublished memoir completed in 2007), p. 153.

9 "My father said that when" (footnote): Gaylord Scherer, interview with author, April 2015.

9 "Whatever my mother wanted": "Roy Fitzgerald Takes Some Time to Reminisce" by Rowland Barber, *TV Guide*, vol. 20, no. 18, April 29, 1972, pp. 24–28.

10 "Back in a small town": Hudson's comments are taken from his interview with Professor Ronald L. Davis, August 24, 1983, which is archived in the Ronald L. Davis Oral History Collection (#276) at the Academy of Motion Picture Arts and Sciences Margaret Herrick Library.

11 "The defendant, Roy H. Scherer": Divorce Decree, Katherine Scherer vs. Roy H. Scherer, the Circuit Court of Cook County, December 6, 1932.

11 "She was mother, father, and big sister": Hudson and Davidson, *Rock Hudson: His Story*, p. 19.

13 "I once asked my stepfather": Hudson and Davidson, *Rock Hudson: His Story*, p. 17.

13 "He was a drunk": Oppenheimer and Vitek, *Idol: Rock Hudson*, p. 6.

13 "We used to see Roy": Hudson and Davidson, *Rock Hudson: His Story*, p. 19.

14 "Years later, I was skin diving" (footnote): "A Change of Pace for Rock Hudson" by Kevin Thomas, *Los Angeles Times*, September 21, 1987, p. E-1.

14 *"Well that cinches it"*: Hudson, interview with Professor Ronald L. Davis, August 24, 1983.

14 "He used to beat Roy savagely": "Heading for a Wedding?" by Imogene Collins, *Modern Screen*, August 1954, p. 58.

14 "Skokie Junior High": Suzanne Guyot's comments are taken from the documentary, *Rock Hudson: Dark and Handsome Stranger*, which was directed by Andrew Davies and André Schäfer and released in October 2010 by Florianfilm GmbH.

15 "We were in the same class" . . . "We used to sleep": "Never Before Revealed . . . Childhood of Rock Hudson" by William Dick, *National Enquirer*, September 13, 1977, p. 18.

15 "I remember when Roy": Robert Willett, interview with author, May 10, 2015.

16 "The epic of the Woods of Winnetka" (footnote): "Burning Love of Carol G. for Fireman Told" by Virginia Gardner, *Chicago Daily Tribune*, March 12, 1937, p. 1.

17 "Extreme and repeated cruelty" . . . "A severe beating" . . . "It is further ordered": Divorce Decree, Katherine Fitzgerald vs. Wallace Fitzgerald, Superior Court of Cook County, July 22, 1941.

Chapter 2: Green Gin

18 "At New Trier, Roy sat behind": Bill Markus, correspondence with author.

19 "Why was he not in": Philip "Bud" Davis, interview with author, May 4, 2015.

19 "There were very few": Arce, *The Secret Life of Tyrone Power*, p. 254.

19 "We laughed all the time": Jim Matteoni's remarks are taken from *This Is Your Life: Rock Hudson*, which was originally broadcast on NBC on December 17, 1952.

20 "If we could get near": Patrick McGuire, interview with author, January 15, 2016.

20 "He chased girls": Hudson and Davidson, *Rock Hudson: His Story*, 1986, p. 20.

20 "no overtures or" . . . "If we had been out": Patrick McGuire, interview with author, January 15, 2016.

20 "When I knew him": Philip "Bud" Davis, interview with author, May 4, 2015.

21 "Roy was more taken": Oppenheimer and Vitek, *Idol: Rock Hudson*, p. 11.

21 "She and I were enemies" . . . "We both had a little problem": Patrick McGuire, interview with author, January 15, 2016.

22 "Sliced a Piper Cub": *Star Stories: Rock Hudson* by Jane Ardmore, p. 13.

22 "For this exploit": Remarks made by Ralph Edwards and Rock Hudson are taken from *This Is Your Life: Rock Hudson*, which was originally broadcast on NBC on December 17, 1952.

23 "He told me that he'd had": Bob Preble's comments are taken from the documentary, *Rock Hudson: Acting the Part*, which was originally broadcast on the A&E Network on March 7, 1999 (Peter Jones Productions).

24 "If Roy had a son": "The Search for Rock Hudson's Secret Son" by George Carpozi, Jr., *Star* magazine, March 30, 1990, pp. 18–19.

24 "I have a letter": Alice Waier, interview with author, January 12, 2018.

25 "After my discharge, I returned": "My Real Crazy Career" by Rock Hudson, as told to Maurice Zolotow, *The American Weekly*, March 25, 1956, p. 9.

25 "When Rock worked for me": "The Rock Hudson Story" by Joe Hyams, *Photoplay*, February 1957, p. 92.

25 "Delivering the mail": "My Real Crazy Career" by Rock Hudson, as told to Maurice Zolotow, *The American Weekly*, March 25, 1956, p. 10.

26 "Davey, John . . . 'Imagine—all those letters'": Samuel Steward's "Stud File" is contained in the Samuel Steward Papers (1930–2003) archived at the Beinecke Rare Book & Manuscript Library, Yale University.

26–27 "After I got out" . . . "I didn't quite flip": Rock Hudson, interview with Professor Ronald L. Davis, August 24, 1983.

Chapter 3: A Unique Appeal

28 "They weren't exactly": Jerry Scherer, interview with author, May 2015.

29 "Not very stable stuff": *Star Stories: Rock Hudson* by Jane Ardmore, p. 16.

29 "First of all": Alice Waier, interview with author, January 2015.

29 "With the G.I. Bill": Hudson interview with Professor Ronald L. Davis, August 24, 1983.

29 "Rock vacuumed": Mark Miller's comments are taken from the documentary, *Rock Hudson: Acting the Part*, which was originally broadcast on the A&E Network on March 7, 1999 (Peter Jones Productions).

30–31 "I had a room but" . . . "I thought, 'I'll never get'": Transcript of Pete Martin interview with Rock Hudson (background for "I Call on Rock Hudson," *Saturday Evening Post*, July 23, 1960).

30 "In my mind": Ken Maley, interview with author, January 26, 2015.

31 "It was very difficult" . . . "I kind of talked": Hudson interview with Professor Ronald L. Davis, August 24, 1983.

32 "When I was young": Kare Grams, interview with author, August 2, 2016.

32 "He was, I guess": Hudson interview with Prof. Ronald L. Davis, 1983.

32 "I could definitely see": Richard Hodge, interview with author, August 11, 2016.

33 "Kenny liked sailors": Mark Miller, *Trio of Forever Friends* (unpublished memoir completed in 2007).

33 "They were a good team": Herbert Millspaugh, interview with author, December 2014.

34 "At some point, Uncle Kenneth": Kare Grams, interview with author, August 2, 2016.

34 "The story that": Richard Hodge, interview with author, August 11, 2016.

34 "Ken was pretty devastated": Herbert Millspaugh, interview with author, December 2014.

34 "Part of the heartbreak": Kare Grams, interview with author, August 2, 2016.

35 "He was like the slime" . . . "I'd say that": Hofler, *The Man Who Invented Rock Hudson*, p. 6 (McDowall); p. 159 (Larson).

36 "One way or another" . . . "vacation in purgatory": Hofler, *The Man Who Invented Rock Hudson*, p. 29.

37 "Henry learned a lot": Bob Hofler, interview with author, 2005.

37 "I can always tell": Stine, *Stars & Star Handlers*, 1985.

38 "I always give a green actor": "Rock Hudson: Why he is No. 1," by Eleanor Harris, *Look* magazine, March 18, 1958, p. 52.

38 "Some of Henry's boys": Bob Hofler, interview with author, 2005.

39 "I also saw a face" . . . "He's wholesome": "Rock Hudson: Why He is No. 1," by Eleanor Harris, *Look* magazine, March 18, 1958, pp. 47–48.

40 "He liked my honesty": Hudson interview with Professor Ronald L. Davis, 1983.

40 "to develop a character": Hofler, *The Man Who Invented Rock Hudson*, p. 4.

41 "He's too green, Henry": *The Real Rock Hudson—Fans' Star Library No. 6*, The Amalgamated Press Limited, 1958, p. 39.

41 "He stumbled and giggled": Hofler, *The Man Who Invented Rock Hudson*, p. 17.

41 "Raoul was tough": Hofler, *The Man Who Invented Rock Hudson*, p. 162.

42 "I tend to believe" . . . "Walsh just saw" . . . "It must have": Marilyn Ann Moss, interview with author, February 5, 2015.

42 "he'll be good scenery": Moss, *Raoul Walsh*, p. 281.

43 "It was considered": Jack Larson, interview with author, December 16, 2014.

43–44 "Did you ever have" . . . "Get out the good dice": The quotes are taken directly from the Warner Archive Collection DVD of *Fighter Squadron* (Turner Entertainment/Warner Bros. Entertainment, 2010).

44–45 "Rock had one" . . . "Finally, after many": Jack Larson, interview with author, December 16, 2014.

45 "a *goddamned Christmas* tree": Hofler, *The Man Who Invented Rock Hudson*, p. 164.

45 "It was very sad": Jack Larson, interview with author, December 16, 2014.

45 "I remember when": "Roy Fitzgerald Takes Some Time to Reminisce" by Rowland Barber, *TV Guide*, vol. 20, no. 18, April 29, 1972. Pages 24–28.

45 "I just couldn't": Pat McGuire, interview with author, January 15, 2016.

46 "When I took her" . . . "Save your money": Oppenheimer and Vitek, *Idol: Rock Hudson*, 1986, p. 26.

46 "I remade *High Sierra*": Moss, *Raoul Walsh*, p. 283.

46 "I took him on location": McGilligan, *Film Crazy*, p. 46.

47 "He would wander onto": Mayo and Van Savage, *The Best Years of My Life*, p. 75.

47 "He was certainly very": Kathleen Hughes, interview with author, October 2014.

48 "The last winter of the war": The quotes are taken directly from Rock Hudson's screen test for 20th Century-Fox from July of 1949, which is included in the documentary, *Hollywood Screen Tests, Take 2* (Image Entertainment, 2002, directed by Edith Becker).

Chapter 4: Universal

51 "the biggest moving" . . . "we blow up bridges": Hirschhorn, *The Universal Story*, p. 12.

51 "the least ambitious": Mordden, *The Hollywood Studios*, p. 323.

53 "Universal in those days": Julie Adams, interview with author, December 14, 2014.

53 "His biggest asset is": *Star Stories: Rock Hudson* by Jane Ardmore, 1956, p. 25.

54 "I first met Rock": Piper Laurie, interview with author, November 18, 2014.

54 "Newest Chicagoland contribution": "Tower Ticker" by [Jimmy] Savage, *Chicago Daily Tribune*, October 24, 1949, p. 31.

56 "Anthony Mann was": Hudson interview with Professor Ronald L. Davis, August 24, 1983.

57 "He did a very good job": James Stewart's comments are taken from an interview included on the DVD version of *Winchester '73* (Universal Studios, 2003).

57 "The best thing about Rock": Soren, *Vera-Ellen: The Magic and the Mystery*, p. 135.

58 "Six feet four inches of": *The Real Rock Hudson—Fans Star Library No. 6*, the Amalgamated Press Limited, 1958, p. 48.

58 "We went into a paint store": Soren, *Vera-Ellen: The Magic and the Mystery*, p. 98.

59 "didn't prefer women": Soren, *Vera-Ellen*, p. 134.

59 "Vera's family always": David Soren, correspondence with author, 2017.

59 "Rock was absolutely stricken": Peggy Dow, interview with author, April 2015.

60 "It was right then": "How to Create a Movie Star" by Richard G. Hubler, *Saturday Evening Post*, September 27, 1952, p. 80.

61 "She was madly in love": Kathleen Hughes, interview with author, October 2014.

62 "Henry was a guy": Bob Preble's comments are taken from *E! True Holly-*

wood Story: Rock Hudson, which aired on E!: Entertainment Television on July 11, 1999, season three, episode 27.

63 "We're never attracted": "Bachelor's Bedlam!" by Bob Preble, *Photoplay*, September 1952, p. 82.

63 "I think it was a challenge": Mamie Van Doren's comments are taken from *E! True Hollywood Story: Rock Hudson*, which aired on E!: Entertainment Television on July 11, 1999, season three, episode 27.

63–64 "a little experimenting" . . . "a blast": Hudson and Davidson, *Rock Hudson: His Story*, p. 39.

64 "We were called" . . . "When sex was involved": Mark Miller, *Trio of Forever Friends*, unpublished memoir completed in 2007.

65 "Because instantly": Mark Miller's comments are taken from the documentary, *Rock Hudson: Acting the Part*, which was originally broadcast on the A&E Network on March 7, 1999 (Peter Jones Productions).

66 "We called him 'Claudia'": Miller, *Trio*, p. 17.

66 "We would get in drag" . . . "By using" . . . "We've got to get": Miller, *Trio*, p. 12.

66 "There he was": Miller, *Trio*, p. 86.

67 "Rock went much further": Miller, *Trio*, p. 147.

67 "Rock was under contract": Miller, *Trio*, p. 167.

69 "its heavyweight hero": "The Fat Man Turns to the Films," *New York Times*, May 25, 1951.

69 "It has all the elements": Review of *The Fat Man, The Hollywood Reporter*, March 30, 1951, p. 3.

69 "Stop whatever you have": from *Dear Rock* by Roger Jones, from the Roger W. Jones Papers (Collection #12621), archived at the University of Wyoming/American Heritage Center.

69 "I remember Rock saying": Joyce Holden, interview with author, January 2015.

70 "Sam, you can't do this" . . . "Do you want to be": from *Dear Rock* by Roger Jones (unpublished manuscript), from the Roger W. Jones Papers (Collection #12621), archived at the University of Wyoming/American Heritage Center.

71 "He was very unhappy" . . . "I've found making lots of friends": Oppenheimer and Vitek, *Idol: Rock Hudson*, p. 37 (Laurie); p. 41 (Hedda Hopper).

71–72 "Rock was dating" . . . "I remember the guard": Jerry Scherer, interview with author, April 2015.

72 "A fight story": Keyes, *Scarlett O'Hara's Younger Sister*, 1977.

72 "standard for the course": "The Screen: Three Movies Arrive," *New York Times*, August 20, 1951, p. 14.

72 "I'd say the first": Robert Osborne, interview with author, June 23, 2015.

73 "The studio executives": Frankie Van's comments are taken from *This Is Your Life: Rock Hudson*, which was originally broadcast on NBC on December 17, 1952.

73 "suddenly more like": Oppenheimer and Vitek, *Idol: Rock Hudson*, p. 38.

73 "I was a messenger girl" . . . "Rock fit right into" . . . "He had a": Betty Abbott Griffin, interview with author, January 2017.

74 "a camaraderie seldom seen": "Rock's Mystery Girl" by Maxine Arnold, *Photoplay*, November 1953, p. 110.

74 "Despite the diplomacy" . . . "I surely hope": "Heading for a Wedding?" by Imogene Collins, *Modern Screen*, August 1954, p. 58.

74 "We would laugh": Betty Abbott Griffin, interview with author, January 2017.

Chapter 5: "We Want Hudson!"

76 "I remember watching Jim": Julie Adams, interview with author, December 14, 2014.

77 "pushed, pulled": "Stars of 'Bend of the River' Swarmed in Damp Parade" by Phyllis Lauritz, *The Oregonian*, January 24, 1952, p. 1.

77 "It went to my head": Hudson and Davidson, *Rock Hudson: His Story*, p. 37.

78 "The movie makers threw": "Hollywood in Excelsis and Extremis!" by William M. Tugman, *Eugene Register-Guard*, January 30, 1952, p. 6.

78 "I first met Rock": Bodil Miller, correspondence with author.

79 "He was doing leads now": De Carlo and Warren, *Yvonne*.

79 "After he gained some attention": Robert Osborne, interview with author, June 23, 2015.

80 "It was a charming movie": Piper Laurie, interview with author, November 18, 2014.

81 "Mr. Sirk was": Betty Abbott Griffin, interview with author, January 2017.

81 "I saw a picture": Halliday, *Sirk on Sirk*, p. 99.

81 "I think that": Betty Abbott Griffin, interview with author, January 2017.

81 "Nobody knew Jimmy then": Piper Laurie, interview with author, November 18, 2014.

82 "Horizons West bites the dust": "Horizons West, a Story of Post-Civil War Texas, Opens at Palace," *New York Times*, November 22, 1952, p. 16.

82 "so mean, he once": Paul Trachtman, *The Gunfighters* (Old West series), New York: Time-Life Books, 1974.

83 "Rock Hudson is one of those" (footnote): Universal-International press release, May 6, 1952.

83 "He had a wonderful way": Hudson interview with Professor Ronald L. Davis, August 24, 1983.

84 "You had to give him": Julie Adams, interview with author, December 14, 2014.

84 "absorbing sincerity": Review of *The Lawless Breed*, *The Hollywood Reporter*, November 28, 1952, p. 4.

84 "fairly acceptable": Review of *The Lawless Breed* by Philip K. Scheuer, the *Los Angeles Times*, February 21, 1953.

85 "The best thing you could do": Eric Spilker, interview with author, November 22, 2014.

85 "It was a tumultuous affair": Mark Miller, *Trio*, p. 146.

86 "We lived a very" . . . "If he did": Hudson and Davidson, *Rock Hudson: His Story*, pp. 42–43.

87 "I don't like": De Carlo and Warren, *Yvonne*, p. 169.

88 "six feet four inches" . . . "a fine sense of": "Rock's All Right" by Bryan Forbes, *Picturegoer*, May 14, 1955, pp. 14–15.

88 "I shared rooms with Rock": Moss, *Raoul Walsh*, p. 322.

88 "I didn't feel": De Carlo and Warren, *Yvonne*, p. 169.

89 "As they started": De Carlo and Warren, *Yvonne*, p. 170.

89 "completely undistinguished": "The Screen: Sea Devils" by Bosley Crowther, *New York Times*, July 31, 1953, p. 11.

90 "When we were shooting": Piper Laurie, interview with author, November 18, 2014.

90 "They serve a purpose": "Will Hudson in McMillan Be a TV Rock for NBC?" by Kay Gardella, *New York Daily News*, August 24, 1971, p. 37.

91 "I really didn't want" . . . "Lee Marvin was": Roberta Haynes, interview with author, June 5, 2016.

92 "So that they can": Ross Hunter's comments are taken from his interview with Professor Ronald L. Davis, July 17, 1984, which is archived in the Ronald L. Davis Oral History Collection (#307) at the Academy of Motion Picture Arts & Sciences Margaret Herrick Library.

Chapter 6: Double Technicolor

93 "I looked like Joe College": Hudson and Davidson, *Rock Hudson: His Story*, p. 37.

95 "I felt like such a fool": Undated correspondence from Rock Hudson to George Nader.

95 "forceful" direction: Review of *Taza, Son of Cochise, Variety*, January 20, 1954, p. 6.

95 "It's double-Technicolor": Interview with Rock Hudson by Robert Feidan and Robert Colaciello [*sic*], *Interview*, 1971, pp. 12–13.

96 "like an ass": Hudson interview with Professor Ronald L. Davis, August 24, 1983.

96 "How long before": *Star Stories: Rock Hudson* by Jane Ardmore, p. 34.

96 "I called the studio": Hudson interview with Professor Ronald L. Davis, August 24, 1983.

96 "Without Muhl": Hofler, *The Man Who Invented Rock Hudson*, p. 236.

96 "Not true": Alexandra Muhl, Internet Movie Database posting.

97 "I did it with": Hudson interview with Professor Ronald L. Davis, August 24, 1983.

97 "the most important figure": Douglas, *Magnificent Obsession*, 1929.

98 "Everybody has taken": Ross Hunter interview with Professor Ronald L. Davis, July 17, 1984.

99 "My immediate reaction": Halliday, *Sirk on Sirk*, p. 109.

99 "Rock Hudson was not": "Two Weeks in Another Town: Interview with Douglas Sirk" by Jane Stern and Michael Stern, *Bright Lights Film Journal*, April 30, 2005.

99 "Rock was new": Jane Wyman's comments are taken from the documentary, *Rock Hudson: Acting the Part*, which was originally broadcast on the A&E Network on March 7, 1999 (Peter Jones Productions).

99 "Rock and I were": Gregg Palmer, interview with author, February 4, 2015.

100 *"I'm no actor"*: From "Dear Rock" by Roger Jones (unpublished manuscript), from the Roger W. Jones Papers (Collection #12621), archived at the University of Wyoming/American Heritage Center.

101 "Women wanted to": David Thomson, interview with author, August 8, 2016.

101 "There was this great": Betty Abbott Griffin, interview with author, January 2017.

102 "Released for the first time": Review of *Magnificent Obsession*, *Los Angeles Herald Examiner*, July 22, 1954.

102 "At last, Rock Hudson": "Dramatic, Exalted Film" by Jim O'Connor, *New York Journal American*, August 5, 1954, p. 13.

102 "Bud was very anxious": From "Dear Rock" by Roger Jones (unpublished manuscript), from the Roger W. Jones Papers (Collection #12621), archived at the University of Wyoming/American Heritage Center.

103 "When we were": Arlene Dahl, interview with author, November 1, 2014.

104 "Hollywood's most eligible" . . . "He likes single-breasted": *Modern Screen*.

104 "I noticed that": Arlene Dahl, interview with author, November 1, 2014.

105 "There is nothing": "The Screen: Bengal Brigade vs. Sepoys at Palace" by Bosley Crowther, *New York Times*, November 13, 1954, p. 13.

106 "Rock Hudson was so": Universal-International press release, June 25, 1954.

106 "deeply tanned face": Gates and Thomas, *My Husband, Rock Hudson*, p. 137.

107 "Rock Hudson has resumed": Universal-International press release, June 25, 1954.

107 "Oh, we had great": Betty Abbott Griffin, interview with author, January 2017.

108 "Most of it was shot" . . . "In Hollywood, you have": Halliday, *Sirk on Sirk*, p. 118.

109 "Hudson was playing": Halliday, *Sirk on Sirk*, p. 118.

109 "Hudson is developing": Review of *Captain Lightfoot*, *Los Angeles Times*, March 10, 1955.

Chapter 7: Is Rock Hudson Afraid of Marriage?

111 "Fans are urging": "The Simple Life of a Busy Bachelor," *Life* magazine, October 3, 1955, p. 129.

111 "It Was The Hottest Show": Scott, *Shocking True Story: The Rise and Fall of* Confidential, pp. 159–60.

112 "The descriptions of": O'Hara and Nicoletti, *'Tis Herself*, p. 202.

113 "The virile hero": Scott, *Shocking True Story: The Rise and Fall of* Confidential, p. 79.

113 *"Confidential* approached me": Bob Preble's comments are taken from the documentary, *Rock Hudson: Acting the Part*, which was originally broadcast on the A&E Network on March 7, 1999 (Peter Jones Productions).

114 "It was really terrifying": Michael Childers, interview with author, April 25, 2016.

115 "It is the racy story": Scott, *Shocking True Story: The Rise and Fall of* Confidential, p. 87.

115 "Every month, when *Confidential*": Hudson and Davidson, *Rock Hudson: His Story*, p. 49.

116 "I spent my entire summer": Gates and Thomas, *My Husband, Rock Hudson*, p. 10.

117 "I shouldn't hire": Gates and Thomas, *My Husband, Rock Hudson*, p. 20.

117–19 "Why don't you and Phyllis" . . . "I enjoyed her company" . . . "I wasn't even in town!": Hudson and Davidson, *Rock Hudson: His Story*, p. 51.

119 "The studio is capable": Hofler, *The Man Who Invented Rock Hudson*, p. 232.

119 "I gave Rock a nice background": "Rock Hudson: Why He is No. 1," by Eleanor Harris, *Look* magazine, March 18, 1958, p. 56.

119 "a movie that made me": Gates and Thomas, *My Husband, Rock Hudson*, p. 22.

119 "I discovered that": Gates and Thomas, *My Husband, Rock Hudson*, p. 42.

120 "I could understand why": Hudson and Davidson, *Rock Hudson: His Story*, p. 50.

121 "I finally gave up": Gates and Thomas, *My Husband, Rock Hudson*, p. 45.

122 "Rock Hudson has been enjoying": Gates and Thomas, *My Husband, Rock Hudson*, p. 51.

122 "He brought me home": Gates and Thomas, *My Husband, Rock Hudson*, p. 47.

122 "the house of my dreams": Gates and Thomas, *My Husband, Rock Hudson*, p. 53.

123 "I was thunderstruck": Gates and Thomas, *My Husband, Rock Hudson*, p. 55.

123 "You can have it": Gates and Thomas, *My Husband, Rock Hudson*, p. 72.

125 "I take full credit": Julie Adams, interview with author, December 14, 2014.

125 "meticulous attention": Universal-International Studio Operating Committee—Minutes of Meeting from December 13, 1954; Report by Gilbert Kurland, assistant production manager.

126 "*One Desire* is nothing more": "Soap Opera Triangle Marks One Desire," *New York Times*, September 3, 1955.

126 "Rock Hudson had requested": Universal-International Studio Operating Committee—Minutes of Meeting from November 30, 1954; Report by John Baur.

126 "In spite of a poor story": Douglas Sirk's comments are taken from the documentary, *Behind the Mirror: A Profile of Douglas Sirk*, directed by Sue Mallinson and produced by Mark Shivas (BBC, 1979).

128 "I found it a rich experience": Hudson interview with Professor Ronald L. Davis, August 24, 1983.

129 "We still feel": Letter from Geoffrey M. Shurlock, Motion Picture Association of America to Universal-International executive William Gordon, January 10, 1955.

129 "You know, when you're": Hudson interview with Professor Ronald L. Davis, August 24, 1983.

129 "Rock had matured": William Reynolds, interview with author, December 8, 2014.

130 "In *All That Heaven Allows*": Illeana Douglas, interview with author, May 24, 2016.

131 "As laboriously predictable": Review of *All That Heaven Allows*, *The Monthly Film Bulletin* (British Film Insitute), August 1956.

131 "produced with smartness": "*All That Heaven Allows* Strong in Popular Appeal" by Jack Moffitt, *The Hollywood Reporter*, October 25, 1955, p. 3.

131 "Dear Universal Pictures": Review of *All That Heaven Allows* by Hollis Alpert, *Saturday Review*, December 3, 1955, p. 39.

133 "the ingredients of misunderstanding": Review of *Never Say Goodbye*, *Variety*, February 15, 1956.

Chapter 8: *Giant*

134 "I think Rock Hudson": Steve Hayes, interview with author, September 19, 2016.

135 "I guess I wasn't in": George Stevens, Interview. Date unknown.

136 "The reaction was": Willsmer, *Giant: The Making of an Epic Motion Picture*, p. 9.

136 "To my mind": Willsmer, *Giant: The Making of an Epic Motion Picture*, p. 10.

137 "There was nothing regal": Ferber, *Giant* (Sears Readers Club Edition), 1952, p. 28.

137–38 "We thought about Bill Holden" . . . "He's the best": Willsmer, *Giant: The Making of an Epic Motion Picture*, p. 16.

138 "When I first went": Rock Hudson's comments are taken from the documentary, *George Stevens: A Filmmaker's Journey*, directed by George Stevens, Jr. and released in 1985 by Castle Hill Productions/Warner Bros.

139 "Wonderful, wonderful news": Western Union telegram from Rock Hudson to George Stevens, dated November 4, 1954, archived at the Academy of Motion Picture Arts and Sciences Margaret Herrick Library.

139 "I was very grateful": Rock Hudson's comments were videotaped for the documentary *George Stevens: A Filmmaker's Journey*, directed by George Stevens, Jr. and released in 1985 by Castle Hill Productions/Warner Bros.

139 "Look at the way": Hudson and Davidson, *Rock Hudson: His Story*, p. 58.

139–40 "Frankly, I would rather have" . . . "We are not going to" . . . "Liz Taylor cast herself": Willsmer, *Giant: The Making of an Epic Motion Picture*, p. 19.

140 "We should think": Willsmer, *Giant: The Making of an Epic Motion Picture*, p. 18.

141 "Marfa was": "Location is Everything" by Ben Weber, *Set*, p. 41.

141 "At the time": "A Giant Time" by Lance Avery Morgan, *The Society Diaries*, May-June, 2015, p. 118. See also: www.thesocietydiaries.com.

141 "Rock made me laugh": Elizabeth Taylor's comments are taken from the

television special *TNT Extra: A Very Special Conversation with Elizabeth Taylor*, hosted by Larry King and originally broadcast on the TNT Network on March 13, 1993.

142 "I don't mean to": "Rock Hudson: An Interview" by Sandra Shevey, *Playgirl*, February 1974, p. 55.

142 "It was like": Jane Withers, interview with author, March 6, 2015.

142 "Jimmy was jealous of Rock": "The James Dean I Knew" by Bob Hinkle, online article for www.americanlegends.com.

142 "Stevens is throwing": Gates and Thomas, *My Husband, Rock Hudson*, p. 64.

143 "It was after": Graham, *Giant: The Making of a Legendary American Film*, p. 75.

143 "We were all having": Carroll Baker's comments are taken from the 2003 documentary *Return to Giant*, directed by Jim Brennan and produced by Kirby Warnock.

143 "The lights came up": Willsmer, *Giant: The Making of an Epic Motion Picture*, p. 56.

144 "I had never seen": Gates and Thomas, *My Husband, Rock Hudson*, p. 69.

145 "Elizabeth, the Earth Mother": Willsmer, *Giant: The Making of an Epic Motion Picture*, p. 59.

145 In addition to mourning (footnote): Warner Brothers Inter-Office memo from Tom Andre to Eric Stacey, August 31, 1955, 9:15 a.m.; archived in the Warner Brothers Archives, USC School of Cinematic Arts.

146 "a communist picture": Willsmer, *Giant: The Making of an Epic Motion Picture*, p. 63.

146 "*Giant* is a strong contender": "Screen: Large Subject; The Cast" by Bosley Crowther, *New York Times*, October 11, 1956, p. 51.

146 "an epic film": Review of *Giant*, *The Hollywood Reporter*, October 10, 1956, p. 3.

147 "with *Giant*, Hudson": Review of *Giant*, *Variety*, October 10, 1956, p. 6.

147 "I think Rock Hudson was": Kevin Thomas, interview with author, January 22, 2017.

147 "Dear George, I thought you": Letter from Rock Hudson to George Stevens, May 29, 1962, archived in at the Academy of Motion Picture Arts and Sciences Margaret Herrick Library.

Chapter 9: *Written on the Wind*

150 "The question of whether": Hudson and Davidson, *Rock Hudson: His Story*, p. 61.

150 "Phyllis Gates and Rock Hudson began": Carlyle, *Under the Rainbow*, p. 131.

151 "That was an arranged marriage": Stockton Briggle's comments are taken from the documentary, *Rock Hudson: Acting the Part*, which was originally broadcast on the A&E Network on March 7, 1999 (Peter Jones Productions).

151 "The whole thing": Gates and Thomas, *My Husband, Rock Hudson*, p. 207.

151 "What I heard": Marty Flaherty, interview with author, July 3, 2015.

152 "Phyllis behaved": Christopher Riordan, interview with author, September 8, 2015.

152 "a combination of kitsch": Halliday, *Sirk on Sirk*, p. 110.

152 "this drama of psychic violence": Douglas Sirk's comments are taken from the documentary, *Behind the Mirror: A Profile of Douglas Sirk*, directed by Sue Mallinson and produced by Mark Shivas (BBC, 1979).

154 "Rock Hudson would very": Universal-International press release issued by David A. Lipton, Vice President of Marketing & Publicity.

154 "As usual, I'm": Oppenheimer and Vitek, *Idol: Rock Hudson*, p. 59.

154 "Soap opera beyond": Lauren Bacall's comments are taken from her interview with Mark Cousins for the BBC-TV series *Scene by Scene* (2000), produced by May Miller.

154 "My career": Bacall, *By Myself and Then Some*, p. 252.

155 "He never said a word": Oppenheimer and Vitek, *Idol: Rock Hudson*, p. 59.

155 "Since I was": Stack and Evans, *Straight Shooting*, p. 183.

155 "With *Written on the Wind*, Sirk": David Thomson, interview with author, August 8, 2016.

158 "I have seen": Ebert, *The Great Movies*, p. 511.

158 "That's what I was": Halliday, *Sirk on Sirk*, p. 122.

158 the so-called "flying parson": "News to U From U-I," undated Universal-International Press Release issued by Charles Simonelli, Eastern Advertising and Publicity Department Manager.

158 "I felt that it": "Battle Hymn—25 Orphans Flying Here from Korea," *Citizen-News* (Metropolitan Edition), January 31, 1956.

158 "A little hole": "Dean Hess, Preacher and Fighter Pilot, Dies at 97" by Sam Roberts, *New York Times*, March 7, 2015.

159 "former jailbird": Mike Tomkies, *The Robert Mitchum Story: It Sure Beats Working*, New York: Ballantine Books, 1972, p. 135.

159 "He's the only man": Letter from Colonel Dean E. Hess to William Wilkerson of *The Hollywood Reporter*, May 7, 1956, p. 2.

159 "I had a lot of problems": Halliday, *Sirk on Sirk*, p. 124.

159 "He was there": Halliday, *Sirk on Sirk*, p. 125.

159 "There is a great": Letter to Philip Gerard (Eastern Publicity Manager for Universal-International) from Jack Diamond (Universal Publicity Director), September 4, 1956.

160 "Is Hollywood's": "In Focus: Rock Hudson," *Star News*, February 16, 1957, p. 2.

160 "Perhaps the most": "Screen: All the Cliches; Battle Hymn is Usual Film About Service," by Bosley Crowther, *New York Times*, February 16, 1957, p. 14.

160 "Hudson has great": Review of *Battle Hymn* by James Powers, *The Hollywood Reporter*, December 18, 1956.

161 "Why don't you" . . . "Because he's a": Gates and Thomas, *My Husband, Rock Hudson*, p. 138.

161 "He expected everything": Gates and Thomas, *My Husband, Rock Hudson*.

161 "The minute we got": Clark and Kleiner, *Rock Hudson—Friend of Mine*, p. 72.

161 "I asked Rock": Lee Garlington, interview with author, June 2015.

162 "It is my understanding": MGM Inter-Office Communication from Bud Brown to Joe Finn, June 15, 1956.

163 "The colored boy": Letter from Walter Strohm to William Kaplan (Metro-Goldwyn-Mayer de France), June 18, 1956.

164 "Well, then, we have" . . . "They have decided": Oppenheimer and Vitek, *Idol: Rock Hudson*, p. 61.

164 "One Sunday morning": Hudson interview with Professor Ronald L. Davis, August 24, 1983.

164 "You'll be lucky": Relyea, *Not So Quiet on the Set*, p. 52.

164 "There isn't": Gates and Thomas, *My Husband, Rock Hudson*, p. 144.

165 "Bob, do you think": Daniel, *Tough as Nails: The Life and Films of Richard Brooks*, pp. 117–18.

166 "moments in bwha-nality": Review of *Something of Value*, *Time* magazine, May 20, 1957.

166 "forceful though hard": Review of *Something of Value* by Philip T. Hartung, *Commonweal*.

166 "I don't want": Gates and Thomas, *My Husband, Rock Hudson*, p. 149.

166–67 "Rock, there's a man" . . . "I was surprised" . . . "I learned": *Stepping Stones: The Story of a Girl Who Lived Her Dreams* (unpublished memoir) by Lois Darlene Rupert, archived at the University of Wyoming/American Heritage Center.

Chapter 10: *A Farewell to Arms*

168 "my long tale": Baker, *Ernest Hemingway: A Life Story*.

168 "a high achievement": "Love and War in the Pages of Mr. Hemingway" by Percy Hutchison, *New York Times*, September 29, 1929.

169 "There is too much sentiment": "Helen Hayes, Gary Cooper and Adolphe Menjou in a Film of Hemingway's 'Farewell to Arms'" by Mordaunt Hall, *New York Times*, December 9, 1932.

169 "It broke my heart": Haver, *David O. Selznick's Hollywood*, p. 395.

170 "full of bubbling energy": Hemingway, *A Farewell to Arms*.

170 "Most directors": Haver, *David O. Selznick's Hollywood*, p. 397.

171 "Papa liked": Nolan, *John Huston: King Rebel*, p. 153.

171 "Could you concentrate": Haver, *David O. Selznick's Hollywood*, p. 398.

171 "unplayable and undramatizable": Behlmer, *Memo from David O. Selznick*, p. 471; Letter from David O. Selznick to Robert Chapman, Associate Professor of Playwriting and English at Harvard University.

172 "torturing": Haver, *David O. Selznick's Hollywood*, p. 398.

172 "It's of utmost importance": Telegram from David O. Selznick to Spyros Skouras, President of 20th Century-Fox, September 10, 1956; archived in The David O. Selznick Collection at The Harry Ransom Center, The University of Texas at Austin.

172 "Rock Hudson is the first": Haver, *David O. Selznick's Hollywood*, p. 398.

172 "I did *A Farewell to Arms*": Hudson interview with Professor Ronald L. Davis, August 24, 1983.

173 "I should be less than candid": Grobel, *The Hustons*, p. 446.

173 "In Mr. Huston": Grobel, *The Hustons*, p. 447.

173 "And that was the end": Hudson interview with Professor Ronald L. Davis, August 24, 1983.

173 "He was a very nervous": Grobel, *The Hustons*, p. 447.

173 "I have had to go": Behlmer, *Memo from David O. Selznick*, p. 482; The memo, dated May 6, 1957, is from David O. Selznick to director Charles Vidor.

174 "I had these highly" . . . "We were shooting": Hudson interview with Professor Ronald L. Davis, August 24, 1983.

174 "I flipped over Rock": Elaine Stritch's comments are taken from the DRG Records release *Elaine Stritch: At Liberty*, recorded live on January 10–12, 2002 at the Joseph Papp Public Theater.

174 "The memo indicates": Telegram from director Charles Vidor to producer David O. Selznick; archived in The David O. Selznick Collection at The Harry Ransom Center, The University of Texas at Austin.

175 "Mr. Morris and I": Letter from David O. Selznick to Joe Schoenfeld (editor, *Daily Variety*), June 21, 1957; archived in The David O. Selznick Collection at The Harry Ransom Center, The University of Texas at Austin.

175 "I have never worked": Letter from David O. Selznick to Arthur Fellows, May 29, 1957; archived in The David O. Selznick Collection at The Harry Ransom Center, The University of Texas at Austin.

175 "I do hope that Rock": Letter from David O. Selznick to Henry Willson (Famous Artists Corporation), January 14, 1957; archived in The David O. Selznick Collection at The Harry Ransom Center, The University of Texas at Austin.

175 "Please keep your eye out": Memo from David O. Selznick to cinematographer Piero Portalupi, June 22, 1957; archived in The David O. Selznick Collection at The Harry Ransom Center, The University of Texas at Austin.

175 "It would be in your own": Memo from David O. Selznick to Rock Hudson, June 20, 1957; archived in The David O. Selznick Collection at The Harry Ransom Center, The University of Texas at Austin.

176 "damagingly distracting" . . . "Frightened": Telegram from David O. Selznick to attorney Barry Brannen, July 31, 1957; archived in The David O. Selznick Collection at The Harry Ransom Center, The University of Texas at Austin.

176 "It wasn't a pleasant": Hudson interview with Professor Ronald L. Davis, August 24, 1983.

177 "If there was": Review of *A Farewell to Arms* by William K. Zinsser, *New York Herald-Tribune*.

177 "Sweep and frankness": Review of *A Farewell to Arms*, *Variety*, December 25, 1957.

177 "Hudson is an actor": Review of *A Farewell to Arms*, *The Hollywood Reporter*, December 19, 1957.

177 "The essential excitement": "David O. Selznick's 'A Farewell to Arms';
Hemingway Story Is New Film at Roxy—Rock Hudson, Jennifer Jones
Are Starred" by Bosley Crowther, *New York Times*, January 25, 1958, p. 14.

177 "I received a call" (footnote): *Stepping Stones: The Story of a Girl Who
Lived Her Dreams* (unpublished memoir) by Lois Darlene Rupert, archived at the University of Wyoming/American Heritage Center.

Chapter 11: *The Tarnished Angels*

180 *"Pylon* doesn't work" (footnote): Halliday, *Sirk on Sirk*, p. 136.

180 "They paid Faulkner": "Sirk's *The Tarnished Angels*: *Pylon* Recreated"
by Pauline Degenfelder, *Literature/Film Quarterly*, vol. 5, no. 3, Summer
1977, p. 243.

181 "Strangely enough": Letter from Douglas Sirk to Albert Zugsmith, August
19, 1956; from the George Zuckerman Papers archived at The American
Heritage Center, University of Wyoming.

181 "like a scarecrow": *William Faulkner: Novels* (1930–1935) including *Pylon*
(Library of America Series), p. 791.

181 "the raked disreputable hat": William Faulkner: Novels (1930–1935) including *Pylon* (Library of America Series), p. 800.

181 "I went down into": Rock Hudson's comments are taken from a 1980 interview, which is included in the *Douglas Sirk Filmmaker Collection*, released
by Turner Classic Movies and Universal Home Video in 2010.

181 "It made Douglas so angry and me so angry": Transcript of Pete Martin
interview with Rock Hudson (background for "I Call on Rock Hudson,"
Saturday Evening Post, July 23, 1960).

182 "gallant"/"tender type": Oppenheimer and Vitek, *Idol: Rock Hudson*,
pp. 60–61.

182 "He saw me as a score": Hofler, *The Man Who Invented Rock Hudson*,
p. 307.

183 "Even though he was": William Schallert, interview with author, December 28, 2014.

183 *"The Tarnished Angels* is a stumbling": Review of *The Tarnished Angels*,
Variety, November 20, 1957, p. 6.

183 "Mr. Faulkner's faded story": "Screen: Faulkner Tale; 'The Tarnished Angels' at the Paramount" by Bosley Crowther, *New York Times*, January 7,
1958, p. 31.

183 "Douglas Sirk took a": Review of *The Tarnished Angels* by Dave Kehr, *Chicago Reader*, undated online article.

184 "I was with a bunch": Armistead Maupin, interview with author, April 23,
2015.

185 "I didn't think the story": "Confessions of a Working Actor" by Rock Hudson, as told to Richard G. Hubler, p. 8. The manuscript is archived at the
Howard Gotlieb Archival Research Center, Boston University.

185 "They just wanted Rock": Oppenheimer and Vitek, *Idol: Rock Hudson*, p. 66.

186 "the absolute worst" . . . "He took a good book" . . . "Rock was then": Martin and Charisse, *The Two of Us*, p. 212.

187 "Whenever Rock had time off": Gates and Thomas, *My Husband, Rock Hudson*, p. 195.

187 "One of the biggest surprises": "Louella Parsons in Hollywood," *Los Angeles Examiner*; excerpted in Gates and Thomas, *My Husband, Rock Hudson*, p. 197.

187 "Do you want me to do": Letter from Hedda Hopper to Jack Podell (editor, *Motion Picture Magazine*), July 3, 1958, archived at the Margaret Herrick Library, Academy of Motion Picture Arts and Sciences.

188 "That would only": Gates and Thomas, *My Husband, Rock Hudson*, p. 214.

188 "I was hired": Otash, *Investigation Hollywood!*, p. 31.

188–89 "How long after" . . . "No, I can't deny it": Otash, *Investigation Hollywood!* pp. 32–37.

189 "What has Phyllis contributed": "Exclusively Yours" by Radie Harris, *Photoplay*, April 1958, p. 60.

190 "Hi Hon—All's I need": Flaherty, *"At Home" with Rock Hudson–Volume II.*

190 "I was briefly": Smith, *Natural Blonde*, pp. 146–47.

192 "Rock Hudson discovered me" . . . "In all the magazines": Cynthia Chenault, interview with author, November 3, 2015.

193 "Rock Hudson gives a sympathetic": Review of *This Earth Is Mine*, *Variety*, April 22, 1959.

Chapter 12: *Pillow Talk*

194 "No one wanted": Hotchner, *Doris Day: Her Own Story*, p. 188.

196 "One of the most": David Thomson's comments are taken from the documentary "Back in Bed with Pillow Talk," included on the 50th Anniversary Edition of *Pillow Talk* (Universal Studios Home Video, 2009).

196 "I felt that it was": Hotchner, *Doris Day: Her Own Story*, p. 188.

196 "I liked those scripts": Hotchner, *Doris Day: Her Own Story*, p. 185.

197 "In Ross's office": Hudson interview with Professor Ronald L. Davis, August 24, 1983.

197 "a couple of 1960 Cadillacs": Review of *Pillow Talk*, *Time* magazine, October 19, 1959, p. 106.

197 "The reason why they": Thomas Santopietro, interview with author, December 14, 2015.

198 "I honestly don't think": Doris Day, correspondence with author, December 19, 2014.

198 "He discovered": Tony Randall's comments are taken from his interview for the Turner Classic Movies Archival Project; the interview was taped on October 29, 2003 and it is archived at the Academy of Motion Picture Arts and Sciences Film Archive.

199 "In the original script": Barrios, *Screened Out*, p. 277.

199 "The entire sequence": Letter from Geoffrey M. Shurlock (of the Motion Picture Association of America) to Mrs. Kathryn McTaggart (Universal-International), February 4, 1959.

199 "a good, wholesome film": Memo from Mrs. Dean Gray Edwards, President of the Federation of Motion Picture Councils, Inc., September 1959.

200 "The most exciting thing": "Hunter & Melcher Prod'n Chockful of Fine Performances" by Jack Moffitt, *The Hollywood Reporter*, August 12, 1959, p. 3.

200 "Being nominated": Doris Day, correspondence with author, December 19, 2014.

200 "Thank God": "I Call on Rock Hudson" by Pete Martin, *Saturday Evening Post*, July 23, 1960, p. 74.

201 "Rock had a monstrous crush": Lee Garlington, interview with author, June 2015.

201 "I don't know anybody": Oppenheimer and Vitek, *Idol: Rock Hudson*, p. 67.

202 "The whole 'Newport Bums' crowd" . . . "Later, when she": *Dear Rock* by Roger Jones (unpublished manuscript), from the Roger W. Jones Papers (Collection #12621), archived at the University of Wyoming/American Heritage Center.

203 *"Fag-got!"*: Flaherty, *"At Home" with Rock Hudson, Behind The Walls of his Life*, p. 68.

203 "There are times": "I'm Rock's Best Gal But He Treats Me Like a Dog" by Jane Ardmore, *Photoplay*, February 1960, pp. 48–49.

204 "Rock was making *Pillow Talk*" . . . "About a week" . . . "I remember him": Bill Dawson, interview with author, July 14, 2015.

206 "an interesting performance": Review of *The Big Party* by John Lardner, *New Yorker*, November 21, 1959, pp. 122–28.

206 "painfully contrived": Review of *The Big Party by Revlon, Variety*, October 14, 1959.

206 "It sounded like": "Rock Hudson Will Test T.V. Temper Again," *Los Angeles Times*, September 21, 1966, Part IV, p. 20.

207 "Strange on the range": Capsule review of *The Last Sunset* from Leonard Maltin's *2002 Movie & Video Guide*, New York: Signet, 2002, p. 768.

208 "I have to do your picture": Douglas, *The Ragman's Son*, p. 330.

208 "I was only": Adell Aldrich, interview with author, July 2016.

209 "Dalton Trumbo . . . quit his": *Robert Aldrich: Interviews*, Edited by Eugene L. Miller and Edwin T. Arnold, University Press of Mississippi, 2004, p. 47.

209 "uncharacteristically haphazard": Cook, *Trumbo*, p. 278.

209 "I had a problem": Douglas, *The Ragman's Son*, p. 328.

209 "Rock Hudson emerged": *Robert Aldrich: Interviews*, edited by Eugene L. Miller and Edwin T. Arnold, University Press of Mississippi, 2004, p. 48.

209 "A routine combination": "Douglas and Hudson in 'The Last Sunset'" by Bosley Crowther, *New York Times*, June 15, 1961, p. 51.

210 "This is not so much": "Ha, Ha, Ha," *Newsweek*, July 3, 1961, p. 72.

210 "Aldrich's film is": *Time Out London*, undated online review by ATU.

210 "It is as frightful": Ceplair and Trumbo, *Dalton Trumbo: Blacklisted Hollywood Radical*, p. 423.

210 "That's a film": Hudson interview with Professor Ronald L. Davis, August 24, 1983.

211–12 "That night, my navy buddy" . . . "I was a bit tipsy" . . . "Henry took me": Glenn Jacobson, interview with author, May 25, 2017.

213 "large scale homosexual orgies": Buford, *Burt Lancaster: An American Life*, p. 176; the source is an FBI Office Memorandum, SAC [Special Agent "C"] (94–558) to Director, FBI (63–4296), Re: CRIMDEL—CRS, February 16, 1960.

214 "A friend and I" . . . "The lights were turned off": Robert Harmon, interview with author, January 15, 2015.

215–16 "We were *Pillow Talk*" . . . "What's very interesting": Joel Grey, interview with author.

216 "I don't think": "Twilight of the Goddess" by James Reginato, *Vanity Fair*, February 2015, p. 133.

216 "a superb comedienne": "The Screen: Comedy-Romance in Italy: 'Come September' Is at the Music Hall" by Bosley Crowther, *New York Times*, September 8, 1961, p. 34.

216 "Hudson comes through": Review of *Come September, Variety*, June 28, 1961.

217 "*Lover Come Back* is very": Thomas Santopietro, interview with author, December 14, 2015.

218 "*Pillow Talk* was such a success": Tony Randall's comments are taken from his interview for the Turner Classic Movies Archival Project; the interview was taped on October 29, 2003 and it is archived at the Academy of Motion Picture Arts and Sciences Film Archive.

218 "A springy and spirited": "Screen: 'Lover Come Back' Opens at Music Hall: Rock Hudson and Doris Day Are Co-Starred, Bright Comedy Recalls Their 'Pillow Talk,'" *New York Times*, February 9, 1962, p. 21.

218 "The best romantic-comedy team": "Lovers Come Back" by James Wolcott, *Vanity Fair*, April 2000.

218 "A strange romance" . . . "Right now, five will": "Rock and Marilyn: How They Met, How They Love, Why They Keep it Secret" by Ruth Waterbury, *Photoplay*, January 1962, pp. 60–63.

218–19 "He's the very, very best" . . . "She's one of those girls": Parish and Bowers, *The MGM Stock Company*, p. 476.

219 "this handsome, six-foot-whatever": Oppenheimer and Vitek, *Idol: Rock Hudson*, p. 96.

219 "Marilyn Maxwell's estranged husband": "The Forgotten Marilyn" by Sara Jordan, *Midwest Today* magazine, p. 32.

220 "She was in love with him": Hudson and Davidson, *Rock Hudson: His Story*, p. 88.

220 "When you'd see": Matt Davis, interview with author, June 2016.

220 "I could never count": *Stepping Stones: The Story of a Girl Who Lived Her Dreams* (unpublished memoir) by Lois Darlene Rupert, archived at the University of Wyoming/American Heritage Center.

221 "There was nothing": "Marilyn Maxwell Just 'Rides Away' From Show" by Bob Thomas, *The Corpus Christi Caller-Times*, November 19, 1961, p. 63.

221 "My mom went through" . . . "When I came home": Matt Davis, interview with author, June 2016.

222 "most crucial" . . . to me, it's like": "Hudson Sees Physician Role Crucial One of His Career," *New York Morning Telegraph*, August 24, 1961.

223 "Interminable": Capsule review of *The Spiral Road*, Leonard Maltin's *2002 Movie & Video Guide*, New York: Signet, 2002, p. 1,289.

223 "his finest to date": Review of *The Spiral Road*, *Boxoffice*, June 4, 1962.

224 "I had a producer friend": Earl Holliman, interview with author, January 16, 2015.

225 "I never in my life" (footnote): Clark and Kleiner, *Rock Hudson—Friend of Mine*, p. 87.

225 "I have to say": Ken Jillson, interview with author, April 2, 2017.

226 "Oh, my god, that house": Cathy Hamblin, interview with author, May 3, 2017.

226 "Over ninety percent": Marty Flaherty, interview with author, July 3, 2015.

227 "Everything in that": Cathy Hamblin, interview with author, May 3, 2017.

227 "I couldn't believe": Ken Jillson, interview with author, April 2, 2017.

Chapter 13: *Strange Bedfellows*

228 "You have worked": Otash, *Investigation: Hollywood!*, p. 35.

228 "How do you resist": Otash, *Investigation: Hollywood!*, p. 37.

229 "If you want to talk" . . . "The horse industry" . . . "The story that": Dr. Jonathan Coleman, interview with author, June 11, 2017.

230 "That space has" (footnote): Dr. Jonathan Coleman, interview with author, June 11, 2017.

230 "I knew a lot": Robert Morgan, interview with author, June 9, 2017.

231 "This is how" . . . "Of course, Lonnie and Jim's": Shannon Ragland, interview with author, January 20, 2017.

232 "The way that the story": Robert Morgan, interview with author, June 9, 2017.

232 "Rock didn't want" (footnote): Hofler, *The Man Who Invented Rock Hudson*, p. 364.

232–33 "I never had a player admit" . . . "One of the": Shannon Ragland, interview with author, January 20, 2017.

233 "This would have been": Shannon Ragland, interview with author, January 20, 2017.

233 "The whole town": Otash, *Investigation: Hollywood!*, p. 35.

234 "I got a call" . . . "He wanted to": Hofler, *The Man Who Invented Rock Hudson*, p. 364.

235 "Brave wives": Mary Peach, interview with author, March 11, 2015.

235 "As we got further": Delbert Mann's comments are taken from the documentary *Rock Hudson: Acting the Part*, which was originally broadcast on the A&E Network on March 7, 1999 (Peter Jones Productions).

236 "I think they cast": Mary Peach, interview with author, March 11, 2015.

236 "His dresser and my": Mary Peach, interview with author, March 11, 2015.

236 "It was a classic example": Davis, *Words into Images: Screenwriters on the Studio System*, p. 99.

237–39 "Rock met me" . . . "A rogue": *Stepping Stones: The Story of a Girl Who Lived Her Dreams* (unpublished memoir) by Lois Darlene Rupert, archived at the University of Wyoming/American Heritage Center.

239 "He made very": Bego, *Rock Hudson: Public and Private*, p. 96.

239 "Before she was signed": *Stepping Stones: The Story of a Girl Who Lived Her Dreams* (unpublished memoir) by Lois Darlene Rupert, archived at the University of Wyoming/American Heritage Center.

240 "This is really": Erich Kuersten, correspondence with author, August 23, 2017.

240 "I wanted to be": Lee Garlington, interview with author, June 2015.

241 "Hollywood in those days" . . . "Around the lot" . . . "Word kind of got out": Lee Garlington, interview with author, June 2015.

241–42 "That was very" . . . "He invited me over" . . . "If we wanted": Lee Garlington, interview with author, June 2015.

242–43 "We were not" . . . "I usually requested" . . . "When we came back": Lee Garlington, interview with author, June 2015.

243 "In a way" (footnote): "I Slept in Rock Hudson's Bed" by Alan Somers, *Photoplay*, January 1964, p. 89.

243–44 "Inside a drawer" . . . "I am a very independent" . . . "He had a lot": Lee Garlington, interview with author, June 2015.

244–45 "mysterious friendship" . . . "No comment": "Rock Hudson & Lee Majors," *Globe* magazine, October 1, 1985.

245 "The truth of the matter" . . . "Handsome, blond" . . . "a professor at": "Miracle at Middlesboro" by Flora Rand, *TV Radio Mirror*, 1966.

245 "That's basically": Lee Garlington, interview with author, June 2015.

246 "I would say that your faith": Letter from Colonel Eben C. Henson (Pioneer Playhouse founder) to Rock Hudson, July 25, 1962.

247 "Rock Hudson put Lee Majors": "Rock Hudson & Lee Majors," *Globe* magazine, October 1, 1985.

247 "*Send Me No Flowers* is one of those": "The Theater: New Play on Broadway," *Time* magazine, December 19, 1960.

248 "*Send Me No Flowers* is so much weaker": Thomas Santopietro, interview with author, December 14, 2015.

249 "For Rock Hudson and Doris Day, the third": "Warmed-Over Hudson and Day," undated *Cosmopolitan* review.

251 "There was a note": Joseph Sirola, interview with author, July 6, 2015.

251 "We did two films": Rock Hudson to Professor Ronald L. Davis, August 24, 1983.

251 "generally labored and witless": "'Strange Bedfellows' Opens: Comedy Stars Hudson and Gina Lollobrigida" by Bosley Crowther, *New York Times*, March 11, 1965, p. 38.

251 "Rock Hudson . . . did not": Clark and Kleiner, *Rock Hudson—Friend of Mine*, page 6.

252 "Tom had this very": Marty Flaherty, interview with author, July 3, 2015.

252 "Uncle Tom's philosophy": Cindy Clark, interview with author.

252 "very stern and": Ray Clark, interview with author, March 10, 2017.

253 "It is quite evident" (footnote): Certificate dated November 25, 1952 and signed by Captain Arthur M. Sternberg (USAF), Psychiatric Section, Ellington Air Force Base, Texas; Air Force file on Tommy Harold Clark.

253 "He could have gone": Oppenheimer and Vitek, *Idol: Rock Hudson*, p. 115.

253 "One day, I would": Clark, *Rock Hudson—Friend of Mine*, p. 52.

256 "[Rock's] masculinity is on trial": Russo, *The Celluloid Closet*, p. 161.

256 "He offered a totally smooth": Caron, *Thank Heaven*, p. 170.

256 "What bothers me": "Meet Rock of Gibraltar" by Wanda Hale, *New York Daily News*, March 29, 1965.

257 "It is hard to imagine": "Special Favor" by Richard F. Shepard, *New York Times*, August 25, 1965, p. 40.

257 "The things I had to do": Bego, *Rock Hudson: Public and Private*, p. 98.

258 "From the first day I met him" . . . "I'm a bit" . . . "Of course, he was": Claudia Cardinale, interview with author, April 15, 2016.

259 "The team who fashioned": "Screen . . . Broad Farce Arrives at Three Theaters" by Robert Alden, *New York Times*, May 26, 1966, p. 55.

Chapter 14: *Seconds*

260 "We just don't know what": Clark, *Rock Hudson—Friend of Mine*, p. 146.

261 "I would hesitate": David Ely, interview with author, April 10, 2015.

261 "He was fascinated": Evans Frankenheimer's comments are taken from the documentary *A Second Look*, which was produced by Susan Arosteguy and featured on the 2013 Criterion Collection DVD of *Seconds*.

261 "I had a play": Lewis John Carlino, interview with author, January 9, 2015.

262 "Laurence Olivier?" (footnote): David Ely, interview with author, April 10, 2015.

262 "Rock's performance": Lewis John Carlino, interview with author, January 9, 2015.

263 "We wanted to beat him": John Frankenheimer's comments are taken from an audio commentary the director recorded in 1997, which is featured on the Criterion Collection DVD of *Seconds*, released in 2013.

263 "If you look at it" . . . "I came up with": John Frankenheimer's comments are taken from the documentary *Rock Hudson: Acting the Part*, which was originally broadcast on the A&E Network on March 7, 1999 (Peter Jones Productions).

263 "Something happened to Rock": Salome Jens's comments are taken from the documentary, *Rock Hudson: Dark and Handsome Stranger*, which was directed by Andrew Davies and André Schäfer and released in October 2010 by Florianfilm, GmbH.

265 "Frankenheimer told me": Salome Jens's comments are taken from the documentary, *A Second Look*, which was produced by Susan Arosteguy and featured on the 2013 Criterion Collection DVD of *Seconds*.

265–66 "That was a ritual" . . . "He had a very" . . . "It was actually": Lewis John Carlino, interview with author, January 9, 2015.

266 "Director John Frankenheimer and veteran": "Cinema: Identity Crisis," *Time* magazine, October 14, 1966, p. 117.

267 "The movie went from": John Frankenheimer's comments are taken from an audio commentary the director recorded in 1997, which is featured on the Criterion Collection DVD of *Seconds*, released in 2013.

268 "When Dale Olson took over": Kevin Thomas, interview with author, January 22, 2017.

268 "Rock Hudson is completely": "Rock Hudson: Why he is No. 1," by Eleanor Harris, *Look* magazine, March 18, 1958, p. 48.

268 "I don't think anybody has made me": "I Call on Rock Hudson" by Pete Martin, *Saturday Evening Post*, July 23, 1960, p. 74.

268 "Rock was complaining": Lee Garlington, interview with author, June 2015.

270 "Rock was just": Arthur Hiller, interview with author, March 17, 2015.

270 "best performance": "'Tobruk' Arrives at 2 Theaters: Criterion and Sutton" by Howard Thompson, *New York Times,* February 9, 1967, p. 33.

270 "I had to make a decision": Bego, *Rock Hudson: Public and Private*, p. 105.

271 "Jack was very good-looking": Cathy Hamblin, interview with author, May 3, 2017.

272 "When I hear": Ken Jillson, interview with author, April 2, 2017.

273–74 "I have no objection" . . . "A bunch of claptrap": Lovell, *Escape Artist: The Life and Films of John Sturges*, p. 264.

274 "Marty, I'd like to": Clark and Kleiner, *Rock Hudson—Friend of Mine*, p. 148.

274 "stern" . . . "heart of gold" . . . "We had shot": William Hillman, interview with author, September 20, 2015.

275 "It was the last": Mark Miller's comments are taken from the documentary *Rock Hudson: Acting the Part*, which was originally broadcast on the A&E Network on March 7, 1999 (Peter Jones Productions).

275 "Another good": "The Screen: 'Ice Station Zebra' at the Cinerama" by Renata Adler, *New York Times*, December 21, 1968, p. 49.

275 "It's terrible": Review of *Ice Station Zebra* by Pauline Kael, *New Yorker,* January 4, 1969.

276 "We worked in Rome": Claudia Cardinale, interview with author, April 15, 2016.

277 "a soggy caper twist": "'A Fine Pair' and 'Charro' on Double Bill in Neighborhoods" by Roger Greenspun, *New York Times,* September 4, 1969.

277 "Why don't you hold" . . . "Why don't you turn" . . . "I started thinking" . . . "I like you": Hudson and Davidson, *Rock Hudson: His Story*, p. 111.

278 "What Rock does": Davis, *Duke: The Life and Image of John Wayne*, p. 290.

278 "It never bothered me": Eyman, *John Wayne: The Life and Legend*, p. 452.

279 "A rerun of": Review of *The Undefeated, Variety*, October 1, 1969.

279 "One of the most": Royce, *Rock Hudson: A Bio-Bibliography*, p. 143.

281 "great natural talent": Hudson and Davidson, *Rock Hudson: His Story*, p. 112.

281 "I heard he was": Mark Colleano, interview with author, March 15, 2016.

282 "An overly long": Review of *The Hornet's Nest* by John C. Mahoney, *Los Angeles Times*, October 2, 1970, Part IV, p. 14.

282 "I was really sad": Mark Colleano, interview with author, March 15, 2016.

Chapter 15: Whistling Away the Dark

284 "I think that the people": Peter Bart, interview with author, July 17, 2012.

285 "Blake and I had worked": William Peter Blatty, interview with author, April 29, 2015.

286 "Their supposedly steamy": Bart, *Infamous Players*, viii.

286 "Sometimes we wait": "Filming, or How to Get Rained on Anywhere" by Mary Blume, *International Herald Tribune*, August 9, 1968.

287 "U.S. Go Home!"—"Paramount Crew Told to Go Home," *Los Angeles Times*, July 25, 1968.

287 "The 'Star' who is beginning": "Julie's Snow Job in New York City" by Joyce Haber, *Los Angeles Times*, February 12, 1969.

287 "Miss P and P": Windeler, *Julie Andrews: A Life on Stage and Screen*, p. 166.

287 "They should give Haber": Windeler, *Julie Andrews: A Life on Stage and Screen*, p. 167.

287 "When he did the movie": Dennis Holahan, interview with author, January 13, 2015.

288 "It's really too bad": Robert Osborne, interview with author, June 23, 2015.

288 "I loved and respected Blake": William Peter Blatty, interview with author, April 29, 2015.

289 "Blake Edwards' attempted spoof": Review of *Darling Lili* by Judith Crist, *New York* magazine, July 27, 1970.

289 "The overall effect": "How Darling Was My Lili" by Arthur Knight, *Saturday Review*, July 18, 1970.

289 "It is certainly no effort": "'Darling Lili' Has World War I Setting" by Charles Champlin, *Los Angeles Times*, June 24, 1970, p. F-1.

289 "Hudson's performance": "Films in Focus" by Andrew Sarris, *The Village Voice*, August 13, 1970, p. 47.

289 "*Darling Lili* was": Evans, *The Kid Stays in the Picture*, p. 134.

289–90 "an 8-year-old ragamuffin" . . . "One day, out of" . . . "I've thought of": "I Want to Be Your Daddy" by Henry Gris, *Photoplay*, December, 1972, pp. 72–99.

291 "Rock came home": Clark and Kleiner, *Rock Hudson—Friend of Mine*, p. 76.

291 "Rock and Rod Join Forces": *Los Angeles Times*, January 24, 1970, p. A9.

292 a "mush huckster": Nora Ephron, *Wallflower at the Orgy*, New York: The Viking Press, 1970, p. 67.

292 "staggeringly awful": *Kirkus Reviews*, May 1969.

293 "You paid $80,000 to cut that record" (footnote): from *Dear Rock* by Roger Jones (unpublished manuscript), from the Roger W. Jones Papers (Collection #12621), archived at the University of Wyoming/American Heritage Center.

293 "It was such a farce": David Nutter, interview with author, February 17, 2015.

293 "I'm 45 years old": "Rock's a Passionate, Complex Man" by Toni Holt, *Hollywood Citizen News*, June 20, 1970.

294 "thousands of copies": "Rock's Record Gathers Dust," *Baltimore Evening Sun*, July 30, 1971.

295 "To me, he's a very": "Rock Hudson: Superstar at 46" by Jerry Parker, *Chicago Sun-Times*, August 15, 1970, pp. 40–42.

295 "There is only one way": Roger Vadim's comments are quoted in Leonard Maltin's notes for the Museum of Modern Art's American Film Comedy series from 1976.

296 "It must be hard": Interview with Rock Hudson by Robert Feidan and Robert Colaciello [*sic*], *Interview*, 1971, pp. 12–13.

297 "Rock Hudson was very": Diane Sherry Case, interview with author, October 19, 2015.

297 "Rock and John David Carson were": Barbara Leigh, interview with author, November 24, 2015.

298 "Louis B. Mayer would have": Germaine Szal, correspondence with author.

298 "one of the most": "No Hollywood Film Has Broken So Many Taboos," Internet Movie Database review, posted March 20, 2008 by t1480.

298 "The re-cutting ruined": Clark, *Rock Hudson—Friend of Mine*, p. 149.

298 "MGM slashed it": "Rock Hudson: An Interview" by Sandra Shevey, *Playgirl*, February 1974, p. 55.

298 "Roger Vadim's first": Review of *Pretty Maids All in a Row* by Rex Reed, *New York Daily News*, April 30, 1971.

298 "Sleazy, Crude, Lecherous": Review of *Pretty Maids All in a Row* by Kathleen Carroll, *New York Daily News*, April 29, 1971.

298 "remarkably good": "Hudson Stars in Vadim's 'Pretty Maids'" by Roger Greenspun, *New York Times*, April 29, 1971, p. 46.

298 "Vadim was an outrageous guy" (footnote): Kevin Thomas, interview with author, January 22, 2017.

298 "A hilarious and outrageous": Review of *Pretty Maids All in a Row* by Kevin Thomas, *Los Angeles Times*, May 12, 1971.

299 "one of the stupidest": "Film: Bananas/Pretty Maids" by Andrew Sarris, *The Village Voice*, May 6, 1971, p. 65.

299 "The truth is" (footnote): "Rock Hudson Blames 'Sickies' for Rumors He Wed Jim Nabors" by Marilyn and Hy Gardner, *The Youngstown Vindicator*, September 1, 1985, p. C-19.

300 "All of this was started": Tony Melia, interview with author, September 23, 2015.

300 "perversion in Hollywood": "The Truth About The Rock Hudson-Jim Nabors Marriage Rumors" by John Samson, *National Examiner*, November 29, 1971, p. 7.

301 "I'll tell you": "I Did Not Marry Jim Nabors" by Carol Welles, *Photoplay*, November 1971, pp. 62–63.

301 "When Roy was finished": Tony Melia, interview with author, September 23, 2015.

301 "I remember the summer": Craig Muckler, interview with author, January 13, 2016.

302 "I wish I'd been": Hudson and Davidson, *Rock Hudson: His Story*, p. 116.

302 "I was so mad": Cathy Hamblin, interview with author, May 3, 2017.

Chapter 16: *McMillan & Wife*

304 "Illustrated radio": Oppenheimer and Vitek, *Idol: Rock Hudson*, p. 121.

304 "Rock and his agent": Paul Mason, interview with author.

305 "Instant Mouth": "Lunch Ended Up a Smashing Success!" by Arnold Hano, *TV Guide*, February 17, 1973, p. 30.

305 "We presented Rock": Paul Mason, interview with author.

305 "I was in North Beach": John Schuck, interview with author, March 12, 2015.

306 "A nifty blend": Review of *McMillan & Wife*, *Variety*, September 22, 1971.

306 "Our first season": John Schuck, interview with author, March 12, 2015.

306 "Television brought Rock": Germaine Szal, correspondence with author.

307 "There was real chemistry": John Schuck, interview with author, March 12, 2015.

307 "She taxed him": Oppenheimer and Vitek, *Idol: Rock Hudson*, p. 125.

307 "On screen, they were": Paul Mason, interview with author.

307 "We didn't go": Carole Cook, interview with author, August 5, 2015.

308 "I think it was probably" . . . "I do remember us" . . . "just one of those": Kenneth Griggs, interview with author, September 2, 2015.

309 "He wasn't awfully": Nick Tosches, *Dino: Living High in the Dirty Business of Dreams*, p. 404.

310 "A tale that": "Coming Out of 'Showdown' Saddle-Sore" by A. H. Weiler, *New York Times*, November 22, 1973, p. 51.

310 "the full movie star aura": George Nader diary entry (undated).

310–11 "There was, at one time" . . . "I had a house" . . . "Kay and I": Tony Melia, interview with author, September 23, 2015.

312 "informal": "Princess Grace, Stars at Hudson Party" by Kim Blair, *Los Angeles Times*, August 15, 1967, p. E1.

312 "He just said" . . . "Of course, I was just": Carol Burnett, interview with author, December 9, 2015.

313 "I remember thinking" . . . "Gower Champion wanted" . . . "Well, right from": Carol Burnett, interview with author, December 9, 2015.

314 "I have this unforgettable image": Armistead Maupin, interview with author, April 23, 2015.

315 "Rock always had": Lee Garlington, interview with author, June 2015.

315 "It didn't bother me": Hudson and Davidson, *Rock Hudson: His Story*, p. 131.

316 "Tom is obviously": George Nader diary entry, September 3, 1985.

316 "He never questioned": Marty Flaherty, interview with author, July 3, 2015.

317 "We drank a lot": Hudson and Davidson, *Rock Hudson: His Story*, p. 98.

318 "I've always been looking": Hudson and Davidson, *Rock Hudson: His Story*, p. 129.

318 "He took control of Rock": Bob Preble's comments are taken from *E! True Hollywood Story: Rock Hudson*, which aired on E!: Entertainment Television on July 11, 1999, season three, episode 27.

318 "At first, I wasn't": Oppenheimer and Vitek, *Idol: Rock Hudson*, p. 117.

318 "You better believe": Judy Kaye, interview with author, January 29, 2015.

319 "In the early days": Armistead Maupin, interview with author, April 23, 2015.

319 "I would say that mentally": Ken Maley, interview with author, January 26, 2015.

321 "I put Rock into": Clark and Kleiner, *Rock Hudson—Friend of Mine*, p. 144.

321 "When a scene demands": "People: Rock Hudson Spouts Off," *Time* magazine, June 2, 1975, p. 33.

321 "In the most demanding part": Review of *Embryo, Los Angeles Times*, May 28, 1976, Part IV, p. 22.

323 "As soon as they said": Clark and Kleiner, *Rock Hudson—Friend of Mine*, p. 209.

323 "Trevor and Hudson": Review of *John Brown's Body* by Ron Pennington, *The Hollywood Reporter*, May 7, 1976, p. 23.

323 "Hudson proves himself": Review of *John Brown's Body* by Bill Edwards, *Variety*, May 6, 1976.

324 "I was in the chorus": Florence Lacey, interview with author, March 19, 2015.

324 "When we finished": Peter Kevoian, interview with author, March 19, 2015.

325–26 "The moment he" . . . "The very first episode" . . . "He was surrounded": Armistead Maupin, interview with author, April 23, 2015.

326–27 "Rock thought San Francisco" . . . "I remember standing" . . . "The word would go out that": Ken Maley, interview with author, January 26, 2015.

327 "I knew a lot of": Wes Wheadon, interview with author, June 25, 2017.

328 "At the appropriate day and time" . . . "The main hosts": Ken Maley, interview with author, January 26, 2015.

328 "In a way, Rock was": Wes Wheadon, interview with author, June 25, 2017.

328 "I don't think Rock was": Mark Tillman-Briggle, interview with author, June 21, 2017.

329 "a fuddy-duddy": Hudson and Davidson, *Rock Hudson: His Story*, p. 152.

329 "It's funny, I guess": Lauren Bacall's comments are taken from a chapter that was dropped from the publication version of *Who the Hell's in It* by Peter Bogdanovich. In the uncorrected proof of the manuscript, Bacall's comments appear in chapter 12, page 309.

329 "Believe it or not but": Tony Kiser, interview with author, May 23, 2016.

330 "Rock was an amazing": Peter Kevoian, interview with author, March 19, 2015.

330 "I don't like": Oppenheimer and Vitek, *Idol: Rock Hudson*, p. 123.

331 "The networks get scared": Hudson interview with Professor Ronald L. Davis, August 24, 1983.

331–32 "empty hit" . . . "homoerotic three-person": Hudson and Davidson, *Rock Hudson: His Story*, p. 144.

332 "It was almost a sexual thing": Hudson and Davidson, *Rock Hudson: His Story*, p. 145.

332 "From the beginning": Robert Ousley, interview with author, February 20, 2015.

333 "I had never really": John Leslie Wolfe, interview with author, February 25, 2015.

333 "That's French for": Michael Licata, interview with author, March 15, 2015.

333 "It affected him deeply": Robert Ousley, interview with author, February 20, 2015.

334 "Your mother's had a" . . . "Why won't my son": Hudson and Davidson, *Rock Hudson: His Story*, p. 147.

335 "When Katharine died": Clark and Kleiner, *Rock Hudson—Friend of Mine*, p. 83.

335 "I was an only child": "Rock Hudson: Missing Marilyn & Mom," *New York Daily News*, May 7, 1978.

Chapter 17: Blue Snow

338 "dewrote": "The Young Directors: Who Is Using Whom?" by Patricia Goldstone, *Los Angeles Times*, December 17, 1978.

338 "Sounds awful": Clark and Kleiner, *Rock Hudson—Friend of Mine*, p. 144.

338 "I told him that this happened": Clark and Kleiner, *Rock Hudson—Friend of Mine*, p. 27.

338 "about as right as Whoopi": Clark and Kleiner, *Rock Hudson—Friend of Mine*, p. 148.

338–39 "The only thing that I have" . . . "He was a total": Jerry Douglas, interview with author, January 13, 2015.

339 "Roger Corman appears to have": "The Young Directors: Who Is Using Whom?" by Patricia Goldstone, *Los Angeles Times*, December 17, 1978.

340 "looked like it was": Clark and Kleiner, *Rock Hudson—Friend of Mine*, p. 145.

340 "We had some bad": Jerry Douglas, interview with author, January 13, 2015.

340 "It was so bungled": Lambert, *Mainly About Lindsay Anderson*, p. 284.

340 "After theatre managers add up": "Burying Art Alive In 'Avalanche'" by Gary Arnold, *Washington Post*, September 23, 1978.

341 "Hudson makes a good": Review of *Avalanche* by Robert Osborne, *The Hollywood Reporter*, August 30, 1978.

341 "an exposé and a salute": Review of *Wheels*, by John Reed, *New York Times*, September 19, 1971.

342 "Not on your life!": Clark, *Rock Hudson—Friend of Mine*, p. 27.

342 "I remember Rock told me": Howard McGillin, interview with author, February 5, 2016.

343 "It takes a while": Review of *Wheels* by Howard Rosenberg, *Los Angeles Times*, May 6, 1978.

344 "It's terrible, Rock": Clark and Kleiner, *Rock Hudson—Friend of Mine*, p. 212.

344 "a 2 ½ hour" . . . "I had the luxury": "Time Passes, Rock Endures" by Michael J. Bandler, *Chicago Tribune Magazine*, July 8, 1979, Section 9, p. 29.

344 "Damned near perfect": "Rock's On Board," *Chicago Sun-Times*, Entertainment Extra (advertising supplement), July 13, 1979.

345 "I salute him": Judy Kaye, interview with author, January 29, 2015.

346 "I was excited as hell": "Time Passes, Rock Endures" by Michael J. Bandler, *Chicago Tribune Magazine*, July 8, 1979, Section 9, p. 27.

346 "When I heard that Rock": "Time Passes, Rock Endures" by Michael J. Bandler, *Chicago Tribune Magazine*, July 8, 1979, Section 9, p. 26.

346 "Hal was very difficult" . . . "He never showed any": Oppenheimer and Vitek, *Idol: Rock Hudson*, p. 139.

346 "I never saw Hal": Judy Kaye, interview with author, January 29, 2015.

347 "Judy Kaye is the life": "Well-Engineered Nostalgia" by J. Linn Allen, *Chicago Reader*, Section 1, p. 42.

347 "Hudson is the most likable": Review of *On the Twentieth Century* by Dan Sullivan, *Los Angeles Times*, August 30, 1979.

348 "The critics were actually kinder": Clark and Kleiner, *Rock Hudson—Friend of Mine*, p. 215.

348 "We talked about the impact" . . . "You had to find": Charles Fries, correspondence with author, May 31, 2016.

348 "a lot more Martians": Review of *The Martian Chronicles* by Gail Williams, *The Hollywood Reporter*, January 28, 1980.

349 "On the one hand": Charles Fries, correspondence with author, May 31, 2016.

350 "When we were casting" (footnote): Barry Sandler, interview with author, February 20, 2015.

350 "I had known Rock" . . . "I was a huge": Barry Sandler, interview with author, February 20, 2015.

351 "A Yalta Conference": "Hollywood Crack'd" by Gerald Peary, *Real Paper*, January 18, 1981, p. 17.

351 "I was part of a roundtable": Gerald Peary, correspondence with author, October 15, 2015.

351 "total sleaze" . . . "It just wasn't very good": Lou Antonio, interview with author, July 2016.

352 "When I first read it": Rock Hudson's comments are taken from his appearance on *The Paul Ryan Show* in 1982.

352 "I said I'd never" . . . "I like to work": "One Year After Heart Surgery, Rock Hudson is Rolling Again," *People* magazine, November 15, 1982, p. 148.

353 "NBC asked me": John Wilder, interview with author, November 29, 2016.

353 "Events happen" . . . "He was so": Jack Scalia, interview with author, November 22, 2016.

354 "I won't say": John Wilder, interview with author, November 29, 2016.

354 "There was chaos": Hudson and Davidson, *Rock Hudson: His Story*, p. 156.

354 "I was working when" . . . "I didn't want to": "One Year After Heart Surgery, Rock Hudson is Rolling Again," *People* magazine, November 15, 1982, p. 147.

355 "I went to see him": Jack Scalia, interview with author, November 22, 2016.

355 "We read them": Clark and Kleiner, *Rock Hudson—Friend of Mine*, p. 169.

356 "None of what went on": Jack Scalia, interview with author, November 22, 2016.

356 "rather smug about": "One Year After Heart Surgery, Rock Hudson is Rolling Again," *People* magazine, November 15, 1982, p. 148.

356 "It is very difficult": Clark and Kleiner, *Rock Hudson—Friend of Mine*, p. 177.

357 "When Rock came out" . . . "Claire called me": Mark Miller, *Trio of Forever Friends* (unpublished memoir completed in 2007).

357 "I felt an overpowering": Clark and Kleiner, *Rock Hudson—Friend of Mine*, p. 229.

358 "Did you have" . . . "It was this" . . . "When I found": Michael Kearns, interview with author, February 24, 2015.

359 "There's a little" . . . "I put on 'Marilyn'": These lines are taken from the script of *Rock* by Michael Kearns.

359 "Rock was a brilliant actor": Michael Kearns, interview with author, February 24, 2015.

Chapter 18: Christian

360 "Physically, he fit": Ken Maley, interview with author, January 26, 2015.

361 "putting together a history": Hudson and Davidson, *Rock Hudson: His Story*, p. 164.

361 "To start doing his": "Between Rock and a Hard Place: Marc Christian Tells All" by Barry Adkins, *Au Courant*, January 20, 1986, p. 16.

361 "a very slow and": "Between Rock and a Hard Place: Marc Christian Tells All" by Barry Adkins, *New York Native*, Issue 140, December 23–29, p. 22.

361 "They got right down": Mark Miller, interview with author.

361 "Like a snake": Hudson and Davidson, *Rock Hudson: His Story*, p. 168.

362 "Rock was going": Marty Flaherty, interview with author, July 3, 2015.

363 "Rock, I read that": Clark and Kleiner, *Rock Hudson—Friend of Mine*, p. 145.

363 "I didn't think the part": Oppenheimer and Vitek, *Idol: Rock Hudson*, p. 149.

363 "a very great": Oppenheimer and Vitek, *Idol: Rock Hudson*, p. 150.

364 "I don't think Mitchum": Server, *Robert Mitchum: 'Baby, I Don't Care,'* p. 505.

364 "When I moved into the house": "Between Rock and a Hard Place: Marc Christian Tells All" by Barry Adkins, *Au Courant*, January 20, 1986, p. 7.

365 "At the beginning": Marty Flaherty, interview with author, July 3, 2015.

366 "I liked Marc": Hudson and Davidson, *Rock Hudson: His Story*, p. 167.

366 "I was afraid for Rock": Florence Lacey, interview with author, March 19, 2015.

366 "I met Marc Christian": Ken Jillson, interview with author, April 2, 2017.

366 "Marc Christian—I don't think": Stockton Briggle's comments are taken from *E! True Hollywood Story: Rock Hudson*, which aired on E! Entertainment Television on July 11, 1999, season three, episode 27.

367 "was very well known": Hudson and Davidson, *Rock Hudson: His Story*, p. 168.

367 "I want you to know": Mills, *Between Rock and a Hard Place*, p. 330.

367 "She was Gloria Swanson": Robert Parker Mills, interview with author, August 3, 2015.

367 "We don't understand": Hudson and Davidson, *Rock Hudson: His Story*, p. 164.

367 "I asked him about": Gunther Fraulob, interview with author, March 3, 2017.

368 "You'd have thought" . . . "no warmth or caring": Hudson and Davidson, *Rock Hudson: His Story*, p. 171.

368 "You've got to": Hudson and Davidson, *Rock Hudson: His Story*, p. 173.

368 "A brief affair": Rupert Allen's comments are taken from *E! True Hollywood Story: Rock Hudson*, which aired on E!: Entertainment Television on July 11, 1999, season three, episode 27.

369 "The fat hit the fire": George Nader diary entry, February 3, 1984.

369 "I'm not the suing type": Clark and Kleiner, *Rock Hudson—Friend of Mine*.

370 "Ron talked like": Transcript: Marc Christian deposition, page 728, from the David Stenn Collection, archived at the Margaret Herrick Library, Academy of Motion Picture Arts and Sciences.

371 "Whenever we met" . . . "During one of" . . . "I had just": Gunther Fraulob, interview with author, March 3, 2017.

371 "It was getting close" . . . "My parents were": Gunther Fraulob, interview with author, March 3, 2017.

372 "You're thin, also": Hudson and Davidson, *Rock Hudson: His Story*, p. 176.

372 "the beginning of where": Mark Miller, *Trio of Forever Friends* (unpublished memoir completed in 2007), p. 211.

372–73 "An inner voice said" . . . "I thought it was": Hudson and Davidson, *Rock Hudson: His Story*, p. 178.

373 "so filthy": Mills, *Between Rock and a Hard Place*, p. 366.

374–75 "He—[Hudson]—could" . . . "You're absolutely right": Mills, *Between Rock and a Hard Place*, p. 369.

375 "We recently had": George Nader diary entry, June 8, 1984.

375 "Only one person": Mark Miller, *Trio of Forever Friends* (unpublished memoir completed in 2007), p. 213.

375 "Rock intimated that" (footnote): Oppenheimer and Vitek, *Idol: Rock Hudson*, p. 156.

376 "Not in your condition": Mark Miller, *Trio of Forever Friends* (unpublished memoir completed in 2007), p. 215.

376 "The next week": Jimmy Hawkins, interview with author, August 8, 2016.

376 "He loved the": Jimmy Hawkins, interview with author, August 8, 2016.

377 "From the beginning": Oppenheimer and Vitek, *Idol: Rock Hudson*, pp. 160–62.

377 "He'd call me in the morning": Sharon Stone's comments are taken from *E! True Hollywood Story: Rock Hudson*, which aired on E!: Entertainment Television on July 11, 1999, season three, episode 27.

378 "We became close friends": Madison Mason, interview with author, January 13, 2015.

378 "I was married to" . . . "He didn't want to be": Dennis Holahan, interview with author, January 13, 2015.

378 "Everybody asks about": "Rock Hudson on his Health, TV, 'Dynasty'" by Jon Anderson, *Chicago Tribune*, February 17, 1985.

379 "I don't have AIDS": George Nader diary entry, June 12, 1984.

380 "story conferences": George Nader diary entry, September 9, 1984.

380 "devising and bequeathing": George Nader diary entry, August 16, 1984.

381 "I think they manipulated": Robert Osborne, interview with author, June 23, 2015.

381 "When Sheft told me" . . . "I think that": Clark and Kleiner, *Rock Hudson—Friend of Mine*, p. 234.

382 "I remember when Rock" . . . "He never sat me down": "Between Rock and a Hard Place: Marc Christian Tells All" by Barry Adkins, *Au Courant*, January 20, 1986, p. 7.

382 "Q: Did you have any reason" (footnote): Mills, *Between Rock and a Hard Place*, p. 134.

382 a "successful business trip": George Nader diary entry, August 26, 1984.

382 "middle stages of AIDS": Oppenheimer and Vitek, *Idol: Rock Hudson*, p. 167.

382 "If Rock had agreed": Hudson and Davidson, *Rock Hudson: His Story*, p. 185.

383 "guardedly optimistic": George Nader diary entry, September 10, 1984.

383 "I was on the street in Paris": Robert Osborne, interview with author, June 23, 2015.

383 "Oh, so so": George Nader diary entry, September 27, 1984.

383 "Rock has AIDS": Hudson and Davidson, *Rock Hudson: His Story*, p. 185.

384 "He was a little too": Oppenheimer and Vitek, *Idol: Rock Hudson*, p. 168.

384 "There was no such thing": John Poer, interview with author, August 7, 2015.

385 "Please don't feel" . . . "What the hell": Hudson and Davidson, *Rock Hudson: His Story*, pp. 186–87.

386 "I remember that the director": John Poer, interview with author, August 7, 2015.

386 "In retrospect": Evans, *Recipes for Life: My Memories*, p. 163.

386 "I asked him if the cameraman": Transcript: Marc Christian deposition, p. 735, from the David Stenn Collection, archived at the Margaret Herrick Library, Academy of Motion Picture Arts and Sciences.

386 "Perhaps it's my imagination": George Nader diary entry, February 5, 1985.

387 "Room-temperature passion": "Benefits and Backlash: The Reaction to Rock Hudson" by Michael Musto, *The Village Voice*, August 13, 1985, p. 24.

387 "What do I do?": Hudson and Davidson, *Rock Hudson: His Story*, p. 7.

387 "My official statement": "Rock Hudson Has Cancer," *New York Times*, July 24, 1985, p. C16.

387 "As far as we know": "Rock Hudson stable after tests," *The Orange County Register*, July 25, 1985, p. A14.

387 "What I know": "Hospital Denies Hudson Cancer Report," Special to *New York Times*, July 25, 1985, p. C21.

388 "I said, 'Rock, you look'": Dale Olson's comments are taken from *E! True Hollywood Story: Rock Hudson*, which aired on E!: Entertainment Television on July 11, 1999, season three, episode 27.

388 "When I entered": Hudson and Davidson, *Rock Hudson: His Story*, p. 8.

388 "Where's Ron?" . . . "I shipped him home" . . . "There are photographers": Mark Miller, *Trio of Forever Friends* (unpublished memoir completed in 2007), p. 293.

388 "Mr. Rock Hudson has Acquired Immune" . . . "He came to Paris": "Hudson Said to Recover From AIDS Symptoms," *New York Times*, July 26, 1985.

388 "The last test": "Hudson's AIDS confirmed; diagnosis was made last year," *San Diego Union*, July 26, 1985.

389 "Did you throw it": Mark Miller, *Trio of Forever Friends* (unpublished memoir completed in 2007), p. 296.

389 "I just remember having": Howard McGillin, interview with author, February 5, 2016.

390 "I'm watching the television": Marc Christian's comments are taken from an episode of *Larry King Live* entitled "Rock Hudson's Ex-Lover Speaks Out," which aired on CNN on March 29, 2001.

390 "I was checked out": "Between Rock And a Hard Place" by Barry Adkins, *New York Native*, Issue 140, December 23–29, p. 21.

390 "I thought I was": "The Price of Betrayal" by Paula Chin and Dan Knapp, *People* magazine, March 6, 1989, p. 182.

390 "Marc Christian knew Rock": Marty Flaherty, interview with author, July 3, 2015.

Chapter 19: This Is Your Life

391 "I tell Tom he is": George Nader diary entry, p. 317.

392 "I tried to visit him": "Rock Hudson's Lover Talks," *New York Daily News*, December 6, 1985, p. 11.

393 "Well, Rock asked me": Clark and Kleiner, *Rock Hudson—Friend of Mine*, p. 246.

393 "When Marc met with": Brent Beckwith, interview with author, June 7, 2016.

393 "marriage with no": "Marvin Mitchelson, 76, Father of Palimony, Is Dead" by Patrick Healy, *New York Times*, September 20, 2004.

393 "Trust me, you'll be": Hudson and Davidson, *Rock Hudson: His Story*, p. 213.

393 "I have no intention" . . . "If you go to court" . . . "If we allege it": Transcript: Marc Christian deposition, p. 808, from the David Stenn Collection, archived at the Margaret Herrick Library, Academy of Motion Picture Arts and Sciences.

394 "Why don't we": Marty Flaherty, interview with author, July 3, 2016.

394 "I had a perfectly lucid" . . . "Hudson signed" (footnote): "The Dispute On Hudson's Final Days: Friends Disagree Over Actor's State of Mind" by Carla Hall, *Washington Post*, October 9, 1985, B-3, Col. 1.

395 "He had good days": "Encounters With a Man of Mystery" by Carla Hall, *Washington Post*, July 23, 1986.

395 "People deserted him" . . . "You never knew": Marty Flaherty, interview with author, July 3, 2016.

395 "It's Dean!": Hudson and Davidson, *Rock Hudson: His Story*, p. 220.

396 "When I saw my brother": Alice Waier, interview with author, January 2015.

396 "Rock had always said" (footnote): "Rock Hudson's Lover Talks," *New York Daily News*, December 6, 1985, p. 11.

396 "Do you realize": "Ex Wheel of Fortune Hostess, Susan Stafford Reveals How Hollywood Superstar, Rock Hudson, Received Christ Just Hours Before He Died from Complications From AIDS" by Dan Wooding, Assist News Service, October 19, 2015, posted on CrossMap.com.

397 "Shirley Boone . . . racing in": "Between Rock and a Hard Place" by Barry Adkins, *New York Native*, Issue 140, December 23–29, p. 23.

397 "One has to imagine": Mark Miller, *Trio of Forever Friends* (unpublished memoir completed in 2007), pp. 337–38.

397 "Oh, for goodness": Mark Miller, *Trio of Forever Friends* (unpublished memoir completed in 2007), p. 338.

398 "She is most cordial": George Nader diary entry, September 28, 1985.

398 "People have told me": Oppenheimer and Vitek, *Idol: Rock Hudson*, pp. 221–22.

399 "Rock Hudson never" . . . "The statement was not": "Rock's 'quote' wasn't his: pal" by Marilyn Beck, *New York Daily News*, October 4, 1985, p. 4.

399 "There is no truth": Transcript of Rona Barrett report for *Entertainment Tonight*, excerpted in Flaherty, *"At Home" With Rock Hudson*, p. 275.

399 "Elizabeth was just": Wes Wheadon, interview with author, June 25, 2017.

400 "agreed wholeheartedly": "The Dispute On Hudson's Final Days: Friends Disagree Over Actor's State of Mind" by Carla Hall, *Washington Post*, October 9, 1985, B-3, Col. 1.

400 "It was the single most important": "Rock Hudson's Death, the Turning Point of AIDS," NewsNight report for CNN by Sandy Kenyon.

400 "I said to myself": Clark and Kleiner, *Rock Hudson—Friend of Mine*, p. 254.

401 "final ministry": George Nader diary entry, September 21, 1985.

401 "Jesus told me": Clark and Kleiner, *Rock Hudson—Friend of Mine*, p. 254.

401 "Thanks for that": Clark and Kleiner, *Rock Hudson—Friend of Mine*, p. 262.

401 "Liz, what would": George Nader diary, October 1, 1985.

402 "I'm going downstairs" . . . "No, I don't": Clark and Kleiner, *Rock Hudson—Friend of Mine*, p. 262.

402 "I got a call from": Ken Jillson, interview with author, April 2, 2017.

403 "I didn't go to the service": George Nader diary entry, October 19, 1985.

403 "I get to be": Miller, *Trio*, p. 343.

403 "The Elizabeth Taylor Quaker Memorial": George Nader diary entry, October 19, 1985.

403 "Rock would have wanted": Hudson and Davidson, *Rock Hudson: His Story*, p. 226.

404 "He wanted to know" . . . "He was very charming" . . . "Christian and I had": Gunther Fraulob, interview with author, March 3, 2017.

404 "blackmail and coerce" (footnote): "Hudson's Estate Files Countersuit Vs. 'Lover,'" *Variety*, March 19, 1986, p. 2.

405 "Marc, have you" (footnote): Marc Christian's comments are taken from his appearance on *Donahue*, February 27, 1989.

405 "Marc asked for $300,000": Brent Beckwith, interview with author, June 7, 2016.

405 "I didn't want to drag": Gunther Fraulob, interview with author, March 3, 2017.

406 "After the trial was over": Paul Cohen, interview with author, December 3, 2017.

406 "nowhere near" (footnote): Robert Parker Mills, interview with author, August 3, 2015.

406 "Everyone at the service": Gunther Fraulob, interview with author, March 3, 2017.

406 "Elizabeth Taylor and Stockton": Mark Tillman-Briggle, interview with author, June 21, 2017.

407 "Tom Clark took": Stockton Briggle's comments are taken from the documentary, *Rock Hudson: Dark and Handsome Stranger*, which was directed by Andrew Davies and André Schäfer and released in October 2010 by Florianfilm, GmbH.

408 "A lonely seagull": George Nader diary entry, October 20, 1985.

408 "After he died, the one memory": Peter Kevoian, interview with author, March 19, 2015.

BIBLIOGRAPHY

Adams, Julie, with Mitchell Danton. *The Lucky Southern Star: Reflections from The Black Lagoon*. Los Angeles: Hollywood Adventures Publishing, 2011.

Alleman, Richard. *The Movie Lover's Guide to New York*. New York: Harper & Row, 1988.

Amburn, Ellis. *The Most Beautiful Woman in the World: The Obsessions, Passions and Courage of Elizabeth Taylor*. New York: HarperCollins, 2000.

Arce, Hector. *The Secret Life of Tyrone Power*. New York: William Morrow and Company, 1979.

Bacall, Lauren. *By Myself and Then Some*. New York: HarperEntertainment, 2005.

Baker, Carlos. *Ernest Hemingway: A Life Story*. New York: Charles Scribner's Sons, 1969.

Barrios, Richard. *Screened Out: Playing Gay in Hollywood from Edison to Stonewall*. New York: Routledge, 2003.

Bart, Peter. *Infamous Players*. New York: Weinstein Books, 2011.

Bast, William. *Surviving James Dean*. Fort Lee, NJ: Barricade Books, 2006.

Bego, Mark. *Rock Hudson: Public and Private*. New York: Signet/New American Library, 1986.

Behlmer, Rudy. *Memo from David O. Selznick*. New York: The Viking Press, 1972.

Benét, Stephen Vincent. *John Brown's Body*. New York: Dramatists Play Service, 1961.

Bogdanovich, Peter. *Who the Hell's In It*. New York: Alfred A. Knopf, 2004.

Bowers, Scotty, with Lionel Friedberg. *Full Service*. New York: Grove Press, 2012.

Buford, Kate. *Burt Lancaster: An American Life*. New York: Alfred A. Knopf, 2000.

Carlyle, John. *Under the Rainbow: An Intimate Memoir of Judy Garland, Rock Hudson & My Life in Old Hollywood*. New York: Carroll & Graf Publishers, 2006.

Caron, Leslie. *Thank Heaven*. New York: Viking Penguin, 2009.

Ceplair, Larry, and Christopher Trumbo. *Dalton Trumbo: Blacklisted Hollywood Radical*. University Press of Kentucky, 2014.

Clark, Tom, and Dick Kleiner. *Rock Hudson—Friend of Mine*. New York: Pharos Books, 1989.

Collins, Joan. *Second Act*. New York: St. Martin's Press, 1996.

Cook, Bruce. *Trumbo*. New York: Grand Central Publishing, 2015.

Dalton, David. *James Dean: The Mutant King*. New York: St. Martin's Press, 1974.

Daniel, Douglass K. *Tough as Nails: The Life and Films of Richard Brooks*. Madison, Wisconsin: The University of Wisconsin Press, 2011.

Davis, Ronald L. *Duke: The Life and Image of John Wayne*. Norman, Oklahoma: University of Oklahoma Press, 1998.

————. *Words into Images: Screenwriters on the Studio System*. Jackson, Mississippi: University Press of Mississippi, 2007.

De Carlo, Yvonne, with Doug Warren. *Yvonne*. New York: St. Martin's Press, 1987.

Douglas, Kirk. *The Ragman's Son*. New York: Simon and Schuster, 1988.

Douglas, Lloyd C. *Magnificent Obsession*. New York: P.F. Collier & Son Corporation, 1929.

Ebert, Roger. *The Great Movies*. New York: Broadway Books, 2002.

Ehrenstein, David. *Open Secret: Gay Hollywood 1928–1998*. New York: William Morow, 1998.

Evans, Linda. *Recipes for Life: My Memories*. New York: Post Hill Press, 2015.

Evans, Peter William. *BFI Film Classics: Written on the Wind*. London: Palgrave Macmillan, 2013.

Evans, Robert. *The Kid Stays in the Picture*. New York: Hyperion, 1994.

Eyman, Scott. *John Wayne: The Life and Legend*. New York: Simon & Schuster, 2014.

Ferber, Edna. *Giant*. New York: Doubleday, 1952.

Ferguson, Michael. *Idol Worship: A Shameless Celebration of Male Beauty in the Movies*. Sarasota, Fla.: STARbooks Press, 2003.

Flaherty, Martin. *"At Home" with Rock Hudson: Behind the Walls of His Life*. La Pine, Oregon: CreateSpace Independent Publishing Platform, 2011.

————. *"At Home" with Rock Hudson—Volume II*. La Pine, Oregon: CreateSpace Independent Publishing Platform, 2013.

Gates, Phyllis, and Bob Thomas. *My Husband, Rock Hudson*. New York: Doubleday & Company, 1987.

Grady, Billy. *The Irish Peacock: Confessions of a Legendary Talent Agent*. New Rochelle, NY: Arlington House, 1972.

Graham, Don. *Giant: The Making of a Legendary American Film*. New York: St. Martin's Press, 2018.

Grey, Joel, with Rebecca Paley. *Master of Ceremonies: A Memoir*. New York: Flatiron Books, 2016.

Grobel, Lawrence. *The Hustons*. New York: Avon Books, 1989.

Hailey, Arthur. *Wheels*. New York: Doubleday & Company, 1971.

Halliday, Jon. *Sirk on Sirk*. London: Faber and Faber Limited, 1997.

Haver, Ronald. *David O. Selznick's Hollywood*. New York: Bonanza Books, 1980.

Helms, Alan. *Young Man from the Provinces: A Gay Life Before Stonewall*. New York: Avon Books, 1995.

Hirschhorn, Clive. *The Films of James Mason*. New Jersey: Citadel Press, 1977.

————. *The Universal Story*. New York: Crown Books, 1983.

Hemingway, Ernest. *A Farewell to Arms*. New York: Charles Scribner's Sons, 1929.

Hofler, Robert. *The Man Who Invented Rock Hudson*. New York: Carroll & Graf, 2005.

Hotchner, A.E. *Doris Day: Her Own Story*. New York: William Morrow and Company, Inc., 1976.

Hudson, Rock, and Sara Davidson. *Rock Hudson: His Story*. New York: William Morrow and Company, 1986.

Hunter, Tab, and Eddie Muller. *Tab Hunter Confidential*. Chapel Hill, N.C.: Algonquin Books of Chapel Hill, 2005.

Kaufman, David. *Doris Day: The Untold Story of the Girl Next Door*. New York: Virgin Books, 2008.

Kendrick, Baynard. *Lights Out*. New York: William Morrow & Co., 1945.

Keyes, Evelyn. *Scarlett O'Hara's Younger Sister—My Lively Life In and Out of Hollywood*. Secaucus, N.J.: Lyle Stuart, Inc., 1977.

Koetting, Christopher T. *Mind Warp: The Fantastic True Story of Roger Corman's New World Pictures*. Bristol (UK): Hemlock Books Limited, 2009.

Lambert, Gavin. *Mainly About Lindsay Anderson*. New York: Alfred A. Knopf, 2000.

Laurie, Piper. *Learning to Live Out Loud: A Memoir*. New York: Crown Archetype, 2011.

Lovell, Glenn. *Escape Artist: The Life and Films of John Sturges*. Madison, Wisconsin: The University of Wisconsin Press, 2008.

Mann, William J. *Behind the Screen: How Gays and Lesbians Shaped Hollywood*. New York: Viking, 2001.

Martin, Tony, and Cyd Charisse, as told to Dick Kleiner. *The Two of Us*. New York: Mason/Charter, 1976.

Martinett, Ronald. *The James Dean Story*. New York: Birch Lane Press, 1995.

Mayo, Virginia, as told to LC Van Savage. *The Best Years of My Life*. Chesterfield, Mo: BeachHouse Books, 2002.

McCarthy, Todd. *Howard Hawks: The Grey Fox of Hollywood*. New York: Grove Press, 1997.

McGilligan, Patrick. *Film Crazy: Interviews with Hollywood Legends*. New York: St. Martin's Press, 2000.

Mercer, John. *Rock Hudson*. London: Palgrave (on behalf of BFI), 2015.

Mills, Robert Parker. *Between Rock and a Hard Place: In Defense of Rock Hudson*. Bloomington, Indiana: AuthorHouse, 2010.

Mordden, Ethan. *The Hollywood Studios*. New York: Alfred A. Knopf, 1988.

Morella, Joe and Edward Z. Epstein. *Jane Wyman*. New York: Delacorte Press, 1985.

Morley, Sheridan. *James Mason: Odd Man Out*. New York: Harper & Row, 1989.

Moss, Marilyn Ann. *Raoul Walsh—The True Adventures of Hollywood's Legendary Director*. Lexington, Kentucky: The University Press of Kentucky, 2011.

Navasky, Victor S. *Naming Names*. New York: The Viking Press, 1980.

Nolan, William F. *John Huston: King Rebel*. Los Angeles: Sherbourne Press, Inc., 1965.

O'Hara, Maureen, with John Nicoletti. *'Tis Herself.* New York: Simon & Schuster, Inc., 2004.

Oppenheimer, Jerry, and Jack Vitek. *Idol: Rock Hudson, The True Story of an American Film Hero.* New York: Villard Books, 1986.

Otash, Fred. *Investigation Hollywood!* Chicago: Henry Regnery Company, 1976.

Parish, James Robert and Ronald L. Bowers. *The MGM Stock Company.* New York: Bonanza Books, 1973.

Ragland, Shannon. *The Thin Thirty.* Louisville, Kentucky: The Set Shot Press, 2007.

Reed, Rex. *People Are Crazy Here.* New York: Delacorte Press, 1974.

Relyea, Robert E., with Craig Relyea. *Not So Quiet on the Set: My Life in Movies During Hollywood's Macho Era.* New York: iUniverse, Inc., 2008.

Reynolds, Michael. *Hemingway: The Final Years.* New York: W. W. Norton & Company, 1999.

Royce, Brenda Scott. *Rock Hudson: A Bio-Bibliography.* Westport, Connecticut: Greenwood Press, 1995.

Ruark, Robert C. *Something of Value.* New York: Doubleday & Company, 1955.

Russo, Vito. *The Celluloid Closet: Homosexuality in the Movies.* New York: Harper & Row, 1987.

Santopietro, Tom. *Considering Doris Day.* New York: Thomas Dunne Books, 2007.

Scott, Henry E. *Shocking True Story: The Rise and Fall of* Confidential. New York: Pantheon Books, 2010.

Server, Lee. *Robert Mitchum: "Baby, I Don't Care."* New York: St. Martin's Press, 2001.

Shapiro, Peter. *Turn the Beat Around: The Secret History of Disco.* London: Faber and Faber, 2005.

Smith, Liz. *Natural Blonde: A Memoir.* New York: Hyperion, 2000.

Soren, David, with Meredith Banasiak and Bob Johnston. *Vera-Ellen: The Magic and the Mystery.* Fredericksburg, VA: Luminary Press, 2003.

Spring, Justin. *Secret Historian: The Life and Times of Samuel Steward.* New York: Farrar, Straus and Giroux, 2010.

Spoto, Donald. *A Passion for Life: The Biography of Elizabeth Taylor.* New York: HarperCollins, 1995.

———. *Rebel: The Life and Legend of James Dean.* New York: HarperCollins, 1996.

Stack, Robert with Mark Evans. *Straight Shooting.* New York: Macmillan Publishing, 1980.

Stine, Whitney. *Stars & Star Handlers.* Santa Monica, Calif.: Roundtable Publishing, 1985.

Taylor, Elizabeth. *Elizabeth Taylor: An Informal Memoir.* New York: Harper & Row, 1964.

Teeman, Tim. *In Bed With Gore Vidal.* New York: Magnus Books, 2013.

Thomson, David. *The New Biographical Dictionary of Film.* New York: Alfred A. Knopf, 2002.

Tosches, Nick. *Dino: Living High in the Dirty Business of Dreams.* New York: Dell Publishing, 1992.

Vagg, Stephen. *Rod Taylor: An Aussie in Hollywood*. Albany, Georgia: Bear Manor Media, 2010.

Wasson, Sam. *A Splurch in the Kisser: The Movies of Blake Edwards*. Middletown, Connecticut: Wesleyan University Press, 2009.

Wiley, Mason, and Damien Bona. *Inside Oscar: The Unofficial History of the Academy Awards*. New York: Ballantine Books, 1986.

Willsmer, Trevor. *Giant: The Making of an Epic Motion Picture*. Los Angeles, CA: Project Marketing/Time Warner Entertainment, 1996.

Wilson, John. *The Official Razzie Movie Guide*. New York: Time Warner Book Group, 2005.

Windeler, Robert. *Julie Andrews: A Life on Stage and Screen*. Secaucus, N.J.: Birch Lane Press, 1997.

INTERVIEWS

Julie Adams, Adell Aldrich, Richard Anderson, Lou Antonio, Lauren Bacall, Peter Baldwin, Peter Bart (2012 interview), Brent Beckwith, William Peter Blatty, Carol Burnett, Claudia Cardinale, Lewis John Carlino, Diane Sherry Case, Wally Cech, Cynthia Chenault, Michael Childers, Cindy Clark, Ray Clark, Paul Cohen, Dr. Jonathan E. Coleman, Mark Colleano, Cora Sue Collins, Carole Cook, Arlene Dahl, Matt Davis, Philip "Bud" Davis, Professor Ronald L. Davis, William Dawson, Doris Day, Illeana Douglas, Jerry Douglas, Peggy Dow, David Ely, Betty Engelman, Martin Flaherty, Gunther Fraulob, Joel Freeman, Charles Fries, Constance Garcia-Singer, Lee Garlington, Joel Grey, Betty Abbott Griffin, Kenneth Griggs, Cathy Hamblin, Robert Harmon, Jimmy Hawkins, Steve Hayes, Roberta Haynes, Arthur Hiller, Richard Hodge, Robert Hofler (2005 interview), Dennis Holahan, Joyce Holden, Earl Holliman, Virginia Hougasian, Kathleen Hughes, Tab Hunter, Glenn Jacobson, Ken Jillson, Judy Kaye, Michael Kearns, Peter Kevoian, Tony Kiser, Florence Lacey, Jack Larson, Piper Laurie, William Layer, Barbara Leigh, Nancy Leman, Dan Leonard, Michael Licata, Ken Maley, Ron Masak, Madison Mason, Paul Mason, Armistead Maupin, Taman McCall, Joe McElhaney, Howard McGillin, Patrick McGuire, Tony Melia, Bodil Miller, Mark Miller, Robert Parker Mills, Herbert Millspaugh, Robert Morgan, Marilyn Ann Moss, Craig Muckler, Lynn West Mullen, Noreen Nash, David Nutter, Robert Osborne, Robert Ousley, Gregg Palmer, Mary Peach, John Poer, Harper Poling, Shannon Ragland, Rex Reason, William Reynolds, Christopher Riordan, Ann Robinson, Barry Sandler, Thomas Santopietro, Jack Scalia, William Schallert, Gaylord Scherer, Jerry Scherer, Liz Scherer, John Schuck, Wallace Sheft, Joseph Sirola, Derline Smithson, Kenneth Soderblom, Dr. David Soren, Angela Stevens, Kevin Thomas, David Thomson, Maeve Thunderchild, Mark Tillman-Briggle, Dr. Margaret E. Towner, Alice Waier, Clint Walker, Ruth Holland Walsh, Dr. Wes Wheadon, John Wilder, Robert Willett, Jane Withers, John Leslie Wolfe.

INDEX

NOTE: *Italic page numbers* indicate a photograph; an *"n"* following a page number indicates a note on that page.

ABOUT THE AUTHOR

MARK GRIFFIN is the author of *A Hundred or More Hidden Things: The Life and Films of Vincente Minnelli*. Griffin's interviews, reviews, and essays have appeared in scores of publications, including the *Boston Globe*, *MovieMaker*, and *Genre*. He recently appeared in the documentaries *Gene Kelly: To Live and Dance* and *Mythical Couples: Judy Garland and Vincente Minnelli*.